THE IRWIN
ASSET ALLOCATION SERIES
FOR INSTITUTIONAL
INVESTORS

EQUITY STYLE MANAGEMENT

EVALUATING AND SELECTING INVESTMENT STYLES

ROBERT A. KLEIN AND JESS LEDERMAN, EDITORS

IRWIN
Professional Publishing®
Chicago • London • Singapore

To Wyoming State Treasurer Stan Smith

Contents

Author Biographies   *ix*

Preface   *xix*

Part I   Origins of Equity Style   **1**

1. *Basic Issues and Key Elements for Equity Style Management*   **3**

   Bruce D. Westervelt, CFA, Executive Director,
      First Madison Advisors
   Thomas J. Schwab, Executive Director, First Madison Advisors

2. *Footprints in the Sand: Return-Based Style Analysis*   **19**

   Diana L. Lieberman, Vice President,
      Strategic Investment Solutions, Inc.

Part II   Definitions of Style   **47**

3. *The Sponsor's Perspective*   **49**

   William J. De Allaume, CFA, Asset Consulting Group,
      Bankers Trust Co.

4. *Equity Style Management: The Case of Growth and Value*   **67**

   Eric H. Sorensen, Ph.D., Managing Director,
      Salomon Brothers Inc
   Craig J. Lazzara, CFA, Vice President, Salomon Brothers Inc

5. *Value/Growth Considerations in International*
    Investing: Two Perspectives   *85*

    John P. Meier, Vice President,
        Strategic Investment Solutions, Inc.
    Andre Bertolotti, Product Manager, BARRA Inc.
    David Umstead, Ph.D., CFA, Managing Director,
        Boston International Advisors, Inc.

6. *Understanding the Style Benchmarks*   *143*

    Claudia E. Mott, First Vice President,
        Director of Small-Cap Research,
        Prudential Securities Inc.
    Daniel P. Coker, Assistant Vice President,
        Prudential Securities Inc.

7. *Do We Need Mid-Cap? An Examination*
    of the EAI Database   *181*

    Elizabeth E. Nevin, Vice President, Director, U.S. Equities,
        Evaluation Associates, Inc.

8. *Mid-Cap Investing by Investment Managers*   *191*

    Daniel J. Cardell, CFA, Director of Equities,
        Bank of America

9. *Exploring the Cycles of Small-Cap Style Performance*   *217*

    Claudia E. Mott, First Vice President,
        Director of Small-Cap Research,
        Prudential Securities Inc.
    Kevin C. Condon, Associate Vice President,
        Prudential Securities Inc.

10. *The Presence of Value in Small-Cap Equities*   *235*

    Satya Dev Pradhuman, Vice President, Merrill Lynch & Co.
    Suzanne M. Crosby, Ph.D., Analyst, Standard & Poor's

Part III The Different Approaches to the Investment Process   249

11. *The Evolution of Equity Indexation in the U.S. Market*   *251*

Arlene M. Rockefeller, CFA, Managing Director,
State Street Global Advisors
Anne B. Eisenberg, Vice President,
State Street Global Advisors

12. *Historical Tendencies of Equity Style Returns and the Prospects for Tactical Style Allocation*   *259*

Douglas W. Case, CFA, Director of Equity Portfolio
Management, LBS Capital Management
Steven Cusimano, CFA, Senior Portfolio Manager,
Florida State Board of Administration

13. *How Does Stock Selection Criteria Performance Vary across Investment Style Universes?*   *289*

Gregory J. Forsythe, CFA, President,
Chicago Investment Analytics, Inc.

14. *Equity Style Timing and Allocation*   *297*

Stephen C. Fan, Ph.D., Vice President, Vestek Systems, Inc.

15. *Country-Selection Style*   *333*

Rosemary Macedo, Senior Vice President, Quantitative Research,
Bailard, Biehl & Kaiser

16. *Don't Leave Excess Return on the Table: The Case for Active Style-Management*   *357*

Lawrence J. Marks, CFA, Managing Director,
Harbor Capital Management Company, Inc.

17. *Style Trends in Institutional Investment*   *367*

Michael Markov, President, Markov Processes, Inc.

18. *Portfolio Applications Using Synthetic*
    Convertible Bonds   385

    Daniel J. Bukowski, Director of Quantitative Research,
      Kemper Financial Services
    William M. Knapp, Ph.D., Vice President and Quantitative Analyst,
      Kemper Financial Services

Part IV   Aggregate Fund (Sponsor) Issues   397

19. *Reversing Manager-Selection Failure:*
    Using Style Allocation to Improve Fund Returns   399

    David J. Kudish, President, Stratford Advisory Group, Inc.

20. *Managing Equity Style Exposure:*
    A Plan Sponsor's Experience   421

    Robert A. Birch, Assistant Director of Finance,
      Central Pension Fund, International Union of Operating
      Engineers and Participating Employers

21. *Controlling Misfit through the Use of Dynamic*
    Completeness Funds   433

    Jeffery V. Bailey, Principal, Richards & Tierney, Inc.
    David E. Tierney, Ph.D., Principal, Richards & Tierney, Inc.

22. *Driving Factors Behind Style-Based Investing*   479

    Kenneth L. Fisher, President and Chief Executive Officer,
      Fisher Investments, Inc.
    Joseph L. Toms, Senior Vice President and Director of Research,
      Fisher Investments, Inc.
    W. Kevin Blount, Research Analyst, Fisher Investments, Inc.

    Index   507

Author Biographies

Jeffery V. Bailey
Jeffery Bailey is a principal of Richards & Tierney, Inc., which specializes in applying quantitative risk control techniques to enhance the performance of plan sponsor portfolios. Mr. Bailey was formerly the assistant executive director of the Minnesota State Board of Investment, where he directed the external manager operations, developed investment policy for the board's portfolios, and measured and evaluated the performance of investment managers. Mr. Bailey co-authored the textbooks *Investments* and *Fundamentals of Investments* with William Sharpe and Gordon Alexander.

Mr. Bailey earned his B.A. in economics from Oakland University and his M.A. in economics and his M.B.A. in finance from the University of Minnesota.

Andre Bertolotti
Andre Bertolotti is a product manager and consultant with BARRA Inc., where he is responsible for all global equity products. Mr. Bertolotti is involved in the design and development of multifactor-based models for risk management and performance attribution of equity securities in developed and emerging markets. He consults with money managers and plan sponsors in the area of equity modeling, portfolio construction and optimization, and performance attribution. Prior to joining BARRA, Mr. Bertolotti worked with a consulting firm in the field of transportation and infrastucture development.

Mr. Bertolotti earned a B.S. magna cum laude from Virginia Polytechnic Institute and an M.Eng. from the University of California at Berkeley. He received an M.B.A. in finance from the University of California at Berkeley.

Robert A. Birch
Robert Birch has served as the assistant director of finance for the Central Pension Fund of the International Union of Operating Engineers and Participating Employers, where he participates in investment policy formation, asset/liability modeling, asset allocation, investment performance evalua-

tion, and manager monitoring. In addition, Mr. Birch has been instrumental in the fund's development of an equity style management process designed to minimize unintended style biases.

Mr. Birch earned his undergraduate degree from the University of Utah and his M.B.A. from the George Washington School of Business and Government.

W. Kevin Blount

Kevin Blount is a research analyst at Fisher Investments, Inc., which he joined in 1993. His areas of responsibility include performance analysis of securities, money managers, mutual funds, and consultants. Previously he was employed by a team of Paine Webber brokers.

Mr. Blount earned his bachelor's and master's degrees in engineering from Stanford University.

Daniel J. Bukowski

Dan Bukowski is the director of quantitative research at Kemper Financial Services in Chicago where he oversees research in equities, fixed income, and derivatives. Prior to joining Kemper, Mr. Bukowski was at IDS Financial Services in Minneapolis in the asset/liability management group.

Mr. Bukowski earned both his B.A. and M.B.A. from the University of Chicago and serves on the board of directors of the Chicago Quantitative Alliance.

Daniel J. Cardell

Daniel Cardell is director of equities at Bank of America in Chicago. He is responsible for the Funds Management Group, which handles over $3 billion of active equity investments. The equities are managed using internally developed quantitative techniques for asset selection and portfolio construction. Before joining the former Continental Bank in 1989, Mr. Cardell's prior experience was with the investment staffs of Equibank, Maryland National Bank, and Mellon Bank.

Mr. Cardell earned his B.S. in finance at Wilkes University and his M.B.A. from the University of Pittsburgh. He is a chartered financial analyst and a member of the board of directors of the Chicago Quantitative Alliance.

Douglas W. Case

Doug Case is director of equity portfolio management at LBS Capital Management, a money management firm utilizing artificial intelligence approaches to market analysis, stock selection, and portfolio management for private and institutional clients. Mr. Case began his career at the Florida State Board of Administration, where he was responsible for internal quantitative equity strategies and assisted in aggregate equity portfolio risk management.

Mr. Case is a graduate of the University of Pittsburgh and Florida State University's Graduate School of Business. In addition, he is a chartered financial analyst, a member of the AIMR, and a member of the Chicago Quantitative Alliance.

Daniel P. Coker

Daniel Coker is an assistant vice president with Prudential Securities Small-Cap Research Group. In addition to maintaining the department's quantitative models he has done many "Focus on a Factor" studies, which test the historical usefulness of basic factors used in stock selection.

Mr. Coker earned his B.A. magna cum laude from Drew University in Madison, New Jersey.

Kevin C. Condon

Kevin Condon is a junior quantitative analyst and an associate vice president for Prudential Securities in New York, where he is responsible for the analysis of investment strategies across core, growth, and value universes.

Mr. Condon received a B.S. in business administration from the University of Massachusetts at Lowell and an M.B.A. from Boston University. He is a member of the Association of Investment Management & Research, the New York Society of Securities Analysts, and the Society of Quantitative Analysts.

Suzanne M. Crosby

Suzanne Crosby is an analyst in the Index Products and Services Department at Standard & Poor's. Dr. Crosby assists in the maintenance and management of the S&P SmallCap 600 Index and its related products and services. Prior to joining S&P, Dr. Crosby was an assistant professor of finance and business economics at Iona College.

Dr. Crosby earned her B.S. and Ph.D. in economics at Northern Illinois University. She is a member of the American Economics Association.

Steven Cusimano

Steve Cusimano is a senior portfolio manager for the Florida State Board of Administration, which manages the $42 billion Florida Retirement System pension fund. Mr. Cusimano is responsible for the development and management of all internal quantitatively driven equity portfolios, the assets of which total approximately $9.5 billion.

Mr. Cusimano graduated with honors from the University of Florida. He is a chartered financial analyst and a member of the Association for Investment Management and Research and the Chicago Quantitative Alliance.

William J. De Allaume

Bill De Allaume has six years of investment experience with Bankers Trust Company. In its Asset Consulting Group, Mr. De Allaume has worked with institutional clients in assessing the contribution of individual investment managers and in evaluating a fund's structural allocation among managers and asset classes. Mr. De Allaume has worked extensively in applying quantitative techniques to the process of equity style analysis, and has developed products specifically for the plan sponsor market.

Mr. De Allaume earned his B.S. from Montclair State University and is currently pursuing graduate studies at the University of Chicago. He is a chartered financial analyst.

Anne B. Eisenberg

Anne Eisenberg is vice president of U.S. structured products at State Street Global Advisors, where she is responsible for directing and implementing quantitative applications in futures investment management. In addition to managing State Street's commingled S&P 500 Index Fund, Ms. Eisenberg is also responsible for managing the commingled S&P 500 Futures Fund and several extended market portfolios.

Ms. Eisenberg earned her B.A. at Tufts University and her M.B.A. at Boston University.

Stephen C. Fan

Stephen Fan is the director of research and consulting services at Vestek Systems, where he directs all quantitative research, equity and fixed income product development, and consulting activities. He is also currently associate professor of finance in the industrial engineering and engineering management department at Stanford University. Dr. Fan has served as a portfolio strategist at the Electric Power Research Institute and has conducted research in finance at the Graduate School of Business at Stanford University.

Dr. Fan earned his Ph.D. in engineering and economic systems with a specialty in international finance at Stanford University.

Kenneth L. Fisher

Ken Fisher is CEO of Fisher Investments, Inc., which he founded more than 20 years ago. He oversees the firm's ongoing research into factors affecting market performance. Mr. Fisher is widely noted for his pioneering theoretical work on price/sales ratios and his general stock market writing. He has written three books on the stock market, *Super Stocks, The Wall Street Waltz,* and *100 Minds That Made the Market.* Since 1984 he has written the "Portfolio Strategy" column for *Forbes* magazine.

Gregory J. Forsythe

Gregory Forsythe is president and research director of Chicago Investment Analytics, Inc., a specialized firm focusing exclusively on quantitative stock selection research. Prior to cofounding CIA in 1991, Mr. Forsythe was a vice president at Zacks Investment Research, serving in various research, consulting, and product management capacities. Mr. Forsythe started his business career at Union Carbide Corporation as an industrial engineer.

Mr. Forsythe earned his B.S. in industrial engineering at Purdue University and his M.B.A. in finance at the University of Chicago. He is a member of the AIMR and the Investments Analysts Society of Chicago as well as a board member of the Chicago Quantitative Alliance.

William M. Knapp

William Knapp is a vice president and quantitative analyst at Kemper Financial Services in Chicago, where he oversees research in equities and derivative securities. Prior to joining Kemper, Dr. Knapp was an investment strategist for ANB Investment Management in Chicago.

Dr. Knapp earned his B.S. from Drake University and his Ph.D. from the University of Wisconsin in Madison.

David J. Kudish

David Kudish is president and managing director of Stratford Advisory Group. He is responsible for fundamental research on market cycles and style trends in the capital markets. After serving on active duty in the U.S. Air Force, Mr. Kudish formed and was a managing partner of the investment consulting practice at Hewitt Associates. Mr. Kudish is also a past member of the board of directors of the ABT Group of Mutual Funds and served as chairman of its investment committee.

Mr. Kudish earned his B.S. with honors from the University of Rochester and his M.S. from the University of Minnesota under a National Science Foundation grant.

Craig J. Lazzara

Craig Lazzara is a vice president with Salomon Brothers, where his responsibilities include working with clients on applications of the firm's quantitative equity research. Previously, he was president of Vantage Global Advisors, managing $2 billion in quantitatively disciplined equity, tactical asset allocation, and currency management strategies. Mr. Lazzara was a managing director of TSA Capital Management, with responsibilities for both applied research and client relations. Earlier, he was a vice president and portfolio manager for Mellon Bank and T. Rowe Price Associates.

Mr. Lazzara is a graduate of Princeton University and the Harvard Business School.

Diana L. Lieberman

Diana Lieberman is a vice president and consultant at Strategic Investment Solutions. Prior to joining Strategic, Ms. Lieberman was a senior associate and consultant with William F. Sharpe Associates, where she was a key participant in developing and refining the use of the return-based style analysis system and responsible for client relationships. Ms. Lieberman was also a consultant at Montgomery Securities, where she developed and implemented asset allocations, investment manager selections, and performance monitoring systems for use with Montgomery's high-net-worth clients.

Ms. Lieberman earned an A.B. in economics from Stanford University, and is a CFA candidate.

Rosemary Macedo

Rosemary Macedo is vice president of quantitative research at Bailard, Biehl & Kaiser, where her primary focus is on developing quantitative models for international equities, and on integrating this quantitative information with more traditional qualitative inputs to formulate portfolio strategy. Prior to joining Bailard, Biehl & Kaiser, Ms. Macedo was affiliated with First Quadrant, where she developed models for equity style selection and asset allocation.

Ms. Macedo earned her B.S. in independent studies from the California Institute of Technology.

Michael Markov

Michael Markov is president of Markov Processes, which specializes in the development of quantitative financial software and securities research using quantitative methods. His firm designed and developed Zephyr Associates Style Advisor, a style and performance evaluation system that is now used by major pension funds, foundations, and consultants in the United States and abroad.

Mr. Markov earned an M.S. in mathematics from Kharkov University, Ukraine. Mr. Markov has also spent a number of years in Russia teaching mathematics and statistics as well as developing data analysis software.

Lawrence J. Marks

Lawrence Marks is a founder and managing director of Harbor Capital Management Company Inc., which combines growth stocks and value stocks in separately managed portfolios with one portfolio manager responsible for both portions. His 35-year career includes stints as a research analyst, portfolio manager, economist, and director of research.

Mr. Marks earned a B.S. in economics from the Wharton School at the University of Pennsylvania and an M.B.A. from New York University. He is a chartered financial analyst and a trustee of the Beth Israel Hospital Corporation in Boston as well as a member of its finance and investment subcommittees.

John P. Meier

John Meier is a vice president and director of quantitative consulting for Strategic Investment Solutions, Inc. and has responsibility for the firm's systems and technology as well as directing client's strategic planning activities and researching quantitative investment strategies. From 1988 to 1994, Mr. Meier was a senior product manager at BARRA, responsible for equity risk management and valuation models and services covering over 40 markets around the world. Prior to joining BARRA, Mr. Meier spent nine years with the Standard Oil Company in Anchorage, Cleveland, and San Francisco as a senior production and process engineer. He also worked as an analyst with Liquidity Fund Investment Corp., developing a mutual fund of publicly traded real estate securities.

Mr. Meier earned a B.S. degree in chemical engineering from Michigan State University and an M.B.A. in finance from the University of California at Berkeley.

Claudia E. Mott

Claudia Mott is a first vice president and director of small-cap research at Prudential Securities Inc. She provides quantitative research to the small-cap investment community in the form of stock valuation and earnings surprise models, topical studies, and screens, and is well known for her work on the various benchmarks used to measure small-cap performance. Over the past two years, Ms. Mott has broadened her research to include the mid-cap sector of the market. Ms. Mott joined Prudential Securities in 1986 as a quantitative analyst supporting the existing large-cap quantitative model and related screening software. Prior to joining Prudential Securities, she was a senior consultant for Interactive Data Corporation in Boston and a financial analyst for Boston Gas Company.

Ms. Mott earned a B.B.A. cum laude from the University of Massachusetts at Amherst and an M.B.A. from Boston University.

Elizabeth E. Nevin

Elizabeth Nevin directs U.S. equity manager research at Evaluation Associates, Inc. Ms. Nevin leads the firm's professional activities in the structuring of U.S. equity portfolios, manager evaluations, and due diligence activities as well as domestic equity searches. She joined Evaluation Associates in 1989.

Prior to joining Evaluation Associates, Ms. Nevin held several positions at Penn Central Corporation, including inventory accountant, treasury analyst, and pension plan administrator. Ms. Nevin managed relationships with all of the plan's external managers as well as serving as liaison with the master custodian.

Ms. Nevin holds a B.A. from the College of New Rochelle and an M.B.A. from Iona College.

Satya Dev Pradhuman

Satya Pradhuman is vice president and senior quantitative analyst at Merrill Lynch & Company. Mr. Pradhuman is responsible for the research and development of small- and mid-cap equity and equity-related derivative strategies. Prior to joining Merrill Lynch in 1989, Mr. Pradhuman worked at E.F. Hutton and Shearson Lehman.

Mr. Pradhuman earned his B.S. from Union College and his M.B.A. in finance from New York University. He is a member of the Chicago Quantitative Alliance.

Arlene M. Rockefeller

Arlene Rockefeller is a managing director and unit head of U.S. structured products at State Street Global Advisors, where she is responsible for managing the Russell 1000 and 2000 funds, the equal-weighted S&P 500 fund, several restricted funds, and the MULDEX funds, as well as being involved with the computerized implementation of new products.

Ms. Rockefeller earned her undergraduate degree as well as an M.I.S. degree from the University of Chicago and her M.B.A. from Boston University.

Thomas J. Schwab

Thomas J. Schwab is an executive director of First Madison Advisors, where he is primarily responsible for business strategy and portfolio management. A founder of First Madison Advisors in 1990, he has worked for Smith Barney Inc. since 1976. Previously, he worked for Goldman, Sachs & Co. and the New York Stock Exchange.

Mr. Schwab holds an M.B.A. in finance from New York University and a B.B.A. from the University of Notre Dame.

Eric H. Sorensen

Eric Sorensen is a managing director of Salomon Brothers Inc. He joined Salomon Brothers in 1986 and currently heads Salomon's Equity Portfolio Analysis and Derivatives Research Group. He leads a team of approximately 30 analysts in the creation and implementation of derivatives and quantitative investment strategies, including global asset allocation, currency hedging, equity portfolio construction, stock ranking models, and hedged trading strategies. He was formerly head of the department of finance and real estate at the University of Arizona, and was professor of finance between 1977 and 1986.

Dr. Sorensen earned his Ph.D. in finance at the University of Oregon in 1977. He has published over 40 articles in professional and academic journals. He serves on the editorial boards of the *Financial Analysts Journal,* the *Journal of Portfolio Management,* and the *Financial Management Journal.* Dr. Sorensen also served as an Air Force jet pilot and officer from 1969 to 1974.

David E. Tierney

David Tierney is a cofounder and a principal of Richards & Tierney, Inc., which specializes in applying quantitative risk control techniques to enhance the performance of plan sponsor portfolios. Formerly, Dr. Tierney was administrative manager of investments for Amoco Corporation's pension fund, where he directed and coordinated the activities of the investment managers, controlled the pension fund's accounting and auditing functions, measured and analyzed the performance of the fund's investment managers, and conducted research into improved methods of pension management. Dr. Tierney has taught at the University of Chicago's Graduate School of Business.

Dr. Tierney earned his B.S., with distinction, in engineering science from Northwestern University and his M.S. and Ph.D. in applied statistics from the University of Wisconsin.

Joseph L. Toms

Joe Toms is director of research and a shareholder of Fisher Investments, Inc., which he joined in 1985. He has developed extensive research on style analysis based on size and valuation as well as the performance attributes of small-cap stocks. Previously he worked for L. H. Friend & Co. and for Prudential-Bache Securities.

Mr. Toms graduated with a degree in finance from the University of California at Santa Barbara and studied finance at Cambridge University.

David A. Umstead

David Umstead is a founder and managing director of Boston International Advisors, where he concentrates on strategy research. From 1975 to 1978, Dr. Umstead taught at the Wharton School of Finance at the University of Pennsylvania while providing services to The Hartford Fire Insurance Company and The Boston Company. In 1978, Dr. Umstead was named a vice president and director of quantitative research for the Putnam Management Company in Boston, where he was leader of a group dedicated to providing quantitative research support. He also served as a portfolio manager for the Putnam International Equities Fund and was a member of the international investment policy committee. Following Putnam, Dr. Umstead joined State Street Bank and Trust Company in 1984 as vice president and head of the international investment department. Under his tenure, the international department expanded from four accounts and assets of $400 million to 33 accounts and assets of over $2.3 billion.

Dr. Umstead is a chartered financial analyst and a member of the Association for Investment Management and Research and the Boston Security Analysts Society. Dr. Umstead earned a B.S. from the University of Vermont, an M.S. from MIT, and M.B.A. from Boston University, and a Ph.D. in finance from the University of North Carolina at Chapel Hill.

Bruce D. Westervelt

Bruce D. Westervelt is an executive director of First Madison Advisors, where he is primarily responsible for research, model development, portfolio implementation, and investment strategy. A founder of First Madison Advisors in 1990, he has worked for Smith Barney Inc. since 1981. He is a chartered financial analyst and a member of the AIMR.

Mr. Westervelt holds a B.B.A. in finance from the University of Wisconsin.

Preface

The Irwin asset allocation series for institutional investors is dedicated to exploring both the theory and real-world application of cutting-edge topics. *Equity Style Management* follows *Hedge Funds: Investment and Portfolio Strategies* as the second book in this exciting and innovative series.

Portfolio managers have only recently come to realize that decisions about equity investment *styles* can have a dominant impact on equity-portfolio performance. *Equity Style Management* is devoted to a comprehensive analysis of this phenomenon, with an emphasis on practical utilization. It is the result of a year of effort by 35 of the brightest and most successful experts on equity investment. Every aspect of style management is examined in detail: growth and value; small-, medium-, and large-cap stocks; country selection style; equity style benchmarking and indexation; timing of style switches; active versus passive style management; and manager selection.

Many thanks must be given to each of the contributing authors for the time and energy they took from their hectic schedules. We are also grateful to the superb staff at Irwin Professional Publishing and to Kirsten Stigberg at Precision Graphics, who made the timely publication of this important book possible.

Jess Lederman
Robert Klein

PART I

Origins of Equity Style

Basic Issues and Key Elements for Equity Style Management

Bruce D. Westervelt, CFA, Executive Director
First Madison Advisors

Thomas J. Schwab, Executive Director
First Madison Advisors

Ninety-seven percent of a portfolio's return can be explained by style exposure. This notion, developed by the Nobel laureate William F. Sharpe, is causing a complete reexamination and rethinking of how portfolios are managed. Because allocation between asset classes (stocks, bonds, cash, etc.) is widely accepted as the key determinant of performance for an entire fund, the concept of equity style allocation as the key driver of equity performance is intuitively appealing. However, as with all straightforward concepts in investing, the important nuances of equity style allocation (interchangeably termed "equity style management") require consideration. This anthology covers a variety of methods for identifying, measuring, controlling, and taking advantage of equity style. This chapter will discuss the important elements and issues for equity style management. It will begin with academic research and viewpoints, then review different applications and common questions concerning equity style management. Finally, the realities and challenges affecting implementation of equity style management will be examined. Equity style management is destined to become widely understood and broadly accepted as the most important decision for the equity asset class.

Academic Foundations

A Serial Walk down Wall Street

Much of the modern view of equity style management has been shaped by well-known academic researchers. Recently, Burton G. Malkiel (author of the popular book *A Random Walk Down Wall Street*) has stated in his research "there appeared to be a considerable degree of predictability of stock returns on the basis of certain fundamental ratios and variables. Stock returns appeared to be predictable on the basis of such variables as initial dividend yields, market capitalization (size), price/earnings ratios, and price/book value ratios. Of course, return predictability need not imply inefficiency of equity markets. Time-series tests of return predictability may reflect rational variation through time in expected returns. . . . The apparent robustness of certain predictable patterns has led to a view that our 1970s belief in the simplistic efficient-markets constant-returns model was unwarranted."[1] These predictable patterns indicate that trends (serial correlation) in the returns for segments of the market exist. Therefore, the random-walk theory, which states that future directions cannot be predicted on the basis of past actions, is flawed.

Significant New Research

The work of French and Fama, "The Cross-Section of Expected Stock Returns,"[2] contributed to this new way of thinking. The research found that size and book market value accounted for differences in return for segments of the market. It further suggested that expected returns for different portfolio strategies could be estimated from historical returns of portfolios of similar size and book market values. This work and the research of others have reached the same conclusion. Specifically, segments of the market act differently over time and pattern predictability exists.

Application of This New Finance Technology

The factors that shaped this broader definition of the efficient market also drive the equity style allocation (management) process. Best illustrated in the widely quoted Bill Sharpe article "Asset Allocation:

---

[1] Malkiel, Burton G. "Returns from Investing in Equity Mutual Funds 1971–1991." Center for Economic Policy Studies *Working Paper No. 15*, Princeton University, December 1993, pp. 1–2.

[2] Fama, Eugene F., and French, Kenneth R. "The Cross-Section of Expected Returns." *The Journal of Finance*, June 1992, pp. 427–465.

Management Style and Performance Measurement,"[3] size and growth-value characteristics can explain a huge portion of the returns of an equity portfolio. The bulk of the returns of a diversified equity portfolio is a function of these factors. This suggests that the most critical issue for a holder of a diversified equity portfolio is the equity style exposure of the portfolio versus a broad benchmark index.

Some observers may be troubled by the notion that the risk of an equity-style-driven investment process is often equal to that of the market but that the process is still able to generate excess returns. What generally occurs is that the portfolio is at a lower risk (beta) level than the market half of the time while at a higher risk level the rest of the time. Over time, the two offset each other giving market-like risk. However, in the short run the risk of being different from the market must be accepted to achieve excess return.

Is "Style Neutral" an Acceptable Paradigm for Portfolio Construction?

If the risk of being different from the market must be accepted to achieve excess returns, then a commonly used approach to portfolio structure, equity style neutrality, must be rethought. The equity-style-neutral approach ignores the potential gains from equity style management and only relies on stock selection as the source of excess returns. A sponsor's aggregate portfolio in an equity-style-neutral structure approximately replicates the market by size (Figure 1-1) and industry weights.

Sponsors and consultants become frustrated when diligent research and careful manager-selection techniques produce only mediocre results. Bill Sharpe, in his article and in subsequent references, sheds light on why this phenomenon occurs. In his analysis of Fidelity's Magellan fund and other funds, Sharpe finds that 97% of a portfolio's return is explained by equity style exposure, leaving only 3% to come from stock selection. Therefore, if a sponsor's portfolio is always equity style neutral, it will experience index-like returns plus

---

[3] Sharpe, William F. "Asset Allocation: Management Style and Performance Measurement." *The Journal of Portfolio Management*, Winter 1992, pp. 7–19.

FIGURE 1-1.   Traditional Style-Neutral Approach

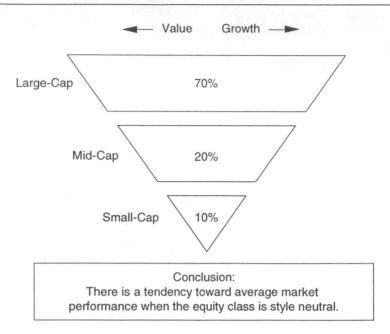

Source: First Madison Advisors.

or minus a small amount from stock selection. Sponsors who adhere to an equity-style-neutral approach sometimes question active management and sophisticated analysis because their funds, net of all costs, have produced the same results as an inexpensive and effortless market index fund.

Is a "Static Tilt" the Answer?

Some participants who argue against the equity-style-neutral approach favor a constant or static tilt to growth or value for the aggregate portfolio. Typically, a value-tilt advocate will argue that value tends to outperform on an absolute and risk-adjusted basis over time (largely true over the last 15 years). A growth partisan will say that growth is a way to "out-grow" the market. Both parties will probably agree that, over discrete time frames, the aggregate equity portfolio will experience over or under performance as a result of any constant tilt. Unless this static tilt is managed in some way, the familiar battle cry, "but my style was out of favor," will soon be heard. Separately, those of the growth persuasion who have been waiting off and on for 15 years, may soon have their day in the sun.

Style Allocation Rivals Asset-Class Allocation in Importance and Opportunity

In First Madison's research piece, "The Importance of Equity Style Allocation,"[4] the opportunity to add value through allocation was examined. This two-part study analyzed potential returns from asset class allocation and equity style allocation over the 15-year period 1980 through 1994. The opportunity to add value through allocation was assessed by examining the returns generated from allocating assets between four asset classes (long bond, intermediate bond, S&P 500, and cash) as well as the returns generated from allocating assets between four equity styles (large-cap value, large-cap growth, small-cap value, and small-cap growth).

The study found that over the 15-year period, the return of a normal 60% stocks, 35% bonds, and 5% cash portfolio was 13.20%. However, if one could perfectly shift to the best asset class each quarter, the annualized rate of return exploded to 31.93%. The opportunity to add value through asset class allocation was, therefore, the difference of 18.73% (Figure 1-2). Obviously, not all of these returns can be achieved through asset class allocation, but one can see that asset class allocation is important.

The study went on to hypothesize that unless a great deal of difference exists among the returns of various equity styles, no attempt should be made to shift among them. The annualized return of the Wilshire 5000, an all equity proxy, was 13.98% over the 15-year time frame. Perfectly timed shifting among the four equity styles caused annual returns to mushroom to 29.67%. The difference, 15.69%, represents the opportunity to add value through equity style allocation within an equity portfolio. Again, the returns from either perfect asset class allocation or perfect equity style allocation presented above are unattainable best-case scenarios. However, one can see that the magni-

---

[4] First Madison Advisors. "The Importance of Style Allocation," January 1995. Additional equity style management data is available from the firm on request. (P.O. Box 1498, Madison, WI 53701.)

FIGURE 1-2. The Importance of Equity Style Allocation for the 15 Years December 31, 1979 through December 31, 1994

By taking only the best quarter for one of the asset classes each quarter in Asset Allocation and Equity Style Allocation, respectively, and linking them together, the potential to add extra return through shifting is revealed.

Asset Allocation		Equity Style Allocation	
Long bond	Intermediate bond	Large Value	Large Growth
Cash	S&P 500	Small Value	Small Growth
Best of asset allocation	31.93%	Best of style allocation	29.67%
Versus traditional 60/35/5 mix	13.20%	Versus Wilshire 5000	13.98%
Maximum potential from shifts	18.73%	Maximum potential from shifts	15.69%

Conclusion: Style allocation rivals asset allocation in potential.

Source: First Madison Advisors.

tude of increased returns from equity style allocation rivals that of asset class allocation in relative importance and opportunity (Figure 1-3).

Isn't Equity Style Allocation Market Timing?

The parallels of equity style allocation and asset class allocation are many. However major differences exist. Detractors of equity style allocation may view it as a form of "market timing," and cite studies that show that being out of the market for just a handful of the best days can drop returns significantly. Equity style allocation, however, is always fully invested in the market, so "market timing" is not an issue. Detractors may continue by suggesting that attempts to shift between equity styles comprise timing those styles and that may be difficult. This argument typically originates with sponsors who hire traditional active managers to pick (or "time") stocks. In fact, analyzing styles is similar to analyzing stocks. With today's risk-management software, broad segments of the market, each representing an equity style, can be viewed as "composite assets," whereby all constituents of a market segment or style are viewed as a single unit. Traditional fundamental analysis data can be generated for composite assets or styles, which significantly enhance the ability to model and predict outcomes. Having more hard data available with which to work means equity style allocators should have a higher degree of success than asset class allocators in their active process.

FIGURE 1-3.   Opportunity for Gain from Style Allocation

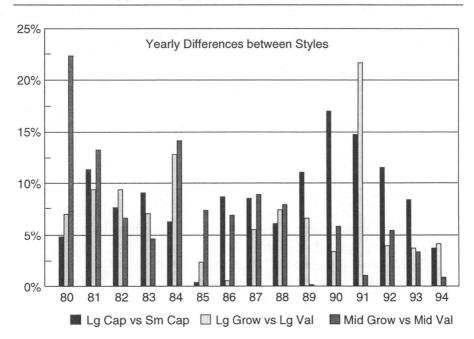

Source: First Madison Advisors.

Implementation Issues

Critical to executing an equity style management process is capturing the returns of the intended equity style exposures. Passive management believers suggest that the only way to proceed is with passive portfolios that have the advantages of low cost and are clearly defined. Active management believers criticize the use of passive management by pointing out that the opportunity to gain significant extra return from the active process is not considered. Most often the right approach is somewhere in the middle. The question is how to ensure that active-style tilts will capture the returns and add the value from traditional active management. Naturally, it depends on the nature of the portfolio to which it is applied. The current structure of a portfolio and how much this structure will be allowed to change as a practical matter are important factors. Often the largest consideration with regard to change stems from politics or biases within the organization, and the actual correctness of what should be done often takes a back seat.

The Ramifications of Shifting Funds between Individual Managers

The actual shifting of funds between managers requires not only a high degree of skill, but tact as well. Dislocations of funds at untimely moments can cause the returns of the individual portfolios and the aggregate to suffer. This may occur for a couple of reasons. First, the manager being reduced will probably be asked to sell what he or she sees fit, leading to a cash buildup that may cause undesirable results. Second, the manager with the increased allocation must make decisions based on timely analysis of information and must act quickly. This leads to market impact, a cost incurred both with the original investment and with the shifting of funds.

When funds are frequently shifted between active managers and they are forced to bear interruptions in their investment process, are the managers getting a fair shake in their performance assessment? Removing funds as a reward for good performance (largely a function of equity style) may not foster a positive working relationship. Additionally, with the amount of focus on cost control and accounting for the expenses of the plan, knowing what expenses were naturally assignable to the individual manager's process and what was a function of the dynamic structure would be virtually impossible. Sponsors who prefer to take the responsibility for the outcome of the plan by making the allocation decision may place themselves at odds with their managers. Underperformance has to rest with someone, and the macromanagement decision-maker may not like having to take that responsibility. This is especially true when the individual managers have done well versus their style benchmarks but the fund was allocated incorrectly.

Incorporating Equity Style Management

The three most common structures for funds are first, a fund composed of multiple active managers; second, a fund with a core index surrounded by active and/or passive managers; and third, a single-manager fund with active or passive management. For each of these cases the introduction of style management will be different. However, the goal, to achieve the gains from style management while minimizing the disruption to the current fund structure, will always be the same. The biases and politics that led to an existing manager configuration are not likely to change and should be the paradigm for a new structure that will include equity style management.

The Multimanager Fund

The multimanager fund is the most common. In the construction of a multimanager fund, a diverse group of managers is typically put together, with or without the aid of a consultant, based on some logical fit between the individual managers. That fit is most often an equity-style-neutral or static-tilt configuration. To introduce equity style management, one could hire a firm to direct the shifting of funds between managers. If one's situation is inflexible, this may be the best course to take. Earlier comments regarding the shifting of funds between managers indicated direct and indirect expenses associated with this method of equity style management. The risk of missing a targeted equity style tilt due to an active manager's portfolio construction also exists. If funds are available, or if a manager has done poorly versus his or her respective equity style benchmark and is a candidate for replacement, adding an equity style allocation manager becomes a possibility. By positioning this equity style manager in the core slot, the automatic tilting of the fund can be achieved with a minimum of dislocation, expense, and effort.

The Core Index Plus Multiple Managers Fund

The fund with a core index surrounded by active and/or passive managers is the easiest for introducing an equity style manager. The pros and cons of a "macro" style manager for this structure are about the same as previously discussed. With a core-index configuration, an individual equity style manager can be installed by simply reallocating a percentage of the index to the equity style manager. The mix of managers is unaffected, and since most equity style managers use passive portfolios to accomplish their equity style tilt, the same efficiency and diversification associated with indexing remains. Conceptually, an investment committee would not be required to change their thinking about this portion of the fund. However, at a deeper level some rather interesting things happen to the characteristics of the fund.

Often, this type of fund has an overall equity style bias. This predisposition to a particular equity style is something that is not going to change in the short run and turns into quite a battle with the investment committee if one attempts to do so. The advantage of having a core equity style manager is that the bias remains undisturbed, but is modified through time in a positive way. If, for example, the fund's bias is toward large-cap value and the equity style allocator is tilted in the same direction, the alpha (extra return) is amplified by this larger-than-average weighting to that equity style. Conversely, when the equity style allocator is in a small-cap growth mode, the potential negative impact of the static large-cap value bias is offset. This, of course, would help avoid periods of underperformance for the overall portfolio that would certainly occur if the shift had not been implemented. The static bias of the fund over time would still have an impact regardless of equity style allocation, but in the short run the fund would tend to generate smoother performance. Moreover, the largest opportunity to add value and extra return to the aggregate equity portfolio is through shifting equity style exposures over time. At the aggregate level the fund will experience subtle benefits from equity style management that go beyond extra return.

The Single-Manager Fund

The single-manager equity fund is the most challenging situation. Single-manager funds are typically of smaller size and have biases and politics that are entrenched. Attempting to change the structure or trying to convince a committee that may not be highly sophisticated of the merits of equity style allocation can be difficult. If the lone manager is questioned whether equity style consideration plays an important role in the investment process, the answer invariably is yes. One should question that if this is true, has the manager ever brought this to the board's attention before? In any case, is equity style the true driver of the manager's process? Usually, the only hope of introducing equity style management in a single-manager fund is to wait for underperformance by the manager. Ironically, when poor results occur, the manager is likely to explain the underperformance by saying that the fund's equity style was out of favor at the time. This would be the ideal time to request further clarification of the manager's equity style, and how that style led to underperformance.

If a lone manager is underperforming, the stage has been set to highlight to a committee the differences in equity style. Specifically, one can identify the inefficiencies of a fund's current structure, and how, through equity style allocation, the fund can achieve the same buffering effect available to large multimanager funds. Time and patience may be required to convince a committee of the need for equity style management. With only one manager, macro-style management is not an option and the only form of implementation available is to hire an individual equity style manager with some portion of available funds. In the future many single-manager funds which are equity style allocation driven will exist, and complete adoption of equity style management will be commonplace.

Large Funds Can Achieve Meaningful Results with Equity Style Management

A concern, particularly for large funds using any of the above mentioned configurations, is how much of an allocation is needed to generate significant impact on the overall equity fund through equity style management. The right answer depends on the objectives of the specific fund. As a practical matter, the sheer size of a fund may dictate that an individual equity style manager in concert with macro equity style management is the best solution.

Constructing an Equity Style Management Portfolio

Having covered first, the academic validity of equity style management; second, the possible scenarios for implementation to the aggregate portfolio; and finally, the pluses and minuses of macro-style management versus an individual equity style management portfolio; we can now move to the key points of the equity style management portfolio itself. Reiterating comments from the opening paragraph, although equity style management is straightforward, the nuances are numerous, varied, and critical.

Equity style management portfolios are available in different forms. For example, assume a search for equity style managers produces three candidates. One manager uses equity style indices trademarked by ABC Consulting, the second uses XYZ Consultant's indices, and the third develops custom portfolios (indices) to implement his equity style management process.

Critical Differences in Equity Style Portfolios

Assume that ABC Consulting's indices are known for high turnover and actively managed industry concentrations, while XYZ Consultant's indices use only price to book for their definition of growth versus value. Should one care if custom portfolios are used? If an equity style manager has to deal with arbitrary changes in industry mix over time, his modeling will not be accurate. If an index has high turnover, it will be expensive and can miss the returns of the sector it is designed to replicate (Figure 1-4). If price to book, a lagged accounting artifact, is the only criteria for value, the correlation between the value segment and a broad index may be as high as 98%, thereby seriously dampening the equity-style-shift effort. Custom indices that consistently and efficiently replicate style segments can play an important role for effective implementation of an equity style management process.

An Equity Style Management Investment Process Must Be Structurally Sound

After the decision is made to implement equity style management and the nuances of equity style indices or vehicles available for implementation have been considered, the final and most important step is to

---

FIGURE 1-4. Critical Differences in Equity Style Portfolios

---

1. If the turnover rate of stocks in the portfolio is high
   - May miss the returns for the market segment
   - Expensive (transaction costs and market impact)

2. Overly simplistic value definition
   - Example: Price/book, often used to separate growth and value, is a lagged indicator—an "accounting artifact."

3. Industry concentrations
   - Indexes that single out industries as value ignore the value stocks of other industries, introducing bias into the portfolio.

Source: First Madison Advisors.

identify an equity style management process that is structurally sound. A myriad of ways exist to model the equity style segments, and a manager's process must be both intuitive and academically correct.

Requirements for the Equity Style Management Process

On the basis of current technology, the first requirement of the investment process would be the manager's use of a multivariate (multifactor) framework. Recent research indicates that *ex ante* the amount of return explained by beta, a univariate or single-factor model, is only slightly above 50%. Multifactor models explain a great deal more. In a related issue the concept of linearity must be addressed as well. Beta and some multifactor models assume linearity as a given, which is probably not a good idea, given the general acceptance of the fact that equity returns are not normally distributed.

The non-normal distribution of returns and the presence of serial correlation that leads to the "predictable stock returns based on fundamental ratios and variables" noted by Burton G. Malkiel by definition indicate identifiable trends. Several elements should be considered. How does a manager's model incorporate trend into the process? Does the model do a good job of identifying when conditions are at the extremes (in the error terms)? Can the model ignore noise when extreme conditions are not present?

Expense Control

Another nuance to consider is whether a manager's model tends to shift frequently. Cost minimization and risk control are important issues to the end user. A process that attempts to capture small short-term movements can easily be swamped by transaction expenses (both direct and market impact). A short-term process also runs the risk of missing more important long-term equity style trends that do not need to be micromanaged. Keep in mind that an expensive and volatile process undermines the key point of what equity style allocation is all about; maximizing return while minimizing risk.

A Dynamic Process for Dynamic Markets

Finally, the difference between dynamic equity style allocation versus tactical equity style allocation must be addressed. Dynamic allocation is reactive to the current environment where tactical allocation requires prediction of expected returns. Both methodologies are constantly utilizing new data in their process but in different ways.

George Soros, known for his market savvy, communicated what he felt was a major key to his success in his speech entitled "The Theory of Reflexivity" for the MIT Department of Economics in April 1994.[5] Soros commented, "I must state at the outset that I am in fundamental disagreement with the prevailing wisdom. The generally accepted theory is the financial markets tend towards equilibrium, and on the whole, discount the future correctly. I operate using a different theory, according to which financial markets cannot possibly discount the future correctly because they do not merely discount the future, they help to shape it. In certain circumstances, financial markets can affect the so-called fundamentals which they are supposed to reflect. When that happens, markets enter into a state of dynamic disequilibrium and behave quite differently from what would be considered normal by the theory of efficient markets."

Tactical versus Dynamic Equity Style Allocation

A tactical process cannot deal with extreme conditions the way a dynamic process can. This, of course, is where large amounts of excess returns are available and what Soros suggests is the key to his success. By raising exposure prematurely to an equity style that is underperforming, the portfolio will have significantly limited the possibility of generating extra return. Tactical equity style allocation requires absolute estimates of economic events and premiums for the market and its segments, whereas dynamic equity style allocation requires only the relative probability of a conditional state being present. Analysts who are in the business of generating absolute estimates often poke fun at themselves by using the humorous phrase, "Predict, and predict often." Because the interrelationships between economic variables are not static, analysts need to revise their forecasts constantly. This volume of change in estimates leads to implementation error, resulting in poor performance. A dynamic process that gives heed to trends in the market is less susceptible to estimation errors.

---

[5] Soros, George. "The Theory of Reflexivity." Address to the MIT Economics World Economy Laboratory Conference, Washington D.C. April 26, 1994.

Conclusion

Equity style management is a straightforward intuitive process destined to become widely known as the most important decision affecting performance of the equity asset class. This chapter has touched on many of the basic issues and key elements of equity style management, and some of the real challenges faced in actually implementing this type of process. Since the concept is academically correct and intuitively appealing, broad acceptance and use lie ahead. The effort to understand and utilize equity style management must be diligently pursued, and as with all key investment concepts that stand the test of time, those that master and incorporate them will lead the way.

Footprints in the Sand: Return-Based Style Analysis

Diana L. Lieberman, Vice President
Strategic Investment Solutions, Inc.

The investment management field is constantly evolving. The increasing sophistication and responsibilities of fund sponsors are the primary impetus to this evolution. The emergence of equity styles is a perfect example of this transition. Establishing equity style indices can be routine, determining an investment manager's style is not as straightforward. There are various techniques that assist in categorizing managers by style. Return-based style analysis (style analysis) is becoming a popular tool. Its popularity is due to quickness, ease of use, and communication ability. While the appeal of the analysis is its simplicity, it is important to have an understanding of the mechanics and the inputs behind the analysis to utilize the full benefits of the tool.

Style-analysis users do not need to know all the technical aspects, but they should have an understanding of the overall concept. Once there is a general understanding of the program, issues regarding the proper inputs need to be clarified. These issues include choosing the appropriate indices, the appropriate time period, and the frequency of the returns.

After these issues have been addressed, the validity of resultant styles can be tested. Such tests include: the degree of variability in a manager's style with the additional years of data, the value added of

I would like to thank Michael Beasley, Barry Dennis, and Lou Kingsland of Strategic Investment Solutions, Inc. and John Freeman of Martingale Asset Management for their helpful input.

using style analysis compared to a broad-market index, and a reality check comparing mutual funds' styles with their classifications.

The results from the analysis are useful in not only determining individual manager styles, but also in determining a fund's effective asset mix. The style-analysis results are extremely useful in simply communicating these and other complex investment issues.

Although style analysis is helpful, it has its limitations. Once these are understood, style analysis becomes a powerful tool to gain insight into the issues that affect the fund sponsor's most important decision: asset allocation.

Equity Style Determination Techniques

In past decades, manager classification was not difficult because only one or two equity styles were defined. This task has become more cumbersome with the proliferation of investment manager styles. To improve diversification and performance monitoring, fund sponsors and their consultants have devised methods to determine (or verify) investment manager styles. Two such approaches are portfolio characteristics and return-based analysis.

Portfolio Characteristic Approach

The portfolio characteristic approach classifies investment managers based on their investment approach and point-in-time characteristics of the securities within the portfolio (usually current portfolio). Portfolio characteristics such as P/E, price/book, earnings growth, and market capitalization are determined. These, in conjunction with the investment manager's stated approach, are compared to either a benchmark (e.g., S&P 500 Index) or a peer group to determine the appropriate classification.

The portfolio characteristic approach is labor intensive and can be judgmental. Portfolios change over time. Point-in-time categorizations may result in significant style "drift," with or without transaction activity. Such "drift" would render long-term stylistic comparisons useless. One solution is to calculate these characteristics at different points in time and use multiple portfolios to classify the investment manager. One drawback to this strategy is that the data and analysis requirements increase.

FIGURE 2-1. Large/Small, Value/Growth
Annual returns, 1984 through 1993

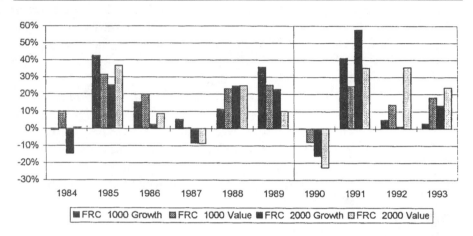

Return-Based Analysis

The second approach relies on only an investment manager's historical returns to determine the appropriate style classification. Figure 2-1 illustrates how large, small, value, and growth indices produce different return patterns.

If a large percentage of the investment manager's returns can be explained by these four factors, this information can be used to determine the manager's classification. For instance, if combining 90% of a large-growth index and 10% of a small-growth index closely replicates the manager's return pattern, then it is most likely a large-growth manager. This approach focuses solely on past returns, and does not investigate the portfolio holdings (opposite to the portfolio characteristic approach).

While it is not important to know the technicalities of the actual analysis, it is crucial to have a general understanding of the principle behind the analysis.[1] Return-based style analysis is similar to a regression analysis, but technically is a quadratic optimization program. In

[1] For a detailed explanation of return-based style analysis see: Sharpe, William. "Determining a Fund's Effective Asset Mix." *Investment Management Review*, November/December 1988.

a sense, the manager's historical returns are regressed upon various chosen indices. Nobel laureate William F. Sharpe refers to manager's past returns as "tracks in the sand." The resultant style is the mixture of indices' returns that match the portfolio's returns the closest.[2] The program tests every possible combination of selected indices to determine the best fit. The mix with the minimum tracking variance suggests the most relevant style.

The selected style is represented by the loadings (or weightings) on the indices. How well the pattern of the style's returns tracks the pattern of the manager's returns is measured by the R-squared.[3] An R-squared of 0.95 is interpreted as the style explaining 95% of the managers historic return pattern. Style analysis is a quantitative method that decomposes the proportion of the return attributed to the market into size and style.

Return-Based Style Analysis Inputs

Index Issues

Any quantitative model is only as good as its inputs. Return-based style analysis is no exception. First, the overall concept of the analysis needs to be understood. Second, valid manager-returns must be obtained. Third, one must understand the indices chosen for the analysis. The user of the analysis has several choices when determining the suitable indices.

Number of Indices

The proper number of asset classes for the analysis must first be determined. A full model using fixed-income, equity, and interna-

---

[2] For instance, the large-growth manager referred to earlier would have had a 90% loading on the large-growth index, and a 10% loading on the small-growth index, and zero loadings on any other indices which were used in the optimization. The style-return pattern is calculated by multiplying 0.90 times each monthly large-growth index return plus 0.10 times each monthly small-growth index return. This return pattern can then be compared to that of the manager's.

[3] The R-squared is a measure of the correlation between the two return series. The R-squared is actually the adjusted R-squared. The R-squared value is adjusted to account for degrees of freedom lost due to the number of indices used and the number of observations available.

tional indices is appropriate for analysis (1) of managers who use multiple asset classes (i.e., balanced accounts), or (2) when a fund sponsor desires to evaluate the fund's overall asset allocation.[4] If the user is only interested in the equity portion of the fund, then it is preferable to use only equity and cash indices.

Index Characteristics

The selected indices should cover at least the full spectrum of the investment manager's opportunity set and be mutually exclusive. Ideally, the appropriate equity indices combined would equal the equity universe, with mutually exclusivity eliminating overlap.

Using two highly correlated or overlapping indices will produce meaningless results. Table 2-1 is a correlation matrix of the Russell indices over the last five years.

Considering the high degree of correlation, it would be pointless to include the Russell 1000 Index (or Russell 2000 Index) when the value and growth components are in use. The same reasoning applies to why similar indices provided by different vendors (e.g., S&P/BARRA Value Index and Russell 1000 Value Index) should not be used in the same analysis.

Index Effects

It is important to understand the biases associated with various equity indices. These biases will impact the style analysis results. Figure 2-2 illustrates the style for S&P 500 Index using various indices.[5]

---

[4] Sharpe, William. "Asset Allocation: Management Style and Performance Measurement." *Journal of Portfolio Management*, Winter 1992.

[5] Zephyr Associates Inc. Style Advisor software was used for this analysis and all subsequent analyses. All return data were supplied by Zephyr Associates Inc.

TABLE 2-1.   Correlation Matrix, July 1989 through June 1994

	R1000	R2000
FRC1000 Growth	0.97	0.80
FRC1000 Value	0.96	0.82
FRC2000 Growth	0.82	0.97
FRC2000 Value	0.80	0.96

FIGURE 2-2.   S&P 500 Index
July 1991 through June 1994

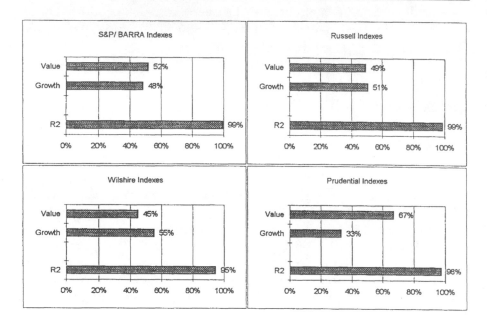

The analyses use three years of monthly data ending June 1994. Indices were classified as large-cap growth and value. The Salomon Brothers three-month T-bill return and the small-cap growth and value components were included in the analysis but are not shown in any of the graphs because all the loadings are zero.[6]

Using either the S&P/BARRA indices and the Russell indices will result in similar style identification. The S&P 500 Index, using either vendor's indices are roughly 50% value and 50% growth. Ninety-nine percent of the returns for the S&P 500 Index are explained by the mixture of these indices.[7]

[6] The S&P 500 Index has a negligible loading (less than 1%) on T-bills using the Russell indices and virtually no change in R-squared when it is excluded.

[7] These results are not surprising because both indices are created similarly. The S&P/BARRA indices do not map the S&P 500 Index 100% because the style value and growth weightings are static and the index weightings are rebalanced semiannually. Both indices use a large-cap universe and divide it into value and growth using similar factors.

The Wilshire indices provide different interpretations of manager's styles compared to the S&P/BARRA indices and the Russell indices. The style mapping using the Wilshire indices indicate the S&P 500 Index has a growth tilt. Wilshire's indices were designed to contain extreme value and growth portfolios. The resultant R-squared of 0.95 represents a high degree of tracking error for an index and indicates that combining these indices, in any combination, does not replicate the S&P 500 Index well. The growth tilt could be caused by the fact that historically the constituents within S&P 500 Index do not contain the extreme value qualities that characterize those in the Wilshire Value Index. The veracity of this growth characterization depends upon the definition of growth and value.

The Prudential indices produce an opposite interpretation of the S&P 500 Index. Mapping the S&P 500 Index into the Prudential indices concludes that the S&P 500 Index has a value tilt. This tilt may be caused by the smaller market-capitalization of the Prudential Growth Index as compared to the Prudential Value Index.[8] Based on these definitions of value and growth, 98% of the S&P 500 Index's return can be explained by this mix.

While in theory, each manager analysis can use different vendor's indices, for consistency and comparability it is best to use the same indices for each asset class (and the same number of asset classes).[9] The correct index choice depends on finding the indices that most closely explain the manager's return pattern (i.e., have the highest R-squared), and the consistency with the user's definition of value and growth.

Appropriate Time Period

Once the indices are researched and chosen, the next issue is selecting the appropriate time period. If an investment manager's returns begin in 1980, should the full period be used? Even though the investment approach and the portfolio manager are stable throughout those years, minimal information is added beyond five years of returns for most manager styles.

---

[8] Prudential Securities. *Benchmark Study V.* September 1994.

[9] All subsequent analyses in the chapter will use the Russell Value and Growth indices and the Salomon Brothers' three-month T-bill return. All analyses use monthly data unless otherwise noted.

A few instances when longer time periods are necessary occur with balanced managers, tactical asset allocators, and managers who style rotate between sectors. The nature of the sector-rotating styles results in a lower R-squared for the style analysis compared to other equity products. The style is always changing, therefore the optimizer will not find one average style with a strong fit. Even though the R-squared will remain low, the market neutral (or average) style can be calculated if enough history is used. If a short time-horizon is used, the style may reflect a tactical decision rather than the long-term style. For example, a balanced manager's stated market-neutral position may be 50% equity and 50% fixed income, but the manager takes tactical positions when appropriate. The eight-year style would reflect the 50/50 allocation, while the three-year style may result in a 65% equity/35% bond allocation due to the portfolio manager's tactical view on the equity market.

The relevancy of the historical returns can be questionable if changes in the portfolio management occurred. Fidelity Magellan had an incredible reign under Peter Lynch, but Jeffrey Vinik's (the current portfolio manager) investment style may differ. Since each observation (return) in the style analysis program is equally weighted, style changes only become apparent when the number of returns using the new style (or portfolio manager) outnumber the old. When portfolio managers change or the process changes considerably, it is best to use the returns pertaining to the new portfolio manager.

The Effects of Using Monthly or Quarterly Data

The appropriate time period also depends on the frequency of the data and the number of indices. Three years of data using monthly returns contain 36 observations, while three years of quarterly returns contain only 12 observations. The style results are not always materially different using only five indices. If 15 asset classes were used, this analysis would be impossible with three years of quarterly data.

While monthly data are preferred for style analysis, if enough observations are available, on average, quarterly returns will suffice. To demonstrate, style analysis was performed on 166 growth-income mutual funds using both monthly and quarterly data.[10] Both five- and three-year time periods ending June 1994 were used. The average of all 166 styles and R-squareds were calculated and are shown in Figure 2-3.

---

[10] *Data source:* Morningstar and Zephyr Associates Inc.

FIGURE 2-3.   Monthly versus Quarterly Returns: 166 Growth-Income Mutual Funds
Ending June 30, 1994

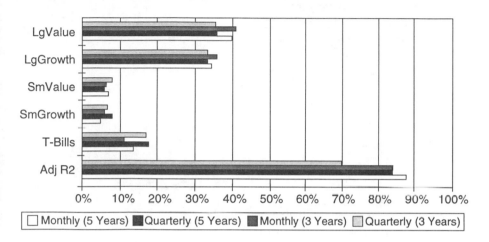

The monthly and quarterly styles are not materially different.[11] Generally the funds would be classified similarly regardless of which returns were used. Although the styles remain similar, the adjusted R-squared drops using the quarterly data for the three-year time period, partially due to the reduction of the number of observations (36 to 12). In the 166 mutual fund sample, there were a few funds whose styles changed by over 50% when substituting quarterly data. Therefore, for the most valid results, one should use monthly data when possible.

Validity of Results

Result Stability

Return-based style analysis is a useful tool only if the results are reliable and stable. For instance, a result that varies drastically with each

---

[11] The distribution of the style adjustments (calculated by summing the absolute difference of both the monthly and quarterly style loading and dividing by two) is narrowly spread around the mean.

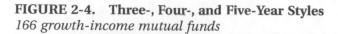

FIGURE 2-4.   Three-, Four-, and Five-Year Styles
166 growth-income mutual funds

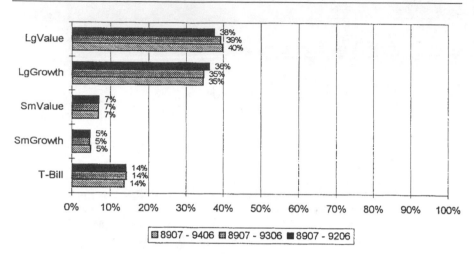

additional year of returns gives little insight into style. A slow progression to a different style is understandable for a manager, but a drastic shift illustrates ambiguous results. The styles for each growth-income fund were calculated using three years of monthly data ending June 1992. Those styles were compared to the new styles after adding an additional 12 months' worth of returns. The four-year styles ended in June 1993. An additional year's returns were added to compare the five-year styles ending June 1994 to the other two time-periods. Figure 2-4 contains the average styles for the three-, four-, and five-year styles ending June 30, 1992, 1993, and 1994, respectively.

   The styles for the growth-income mutual funds are primarily large-cap value and growth, with a slightly smaller capitalization than the Russell 1000 Index. The cash weighting is partially due to the liquidity needs of mutual funds. The mutual fund styles are stable and change minimally by adding additional observations. One can conclude that the resultant styles are reliable.

Informational Content

The validity of these styles can also be gauged by the additional information that is gained using a style benchmark compared to a stan-

FIGURE 2-5.   Percent of Variance Explained by Style and Percent of Variance Explained by S&P 500 Index

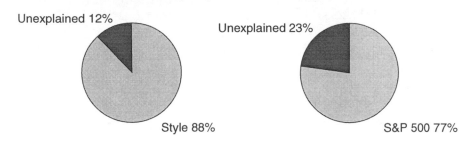

dard benchmark, such as the S&P 500 Index. Figure 2-5 contains the average R-squared obtained using a three-year rolling window style, beginning July 1989, for the 166 growth-income mutual funds. Also depicted is the average R-squared of each fund compared to the S&P 500 Index. This illustrates the additional information obtained by not only adjusting for the market return, but also for style.

The S&P 500 Index explains 77% of the mutual funds' returns. Most growth-income funds are similar to the S&P 500 Index, which is their most common benchmark. An additional 11% of the returns can be explained by using style benchmarks. The style benchmark reduces the unexplained portion of the mutual funds' returns from 23% to 12%. Style analysis becomes extremely useful in providing valid insight into the manager's historic returns, more so than using a standard benchmark.

Style Analysis Applications

Manager Classification

Another validity check is the sensibility of the resultant styles. Style analysis was run on 757 equity mutual funds in Morningstar's database[12] with over three years of data. Each was classified as either

---

[12] *Data source:* Morningstar and Zephyr Associates.

equity-income, growth-income, growth, aggressive growth, and small company. The averages for both style and R-squareds for each Morningstar category are illustrated in Figures 2-6 through 2-10.[13]

Most of these styles are similar to what one would expect, although they do drift from their standard benchmarks. Possible standard benchmarks for each category are:

- Growth-income funds—the S&P 500 Index (50% large growth, 50% large value)
- Growth funds—the Russell 1000 Growth Index (100% large growth)
- Equity-income funds—the Russell Value Index (100% large value)
- Small company—the Russell 2000 Index (50% small growth, 50% small value)

[13] Sharpe, William. "Asset Allocation: Management Style and Performance Measurement." *Journal of Portfolio Management*, Winter 1992.

FIGURE 2-6. Growth (336 Funds)

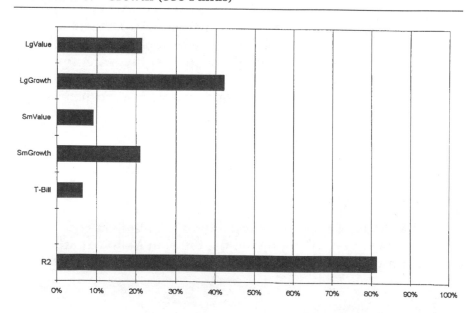

FIGURE 2-7.   Equity-Income (54 Funds)

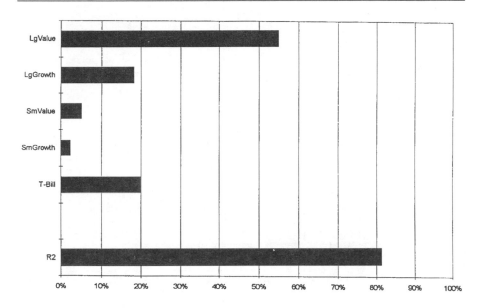

FIGURE 2-8.   Growth-Income (213 Funds)

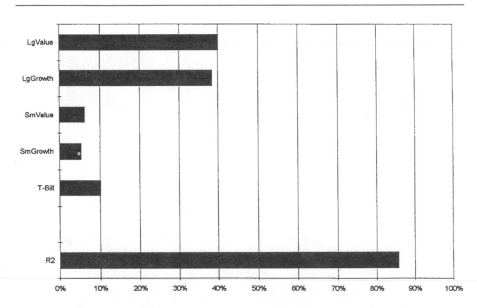

FIGURE 2-9. Aggressive Growth (52 Funds)

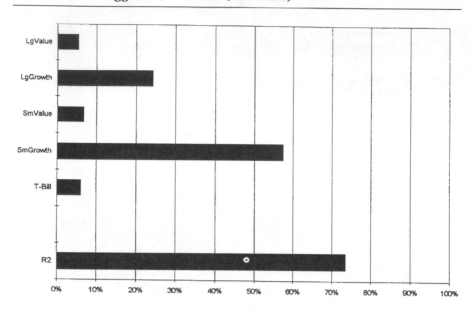

FIGURE 2-10. Small Company (102 Funds)

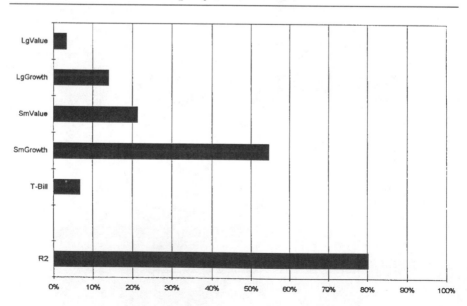

Some of the T-bill weightings in all the categories are attributed to actual cash holdings due to either new cash inflows, or liquidity needs.

Growth Funds: Figure 2-6

Growth is prominent in the funds categorized as growth, but not entirely. Roughly 30% of the style weightings are on the value indices. This does not mean that these are not growth funds. It means the average growth fund does not have growth characteristics as strong as the growth index used (Russell 1000 Growth Index). Most of these funds have more growth characteristics than the S&P 500 Index, but not as much as the Russell 1000 Growth Index. The average fund is smaller in market capitalization than any of the indices. Eighty percent of the typical growth fund's return can be attributed to its style.

Equity-Income Funds: Figure 2-7

Equity-income funds have a significant weighting in large value. Typically these funds hold large value, income-oriented stocks. Even though 20% of the style can be explained by nonvalue characteristics, this does not mean they are not value funds. Approximately 80% of these funds' returns can be attributed to style.

Growth-Income Funds: Figure 2-8

Growth-income funds are similar to the S&P 500 Index in that they are roughly balanced between value and growth, but are smaller in market capitalization. These funds comparatively have the largest percentage (86%) of returns explained by their style.

Aggressive-Growth Funds: Figure 2-9

The aggressive-growth-group style has a large weighting in growth, especially in small growth, although there is some weighting on all the indices. The weighting on both large- and small-cap indices illustrates that these funds could be buying mid-cap stocks, as well as small- and large-cap stocks. Usually these funds focus on companies with a great deal of growth potential. These companies are not usually the larger-capitalization stocks. The R-squared is noticeably smaller than the other categories. Many aggressive-growth portfolios are highly concentrated in very growth-oriented stocks. These funds most likely have stronger growth characteristics than the growth index itself, thus accounting for the lower R-squareds. Had the optimization allowed for short positions to compensate for this constraint (i.e., sold value short), the R-squared would be higher.

Small-Company Funds: Figure 2-10

The small-company category maps similarly to the aggressive-growth group, but slightly smaller and with less growth. The Russell 2000 Index definition of small is very small. The loading on the large-cap indices does not indicate small-cap managers are buying large stocks, but larger stocks than represented by the Russell 2000 Index. The average-adjusted R-squared is 80%, illustrating a good fit for most small-cap funds.

The majority of the styles within the mutual-fund classifications are similar to what one would expect. Granted some funds are misclassified, the majority are among peers. Figures 2-6 through 2-10 illustrate that the styles within each classification do not map perfectly into any publicly available indices. Once a fund is given a broad classification, style analysis helps to refine the classification.

Manager Tilts

One conclusion drawn from Figure 2-6 is that while the average growth mutual fund has a growth bias, it is not 100% growth. A spectrum of growth exists within growth. Figures 2-11 and 2-12 portray the style of three "growth" funds. All three funds are well-known growth funds with large asset bases: Twentieth Century Growth Investors, American Capital Enterprise, and Janus.

The investment criteria for each fund described by Morningstar are as follows:

> *Twentieth Century Growth Investors* seeks capital appreciation. The fund primarily purchases equity securities of large, established companies that meet its standards of earnings and revenue trends. The fund intends to remain fully invested in such securities, as long as viable candidates are present. Up to 10% of the fund's assets may be held in cash. The fund may only purchase securities of

FIGURE 2-11.   Three Growth Funds: Style Weightings

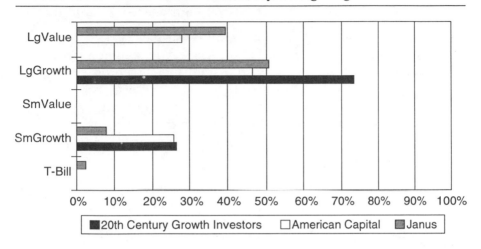

FIGURE 2-12.   Three Growth Funds: Style Mapping

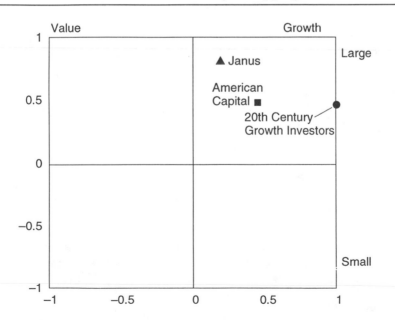

companies with at least three years of operations. The fund also emphasizes securities with a high degree of liquidity.

American Capital Enterprise Fund—Class A seeks capital appreciation. The fund invests primarily in common stocks issued by companies with established records or by companies with new products, new services, or new processes. It may also invest in companies in cyclical industries. The fund may invest a portion of its assets in investment-grade debt securities. It may invest up to 15% of its assets in foreign securities.

Janus Fund seeks capital appreciation consistent with preservation of capital. The fund invests primarily in common stocks of companies and industries that experience increasing demand for their products and services, or that operate in a favorable regulatory climate. It invests in a large number of issuers of any size. No more than 20% of the fund's assets may be invested in foreign securities. The fund may invest, for capital appreciation, in preferred stocks, warrants, government securities, and corporate debt.[14]

All three philosophies seem very similar. The style-analysis results are helpful in differentiating these funds. Figure 2-11 shows the style weightings of each fund. Figure 2-12 maps the equity-only styles (T-bills were constrained to 0%) into two dimensions: market capitalization and value/growth. Funds approaching the north of the chart are larger in capitalization and funds approaching the east contain more growth.

Twentieth Century's style contains a 100% weighting on growth. This is the extreme on the growth spectrum. The market capitalization of the fund's style is smaller than the Russell 1000 Index. Twentieth Century's portfolio historically seems to invest primarily in stocks with very high growth-characteristics. The low market-capitalization probably represents purchasing of mid-cap stocks.

The market capitalization of American Capital's style is similar to Twentieth Century's, but does not have nearly the same growth weights. This fund is in the middle of the growth spectrum. Unlike

[14] Morningstar.

Twentieth Century, the style has some value-like characteristics. The companies American Capital invests in are for the most part not as growth oriented as Twentieth Century's stocks.

Janus fund's return-based style is core-oriented. It has a growth tilt, but less so than the other two funds. The fund has a significant loading on large value (about 38%). Even though the fund can invest in companies of any size, historically the majority of the fund's assets seem to be invested in large-cap stocks.

While all three are growth funds, Twentieth Century has a much higher growth concentration than the other two funds.[15] Twentieth Century is the only fund in which a typical growth benchmark (Russell 1000 Growth Index) would characterize the fund's style appropriately. The fund would still be misrepresented due to the smaller capitalization than the Russell 1000 Growth Index. Once the category to invest is decided, style analysis assists in determining where the fund belongs within the style category.

Style Shift

Some portfolio managers shift their emphasis within their style. A fund's style history can be developed using rolling time periods to calculate its historical styles.[16] The three-year rolling style-histories of two of the largest mutual funds, Delaware Decatur and Fidelity Magellan, are illustrated in Figure 2-13.[17] The smaller symbols are representative of styles based on older returns.

The Delaware Decatur fund has had minimal style-shift; it is and has been a large-cap concentrated value fund. Fidelity Magellan, on the other hand, has had considerable style-shift. During Peter Lynch's reign, Magellan went from a small-cap fund to a large-cap fund. Perhaps this shift was coincident with the increase in the fund's assets. The fund has transitioned from growth to value during the years, but has never been very concentrated in one or the other.

---

[15] Janus and American Capital have the option to invest in investment-grade bonds. This could be a contributing factor to some of the value characteristics, if in the past they have held bonds in their portfolios.

[16] For example, a three-year rolling time period uses the three-year styles from July 1982 to June 1985, August 1982 to July 1985, September 1982 to August 1985, etc., calculated up through the present.

[17] Zephyr Associates.

FIGURE 2-13.   Managers' Style Shift

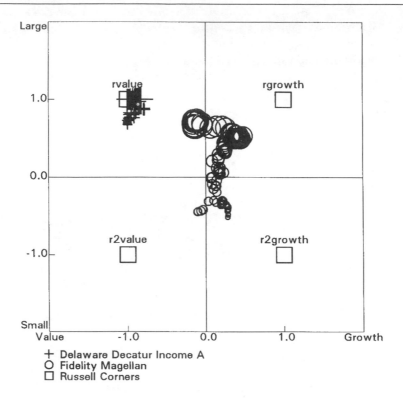

        + Delaware Decatur Income A
        O Fidelity Magellan
        □ Russell Corners

Style-shift information gives insight into investment managers' philosophies. Style shift such as Magellan's would not be appropriate for a manager who was hired with a specific style mandate. This type manager would be expected to demonstrate a more consistent style during all periods. Style shift would be appropriate and expected for a manager hired to adjust for the in-favor style. This analysis provides some proof as to which philosophy the manager follows.

Styles and Total Allocation

Return-based style analysis not only gives insight into individual managers' styles and philosophies, it assists also in determining a fund's overall asset allocation. After determining each manager's style, the styles are weighted by the dollar amount invested within the fund sponsor's portfolio to determine the fund's allocation. Tables 2-2 through 2-5 illustrate the hypothetical ABC Corporation's portfolio of mutual funds.

Table 2-2 contains the styles for each of the mutual funds in this hypothetical portfolio. ABC Corporation has six large-cap funds, three mid-cap funds, and two small-cap funds. Table 2-3 illustrates how managers are weighted by their dollar amounts to obtain the overall equity-allocations. For instance, 15% of ABC Corporation's assets are invested in Vanguard Equity-Income. Each of the loadings for Vanguard's style is multiplied by 0.15. The net effect of investing 15% of ABC's assets with Vanguard adds 12% of large value, 1% large growth and 2% of T-bills to ABC's overall equity-asset allocation. Once this is done for each manager, all the large-value loadings can be summed to determine ABC Corporation's total loading in large value. This is performed for each asset class.

Tables 2-4 and 2-5 break down the ABC Corporation's overall equity-allocation into large- and small-cap aggregates. Weighting the two subcomponents by their dollar amounts yields the total allocation of the fund.

Tables 2-3, 2-4, and 2-5 illustrate the effect of each manager on the fund's asset allocation. While only 5% of ABC Corporation's assets are invested in Skyline Special Equities, it accounts for 67% of the fund's asset allocation in small value, but only 5% of the fund's

TABLE 2-2.   Manager Styles

	Large Value	Large Growth	Small Value	Small Growth	T-Bill
Vanguard Equity-Income	83%	6%			11%
Lord Abbett Value Appreciation	57%	28%	13%	2%	
Transamerica Growth & Income A	51%	49%			
Janus	39%	51%		8%	2%
Twentieth Century Growth Investors		74%		26%	
SunAmerica Blue Chip Growth B	42%		23%	29%	6%
Harbor Growth	5%	26%		70%	
Harbor Capital Appreciation		60%		40%	
Skyline Special Equities		3%	82%	15%	
Montgomery Small Cap		2%		98%	

TABLE 2-3.   Manager Effect and Total Equity Allocation

	Large Value	Large Growth	Small Value	Small Growth	T-Bill	Percent of Fund
Vanguard Equity-Income	12%	1%			2%	15%
Lord Abbett Value Appreciation	5%	3%	1%			9%
Transamerica Growth & Income A	9%	8%				17%
Janus	6%	8%		1%		15%
Twentieth Century Growth Investors		9%		3%		12%
SunAmerica Blue Chip Growth B	2%		1%	1%		5%
Harbor Growth		2%		6%		9%
Harbor Capital Appreciation		5%		3%		8%
Skyline Special Equities			4%	1%		5%
Montgomery Small Cap				5%		5%
Total Equity Allocation	**35%**	**35%**	**6%**	**21%**	**2%**	**100%**

TABLE 2-4.   Large-Capitalization Aggregate

	Large Value	Large Growth	Small Value	Small Growth	T-Bill	Percent of Large
Vanguard Equity-Income	18%	1%			3%	22%
Lord Abbett Value Appreciation	8%	4%	2%			13%
Transamerica Growth & Income A	13%	12%				25%
Janus	9%	11%		2%		22%
Twentieth Century Growth Investors		13%		5%		18%
	47%	**41%**	**2%**	**7%**	**3%**	**100%**

allocation in small growth. Due to Harbor Growth and Montgomery Small Cap's weighting in ABC Corporation's fund, they both have roughly the same net effect on the fund's small-growth allocation even though they have different styles. This type of information on the fund's overall equity-allocation is very useful.

TABLE 2-5. Small-Capitalization Aggregate

	Large Value	Large Growth	Small Value	Small Growth	T-Bill	Percent of Small
SunAmerica Blue Chip Growth B	7%		4%	5%	1%	16%
Harbor Growth	1%	7%		20%		28%
Harbor Capital Appreciation		15%		10%		25%
Skyline Special Equities			13%	2%		16%
Montgomery Small Cap				15%		16%
	8%	23%	16%	52%	1%	100%

Once the overall equity-allocation is calculated, comparisons can be made to ABC Corporation's benchmark. The same is true for the equity subcomponents. ABC's equity-component benchmark is 75% S&P 500 Index, 25% Russell 2500 Index. ABC Corporation's large-cap aggregate benchmark is the S&P 500 Index and small-cap aggregate index is Russell 2500 Index. Figure 2-14 compares ABC Corporation's total benchmark to the Russell 3000 Index. ABC Corporation has chosen to incorporate a small-cap tilt into its equity-asset allocation. This is illustrated by comparing the style for the Russell 3000 Index to the benchmark. No other style tilts are incorporated. This confirms ABC Corporation's strategic decision.

Figure 2-15 graphically illustrates ABC Corporation's actual total equity-allocation, large-cap and small-cap aggregates, along with their respective benchmarks. The large-cap aggregate is in line with its benchmark (Russell 1000 Index) in the value/growth spectrum, but is smaller in capitalization. The small-cap aggregate is in line with the benchmark's capitalization, but a higher growth-concentration. Compared to the fund's overall equity-benchmark, ABC Corporation's total fund has a small capitalization and a growth tilt.

If this deviation from the benchmark is unintentional, ABC Corporation must investigate it further. Once this tilt has been reconfirmed, ABC Corporation might restructure the manager allocation to match the benchmark. Tables 2-3, 2-4, and 2-5 assist in determining each manager's effect on the allocation. Reallocating money from Montgomery Small Cap would not have as much of an effect as reducing Harbor Growth's weight in the fund. Even though the

FIGURE 2-14.   Total Equity Benchmark and Russell 3000

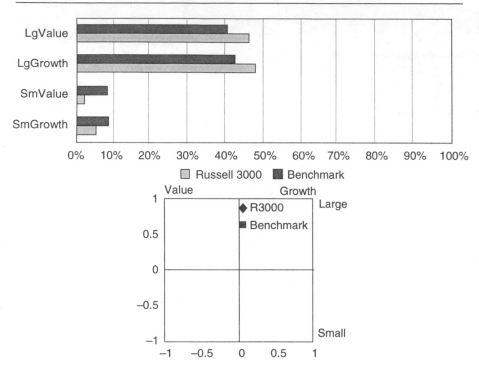

effects on the fund are roughly the same concerning small growth, Harbor Growth has an additional 2% growth-effect due to its weighting in large growth. Perhaps reallocating assets from Harbor (small-cap growth) to a Lord Abbett or Vanguard (large-cap value) would be an appropriate action. While this technique should not be the sole factor in the restructuring decision, it is a reasonable starting point.

Style analysis not only assists in discovering deviations from an asset-allocation policy, but in identifying managers with overlapping or similar styles. Figure 2-16 contains the style mappings of all of ABC Corporation's managers.[18]

Hiring managers with similar styles can add additional costs to a fund, without adding to diversification. These additional costs include

[18] Zephyr Associates.

FIGURE 2-15. Equity Style Allocations

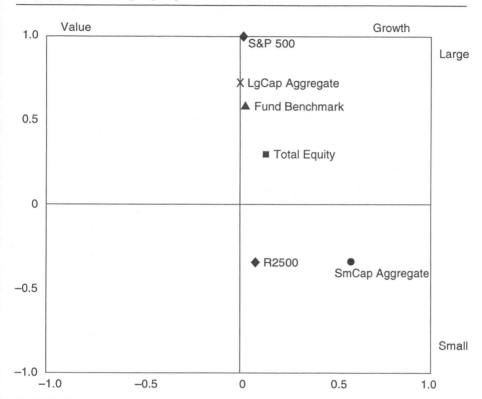

additional monitoring costs, additional custodian costs, an increase in manager fees due to smaller asset-sized accounts and generally the administrative and time costs of a large manager-roster. By reducing the number of managers, ABC Corporation can cut its overall costs, while maintaining (or perhaps lowering) the fund's risk level. Figure 2-16 can alert the fund sponsor to manager redundancy. Tables 2-2 through 2-5 and Figures 2-14 through 2-16 are all useful in delving into and easily understanding the effects of the manager structure on the fund's bottom line.

Style Analysis As a Communication Tool

Early on, the only equity benchmark most boards needed to understand was the S&P 500 Index. The amount of knowledge needed grew

FIGURE 2-16. Managers' Style

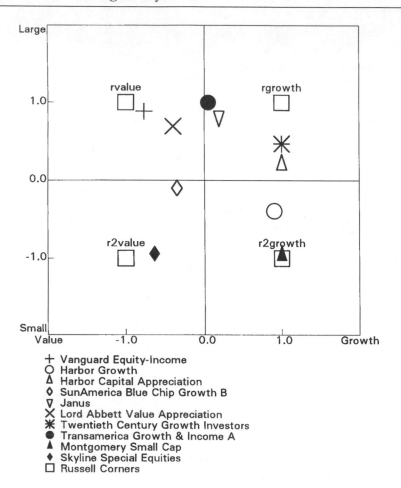

with the evolution of styles. One challenge for fund-sponsor staffs or consultants is to explain issues as clearly as possible. Hopefully, this chapter has shown that return-based style analysis is a useful communication tool in this regard. Rather than overloading the investment board with industry weights and a multitude of other factors, this type of illustration provides a succinct overview of relative exposures. Delving into the individual manager's portfolio and looking at these other factors are still important, but it may be detail which should remain at the staff or consultant level.

In addition to explaining individual managers, style analysis easily communicates the fund's overall structure to the board. By limiting the number of factors, the board can see the effect each manager has on the fund's diversification (Table 2-3). Strategic decisions, such as ABC Corporation's smaller-capitalization tilt compared to the equity universe (Figure 2-14), can be easily illustrated. Mapping each style (Figure 2-16) adds perspective to the styles of each of the managers and their redundancy, once again easily and succinctly.

Caveats

Return-based style analysis is so simple to use, a few caveats need to be addressed. Once these limitations are taken into account, style analysis is an extremely useful tool.

One limitation of this approach to style analysis is that it is based only on historic returns. Therefore any information on the investment manager's current portfolio needs to be obtained using another technique. If an investment manager shifts the style abruptly, it will not be represented immediately using this analysis. The shift will be detected in both the decrease in the R-squared of the style and in the performance of the manager's return net of the style. The net style-performance number could be attributed to good (or bad) stock-picking ability, rather than style shift. Both of these effects would be warning signs.

Return-based analysis does not work with every investment manager and investment style, but on average it gains more insight into investment managers' styles than standard benchmarks. The styles which cannot be represented by this type of analysis are apparent when the R-squared is low (below 60%). The analysis will usually load heavily in T-bills or contain spurious results, both detracting from meaningful interpretation.

Style analysis is an extremely useful tool in analyzing a fund sponsor's manager structure. Yet, it should not be the sole determinant in manager-structure analysis. The impacts of adjusting the fund's structure are not always obvious, and needs to be carefully analyzed. It is crucial to account for the nonstyle-related relationships between managers. The fund's overall characteristics (along with the interrelationships between the fund's managers and the fund) vary depending on the manager allocations. While at first glance, adjusting the fund's manager structure is seemingly easy, there are more complexities than focusing solely on managers' styles.

Conclusion

When used properly, return-based analysis is an effective and powerful tool to analyze investment managers' styles. For style-analysis results to be meaningful, all the underlying data used, including indices and investment-manager returns, must be valid and their overall concept must be understood. As with any analysis, once the results are in, a final reality check needs to be made.

It is important not to rely solely on one type of analysis. The prudent fund-sponsor uses several sources for checks and balances, such as consultants, investment managers, and data vendors. Style analysis is a crucial component of these checks. Style analysis along with experience and good judgment provide useful insight into two of the most important decisions that fund sponsors make: asset allocation, and the investment managers chosen.

References

Hardy, Steve. "Style Analysis, Style Benchmarks and Custom Core Portfolios." *Advances in Asset Allocation*, John Wiley & Sons, Fall 1994.

Sexauer, Steve. *U.S. Equity Style Indexes: Background, Uses, and Potential Misuses.* Morgan Stanley Asset Management Inc. September 1994.

Sharpe, William. "Determining a Fund's Effective Asset Mix." *Investment Management Review*, November/December 1988.

Sharpe, William. "Asset Allocation: Management Style and Performance Measurement." *Journal of Portfolio Management*, Winter 1992.

PART II

Definitions of Style

The Sponsor's Perspective

William J. De Allaume, CFA
Asset Consulting Group, Bankers Trust Co.

Historically, plan sponsors followed somewhat of a piecemeal approach to evaluating their investment portfolio. As long as each manager outperformed "the market," the status quo (and the investment manager's fee) was maintained. By contrast, today's plan sponsors are becoming increasingly sophisticated in determining which managers are in fact adding value through skill in the investment process, and which ones are simply benefiting from luck. Moreover, these sponsors appreciate the importance of looking at the entire plan structure and learning how the pieces fit together.

Equity style analysis is a direct outcome of the plan sponsor's desire to answer two fundamental questions: (1) are my investment managers adding value, and (2) how does my allocation among managers impact the total plan. The former question reflects a desire to isolate an investment manager's truly active decisions, while the question of style allocation recognizes the importance of separating the sponsor's decisions from those of the investment managers.

The earliest application of equity style management was in the area of performance evaluation. Sponsors recognized that similar investment philosophies seemed to move in tandem. For instance, managers investing in companies selling at relatively low price/book ratios would outperform the market overall when these so called "undervalued" stocks performed well. Sponsors needed a way to distinguish between this group effect and an investment manager's active decisions. In making this distinction, managers are not rewarded simply because their style is in favor, and conversely managers are not penalized when their style is out of favor.

There are a number of off-the-shelf benchmarks available for the purpose of performance evaluation. These benchmarks determine which stocks fall into a particular style category based on one or two factors, such as market capitalization and price/book. On the other extreme, some sponsors retain the services of an outside consultant to build normal portfolios for each of their managers. A normal portfolio essentially creates a list of securities from which the manager typically invests, taking into consideration such factors as P/E, liquidity, capitalization, and earnings growth. Then, these securities are weighted in accordance with the manager's weighting scheme (e.g., cap-weighting, equal-weighting). Some managers charge that normal portfolios strip away part of the skill they bring to the process; for example, investing in companies with low price/book ratios and accelerating earnings. Notwithstanding these concerns, sponsors have become increasingly zealous in finding the "right" benchmark for each manager.

More recently, these institutional investors have recognized the importance of comparative universe information based on style. Rather than evaluating a manager's performance within the context of a broad equity-manager universe, each investment manager is compared only to those managers with a similar style. In this way, sponsors are able to gauge a manager's relative performance while observing the opportunity set of investment management firms available in the marketplace. Universe comparisons are similar in many ways to style benchmarking. In each case the goal is to distinguish between the impact of style-factor effects and stock-selection effects. The primary difference is in what defines the investment alternative. In a comparison to a style benchmark, the investor is left with one potential option if the active manager lags the index: terminate the manager and invest in the passive index. By contrast, universe comparisons offer a broad array of options. Investors can not only fall back on a style index, but can choose among other active managers within the same style group as well.

Style management is an evolving area that encompasses both finding the right benchmark and determining the best way to group managers into style universes. While the exact path of this evolution is subject to debate, the direction is clear. At a micro level, plan sponsors want to know whether or not investment managers are adding value. They also want to know if managers are adhering to the investment discipline for which he or she was hired. At the macro level, the concern is more structural; that is, in identifying overlap among managers, a lack of representation (gap) in a particular style, and in determining the overall style-allocation of the fund.

Conventional Approach to Style Identification

There are three broad approaches to style identification for actively managed portfolios. The first is based on an interview with the investment manager. Style is determined based on a qualitative assessment of the manager's investment philosophy. Second, one might look at the holdings of a portfolio and assign a style based on the securities in which a manager invests. In this method, fundamental security information, including such factors as market capitalization, price/book, and price/earnings ratios are considered. Finally, a statistical analysis of a time series of returns for a portfolio can be analyzed. Basically, a portfolio's style is determined by finding a mix of style-index returns that best approximates the managed portfolio's results. We will consider the pros and cons of each of these methods separately, and then propose a modified version of the fundamental approach.

Qualitative Assessment Approach

A qualitative approach to style identification involves either an interview with a portfolio manager or a questionnaire completed by the manager. The goal is to gain insight into the manager's investment philosophy by observing the criteria that the manager considers when making an investment. Although this is a qualitative approach, it may have a quantitative dimension whereby the manager ranks the importance of several criteria, such as measures of value or growth.

An appeal of the qualitative approach is that the manager has input with respect to "which box she is put into." This input may be valuable since a more quantitative approach might overlook a unique factor in the manager's process. The criticism of this approach is that it is extremely subjective, and that it opens the door to conscious or unconscious manipulation on the part of the investment manager. That is, the manager has a vested interest in assuring that she is included in a style group where her performance results are above the median.

Fundamental Characteristic Approach

When a fundamental characteristic approach is employed, the processes of creating a style index and computing a style for an actively managed portfolio are similar. They basically involve the assignment of each stock to a particular style based on criteria cutoffs; the portfolio's style is then based on the weighted average of its constituent holdings. For style indices, these cutoffs are generally relative to a broad universe of stocks. For instance, a small-cap cutoff might be the smallest 10% of the equity market on a capitalization-weighted basis. A trap that many style-universe methodologies fall into is in defining absolute cutoffs—for instance, market capitalization less than $1 billion for a small-cap style. The danger here is that it ignores overall market-movements, which may result in a drastically different group of stocks defining small-cap in bull versus bear markets.

There are a number of different equity styles that can be defined by the characteristics of stocks. Examples include earnings growth, price momentum, yield, value, small-cap, and mid-cap. In determining style groups, there are several questions that must be answered. First, does the style group make sense from an investor's standpoint? This may seem obvious, but there is a potential for style groupings which do not reflect a particular style of investing and therefore have no explanatory power.

For instance, one could create a style comprised of stocks with very low price/book ratios and very high price/book ratios, attempting to capture extreme growth and value characteristics in a single portfolio. It may be an interesting exercise, but it is meaningless from a practical point of view since most investment philosophies are on one end of the spectrum or the other, not both. A second question is which characteristics best capture the style to be defined? Historically, price/book has been used to measure the degree of value or growth, while market capitalization has been used to determine size. But these criteria may not be the best to capture every type of investing. For example, some value managers buy stocks with low P/E ratios and high dividend-yields—stocks that do not necessarily have low price/book ratios. A third concern in creating styles is overlap. This is not a problem when using only one characteristic, but could create confusion if a stock falls into one style based on characteristic A, and another style based on characteristic B.

Single-factor splits, while they may be useful in the creation of style indices, are particularly dangerous when applied to the creation of style universes. The reason is that in creating style universes one must be sensitive to the variety of investment approaches employed in the marketplace. Manager A's definition of growth is different from that of manager B. Of course, it is possible to create a dozen growth styles, each taking into account a particular definition of growth (one based on price/book, one on earnings growth, etc.), but this would limit the usefulness of the final product. Accordingly, most methodologies are based on some hybrid of characteristics. For instance, in determining growth versus value, three characteristics might be considered: price/book, price/earnings, and dividend yield, with each carrying a weight of one-third in the total growth versus value score. With this type of approach, the coverage of various investment philosophies is increased; of course, the danger is in excluding portfolios with a strong bias to only one of the factors (since the factor's impact on the total will be diluted).

In the first-generation style universe, the end product is a classification based on most recent fundamental characteristics. Each stock (and portfolio) falls into a "style bucket" based on its characteristics. The most common buckets are based on value versus growth and small versus large. Within these broad categorizations, there might be steady growth and rapid growth; value and high yield; small-cap and micro-cap. Once a portfolio is dropped into a bucket, its entire history is considered relative to that bucket. This leads to a problem. How can one tell whether or not an investment manager has changed his stripes over the analysis period? For instance, has the manager drifted from mid-cap to large-cap stocks over the past five years? One solution to this problem is to use of an average of a portfolio's characteristics over time, which appears to be the case in most fundamental approaches.

Critics of the fundamental characteristic approach charge that it is subjective, both with respect to the characteristics included and the relative weight of each factor. Often, both of these decisions are made in an arbitrary manner, with little regard to the actual determinants of style that exist among active managers. A second criticism is that most applications of this method offer no indication as to the magnitude of the manager's style bets, they merely identify the end result. This makes it impossible to measure style drift and often leads to unexpected jumps from one style to another as time passes.

Statistical Time-Series Approach

In an attempt to overcome these point-in-time limitations and in an effort to sidestep the process of gathering historical holdings, the statistical time-series approach has gained acceptance. This "return-based" method is usually attributed to the work of William F. Sharpe.[1] A portfolio's "effective asset mix" is based on finding the best combination of indices that explain the portfolio's return. The best combination is the one that maximizes explanatory power (i.e., R-squared) within the context of a quadratic optimization program. The inputs are simple: a time series of returns for both the portfolio and a group of indices. The output is a blend of indices over time. For example, the current style-allocation might be 70% Russell 1000 Growth and 30% S&P 500, while three years ago the mix was 50% Russell 1000 Growth and 50% S&P 500. The conclusion would be that the manager has assumed more of a growth bias.

The statistical time-series approach appears to be more objective than the fundamental characteristic approach, but in reality it suffers from the same problem. The reason is that the end result yields a best fit relative to a style index, which itself is created using some fundamental characteristic approach. Moreover, relying solely on historical performance-results ignores the current position and future prospects of the companies in each style index (unless one takes the position that any future eventuality is immediately reflected in the security's price). Factors such as revised earnings estimates, potential mergers, new competition, and labor problems are by definition excluded from the time-series approach. This is because there is a time lag depending on the rebalancing frequency of each style index; typically, this lag varies from three months to one year.

Current Direction: A Style Map

In evaluating the merits of each of the methodologies discussed above, Bankers Trust Asset Consulting considered three parameters: theoretical soundness, flexibility in the face of an ever changing investment community, and usefulness of the final product to the plan sponsor. Each of these parameters was subject to the constraint of computational efficiency and access to data. Fortunately, given our processing environment and the breadth of our database, the constraints were of only minor concern.

[1] Sharpe, William. "Determining a Fund's Effective Asset Mix." *Investment Management Review,* November/December 1988.

In considering theoretical soundness we eliminated the qualitative approach on the basis of its subjectivity. Simply put, investment managers are not always who they claim to be, so we decided to look at their actual investments in making any determination of style. The theoretical soundness of the return-based method is subject to debate. Our conclusion is that it is only as sound as the style indices underlying the analysis. Accordingly, since there is no style-index series that accounts for all varieties of investment approaches, the method's appeal is seriously tarnished. Moreover, the return-based method is fairly rigid in that once an available basket of indices is selected, it would be difficult to justify the addition of a "better" index, since this would essentially involve rewriting the history of the manager's style. We should note that the return based method is a useful tool, particularly in instances when access to holdings information is impractical.

Our decision to employ a fundamental approach, then, was a function of the method's theoretical appeal, the flexibility with which we could adapt the model to changes in the investment community, and finally the relative ease of accessing holdings information. Our database includes over 2,000 equity portfolios with quarterly-holdings information available on a rolling two-year basis (returns are computed on a monthly basis and stored from a portfolio's inception date). The data can be considered a fair proxy for all equity managers in the separately managed institutional market; for instance, there is ample coverage with respect to sponsor type (corporate, public, jointly trusteed, endowment, foundation, etc.). Plan size ranges from $3.7 million to $5.8 billion, with a median of $72.4 million, while portfolio size ranges from $0.8 million to $325 million, with a median of $20.6 million.

We strove to avoid the trap of subjectivity both with respect to which characteristics to include and in the assignment of appropriate weights for each characteristic. Our process began with identifying the various types of investment strategies employed in the marketplace, and then focusing on those characteristics that best define each strategy. Clearly, identifying strategies in the marketplace is as much an art as it is a science. We considered qualitative factors such as how investment managers characterized their process. In addition, we examined the distribution patterns of individual characteristics in an effort to find areas of concentration among the portfolios in our database.

We considered standard characteristics such as price/earnings, price/book, earnings growth, return on equity, dividend yield, and market capitalization. Additionally, we looked at BARRA[2] factor exposures; specifically size, growth, book/price (B/P), earnings/price (E/P), and yield. We found several data issues with respect to the standard characteristics that limited their appeal in ascertaining investment style. Most notable of these were P/E and market capitalization. An obvious concern with P/E is whether or not to include the impact of negative earnings. (When negative earnings are included, the calculation for the portfolio's P/E is the inverse of the weighted average of each individual security's E/P.) The problem is that both value and growth managers can have high P/E ratios—growth managers in the usual manner of investing in companies with zero or low earnings relative to their price, and value managers if they hold companies with large charges to earnings (and hence negative E/P ratios). In the case of market capitalization, the issue is more theoretical. Market capitalization is the value that investors place on a company. In the context of a dividend discount model, this value is the present value of all future cash flows accruing to all investors. The point is that market capitalization is driven by price, and price is driven by investors' expectations of growth (strictly speaking, growth of dividends). Consequently, using market capitalization as a measure of size includes an imbedded growth factor.

In addition to the specific criticisms of P/E and market capitalization, none of these standard characteristics provide a specific indication of a company's growth prospects. Using BARRA's risk-index exposures (factors) effectively addresses these concerns. The BARRA E2 model includes 13 risk indices which can be used to quantify style bias relative to a broad measure for the market portfolio. Deviations from the market portfolio are expressed in common units: standard deviation from the mean (deviations are computed at both the individual stock and portfolio level). Each risk index might consist of more than one characteristic, in an attempt to more fully explain a particular tendency. For instance, BARRA's E/P factor normalizes earnings and includes the effect of market consensus estimates of a company's future earnings growth (using IBES forecasts). The size factor includes not only market capitalization but asset size and the

---

[2] BARRA is a Berkeley, California–based investment consulting and software development company.

longevity of a firm, which intuitively (and empirically) offers a better measure of large versus small firms. The growth factor measures growth in assets and earnings, and is similar to an internal or sustainable growth rate for a company. The book/price factor is simply the inverse of price/book, while yield is simply a company's dividend yield for the most recent fiscal year. Our analysis has shown that these five BARRA factors are extremely useful in ascertaining a portfolio's investment style.

The decision to include these factors over others was based on the explanatory power that each factor brought to the analysis. This was a function of analyzing scatter distributions in the search for patterns, tempered with a reality check of the investment philosophies known to be prevalent in the marketplace. We decided to examine the universe with respect to two broad parameters: size and valuation. We define valuation as the relative degree of growth versus value bias.

The size parameter was fairly easy, since the BARRA size factor adequately captured the range of small to large portfolios (and individual securities). Determining a portfolio's valuation was more difficult because there is no one universally accepted measure to capture all investment approaches. As expected, the correlations of each of the valuation factors was positive (we defined a positive valuation measure to indicate a growth bias and a negative measure to indicate value), but not high enough to warrant excluding any one of the factors completely. That is, each of the factors—earnings/price, price/book, growth, and yield—had some impact on whether we should consider a portfolio growth or value.

Creating a weighted average of the valuation factors was the natural solution, although determining each factor's relative weight was not as straightforward. Our process began with the premise that the end result should be a fairly even segmentation of the U.S. equity universe as a whole. That is, on the whole we assumed the market portfolio to be neutral with respect to style bias, and that our two parameters—size and valuation—would represent vertical and horizontal deviations from this neutral position. Graphically, the distribution of stocks around this neutral position would fall uniformly into value and growth (the size segmentation is a somewhat more arbitrary decision as to what to consider large versus small).

The determination of which valuation factors were of relatively greater importance began with an iterative process of altering the mix of factors and assessing the explanatory power of each factor. The explanatory power was a function of which characteristics best accounted for performance results. Performance results in this case were "active," meaning that market returns were backed out in an effort to isolate the impact of growth versus value. Our conclusion was that price/book was most important, followed by growth and earnings/price, and finally yield. Next, the process of determining the appropriate weights involved testing scenarios on a stock and portfolio level, then comparing overall portfolio results for a sample group of investment managers to our qualitative expectations of each manager's style.

Admittedly, there is a degree of subjectivity in determining exact factor weights. As a caution, this necessarily requires an on-going monitoring process to ensure future accuracy. Further testing was conducted on a number of market and style indices to confirm that our results were reasonable. In particular, we wanted to make sure that an index series from a given vendor made sense—such as the S&P 500 and its two constituent style-indices, the S&P/BARRA Growth and Value Indices. Our ultimate weighting for valuation was: 40% book-to-price, 25% earnings-to-price, 25% growth and 10% yield.

In the process of our analysis, we observed that as a portfolio's size-factor decreased, the valuation measure increased. This was true for both the valuation measure as a whole and for its individual components. Smaller portfolios (and stocks) exhibited higher growth rates. This empirical observation is not surprising given that smaller companies are expected to have an inherent growth bias (and, many would argue, a higher degree of risk). This presented a problem for our analysis because the goal was to isolate the impact of two parameters: size and valuation. In order to reestablish the distinctiveness of these two parameters, we performed a regression analysis with valuation as the dependent variable and size as the independent variable.

The resulting regression equation is:

Valuation = 0.09 − 0.20 (Size)

The t-statistic for the constant is 0.96, while the t-statistic for the beta coefficient is −25.36.

Figures 3-1 through 3-5 show scatter diagrams for each factor and the valuation measure. (In terms of individual factors, it should be noted that positive values for book/price, earnings/price, and yield are indicative of a value bias, while a positive value for growth

FIGURE 3-1.   Scatter Plot of Earnings/Price versus Size

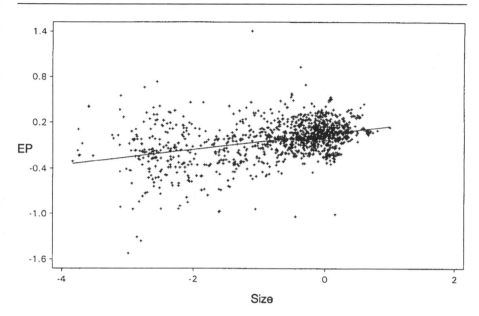

is a growth bias. These individual factors were transformed in the valuation measure such that a positive value indicates a growth bias. Also, in creating the weighted average of individual factors, each value was squared and the result raised to the one-half power. Care was taken to retain the direction (sign) of each factor in the formula.)

The regression equation of this relationship is used to adjust the valuation measure of each portfolio for the impact of size. Thus, as portfolios become smaller, a portion of their valuation measure is deducted because it was merely a function of the size of the portfolio. In making this adjustment, we ensure a linear continuum along the size parameter for the valuation measure. That is, we can identify those portfolios in the small segment of the market with a relative value orientation. Had this adjustment not been made, essentially all small portfolios would end up on the growth end of the spectrum.

In the end, our approach results in two measures for a portfolio and its constituent holdings each quarter, one for size and one for valuation. A significant appeal of this methodology is the flexibility afforded in terms of presentation of data and customization of style groupings. For example, size can be segmented into three groups:

FIGURE 3-2.   Scatter Plot of Book/Price versus Size

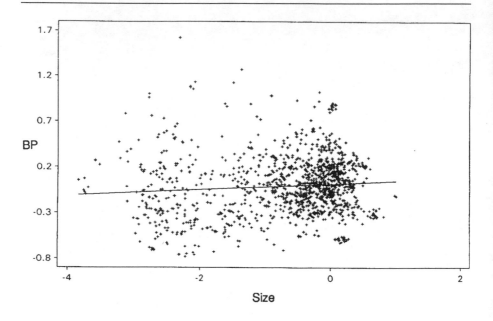

FIGURE 3-3.   Scatter Plot of Yield versus Size

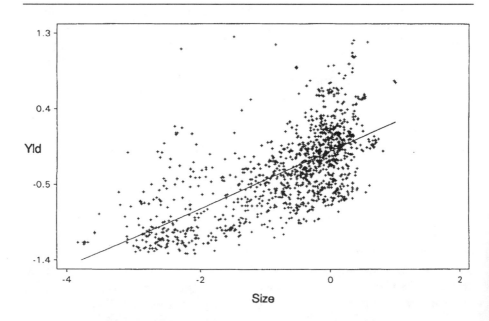

FIGURE 3-4.   Scatter Plot of Growth versus Size

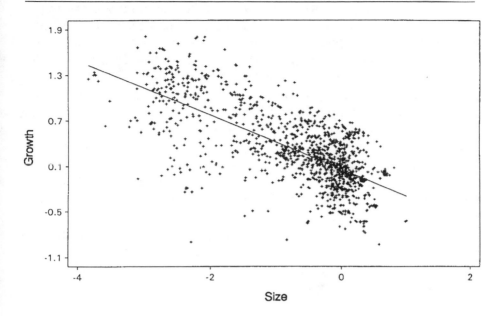

FIGURE 3-5.   Scatter Plot of Raw Value versus Size

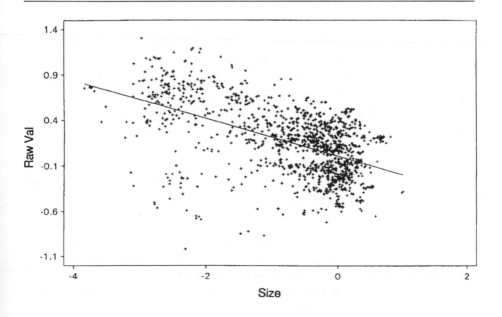

small, mid, and large. A sponsor can then compare the return history of his small-cap manager to the small universe. For a more meaningful comparison, the sponsor might compare this manager to those with a small-value style. As a default, we defined cutoffs along both the size and valuation spectrums, based on a general consensus as to what characterizes small, mid, and large along the y-axis, and value, neutral (or core), and growth along the x-axis.[3] These cutoffs are depicted in a style map, which can be found in Figure 3-6. For illustrative purposes, we also plotted several portfolios and the S&P 500 on the map. Since the overall style of a portfolio has been reduced to two parameters, size and valuation, sponsors have the flexibility to define their own break points. Moreover, once a sponsor has isolated an area of interest on the style map, further detailed analysis can be conducted on the portfolios that fall within that area.

The appeal of the style-map approach is in its visual simplicity. Sponsors can quickly identify gaps in their style allocation (e.g., no small-cap exposure), overlap among managers (e.g., two managers with similar large-value styles), and overall style-bias (which is based on a value weighted average of the constituent portfolios). The style map uses a point to depict the average position over the past two years and cross hatches to represent a portfolio's style range over the period.

In addition to the style map, a second exhibit available with this approach shows style distribution within a portfolio, one for size and one for valuation. Each of these exhibits is a histogram with the y-axis representing the proportion of the portfolio's stocks (value weighted) invested in each range (Figure 3-7). A histogram is helpful in looking beyond the weighted average of a manager's size and valuation measures and into the actual holdings of the portfolio. For instance, it is possible to end up with a neutral style with a portfolio invested in both growth and value stocks.

A third exhibit shows the variation in a portfolio's style over time. As with the distribution analysis, this exhibit is presented both for size and valuation (Figure 3-8). The insight that this exhibit brings

[3] The concept of graphically dividing managers into style quadrants was developed by David Tierney and Kenneth Winston in "Using Generic Benchmarks to Present Manager Style," *The Journal of Portfolio Management*, Summer 1991. The use of this type of presentation in the area of passive-style index management is generally attributed to Wilshire Asset Management.

FIGURE 3-6. XYZ Master Trust Equity Style Spectrum Analysis
Portfolio style map

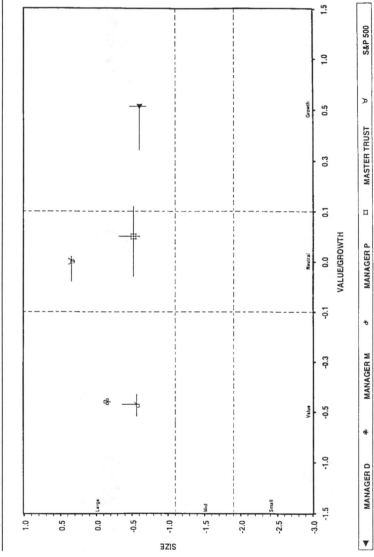

Source: Bankers Trust Company.

FIGURE 3-7. XYZ Master Trust Equity Style Spectrum Analysis
Size distribution, value/growth distribution

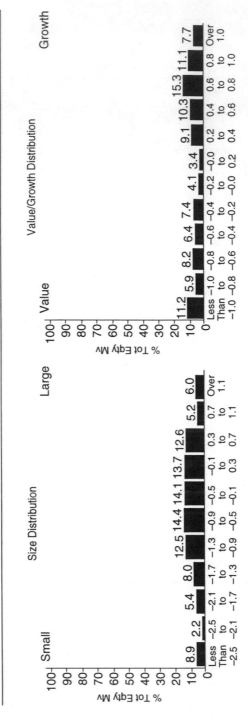

Source: Bankers Trust Company.

FIGURE 3-8. XYZ Master Trust Equity Style Spectrum Analysis

Size history, value/growth history

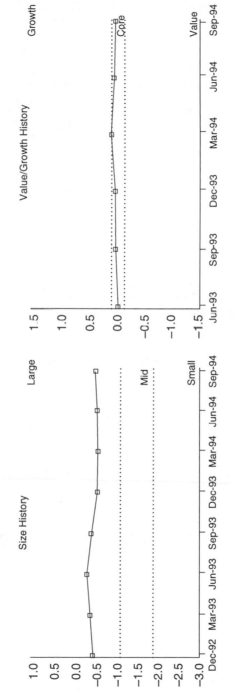

Source: Bankers Trust Company.

to the analysis is in quantifying style drift over time. Often, sponsors are unaware of instances when a manager deviates from the investment style for which she was hired. We have purposely excluded the example of a manager hired as a style rotator. For these managers, specific style comparisons are of little value, and the sponsor would be better served comparing performance results to a neutral or market-like portfolio. In most cases, however, style deviations are deemed unwanted as they make it difficult to manage the structure of the aggregate equity portfolio.

Conclusion

The style-mapping approach that we have developed offers a theoretically sound methodology and an intuitively appealing presentation. Our goal was to provide a framework for plan sponsors to make more informed decisions with respect to style management, taking full advantage of a robust database of fundamental characteristics. The importance of style management within the context of overall plan management has only recently come into the limelight. However, empirical evidence suggests that it is not a new phenomenon. In fact, some studies indicate that style management has a greater impact on total plan performance than asset class allocation.[4] Of course, it is difficult to quantify this impact since it is dependent on a plan's total allocation to equities. One thing is certain, style management has moved to the center of the investment community. It would not be surprising to see this trend expand to other asset classes and to international markets as the decade of the 1990s unfolds.

---

[4] Hardy, Steve. "Style Analysis, Style Benchmarks, and Custom Core Portfolios." *Advances in Asset Allocation.* John Wiley & Sons, Spring 1994.

Equity Style Management: The Case of Growth and Value

Eric H. Sorensen, Ph.D., Managing Director
Salomon Brothers Inc

Craig J. Lazzara, CFA, Vice President
Salomon Brothers Inc

Some Historical Perspective

Investment managers have discussed and debated the notion of growth-stock investing for more than 50 years. In 1939, for example, T. Rowe Price, Jr. argued in *Barron's* that "most corporations pass through a life cycle which, like the human life cycle, has three important phases—growth, maturity and decadence." Understanding this life cycle was the key to identifying stocks that could grow at sustainably high rates. Mr. Price defined a growth stock as a share in a business enterprise "which [has] demonstrated favorable underlying long-term growth in earnings and which . . . [gives] indications of continuing secular growth in the future."[1]

Other successful practitioners of growth stock investing contributed to this literature in the 1950s. David and Thomas Babson argued that a growth stock should be in an industry with above average growth, should demonstrate the ability to increase profits as well as sales, and should have "research-minded" management, low labor-costs, and consistently high profit-margins.[2]

Both of these definitions focus on what it means to be a growth *company*, as opposed to a growth *stock*. Peter Bernstein made this distinction explicit in a 1956 article, arguing that "growth stocks are a

---

[1] Price, T. Rowe, Jr. "Picking 'Growth' Stocks," reprinted in Charles D. Ellis (ed.), *Classics: An Investor's Anthology*, Institute of Chartered Financial Analysts, 1989, pp. 133–121.

[2] Babson, David L., and Thomas E. Babson. "Is Growth Stock Investing Effective?" reprinted in Ellis, ibid., pp. 173–191.

happy or haphazard category of investments which, curiously enough, have little or nothing to do with growth companies."[3] Bernstein's definition of a growth company differs somewhat from those of Price and Babson. More importantly, however, he asked why it mattered to the investor. Do a company's intrinsic growth factors "dominate market value, or at least influence it to such an extent that growth companies are likely to be synonymous with growth stocks, and growth stocks with superior buys?"

Bernstein's answer provided little comfort to the advocates of growth-stock investing: "Nothing beats the discovery of an undervalued stock, no matter what the nature of its business or the past trend of its earnings. But simply purchasing so-called growth stocks tends to lead to the selection of overvalued stocks."[4]

Bernstein's work foreshadowed a significant literature in academic finance. Many authors have characterized stocks by their underlying characteristics or attributes—such data as P/E ratios, price/book ratios, dividend yield, profitability, earnings growth, momentum, and surprise, as well as a variety of technical variables. The overwhelming conclusion of these studies has been that the characteristics typically associated with "value" stocks—low P/E or price/book ratios, for example, or high yields—have also been associated with better than average returns in the long run.[5] There are, of course, periodic exceptions, when relatively expensive growth-stocks outperform relatively cheap value-stocks. In general, however, characteristics associated with "growth" stocks have tended to be predictive of underperformance. This may explain why, as a gross generalization, growth investors like to talk about companies, while value investors like to talk about stocks.

Formal Style-Analysis

In 1959, the Babsons complained that there were "no standard indexes of stocks by types . . . (growth, income, cyclical)."[6] They, and other analysts of that era, used actively managed portfolios as proxies

[3] Bernstein, Peter L. "Growth Companies vs. Growth Stocks," reprinted in Ellis, ibid., pp. 192–214.

[4] Idem., p. 213.

[5] See, for example, Jacobs, Bruce I., and Kenneth N. Levy, "On the Value of 'Value,'" *Financial Analysts Journal*, July–August 1988, pp. 47–62.

[6] Op. cit., p. 173.

for investment style. As the investment business became increasingly institutionalized in the 1960s and thereafter, plan sponsors and consultants tried, with varying degrees of success, to provide objective measurements of investment style. The importance of style analysis became particularly apparent after the growth stock-led rally of 1971–72, its subsequent collapse in 1973–74, and the value-led rebound in the late 1970s. Plan sponsors came to appreciate that the diversification of their assets across manager style was an important contributor in controlling the volatility of their overall returns.

Plan sponsors and investment managers today have a number of alternatives available to help them define investment style. Perhaps the best known are the S&P/BARRA Growth and Value Indices, which were introduced in 1992. These indices are designed with a simple and intuitively appealing rationale. All stocks in the S&P 500 Index are ranked in order of their price to book value ratio. (Investors' willingness to pay a high multiple of book value is considered one indication of a stock's prospective growth rate.) The stocks with the highest ratio of price to book are assigned to the Growth Index until half of the S&P 500's capitalization has been so assigned; the remaining companies compose the S&P/BARRA Value Index. Because growth companies, so defined, are those whose share of capitalization exceeds their share of book value, it requires fewer of them to account for half of the S&P 500's total capitalization. The S&P/BARRA Growth Index has typically contained between 180 and 200 companies, with the remaining 300 to 320 allocated to the Value Index.

With the virtue of simplicity comes a drawback in the S&P/BARRA indices. One variable, the price/book value ratio, assigns every stock uniquely to one of two discrete categories, growth or value. If we assign a numerical score of 1 to the growth stocks and 0 to the value stocks, then the S&P/BARRA growth-value distribution is bimodal. At some critical threshold as a stock's price/book ratio rises, its score will eventually make a quantum leap from zero to one.

This method of portfolio construction produces both predictable and paradoxical results. Most obviously, the weighted-average price/book ratio of the Growth Index is substantially above that of the Value Index.[7] The Growth Index also has a higher P/E ratio, lower yield, and higher average return on equity. All of these results are

---

[7] *Source:* BARRA. As of September 30, 1993, for example, the price/book ratios of the Growth and Value Indices were 4.17 and 1.92, respectively.

consistent with most investors' expectations of the pricing and nature of growth stocks. On the other hand, because the Growth and Value Indices are constructed to have equal total-capitalizations, and because the Growth Index has fewer members, the average capitalization of companies in the S&P/BARRA Growth Index *exceeds* that of the Value Index. This is not an intuitive result, and in fact runs directly counter to the corporate life-cycle paradigm first articulated by T. Rowe Price. Specifically, since it is easier to grow rapidly from a smaller base, it is logical to assume that a typical growth company is smaller than a typical value company.

A More Complex Paradigm

We believe that a more complex model can overcome these difficulties while preserving our ability to make growth and value classifications.[8] Our aim is to assign stocks to growth and value categories, while recognizing that such classifications need not be—indeed, cannot be—strictly bimodal. Most stocks will fall somewhere between the extremes of "pure" growth and "pure" value. If we use our numerical scale of one for growth stocks and zero for value stocks, the distribution will no longer be bimodal; most stocks will be assigned a score between the two extremes. Rather than using only the ratio of price to book value to make these assignments, moreover, we can benefit from using more than one independent variable.

The key to our classification scheme is the specification of growth and value *panels*, the characteristics of which can guide us in the classification of a much broader universe of stocks. Beginning in 1991, we devised two panels to represent, as nearly as possible, the extremes of growth and value. Membership in these panels is determined partly by quantitative characteristics and partly by the judgment of experienced analysts, portfolio managers, and investment strategists. (Table 4-1 shows panel membership at year-end 1994.) Though investment professionals may question the appropriateness of a specific stock's inclusion on either panel, we believe that, taken as a whole, the panels capture the essence of "pure" growth and "pure" value stocks.

---

[8] Bienstock, Sergio, and Eric H. Sorensen, "Segregating Growth from Value: It's Not Always Either/Or," Salomon Brothers Inc., July 1992.

TABLE 4-1. Panel Membership, December 31, 1994

Growth	Value
Amgen	Alexander & Alexander
Automatic Data Processing	Alcan Aluminum
Biogen	Aon Corp.
Bausch & Lomb	Armco
Cracker Barrel Old Country	American Stores
Compaq Computer	Ashland
Cirrus Logic	American Water Works
Cabletron Systems	Briggs & Stratton
Cisco Systems	Black Hills Corp.
CUC International	Bellsouth Corp.
DSC Communications	Caterpillar
Brinker International	Deere & Co.
Forest Laboratories	Duke Power
General Datacomm	Equitable Resources
General Instruments	Ford Motor
Genetech	General Motors
Gap	B.F. Goodrich
Home Depot	GTE Corp.
Informix	Harsco Corp.
International Game Technology	IBM
Intel	JC Penney
Ionics	Pacific Telesis Group
Coca Cola	Phelps Dodge
Medtronic	Pacific Telecom
Motorola	Royal Dutch Petroleum
Microsoft	Raytheon
Oracle	Sears Roebuck
Paychex	Sierra Pacific Resources
Qualcomm	Sun Company
Sbarro	Unilever NV
Silicon Graphics	Westinghouse
Telephone & Data Systems	Exxon
Thermo Electron	Woolworth
United Healthcare	Zions Bancorp

The question of how to classify nonpanel stocks becomes one of measuring how closely an issue resembles the growth panel versus the value panel. We make this determination using four independent variables in a discriminant analysis framework:

- Historical returns: We compute the beta of each stock on the growth panel and the value panel using robust

regression. Our assumption is that a stock which performs more like the growth panel than the value panel is
more likely to be a growth stock than a value stock.

- Historical P/E ratios: As with our treatment of returns,
  we regress the P/E ratio of each stock on those of the
  growth panel and the value panel.
- Historical dividend yields: We regress the dividend yield
  of each stock on those of the growth panel and the value
  panel.
- Consensus growth estimates: We use the IBES five-year
  projected earnings growth rate for each stock in our universe. Where available, this is the single best predictor of
  a stock's growth versus value characteristics.

Since we plan ultimately to assign each stock a score on a zero-
to-one scale, we can think of this score as representing the probability
that the stock is a growth stock (assuming that we preserve our con-
vention of assigning a 1.0 score to "pure" growth stocks). To make
this assignment more meaningful, we must make an assumption
about the distribution of growth stocks across the entire equity popu-
lation. We would not, for example, want to argue that a stock chosen
at random was equally likely to be a growth stock as a value stock. If
the literature on growth-stock selection means anything at all, it
means that true growth tends to be rare, and that growth stocks are
therefore in a minority. (The S&P/BARRA classification, for example,
generally assigns between 35% and 40% of the S&P 500's membership
to the growth category.) We make a more conservative assumption
that only 25% of our universe is more growth-like than value-like—
i.e., that a randomly chosen stock is three times as likely to be a value
stock as a growth stock. The resulting distribution of growth and
value companies is shown in Figure 4-1.

Constructing Growth and Value Indices

Figure 4-1 depicts a realistic view of a world in which only a minority
of stocks are "pure" growth or "pure" value names, with the majority
falling into a middle range. At a point in time, a stock's score can be
thought of as the probability that the stock is a growth stock; over
time, changes in a stock's growth-probability trace the evolution of its

life cycle. Figure 4-2 illustrates this process for IBM and the computer industry, both of which experienced significant declines in their growth probabilities during the 1980s.

These growth probabilities also facilitate the construction of indices of growth and value. Our procedure here is simple: To construct a large-cap growth index, we select the largest 50 stocks in our database with growth probabilities equal to or greater than 0.85. Our large-cap value index, similarly, is composed of the 50 largest stocks with growth probabilities equal to or lower than 0.15. Each index, so constructed, represents an extreme view of its style. If we think of Figure 4-1 as a cumulative-probability distribution, we can think of the Salomon Growth and Value Indices as the extremes of the distribution.

In contrast, the S&P/BARRA Growth and Value Indices, rather than representing only the extremes, together compose the entire S&P 500 Index. We would, accordingly, expect the Salomon Indices to show more divergent behavior than their S&P/BARRA counterparts. Tables 4-2 and 4-3 illustrate this divergence. The correlation between S&P/BARRA Growth and Value Indices, as shown in Table 4-2, is 0.91; the correlation of Salomon Growth and Value is 0.77.

FIGURE 4-1. Growth Stock Probability versus Score for Top 3,000 Stocks

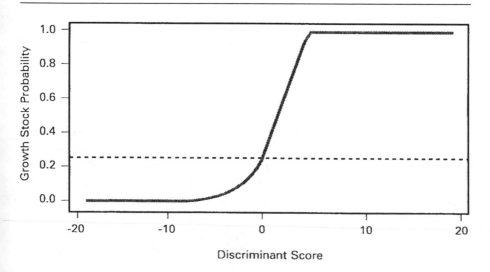

FIGURE 4-2.   Growth Score Migration

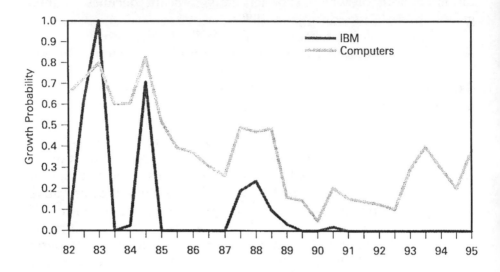

TABLE 4-2.   Uniqueness of Style Indices
Historical correlations of growth and value returns, January 1982 through December 1994

	Salomon Growth	Salomon Value	S&P/BARRA Growth	S&P/BARRA Value
Salomon Growth	1.00			
Salomon Value	**0.77**	1.00		
S&P/BARRA Growth	0.95	0.88	1.00	
S&P/BARRA Value	0.84	0.96	**0.91**	1.00

Table 4-3 translates this correlation insight into returns. We classified the 156 months between January 1982 and December 1994 as either "growth" or "value" months, depending on which style outperformed. In the 81 growth months, the Salomon Growth Index outperformed its value counterpart by an average of 3.14%. The S&P/BARRA Growth Index outperformed in these same months by only 1.05%. Similarly, in value months, the Salomon Value Index outperformed by 2.73%, while the S&P/BARRA Value Index outperformed by only 1.30%. We can observe another facet of the same phenomenon by noting that, in growth months, the Salomon Growth

TABLE 4-3.   Differential Performance in Growth and Value Months
Average monthly returns, January 1982 through December 1994

	Growth Months	Value Months
Number	81	75
Salomon Growth	5.02%	−2.43%
Salomon Value	1.88	0.30
Spread	**3.14%**	**−2.73%**
S&P/BARRA Growth	3.58%	−1.35%
S&P/BARRA Value	2.53	−0.05
Spread	**1.05%**	**−1.30%**
S&P 500	3.07%	−0.69%

Index outperforms the S&P/BARRA Growth Index (and Salomon Value underperforms S&P/BARRA Value). In value months, we see the opposite result: Salomon Value outperforms S&P/BARRA Value (and Salomon Growth underperforms).

Predicting Index Performance

Figure 4-3 shows the performance of the Salomon Growth and Value Indices from 1982 to the present. Growth generally outperformed value during this period, although there have been subperiods when value was the better style.[9] These data stop somewhat short of a comprehensive performance attribution, since the growth and value indices differ along a number of dimensions: market risk, macroeconomic exposures, etc. Nonetheless, given the deliberately extreme nature of these indices, their differential performance can be fairly represented as the differential return to the growth style versus the value style.

It is clearly advantageous to be on the right side of the growth/value divide. Given the potential payoff, it is not surprising that forecasting models have attracted considerable interest. Such models are, at the most general level, of two types:

---

[9] Sorensen, Eric H., and Sergio Bienstock. "The Growth/Value Contest: A Growing American Tradition," Salomon Brothers Inc., October 2, 1992.

FIGURE 4-3.   Performance of Large Growth and Large Value Baskets

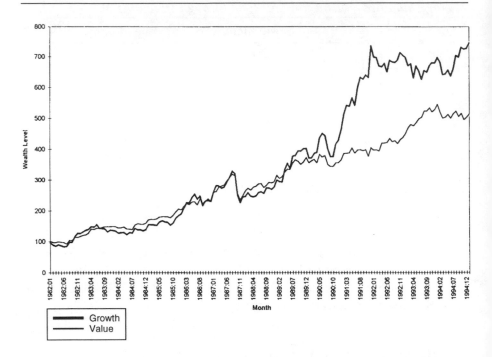

- *Ex ante* models rely exclusively on data which are (or would have been) available in advance of the period for which the forecast is being made. If we are backtesting such a model, our forecast for January 1994 can only be based on data which were in fact readily available on or before December 31, 1993. Only *ex ante* models can be reliably backtested, and great care must be taken to be sure that unavailable data do not corrupt such a test.
- *Ex post* models, in contrast, may rely on contemporaneous data in deriving their forecasts. This makes them impossible to backtest and, in some respects, more difficult to use with confidence. On the other hand, when used properly, *ex post* models can provide a level of market insight which is otherwise unavailable.

Some examples might make these distinctions clearer. Figure 4-4 plots the 1982–94 level of the Salomon Growth/Value relative against

FIGURE 4-4.   Industrial Production versus Growth/Value Relative

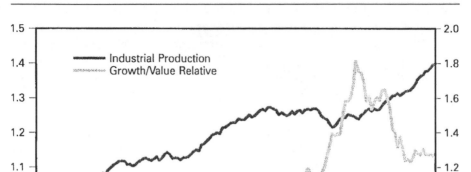

U.S. industrial production.[10] When the Growth/Value relative is rising, growth is outperforming value; when it is falling, value is outperforming growth. Visual inspection of Figure 4-4 suggests that declining or stagnant levels of industrial production are associated with
increases in the Growth/Value relative. Rising industrial production
generally signals a decline in the Growth/Value relative—i.e., a
period when value outperforms growth.

More formal data-analysis confirms our visual impression. The
correlation of monthly changes in industrial production with contemporaneous monthly changes in the Growth/Value relative is approximately –0.35, a statistically significant level. Equally important, industrial production also displays a statistically significant lead effect with
the Growth/Value relative—i.e., the correlation between *this month's*
change in industrial production and next month's change in the
Growth/Value relative is –0.17. Among other things, this means that
industrial production can play an important role in building an *ex ante*
model of the relative performance of growth and value styles.

---

[10] The Growth/Value relative is simply the cumulative return of the Salomon
Growth Index divided by the cumulative return of the Salomon Value Index. Both
indices stood at 100 on January 1, 1982.

From a pure model-building standpoint, it is the leading, rather than the contemporaneous correlation, that is of interest. But this does not make the contemporaneous correlation irrelevant. Indeed, from the standpoint of the many investment managers who do not use formal decision-making models but whose portfolios are nonetheless influenced by the relative performance of the growth and value styles, it may be the more relevant variable of the two.

This is partly because the correlation between industrial production and the Growth/Value relative is much stronger on a contemporaneous than a leading basis. Partly, however, the importance of the contemporaneous correlation is a function of the nature of a manager's investment process. Although many managers are not model-driven, they may nonetheless have views concerning the underlying strength of the economy. If their view is that the economy is likely to expand strongly, indicating increased levels of industrial production, Figure 4-4 and the accompanying statistical analysis tell them that value stocks, not growth stocks, are likely to be in favor. Given the relative magnitude of the contemporaneous and leading correlations, if the manager's (contemporaneous) forecast of the economy is correct, the potential payoff from this insight is likely to be greater than the payoff to an *ex ante* model-driven forecast.[11]

Economic Considerations

Regardless of whether we focus on contemporaneous or leading relationships, any model-building exercise must be firmly grounded in economic theory. We should be very reluctant to accept even strong correlations as evidence of causation absent some plausible theoretical mechanism. Industrial production as a predictor of the Growth/Value relative meets this criterion. If the economy is expanding rapidly, investors have no need to pay growth-stock multiples in order to achieve acceptable levels of earnings growth. During economic stagnation or contraction, however, the higher sustainable earnings-growth potential of growth stocks makes them especially

---

[11] A full discussion of the interaction between required forecasting accuracy and the relative magnitude of contemporaneous and leading correlations is beyond the scope of this chapter.

attractive investments.[12] It is not surprising, therefore, to observe negative correlations between industrial production and the relative performance of growth stocks; when growth is relatively rare, it is more expensive than when it is common.

Interest rates similarly have a plausible economic link to the Growth/Value relative. Since a growth stock's valuation is highly dependent on the discounted value of distant, rather than near-term, dividends, interest-rate changes should affect growth stocks more than value stocks. Growth stocks are, effectively, longer-duration assets than value stocks. It is not surprising, therefore, to find an inverse linkage between changes in long-term interest rates and changes in our Growth/Value relative. Figure 4-5 illustrates the point.

As with industrial production, it is important to rely on more than simply visual observation. More rigorous analysis reveals that the contemporaneous correlation between changes in long-term interest rates and changes in the Growth/Value relative is –0.23. The leading correlation, however, is zero; interest rate changes *this month* tell us nothing about Growth/Value changes *next month*. This means that, on their own, long-term interest-rate changes are unlikely to be

[12] See "The Growth/Value Contest," p. 6.

FIGURE 4-5. Long Rates versus Growth/Value Relative

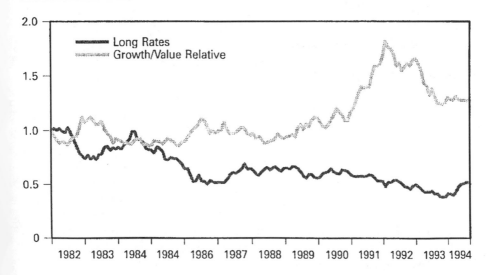

helpful in an *ex ante* forecasting model. On the other hand, a manager who can forecast interest rates could gain additional leverage from that ability by rotating between growth and value styles.

Salomon Brothers Forecasting Model

In 1993, Salomon Brothers developed an *ex ante* forecasting model for the Growth/Value relative. The model includes technical and fundamental explanatory variables, and operates across the entire capitalization spectrum. The model was fit on data from 1982–89, and backtested beginning in July 1990. It is designed to produce monthly categorical forecasts, i.e., to recommend either the growth or value style.

The monthly structure of this model (and others) has occasionally elicited critical comment. It is a rare manager, after all, who has flexibility to shift investment postures 12 times a year. The fact that a model is fit on monthly data, however, does not mean that it changes signals every month. (The average holding period for the Salomon model, in fact, is between three and four months.) Model building and portfolio management are distinct activities, and the optimal horizon for one need not match the optimal horizon for the other. A model builder should choose the horizon which maximizes his or her predictive ability. If the resultant turnover level is unacceptably high, there are a number of ways to constrain turnover while preserving most of the benefit of a model's predictive accuracy. Attenuating turnover should not entail, and does not require, that a model's predictive accuracy be degraded.

Table 4-4, in fact, illustrates several ways in which turnover can be attenuated without altering the model *per se*. The exhibit provides the results of three strategies designed to rotate between the Salomon Growth Index and the Salomon Value Index, around a 50/50 neutral benchmark.

- The pure "bang-bang" strategy puts 100% of the portfolio into the Growth Index or the Value Index, as determined by the model's prediction at the beginning of each month. As a general rule, such bang-bang strategies will maximize turnover and, to the degree that a model's signal is accurate, will maximize returns (gross, and possibly net, of transactions costs).

TABLE 4-4.   Strategy Summary
July 1990 through October 1994 (annualized)

	Pure Bang-Bang	Filtered Bang-Bang	Consecutive Signals
Strategy return	19.4%	17.6%	17.3%
Benchmark return	10.6	10.6	10.6
Incremental return	8.8%	7.0%	6.7%
Annual turnover	369%	277%	242%
Growth tilt	28 mos.	29 mos.	19 mos.
Value tilt	24 mos.	23 mos.	16 mos.
Neutral	—	—	17 mos.

- The filtered bang-bang strategy likewise holds either 100% Growth or 100% Value. It shifts from Growth to Value, or vice versa, only when the absolute value of the predicted return differential is greater than a predetermined threshold (in this case, 1% for the next month). In effect, this rule shifts from one extreme to the other only if the model's signal is sufficiently strong to justify the move (where "sufficiently" is subject to arbitrary definition).
- What we call the "consecutive signals" strategy attenuates turnover by a different mechanism. Rather than requiring a signal of a prespecified magnitude, with this strategy we shift from Growth to Value, or vice versa, only when two consecutive signals so indicate. If consecutive signals "disagree," this strategy holds the 50/50 neutral position.

Table 4-4 summarizes the results of these strategies. The pure bang-bang rule generates the highest return, but also the highest turnover, which is to be expected if there is valuable information in the underlying model. Moving to the consecutive signal rule cuts turnover by better than a third, but reduces incremental value added by more than 200 basis points annually. (Return data are gross of transactions costs. For the large-cap Growth and Value Indices, round-trip transactions costs should amount to no more than 100 basis points, and should probably be closer to half that level.) Importantly, we observe that the value added by style shifts does not derive

TABLE 4-5. Monthly Summary of Value Added
July 1990 through October 1994

	Pure Bang-Bang	Filtered Bang-Bang	Consecutive Signals
Positive Months			
Number	34	33	23
Average	1.73%	1.67%	1.78%
Negative Months			
Number	18	19	12
Average	−1.16%	−1.31%	−1.00%
Neutral Months			
Number	—	—	17

from a systematic bias toward either growth or value. The tilts between the two styles occur with roughly equal frequency.

Table 4-5 sheds more light on the distribution of value added by a style-rotation strategy. Some rotational strategies (in tactical asset allocation, for example) add value fairly infrequently, but by a sufficiently large magnitude that they are worthwhile over time. (Consider, for example, a tactical asset-allocation strategy that kept investors out of the stock market in October 1987.) Table 4-5 shows that the returns to growth-value style rotation are relatively evenly distributed. All three strategies add value about twice as often as they lose it; and the magnitude of the value added in value-added months is substantially greater than the value lost in months of poor performance.

Summary

We have summarized some of the history of growth- and value-equity management, and described our efforts to classify stocks in terms of their growth and value characteristics. Our classification paradigm does not require that all stocks fit into either a growth category or a value category, but rather appreciates that most stocks fall into an intermediate range, rather than into the extremes of "pure" growth or "pure" value. We used our classification scheme to develop indices of growth and value, and demonstrated how investors can rotate between these indices in order to add value to a static style mix.

These results should be useful to three different constituencies:

- Investment managers who are style specialists should be more readily able to identify stocks which fit their specialization. Moreover, by understanding when their style is in or out of favor, specialty managers can better explain, and hedge against, periods of underperformance.
- Investment managers who are not tied either to a growth or value specialization can take advantage of opportunities to shift between styles. This need not entail formal rotation between Growth and Value Indices; opportunistic direction of cash flows is another potential source of value added.
- Finally, plan sponsors can better understand the style biases of their equity managers. This enables them to create benchmarks which correctly measure a manager's style, and to avoid paying active fees for passive-style exposure. Moreover, understanding a fund's style-exposures creates the same opportunities for hedging and opportunistic style-rotation for the plan sponsor as for the investment manager.

Value/Growth Considerations in International Investing: Two Perspectives

PART I: An Analysis of Global Investment Styles

Growth, Value, Small-Cap, Momentum, and Mean Reversion

John P. Meier, Vice President
Strategic Investment Solutions, Inc.

Andre Bertolotti, Product Manager
BARRA Inc.

For the past few years, the U.S. institutional-investing marketplace has experienced a great deal of interest in investment styles for U.S. equity-portfolio management. For the most part, two dimensions of style have been identified and analyzed: size or market capitalization and "value/growth." A lot of work has been done constructing style indices which measure the returns to these styles. In this chapter, we will examine the returns to the value and size styles in countries other than the United States. Furthermore, we will examine a third style, momentum/reversal across countries.

We will use the Financial Times Actuaries World Index™ (FT Index) as our proxy for markets around the world. We will divide the FT Index into portfolios to measure the returns to the styles we are characterizing. We will examine the returns by country to determine if certain styles have created exceptional returns and the volatility of the style returns. We will also examine the correlations of returns to a particular style across countries and finally, outline some of the investment-strategy implications that are suggested by our analysis.

Methodology

In general, our methodology for splitting the FT Index into styles was based on BARRA's Global Equity Risk Model (GEM). GEM covers the 24 equity markets that were included in the FT Index at the time of our analysis. GEM is a multiple-factor model used to identify the volatility of stocks and multiple-country portfolios. Included in the model are factors that identify the "style" of the portfolio: size, success, and value. Before we start describing the process of splitting the index, let's look at how these factors are constructed and why they are useful for our purposes.

First, let's discuss how a BARRA factor is constructed. To create factors, BARRA first determines the measurable characteristic(s) that will go into a factor. These *descriptors* are calculated for every stock in BARRA's GEM universe. The descriptors are then normalized across the model estimation-universe (in the case of GEM it is the FT Index) to a mean of zero and a standard deviation of one.

A further refinement in the normalization process in GEM is that all descriptors are normalized within country. So, for any descriptor, the mean and standard deviation are calculated over the set of stocks in the estimation universe in a single country and the descriptor is normalized accordingly. Furthermore, the capitalization-weighted mean and equal-weighted standard deviation are used.

For example, one of the descriptors in GEM is the dividend yield. To obtain the descriptor dividend-yield for a U.K. stock, BARRA calculates the average yield for all the U.K. companies in the FT Index and the standard deviation of these yields and uses these to normalize all the U.K. stock dividend-yields.

In many cases, factors are made up of several descriptors. The descriptors are combined in a proprietary method and resulting factors are renormalized within each country to a mean of zero and a standard deviation of one. We can use the factor exposures to divide the index by country into two pieces of equal capitalization very easily because the normalization process is by country and the capitalization-weighted mean of the FT Index is zero. All stocks with a positive exposure to the factor represent the style index for that characteristic and all stocks with a negative exposure to the factor represent the style index contrary to that style. Obviously stocks with zero exposures to the factor must be assigned to one of the styles. For this study, splits were completed at greater than or equal to zero and less than zero. Fortunately, the likelihood that the characteristic of a stock will be exactly the same as the market average is very small.

For our value/growth split, we used the GEM value factor. Value comprises four descriptors: dividend yield, reported P/E ratio, forecast P/E ratio, and price/book ratio. WorldScope/Disclosure Partners reported earnings and book value and IBES forecast earnings are used in the calculation of the descriptors. All assets with exposures of zero or greater were assigned to the value style. All others were assigned to growth, or, if you like, nonvalue. The factor's construction resulted in roughly half the capitalization of the FT Index by country in value and half in growth.

For our size or capitalization split, we had to address the problem of companies that issued multiple classes or types of stock. If we just used issue capitalization as our measure of size, it's possible to imagine that a company that issues more than one type of stock could have one issue in the large style and one issue in the small style. However, a more intuitive split would be to split into large and small based on total company-capitalization.

The BARRA size factor comprises one descriptor, natural log of market capitalization using total company-capitalization instead of issue capitalization. Thus, sorting the FT Index by country and the size factor gives us the ordering we are looking for, small-cap companies, not just small-cap issues. We decided on a 90/10 split for our study, the top 90% of the FT capitalization in the large style and the bottom 10% of the capitalization in the small style. Our choice was relatively arbitrary. However, one desirable characteristic of this split is that the two style-portfolios had roughly the same number of issues. So, style performance was less likely to be affected by the performance of any single issue.

Our final split was based on BARRA's success factor. The success factor also contains only one descriptor, relative price-performance over the last 12 months. All issues with exposures of zero or greater, in general all issues that had outperformed the index over the last 12 months, were assigned to momentum. All issues with exposure of less than zero, in general all issues that had underperformed the index over the last 12 months, were assigned to the alternative style, which we will call *mean reversion*. Due to changes in the constituents in the index, however, assets that outperformed (underperformed) the index, may have negative (positive) success exposures depending on the relative performance of the issues that are removed and added to the index over the period.

Our analysis covered the period of January 1988 through July 1994. The style portfolios were rebalanced semiannually at the end of June and December. There was no "buffering" of the cutoff between styles. An asset was assigned to a style based on its factor exposure alone. It didn't matter which portfolio the stock was in for the previous period. For most of the commercial indices, an asset must cross a certain threshold before it moves from one index to the other. The style portfolios were not adjusted between rebalancings for issues that dropped out or were added to the FT Index.

Once we created the different style-portfolios, we calculated their total returns monthly using gross dividends. We ignored any tax withholding on dividends. We calculated the local returns for each style portfolio for each country—for example, the total return in French francs of the French value stocks. We also calculated the active return (return to a portfolio minus return to its benchmark) of each style relative to the FT Index country by country—for example, the total return of the French value stocks minus the total return to the French component of the FT Index in French francs.

Value/Growth Results

Our first style-split analyzed was that of value and growth. In the United States, considerable empirical evidence indicates that low price/book (value) stocks outperformed high price/book (growth) stocks over the last 30 years. We wanted to investigate whether or not the same is true for non-U.S. stocks. For each style portfolio we examined the mean monthly active-return (the return to the style portfolio minus the return to the FT Index component for the country being analyzed), the t-statistic, and the realized risk (annualized standard deviation) of the active returns. We also examined the same characteristics for the spread between the value and growth-style portfolios.

Table 5-I-1 shows these results for the value-style portfolio. In 11 of the 21 countries examined, the value-style portfolio outperformed the FT Index. Are any of the results statistically significant from zero? Basically, no. The returns in Finland and Austria are statistically significant at the 95% level. However, we are looking at 21 countries and would

TABLE 5-I-1.   Active Returns to the Value Style

	Mean Monthly Active Return (%)	t-Statistic	Annualized Standard Deviation (%)
Australia	–0.16	–0.85	5.71
Austria	0.55	1.96	8.63
Belgium	0.28	1.78	4.87
Denmark	–0.55	–2.36	7.16
Finland	–0.12	–0.33	11.27
France	0.11	0.73	4.78
Germany	0.04	0.27	4.18
Hong Kong	0.09	0.49	5.44
Ireland	0.18	0.58	9.51
Italy	0.33	1.87	5.47
Japan	0.20	1.30	4.75
Malaysia	–0.14	–0.61	7.22
Netherlands	–0.11	–0.85	3.85
New Zealand	0.28	0.72	11.94
Norway	–0.10	–0.20	14.87
Singapore	–0.06	–0.37	5.18
Spain	0.19	0.92	6.34
Sweden	–0.27	–0.86	9.56
Switzerland	–0.03	–0.14	5.55
U.K.	0.01	0.15	2.99
U.S.	–0.01	–0.10	3.45

expect that one out of 20 would show statistical significance at the 95% level purely by chance, which was effectively our experience here.

Table 5-I-2 shows these results for the growth-style portfolio. In eight of the 21 countries examined, the growth-style portfolio outperformed the FT Index. Are any of the results statistically significant from zero? Again, only a few of the countries show statistical significance at the 95% level: Denmark (positive), Italy (negative), and Spain (negative).

In Table 5-I-3, we show our results from the return spread between the value- and growth-style portfolios. The spread is the value-portfolio return minus the growth-portfolio return. Looking at the spread, 12 out of 21 countries have positive value-growth spreads. However, again, we see nothing that we can distinguish as statistically different from zero with only Italy and Denmark showing statistical significance at the 95% level.

TABLE 5-I-2.   Active Returns to the Growth Style

	Mean Monthly Active Return (%)	t-Statistic	Annualized Standard Deviation (%)
Australia	0.06	0.44	3.91
Austria	−0.38	−1.26	9.15
Belgium	−0.25	−1.30	6.01
Denmark	0.47	2.48	5.78
Finland	0.10	0.30	10.26
France	−0.14	−1.17	3.59
Germany	−0.07	−0.62	3.55
Hong Kong	−0.02	−0.16	4.52
Ireland	−0.09	−0.31	8.61
Italy	−0.34	−1.96	5.33
Japan	−0.19	−1.36	4.30
Malaysia	0.05	0.26	5.71
Netherlands	0.18	0.91	5.98
New Zealand	−0.19	−0.73	7.92
Norway	0.06	0.20	9.35
Singapore	0.13	0.77	5.09
Spain	−0.37	−2.31	4.98
Sweden	0.39	1.33	8.93
Switzerland	−0.13	−1.00	4.06
U.K.	−0.05	−0.48	3.04
U.S.	−0.01	−0.09	3.29

We should point out that even though the returns to the value- and growth-style portfolios are not significant in statistical terms, they are quite large in investment terms. The average active-returns for the styles are in the range of 10 to 30 basis points per month for a 79-month period. If one had picked the correct style for a country, and held it for the entire period, one would have outperformed the local country by a significant margin. Figures 5-I-1 through 5-I-6 show the cumulative returns to the growth/value spread for France, Germany, Japan, the United Kingdom, the United States, and an international portfolio. The international spread is developed by taking the FT Europe and Pacific Index, splitting, by country, into growth and value according to the methodology outlined, and calculating the difference in U.S.-dollar returns to the two portfolios.

Probably the most interesting graph is Figure 5-I-6, Europe Pacific. The value portfolio outperformed the growth portfolio by

TABLE 5-I-3.   Return Spread between Value and Growth Styles

	Mean Monthly Active Return (%)	t-Statistic	Annualized Standard Deviation (%)
Australia	−0.21	−0.69	9.53
Austria	0.93	1.69	16.91
Belgium	0.54	1.55	10.68
Denmark	−1.01	−2.45	12.74
Finland	−0.22	−0.33	20.76
France	0.25	0.93	8.27
Germany	0.11	0.44	7.59
Hong Kong	0.11	0.35	9.87
Ireland	0.27	0.46	17.83
Italy	0.67	1.95	10.64
Japan	0.39	1.33	9.03
Malaysia	−0.19	−0.47	12.57
Netherlands	−0.28	−0.90	9.64
New Zealand	0.47	0.78	18.37
Norway	−0.16	−0.22	22.75
Singapore	−0.19	−0.61	9.61
Spain	0.56	1.60	10.79
Sweden	−0.66	−1.12	18.01
Switzerland	0.11	0.37	8.84
U.K.	0.06	0.32	5.96
U.S.	0.00	−0.01	6.72

nearly 30% cumulatively over this 6.5-year period, about 3% per year annualized. Other interesting observations are the trends of the value-growth spreads for the countries shown here. Japan shows a relatively consistent positive return to the value-growth spread. However, France, Germany, the United Kingdom, and the United States show much less consistency. In France and Germany, there are periods where neither value or growth consistently outperformed the other. Over the last two to three years, however, both French and German value-portfolios have done very well, with the French value-portfolio outperforming growth by nearly 70% cumulatively and the German value-portfolio outperforming growth by around 35% cumulatively. The United States shows more cycles with growth outperforming for some periods and value outperforming in other periods. The United Kingdom also shows cycles, but the cycles are much shorter and abrupt. The cycles are then fol-

FIGURE 5-I-1. Cumulative Return to France Value/Growth Spread

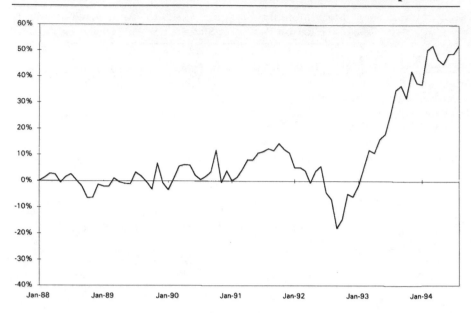

FIGURE 5-I-2. Cumulative Return to Germany Value/Growth Spread

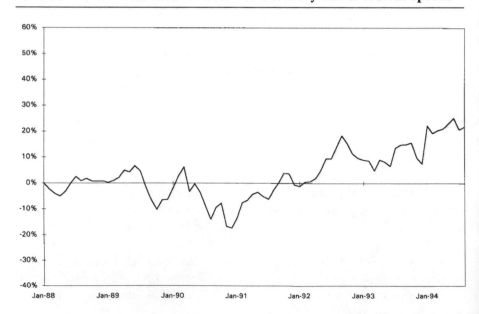

FIGURE 5-I-3.   Cumulative Return to Japan Value/Growth Spread

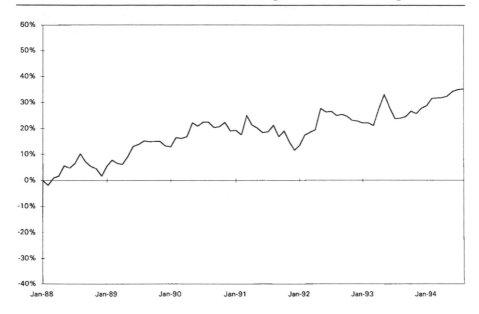

FIGURE 5-I-4.   Cumulative Return to United Kingdom Value/Growth Spread

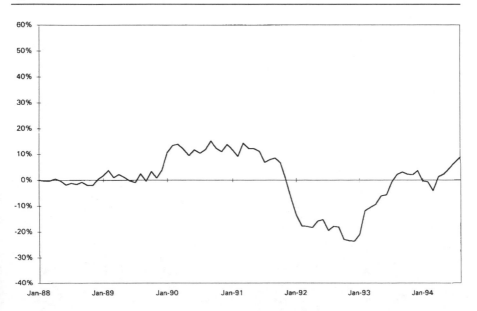

FIGURE 5-I-5.   Cumulative Return to United States Value/Growth Spread

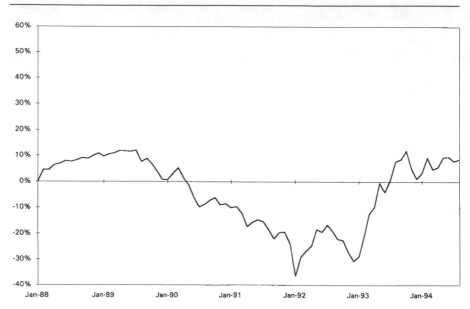

FIGURE 5-I-6.   Cumulative Return to Europe Pacific Value/Growth Spread

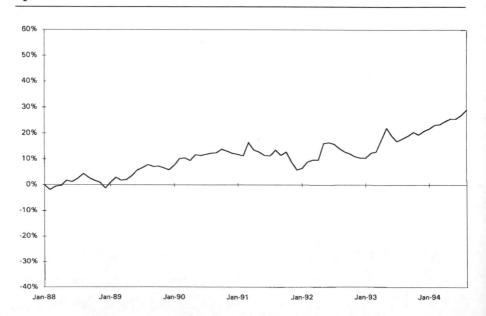

lowed by periods where neither growth nor value outperforms the other.

Correlations of Returns across Countries

Another issue to evaluate is the correlation of an investment style across countries. Are the returns to a style, net of the country return, correlated in any way across countries? If they are not highly correlated then a global or international investment-style strategy could be a diversifying stock-selection strategy, lowering the risk of the overall strategy.

Since the correlation matrices are quite large, we'll focus on the correlations between the larger markets. Table 5-I-4 shows the correlations between the active returns (style portfolio minus the return to the FT Index component for the country being analyzed) to the value portfolios for Japan, Germany, France, Italy, Hong Kong, the United Kingdom, and the United States as well as some other statistics on the entire matrix. The entire matrix can be found in the appendix to this part of the chapter.

From this limited set we can see that the correlations within the value style are very low across countries. The median correlation for all countries is only 0.07. On average, the pure value-returns are vir-

TABLE 5-I-4. **Correlations of Value Active Returns across Countries**

	Japan	Germany	France	Italy	Hong Kong	U.K.	U.S.
Japan	1.00	0.04	0.04	0.01	0.10	0.07	0.18
Germany		1.00	0.13	−0.01	0.03	0.09	0.24
France			1.00	0.07	0.16	0.25	0.35
Italy				1.00	−0.01	0.10	0.14
Hong Kong					1.00	0.03	−0.02
U.K.						1.00	0.30
U.S.							1.00

Statistics for All Countries

Median	0.07
Mean	0.07
Maximum	0.41
Minimum	−0.27

TABLE 5-I-5. Correlations of Growth Active Returns across Countries

	Japan	Germany	France	Italy	Hong Kong	U.K.	U.S.
Japan	1.00	0.02	0.03	−0.02	0.07	0.07	0.20
Germany		1.00	−0.07	0.08	0.03	0.06	0.16
France			1.00	0.03	0.18	0.18	0.25
Italy				1.00	−0.02	0.05	0.14
Hong Kong					1.00	0.06	−0.03
U.K.						1.00	0.24
U.S.							1.00

Statistics for All Countries

Median	0.03
Mean	0.04
Maximum	0.42
Minimum	−0.27

tually uncorrelated with one another. One interesting observation is that within the developed markets, all the countries have a higher correlation to the United States than they have relative to the other major markets but the correlations are still quite low.

Table 5-I-5 shows the correlations between the active returns to the growth portfolios. The entire matrix can be found in the appendix to this part of the chapter.

Again, we see very similar results to those under the value style, as one would expect, since the growth will be mainly just the negative of value. The correlations within the style are very low across countries. The median correlation for growth across all countries is only 0.03, virtually uncorrelated with one another.

Table 5-I-6 shows the correlations of the value- and growth-spread returns. The entire matrix can be found in the appendix to this part of the chapter.

Comparison with Capaul, Rowley, and Sharpe

A similar study was done by Capaul, Rowley, and Sharpe (CRS).[1] How different are the results we report from their results? Before we discuss any comparison, we must point out a few major differences

---

[1] Capaul, Carlo, Ian Rowley, and William F. Sharpe. "International Value and Growth Stock Returns." *Financial Analysts Journal*, January/February 1993.

TABLE 5-I-6. Correlations of Value/Growth Spread Returns across Countries

	Japan	Germany	France	Italy	Hong Kong	U.K.	U.S.
Japan	1.00	0.03	0.04	0.00	0.09	0.07	0.19
Germany		1.00	0.04	0.03	0.03	0.08	0.21
France			1.00	0.05	0.17	0.22	0.32
Italy				1.00	-0.02	0.08	0.14
Hong Kong					1.00	0.04	-0.03
U.K.						1.00	0.27
U.S.							1.00

Statistics for All Countries

Median	0.05
Mean	0.05
Maximum	0.41
Minimum	-0.27

between their study and ours. First, they used price/book to classify stocks as either value or growth whereas we used the BARRA value factor. Second, their study was done over a different time period, January 1981 through June 1992 versus January 1988 through July 1994 for our analysis. Finally, we have different starting universes, the MSCI (Morgan Stanley Capital International) universe of stocks for theirs and the FT Index for ours.

Let us examine some of the statistics on the value/growth spread returns for the two studies that are shown in Table 5-I-7.

TABLE 5-I-7. Comparison of Return Spread between Value and Growth Styles

	Mean Monthly Spread Return (%)		t-Statistic		Annualized Standard Deviation (%)	
	This Study	CRS	This Study	CRS	This Study	CRS
France	0.25	0.53	0.93	1.62	8.27	13.38
Germany	0.11	0.13	0.44	0.48	7.59	10.88
Japan	0.39	0.50	1.33	1.57	9.03	13.03
Switzerland	0.11	0.31	0.37	1.26	8.84	10.03
U.K.	0.06	0.23	0.32	0.81	5.96	11.50
U.S.	0.00	0.11	-0.01	0.67	6.72	6.89

One obse tion is that the mean spread-returns are much lower for our study v . sus the CRS study. Another interesting observation is the difference in the level of risk or volatility of the spread returns. The CRS study has much higher risk except for the United States where the studies used the same indices. Since we have different time horizons, different universes as well as different definitions of value for the other countries we can only say the results are different but not speculate as to why.

Both studies looked at the correlations for the value/growth spread across countries and Table 5-I-8 shows a comparison of the results.

Both studies show very low correlations between countries. The off-diagonal correlations for this study are slightly higher on average for these countries, 0.164, than the CRS study, 0.071. However, the average for all countries examined in this study is only 0.05.

In general, these results are similar, showing positive active-returns to value in a majority of countries, and low correlations between the style-portfolios' active returns across countries.

Small-Cap Stock Results

Investment in small-cap stocks has attracted the interest of investors seeking stocks that as an asset class have outperformed the market. At the international level, this interest is reflected by the increasing number of indices for small-cap firms. For example, Financial Times Actuaries, Morgan Stanley Capital International, and Salomon Brothers are among several investment companies who offer small-stock benchmarks for the global investor.

In this study, small-cap stocks were selected as described above using a consistent approach within each country in order to capture the effect of a small-cap style. As a result, the small-cap stocks of certain countries had greater capitalization than large-cap stocks of other countries, as shown in Figure 5-I-7. The largest stocks in the small-cap group came from the Netherlands, Germany, and Japan. The smallest stocks in the large-cap group were primarily located in Norway, Italy, Belgium, and Finland.

The small-cap effect has been documented in the United States by the work of several researchers, including Ibbotson and Sinque-

TABLE 5-I-8. Comparison of Correlations of Value/Growth Spreads

	France		Germany		Japan		Switzerland		U.K.		U.S.	
	This Study	CRS	This Study	CRS	This Study	CRS	This Study	CRS	This Study	CRS	This Study	CRS
France	1.00	1.00	0.04	-0.07	0.04	0.03	0.19	0.08	0.22	0.34	0.32	0.24
Germany			1.00	1.00	0.03	-0.20	0.17	0.20	0.08	-0.13	0.21	0.08
Japan					1.00	1.00	0.16	0.06	0.07	0.07	0.19	0.01
Switzerland							1.00	1.00	0.25	0.08	0.22	0.03
U.K.									1.00	1.00	0.27	0.26
U.S.											1.00	1.00

FIGURE 5-I-7.   Distribution of Company Capitalization after Split of FT Country Indices into Large- and Small-Cap

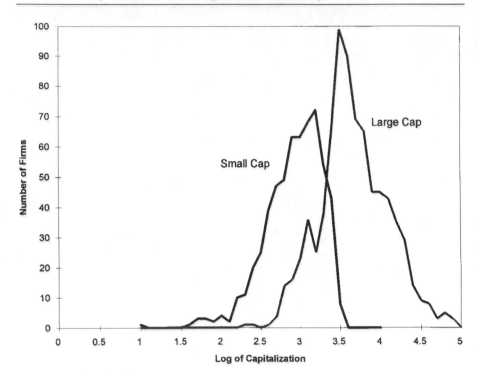

field, and Rosenberg, Reid, and Lanstein. In extending this concept to international stocks we began by creating an international small-cap portfolio and measuring its performance against the FT Index. We found that there is a strong size effect internationally.

The portfolio outperformed the benchmark by an annualized return of 4.4% over the period January 1988 to July 1994. The small-cap effect in Japan was the overwhelming influence, contributing 4.3% of the 4.4% return.

At the country level, the small-cap portfolios outperformed the corresponding FT country index in 14 of the 20 countries considered as shown in Table 5-I-9. Over the 1988–1994 period investigated, the average monthly active return was highest in Finland, at 1.1%, and lowest in Switzerland, at –0.49%. The average monthly active return for all countries was 0.38%.

TABLE 5-I-9. Active Returns to the Small-Capitalization Style

	Mean Monthly Active Return (%)	t-Statistic	Annualized Standard Deviation (%)
Australia	−0.14	−0.47	9.14
Austria	0.26	0.48	16.55
Belgium	0.69	2.27	9.28
Denmark	0.32	0.81	12.31
Finland	1.10	1.15	29.34
France	0.34	1.34	7.80
Germany	0.09	0.29	9.08
Hong Kong	−0.08	−0.28	9.24
Ireland	0.00	−0.01	13.25
Italy	0.28	0.90	9.57
Japan	0.61	1.55	12.00
Malaysia	0.88	1.27	21.49
Netherlands	0.20	0.62	9.82
New Zealand	−0.48	−0.97	15.07
Norway	0.23	0.41	17.11
Singapore	0.17	0.45	11.50
Spain	0.01	0.01	14.30
Sweden	0.36	0.82	13.60
Switzerland	−0.49	−1.34	11.24
U.K.	−0.07	−0.23	8.67

The statistical significance of the average monthly active return for each country was also determined. Belgium, with an average monthly return of 0.69%, was the only country with a t-statistic greater than two. For the other countries, the t-statistic was less than two. In view of the positive average monthly returns, this indicates that empirically there is a small-cap effect but it is not statistically different from zero over the period analyzed.

Again, though the returns to the small-cap style portfolios are not significant in statistical terms, they are quite large in investment terms. The average active-returns for the style are in the range of −50 to +60 basis points per month for a 79-month period. If one had picked the correct style for a country, and held it for the entire period, one would have outperformed the local country by a significant margin. Figures 5-I-8 through 5-I-12 show the cumulative returns to the small-cap spread for France, Germany, Japan, the United Kingdom, and an international portfolio.

FIGURE 5-I-8.   Cumulative Active Return to France Small-Cap

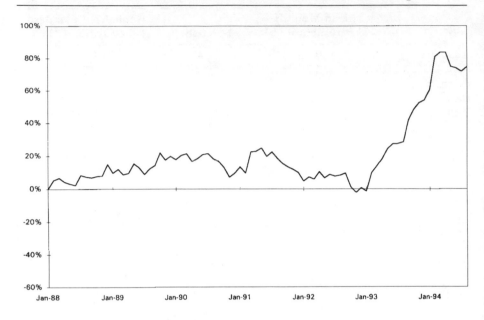

FIGURE 5-I-9.   Cumulative Active Return to Germany Small-Cap

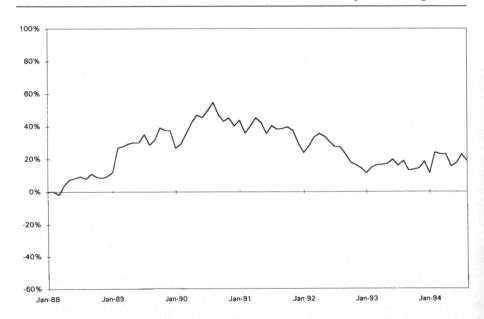

FIGURE 5-I-10.   Cumulative Active Return to Japan Small-Cap

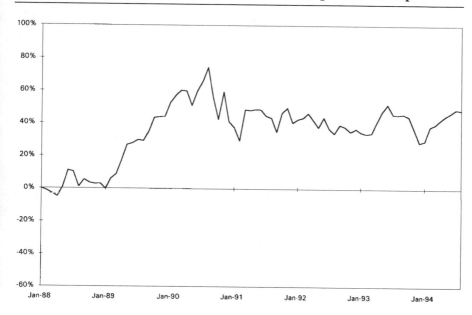

FIGURE 5-I-11.   Cumulative Active Return to United Kingdom Small-Cap

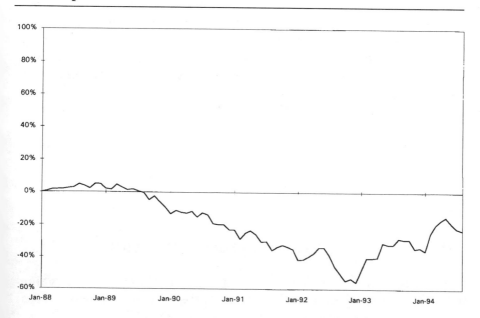

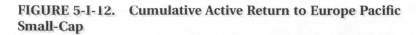

FIGURE 5-I-12.   Cumulative Active Return to Europe Pacific Small-Cap

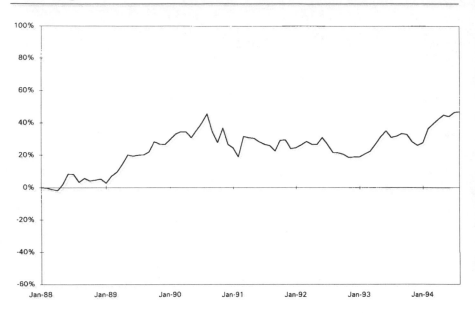

Interesting observations are the trends of the small-cap returns for the countries shown here. Like most of the value/growth spreads, the small-cap returns show trends, sometimes outperforming and other times underperforming the index. However, none of countries show a consistent positive or negative trend. The empirical results we obtained with respect to an international small-cap effect are very dependent on the time period analyzed. Over the entire 79-month time period analyzed, small-cap for Europe and Pacific had a large positive cumulative active-return. However, if we examine just the past four years, small-cap would have been essentially flat. The positive return was obtained during 1988 and 1989. More research is required to determine if there truly is a small-cap effect for other countries.

Correlations of Returns across Countries

The average correlation across all countries was 0.09. This low value indicates that small-cap stock active-returns tend to be uncorrelated between countries, although there were several exceptions where higher positive and negative values netted out to the average. The highest correlation of 0.45 was between Spain and the United Kingdom as well as between Switzerland and the Netherlands. The lowest correlation of –0.27 occurred between Italy and Austria and between Sweden and Belgium. The correlation matrix can be found in the appendix to this part of the chapter.

One might postulate that returns to small-cap stocks of countries within similar regions of the world may be more highly correlated to each other than with countries outside the region if there are common regional factors that influence stock returns. Regional influences however, appear to play a limited role in capturing correlations of small-stock active returns between countries. In Europe, for example, the average correlation of small-cap returns was 0.17. Spanish stocks exhibited the highest average-correlation with a value of 0.26. Austria and Ireland had the lowest correlations with stocks from other countries, with average values of 0.02 and 0.05, respectively.

Among the four Scandinavian countries, Denmark, Norway, Sweden, and Finland, the average correlation was only 0.04. The exception was the correlation of 0.22 between Norway and Finland.

The average correlation between small stocks in the six Pacific-region countries was 0.09. Japan and Hong Kong had the highest correlation with a value of 0.25, while Malaysia and New Zealand were inversely correlated with a value of –0.10.

Return Seasonality

Research on small-cap U.S. stocks by Keim, Roll, and others have found that there is a strong seasonal effect to stock returns. In these studies, stocks listed on the NYSE and AMEX were grouped in 10 portfolios according to capitalization. Returns for the portfolio containing the smallest 10% of the firms were much higher in the month of January than the returns for the remaining nine portfolios, leading to the term "January Effect."

We performed a similar analysis for returns of the small stocks in FT Index over the period January 1988 to July 1994. Returns for each month were calculated net of the FT Index return. The returns were grouped by month and then the average and standard deviation were calculated for each month. In Figure 5-I-13, the average return is

FIGURE 5-I-13.   Seasonal Returns to the Small-Cap Style

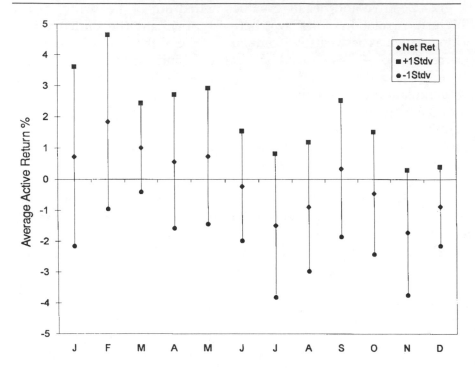

shown with one standard deviation on either side to capture the variability of the monthly returns.

Returns for the month of February were noticeably higher than the FT Index average-return while returns for the months of July and November were lower. The overall seasonal trend of returns for international small stocks is similar to that in the United States in that higher returns are registered at the beginning of the year and lower returns towards the end. But unlike in the United States, the highest return occurs in February and the lowest returns occur on two separate months.

In the United States, the seasonality of small-stock returns has been postulated to be linked to tax-related trading and higher volatility during the month of January. Outside the United States, however, the factors generating this behavior need to be investigated in future research. If indeed there are seasonal effects outside the United States

as shown in Figure 5-I-13, the trend may continue in the future as it
has in the United States.

Momentum/Mean Reversion Results

In the United States, momentum strategies are based on the correlation
of the past eight to 14 months' cumulative return with next month's
return. Momentum, or relative strength as the effect is sometimes called,
can be used by investors as a ranking system when selecting stocks. We
investigated to see if momentum effects exist in markets outside the
United States. Due to the six-month rebalancing period used, the analysis tested whether stocks that outperformed the market during the past
12 months would continue to outperform during the next six months.

Average active returns for stocks selected on the basis of positive
momentum over the past 12 months are shown in Table 5-I-10. When
this style works, investors should buy last year's winners and sell last

TABLE 5-I-10. Active Returns to the Positive Momentum Style

	Mean Monthly Active Return (%)	t-Statistic	Annualized Standard Deviation (%)
Australia	−0.04	−0.48	2.55
Austria	−0.25	−0.93	8.31
Belgium	−0.06	−0.24	7.71
Denmark	0.49	2.18	6.97
Finland	0.26	0.60	13.22
France	0.07	0.61	3.56
Germany	−0.01	−0.06	4.32
Hong Kong	−0.18	−1.17	4.78
Ireland	0.40	1.72	7.19
Italy	0.28	1.40	6.12
Japan	−0.28	−1.54	5.55
Malaysia	−0.05	−0.25	6.85
Netherlands	−0.10	−0.52	5.97
New Zealand	−0.39	−1.49	8.04
Norway	−0.07	−0.25	8.29
Singapore	0.10	0.60	5.08
Spain	0.18	0.96	5.73
Sweden	0.75	2.26	10.23
Switzerland	0.25	1.56	5.02
U.K.	0.05	0.53	3.10

year's losers. The returns were positive in half the countries considered and two countries, Denmark and Sweden, had statistically significant returns at the 95% level.

For stocks with negative momentum (mean reversion) over the past 12 months, returns were positive in seven of the 20 countries considered. Where negative momentum styles work, investors look for stocks that have underperformed the market over the past 12 months because these stocks will tend to outperform the market in the months ahead. In our analysis, no country showed returns statistically significant at the 95% level, as shown in Table 5-I-11.

Correlations of Returns across Countries

The average correlation of positive-momentum returns across countries was 0.1. This low value indicates that positive momentum is

TABLE 5-I-11.   **Active Returns to the Mean Reversion Style**

	Mean Monthly Active Return (%)	t-Statistic	Annualized Standard Deviation (%)
Australia	0.07	0.68	3.24
Austria	−0.05	−0.17	9.13
Belgium	0.17	0.44	11.70
Denmark	−0.36	−1.53	7.29
Finland	−0.03	−0.07	13.95
France	−0.10	−0.75	4.01
Germany	−0.06	−0.38	4.70
Hong Kong	0.16	0.96	5.15
Ireland	−0.37	−1.26	9.07
Italy	−0.08	−0.40	6.18
Japan	0.29	1.73	5.09
Malaysia	0.13	0.40	9.76
Netherlands	0.05	0.21	7.72
New Zealand	0.30	0.75	12.25
Norway	−0.27	−0.70	12.05
Singapore	−0.04	−0.27	4.99
Spain	−0.18	−0.76	7.10
Sweden	−0.38	−0.99	11.61
Switzerland	−0.24	−1.32	5.55
U.K.	−0.09	−0.81	3.45

fairly uncorrelated between countries. Several country pairs, however, had correlations much different than the average. Belgium and Germany had a correlation of 0.5 while Denmark and Japan as well as Austria and Norway had correlation of –0.21.

The correlations for the negative-momentum returns were very similar to those of the positive momentum returns. This result was expected since the return characteristic of the positive-momentum stocks is opposite to that of the negative-momentum stocks. Hence, when one momentum-style has positive active-returns, the other style will have negative returns of the same magnitude. The entire matrices for positive- and negative-momentum returns can be found in the appendix to this part of the chapter.

When returns for positive and negative momentum are considered together within one country, it is possible to determine which trend for return performance is more prevalent. In countries where the positive-momentum style gives positive returns and negative momentum gives negative returns, price momentum works in identifying stocks that will tend to outperform the market in the future. On the other hand, in countries where positive momentum gives negative returns and negative momentum gives positive returns, mean-reversion strategies should be used. The mean-reversion strategy bets that underperforming stocks will outperform the market in the future. Table 5-I-12 summarizes the findings of more in-depth studies on momentum-based trends in major markets. The results found here are similar to the results in those studies. Also included in the table are results from studies performed by BARRA and Salomon Brothers on one-month reversal trends in stock returns.

TABLE 5-I-12. Markets in Which Strategies Tend to Work

	One-Month Reversal	Momentum	Mean Reversion
United States	Yes	Yes	
Japan	Yes		Yes
Germany	Yes	Yes	
United Kingdom	Yes	Yes	
Australia	No		Yes

Sources: BARRA Inc. and Salomon Brothers Inc.

Investment Strategy Implications/Conclusion

The results obtained here indicate that investment styles, value/ growth, large/small, and momentum/mean reversion have different returns associated with them. But the story is far from consistent from country to country. In some countries a particular style will outperform the local benchmark and in others the style will underperform the benchmark. However, the results could just be noise in the investment returns and not a persistent effect that could be expected to continue. In fact, very few of the results obtained here are statistically significant at the 95% level, and those that are statistically significant could be due purely to chance given the number of countries and styles analyzed.

Our study suggests that investment in international small-cap and value stocks will continue to attract the interest of international portfolio managers in search of superior returns due to the empirical evidence that they will outperform other stocks. However, the returns obtained here may not be obtainable in a real portfolio, especially the small-cap results. Low liquidity may hinder investing in small-cap stocks due to difficulty in establishing or liquidating a position in a stock with low trading-volume. Furthermore, the market impact on a stock's price may be great, resulting in large transaction costs and reducing the realized return. These effects were not addressed in our analysis.

Finally, the low correlation of style returns across countries offers possibilities for diversification. Concentrating on a single style across many countries is a diversifying strategy. The correlations across countries are very low even within geographic regions. Thus an investment manager can be more aggressive within each country because the low correlations across countries should result in a portfolio with higher returns per unit of risk.

References

Ibbotson, Roger G., and Rex A. Sinquefield. "Stocks, Bonds, Bills and Inflation: The Past and the Future." Financial Analysts' Research Foundation, 1982.

Keim, Donald B. "Size-Related Anomalies and Stock Return Seasonality: Further Empirical Evidence." *Journal of Financial Economics* 12 no. 1, June 1983.

Roll, Richard. "Vas ist das?" *Journal of Portfolio Management* 9, no. 2, 1983.
Rosenberg, Barr, Kenneth Reid, and Ronald Lanstein. "Pervasive Evidence of Market Inefficiency." *Journal of Portfolio Management* 11 no. 3, 1985.

Appendix

Tables 5-I-13 through 5-I-18 on the next six pages show the investment style correlation matrices for all countries studied.

TABLE 5-1-13. Correlations across Countries: Value

	Aus	Aut	Bel	Den	Fin	Fra	Ger	Hkg	Ire	Ita	Jpn	Mal	Net	Nze	Nor	Sin	Spa	Swe	Swi	UK	US
Australia	1.00	0.05	-0.07	0.04	-0.03	0.04	0.17	-0.06	-0.09	0.04	0.02	-0.07	0.05	-0.12	-0.11	0.03	0.03	0.09	0.12	0.01	0.24
Austria		1.00	0.15	-0.23	0.04	0.29	0.12	0.17	-0.09	0.21	0.16	0.08	0.17	0.12	0.09	0.17	0.01	0.13	0.13	0.14	0.15
Belgium			1.00	-0.23	0.09	0.16	0.05	-0.03	0.14	0.04	-0.01	0.29	0.00	0.01	0.10	0.05	0.08	0.14	-0.03	-0.02	-0.06
Denmark				1.00	-0.01	-0.21	-0.27	-0.01	-0.06	-0.20	0.07	-0.07	-0.14	-0.20	-0.17	-0.02	-0.08	-0.12	0.08	0.07	-0.06
Finland					1.00	-0.10	0.10	0.13	-0.12	0.01	0.09	0.01	0.02	0.11	-0.01	0.24	0.18	0.05	0.02	0.22	-0.12
France						1.00	0.13	0.16	-0.01	0.07	0.04	0.33	0.41	-0.08	0.23	0.08	0.12	0.31	0.25	0.25	0.35
Germany							1.00	0.03	0.05	-0.01	0.04	0.04	0.29	0.09	0.06	0.00	0.08	0.32	0.23	0.09	0.24
Hong Kong								1.00	0.00	-0.01	0.10	0.20	0.08	-0.02	0.02	0.07	-0.06	0.20	0.20	0.03	-0.02
Ireland									1.00	-0.07	-0.04	0.06	0.15	0.09	0.11	-0.15	-0.15	0.00	-0.05	0.15	-0.15
Italy										1.00	0.01	-0.07	-0.16	0.10	0.12	0.15	0.07	0.14	0.11	0.10	0.14
Japan											1.00	0.11	0.21	0.00	0.15	0.06	0.15	0.30	0.18	0.07	0.18
Malaysia												1.00	0.20	0.09	0.15	0.20	0.00	0.09	-0.02	-0.14	-0.01
Netherlands													1.00	-0.04	0.05	0.17	0.12	0.38	0.21	0.40	0.40
New Zealand														1.00	0.05	0.01	0.15	-0.08	-0.10	-0.04	-0.03
Norway															1.00	-0.04	-0.06	0.04	0.16	0.14	-0.07
Singapore																1.00	0.02	0.01	0.18	0.07	0.13
Spain																	1.00	0.14	0.07	0.26	0.14
Sweden																		1.00	0.27	0.15	0.38
Switzerland																			1.00	0.33	0.25
U.K.																				1.00	0.30
U.S.																					1.00

112

TABLE 5-I-14. Correlations across Countries: Growth

	Aus	Aut	Bel	Den	Fin	Fra	Ger	Hkg	Ire	Ita	Jpn	Mal	Net	Nze	Nor	Sin	Spa	Swe	Swi	UK	US
Australia	1.00	0.10	-0.01	0.00	-0.09	-0.02	0.08	-0.06	-0.20	-0.02	0.01	-0.02	0.07	-0.24	-0.11	0.08	0.04	-0.02	0.00	-0.03	0.21
Austria		1.00	0.07	-0.26	-0.09	0.24	0.07	0.10	-0.05	0.14	0.14	0.12	0.29	0.15	0.20	0.08	0.10	0.04	0.07	0.03	0.06
Belgium			1.00	-0.27	0.03	0.08	-0.02	-0.02	0.14	0.05	-0.06	0.21	-0.15	-0.10	0.04	-0.05	0.16	-0.04	-0.14	-0.02	-0.13
Denmark				1.00	-0.02	-0.18	-0.25	-0.06	-0.08	-0.23	0.03	-0.20	-0.27	-0.26	-0.08	0.00	-0.20	-0.14	-0.06	-0.07	-0.09
Finland					1.00	-0.13	0.01	0.11	-0.13	-0.06	-0.01	0.02	0.06	0.18	-0.03	0.09	0.06	-0.09	-0.04	0.24	-0.11
France						1.00	-0.07	0.18	-0.01	0.03	0.03	0.35	0.30	-0.06	0.10	0.09	0.16	0.21	0.07	0.18	0.25
Germany							1.00	0.03	0.00	0.08	0.02	0.01	0.23	0.07	0.18	-0.16	0.01	0.21	0.07	0.06	0.16
Hong Kong								1.00	0.08	-0.02	0.07	0.20	0.11	-0.07	-0.08	-0.06	-0.07	0.16	0.14	0.06	-0.03
Ireland									1.00	-0.10	-0.05	0.00	0.12	0.00	0.19	-0.25	-0.02	-0.02	-0.16	0.15	-0.19
Italy										1.00	-0.02	0.02	-0.19	0.05	-0.01	-0.05	0.04	0.08	0.02	0.05	0.14
Japan											1.00	0.13	0.14	0.03	0.17	0.03	0.01	0.32	0.10	0.07	0.20
Malaysia												1.00	0.15	-0.05	0.02	0.11	0.07	-0.02	0.09	-0.13	-0.01
Netherlands													1.00	0.11	0.15	0.14	0.00	0.32	-0.08	0.35	0.35
New Zealand														1.00	0.29	-0.02	0.07	0.03	0.19	0.07	0.04
Norway															1.00	-0.15	0.04	0.06	0.08	0.18	0.14
Singapore																1.00	0.06	0.01	0.16	0.08	0.14
Spain																	1.00	-0.06	-0.07	0.14	0.08
Sweden																		1.00	0.12	0.14	0.42
Switzerland																			1.00	0.10	0.14
U.K.																				1.00	0.24
U.S.																					1.00

113

TABLE 5-I-15. Correlations across Countries: Growth-Value Spread

	Aus	Aut	Bel	Den	Fin	Fra	Ger	Hkg	Ire	Ita	Jpn	Mal	Net	Nze	Nor	Sin	Spa	Swe	Swi	UK	US
Australia	1.00	0.07	-0.04	0.02	-0.07	0.01	0.13	-0.06	-0.15	0.01	0.02	-0.06	0.07	-0.18	-0.12	0.05	0.02	0.04	0.07	-0.01	0.23
Austria		1.00	0.10	-0.26	-0.02	0.28	0.10	0.15	-0.08	0.18	0.15	0.11	0.25	0.12	0.15	0.11	0.04	0.10	0.10	0.08	0.11
Belgium			1.00	-0.26	0.06	0.11	0.00	-0.03	0.14	0.04	-0.04	0.26	-0.08	-0.06	0.08	-0.03	0.11	0.05	-0.11	-0.03	-0.10
Denmark				1.00	-0.02	-0.21	-0.27	-0.04	-0.08	-0.23	0.05	-0.13	-0.23	-0.26	-0.13	-0.01	-0.16	-0.14	0.02	0.00	-0.07
Finland					1.00	-0.12	0.06	0.13	-0.14	-0.03	0.04	0.01	0.06	0.16	-0.01	0.18	0.13	-0.03	-0.04	0.24	-0.12
France						1.00	0.04	0.17	-0.02	0.05	0.04	0.35	0.36	-0.08	0.20	0.09	0.15	0.27	0.19	0.22	0.32
Germany							1.00	0.03	0.03	0.03	0.03	0.03	0.29	0.10	0.10	-0.07	0.06	0.27	0.17	0.08	0.21
Hong Kong								1.00	0.04	-0.02	0.09	0.20	0.10	-0.05	-0.02	0.00	-0.06	0.19	0.19	0.04	-0.03
Ireland									1.00	-0.09	-0.05	0.04	0.14	0.05	0.16	-0.22	-0.11	-0.01	-0.12	0.16	-0.16
Italy										1.00	0.00	-0.04	-0.18	0.09	0.07	0.04	0.06	0.11	0.08	0.08	0.14
Japan											1.00	0.12	0.17	0.02	0.17	0.05	0.08	0.32	0.16	0.07	0.19
Malaysia												1.00	0.18	0.03	0.11	0.14	0.04	0.04	0.02	-0.13	-0.01
Netherlands													1.00	0.02	0.12	0.17	0.06	0.38	0.08	0.38	0.38
New Zealand														1.00	0.14	-0.04	0.14	-0.04	0.04	0.00	0.00
Norway															1.00	-0.11	0.00	0.05	0.16	0.18	-0.05
Singapore																1.00	0.04	0.01	0.18	0.09	0.14
Spain																	1.00	0.06	-0.01	0.21	0.12
Sweden																		1.00	0.24	0.15	0.41
Switzerland																			1.00	0.25	0.22
U.K.																				1.00	0.27
U.S.A.																					1.00

TABLE 5-I-16. Correlations across Countries: Small-Cap

	Aus	Aut	Bel	Den	Fin	Fra	Ger	Hkg	Ire	Ita	Jpn	Mal	Net	Nze	Nor	Sin	Spa	Swe	Swi	UK
Australia	1.00	-0.20	-0.10	-0.20	0.13	0.31	0.19	0.16	0.00	-0.03	0.03	0.09	0.15	0.09	0.15	0.08	0.05	0.04	0.28	0.10
Austria		1.00	0.00	0.32	-0.07	0.05	0.10	0.00	0.08	-0.27	-0.06	0.03	0.02	-0.05	-0.07	-0.13	0.05	0.22	0.06	0.07
Belgium			1.00	-0.02	0.20	0.28	0.23	0.06	-0.09	0.20	0.33	0.03	0.04	0.07	0.24	-0.02	0.26	-0.27	0.25	0.25
Denmark				1.00	0.06	0.15	0.18	-0.08	-0.15	-0.15	0.07	0.13	-0.01	-0.03	0.04	0.12	0.01	-0.01	-0.03	0.05
Finland					1.00	0.39	0.03	0.13	0.07	0.27	0.41	0.21	0.10	0.16	0.22	0.02	0.30	-0.09	0.12	0.19
France						1.00	0.25	0.10	-0.07	0.15	0.11	0.31	0.10	0.20	0.13	0.02	0.30	0.05	0.38	0.27
Germany							1.00	0.12	-0.07	0.16	0.24	0.12	0.26	0.02	0.01	0.09	0.10	0.09	0.38	0.20
Hong Kong								1.00	0.23	0.06	0.25	0.13	0.20	0.04	-0.15	0.15	0.14	-0.04	0.16	0.17
Ireland									1.00	0.05	-0.08	-0.19	0.19	0.00	0.09	0.04	0.27	0.12	-0.09	0.18
Italy										1.00	0.22	0.18	0.08	0.07	0.00	-0.04	0.33	0.18	0.17	0.26
Japan											1.00	0.12	0.18	0.02	-0.05	0.14	0.26	-0.14	0.14	0.23
Malaysia												1.00	0.09	-0.10	-0.13	0.18	0.13	-0.05	0.07	0.09
Netherlands													1.00	-0.25	0.02	-0.02	0.44	0.08	0.45	0.29
New Zealand														1.00	0.01	-0.04	-0.17	-0.10	-0.09	0.06
Norway															1.00	0.03	0.22	0.01	0.18	0.29
Singapore																1.00	-0.02	-0.06	-0.05	-0.12
Spain																	1.00	0.00	0.32	0.45
Sweden																		1.00	0.20	0.18
Switzerland																			1.00	0.42
U.K.																				1.00

TABLE 5-I-17. Correlations across Countries: Momentum

	Aus	Aut	Bel	Den	Fin	Fra	Ger	Hkg	Ire	Ita	Jpn	Mal	Net	Nze	Nor	Sin	Spa	Swe	Swi	UK
Australia	1.00	0.14	0.10	0.09	0.26	0.04	0.27	0.01	0.10	0.03	-0.01	0.17	-0.05	0.12	0.01	-0.01	0.31	0.02	0.00	0.19
Austria		1.00	0.05	0.06	0.12	0.13	0.12	0.21	0.08	0.10	0.27	0.18	-0.12	0.13	-0.21	0.16	0.15	0.21	-0.03	0.14
Belgium			1.00	0.05	0.03	0.36	0.50	0.12	-0.19	0.08	0.03	-0.01	0.11	0.07	-0.04	-0.11	0.26	0.07	0.02	0.05
Denmark				1.00	0.13	0.05	0.10	0.14	-0.02	-0.07	0.03	0.16	-0.02	0.10	0.01	0.23	0.21	0.41	0.26	0.00
Finland					1.00	0.19	0.12	0.00	0.15	0.24	-0.21	0.23	0.05	0.20	0.23	-0.02	0.18	0.19	0.09	0.18
France						1.00	0.29	0.15	0.13	0.22	-0.06	0.26	0.15	0.10	0.08	0.08	0.31	0.13	0.10	0.24
Germany							1.00	0.05	0.09	0.13	-0.02	0.17	0.08	0.03	-0.07	0.07	0.27	0.27	0.20	0.00
Hong Kong								1.00	-0.01	-0.02	-0.03	0.13	0.13	0.01	-0.16	0.07	0.13	0.14	0.14	0.10
Ireland									1.00	-0.05	0.02	0.14	-0.02	0.11	0.10	0.12	-0.14	-0.02	-0.10	0.18
Italy										1.00	0.03	0.09	0.18	0.28	0.01	-0.02	0.09	0.21	0.01	0.22
Japan											1.00	0.09	-0.05	0.07	0.10	0.12	0.14	0.11	-0.02	0.12
Malaysia												1.00	0.02	0.14	0.14	0.13	0.38	0.09	0.12	0.01
Netherlands													1.00	0.16	0.16	0.13	0.07	0.09	-0.09	0.11
New Zealand														1.00	0.13	0.08	0.09	0.21	0.05	0.19
Norway															1.00	-0.08	0.11	0.02	-0.09	0.01
Singapore																1.00	0.05	0.31	-0.04	-0.05
Spain																	1.00	0.15	0.20	0.27
Sweden																		1.00	0.13	-0.03
Switzerland																			1.00	-0.01
U.K.																				1.00

TABLE 5-I-18. Correlations across Countries: Mean Reversion

	Aus	Aut	Bel	Den	Fin	Fra	Ger	Hkg	Ire	Ita	Jpn	Mal	Net	Nze	Nor	Sin	Spa	Swe	Swi	UK
Australia	1.00	0.07	0.10	0.12	0.12	0.08	0.23	-0.01	0.06	0.00	-0.04	0.19	-0.09	0.05	-0.04	0.15	0.34	-0.05	-0.20	0.14
Austria		1.00	0.04	-0.09	0.07	0.17	0.08	0.19	0.07	0.09	0.19	0.17	-0.13	0.10	-0.26	0.16	0.14	0.19	-0.07	0.10
Belgium			1.00	-0.03	0.30	0.41	0.46	0.11	-0.19	0.16	0.09	0.00	0.05	-0.17	-0.15	-0.04	0.26	0.14	0.08	0.09
Denmark				1.00	0.11	0.13	-0.01	0.18	0.04	-0.07	-0.16	0.29	0.04	0.21	-0.02	0.17	0.24	0.19	0.24	0.08
Finland					1.00	0.40	0.13	0.09	0.11	0.36	-0.08	0.33	0.21	0.19	0.13	0.05	0.24	0.32	0.08	0.28
France						1.00	0.24	0.14	0.15	0.22	0.15	0.26	0.33	0.04	0.01	0.12	0.34	0.20	0.11	0.29
Germany							1.00	0.06	0.07	0.07	-0.04	0.14	0.11	-0.03	-0.08	0.10	0.25	0.16	0.16	-0.09
Hong Kong								1.00	0.03	0.06	-0.02	0.18	0.11	0.13	-0.02	0.21	0.03	0.19	0.15	0.11
Ireland									1.00	-0.04	-0.05	0.13	0.08	0.16	0.12	0.10	-0.15	0.04	-0.26	0.18
Italy										1.00	0.02	0.16	0.13	0.36	-0.06	-0.06	0.18	0.19	-0.03	0.28
Japan											1.00	0.05	-0.03	-0.15	0.06	0.09	0.13	0.09	-0.07	0.08
Malaysia												1.00	0.16	0.15	0.01	0.31	0.37	0.16	0.17	0.11
Netherlands													1.00	0.04	0.13	0.22	0.02	0.12	0.06	0.20
New Zealand														1.00	0.05	0.03	0.01	0.29	-0.08	0.18
Norway															1.00	-0.03	0.05	-0.09	-0.10	0.11
Singapore																1.00	0.14	0.15	0.03	0.00
Spain																	1.00	0.09	0.30	0.18
Sweden																		1.00	-0.01	0.10
Switzerland																			1.00	-0.05
U.K.																				1.00

117

PART II: International Equity Style Management

David Umstead, Ph.D., CFA, Managing Director
Boston International Advisors, Inc.

Numerous studies have documented the performance differences between the value and growth portions of the U.S. equity market. The value half of the U.S. equity market tends to produce considerably higher returns than the growth half. The value/growth spread within the S&P 500 Index, for example, has averaged 320 basis points per year over the last 20 years. It is quite natural to wonder whether similar spreads exist in the international equity markets. The more widespread this phenomenon the more confidence one can have in its persistence. This portion of Chapter 5 focuses on 20 equity-markets in Europe and the Pacific. Boston International Advisors (BIA) has developed a set of value and growth indices for each of these markets, and we shall use these indices to see if value beats growth outside of the United States.

Methodology

Table 5-II-1 is a schematic of the method BIA uses to create its Value and Growth Indices. The process is quite simple.[1] Imagine that Table 5-II-1 represents all stocks in the French stock market. For each stock, we collect two pieces of information: price/book ratio and capitalization. We sort by price/book and sum the capitalization data, starting from the top, until we have accumulated exactly half the capitalization of the French market. We draw a line at this point in the table. All stocks above the line are designated value stocks, and all stocks below the line are growth. We then capitalization-weight the stocks on each list to create value and growth indices for the French market.

---

[1] We use the same methodology as Capaul, Rowley, and Sharpe (1993).

Special thanks to William F. Sharpe, Nobel laureate and professor of finance at Stanford University Graduate School of Business, and Phillip M. Dolan, doctoral student studying under Professor Sharpe, both of whom provided very helpful suggestions on the presentation of this material. Special thanks as well to my colleagues at BIA, who played a key role in this research.

TABLE 5-II-1.   Schematic of the Method BIA Uses to Create Its Value and Growth Indices

Within each market stocks are sorted on price/book and split into value and growth categories. The capitalization of each market is divided equally between each category.

	Company	Cap		Price/Book
	A	$ 2 bil		0.6
	B	10		0.8
	C	1		0.9
	D	15		1.0
Value	E	3	50%	1.1
	F	4		1.2
	G	5		1.5
	H	5		1.7
	I	5		2.0
	J	15		2.1
	K	10		2.4
Growth	L	5	50%	3.4
	M	10		4.6
	N	10		5.2
		$100 bil		

Any stock in Table 5-II-1 with a price/book ratio of 2.0 or less is a value stock, and any stock with a price/book ratio greater than 2.0 is a growth stock. The exact break point between value and growth varies from market to market and even varies over time within a market. In other words, our definition of value is relative rather than absolute. This floating definition allows the value and growth indices to have equal capitalization. This means that when we compare the performance of these indices, we are comparing two investment-strategies that have roughly equal liquidity characteristics and which are therefore equally viable for large institutional investors.

Another important advantage to this technique is that we have apples and apples with respect to country weights when we aggregate regionally. For example, the BIA Europe Value Index has the same country weights as the BIA Europe Growth Index. Since the country factor is typically the most important factor in explaining the volatility of equity returns, it is important to keep country exposures the same when comparing value and growth strategies involving more than one country. If we were to define value in absolute terms, the percentage of capitalization above or below the demarcation line would vary from country to country, and the BIA Europe Growth Index would have different country weights than the Value Index.

BIA International Style-Indices

Figure 5-II-1 shows the performance history for the BIA Europe/ Pacific Value, Growth, and Market Indices. The performance difference between the Value and Growth Indices is dramatic. We see that a dollar invested in the BIA Europe/Pacific Value Index on December 31, 1974 grows to $24.96 by December 31, 1994. This index produces an unhedged return, in U.S. dollar terms, which averages 17.5% per year over this 20-year period. A dollar invested in the BIA Europe/Pacific Growth Index, on the other hand, grows to only

FIGURE 5-II-1. Performance of the BIA Europe/Pacific Value, Growth, and Market Indices
The indices include 20 countries, 14 in Europe and six in the Pacific. The countries are capitalization-weighted as are stocks within countries. Performance, unhedged in U.S. dollar terms, includes both price appreciation and dividends. Dividends are net of withholdings to U.S. tax-exempt investors and adjusted for gross ups where appropriate.

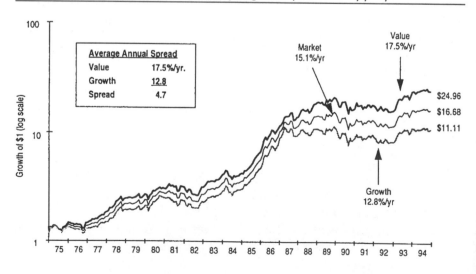

$11.11; an average return of just 12.8% per year. The Value Index out-performs the BIA Growth Index by an average of 466 basis points per year. Furthermore the spread is quite consistent. Note that the vertical axis in Figure 5-II-1 is logarithmic. This helps to highlight the steady divergence between the two indices over the 20-year period.

Table 5-II-2 provides the year-by-year performance for the BIA Europe/Pacific Value and Growth Indices. The Value Index outper-forms the Growth Index 16 years out of 20 and produces lower volatility. The Value Index standard deviation is 17.61% versus 18.14% for the Growth Index. The largest positive value/growth spread is 17.22 percentage points in 1988, and the largest negative is 7.13 percentage points in 1980. The three remaining years with nega-tive spreads are 1984, 1986, and 1991. There is no obvious pattern to

TABLE 5-II-2.   Annual Performance of the BIA Europe/Pacific Value and Growth Indices

The Value Index beats the Growth Index every year but four.

	Value	Growth	Difference
1975	39.41%	30.76%	8.65
1976	5.77	0.34	5.43
1977	24.54	14.30	10.23
1978	35.62	31.16	4.46
1979	5.78	3.77	2.01
1980	19.06	26.20	−7.13
1981	2.77	−7.03	9.80
1982	−1.07	−1.84	0.76
1983	25.40	19.81	5.59
1984	5.89	7.90	−2.01
1985	56.36	54.91	1.45
1986	66.68	68.05	−1.37
1987	27.96	21.35	6.62
1988	33.26	16.04	17.22
1989	15.24	5.65	9.59
1990	−22.75	−24.46	1.71
1991	10.81	12.19	−1.38
1992	−11.78	−14.25	2.47
1993	37.99	24.51	13.47
1994	10.45	4.33	6.12
Annualized			
Return	17.45	12.80	4.66
Standard deviation	17.61	18.14	

the negative-spread years. One negative spread came in a year with phenomenal returns (1986), two in average years (1980 and 1991), and one in a below-average year (1984).

Table 5-II-3 shows rolling five-year comparisons. In this chart we can see that the BIA Europe/Pacific Value Index outperforms the Europe/Pacific Growth Index in every five-year period. The largest differential is for the five years ending in 1989. In this period the Value Index is up 412.13% versus 287.30% for the Growth Index. The smallest differential is for the five years ending in 1984. Here the returns are 60.75% versus 48.89%. The Value Index produces positive returns over all 16 five-year periods; the Growth Index is positive only 13 out of 16.

A careful look at Figure 5-II-1 suggests that 1986 and 1987 need closer scrutiny. The cumulative spread between value and growth narrows considerably during this period. Figure 5-II-2 provides a clearer picture of the spread. Figure 5-II-2 plots the BIA Europe/ Pacific Value Index relative to the BIA Europe/Pacific Growth Index. At each point in time, the Value Index is divided by the Growth

TABLE 5-II-3.   Rolling Five-Year Performance of the BIA Europe/Pacific Value and Europe/Pacific Growth Indices
The Value Index wins over every five-year period.

	Value	Growth	Difference
1979	163.45%	104.12%	59.32
1980	125.00	97.00	28.00
1981	118.62	82.53	36.09
1982	73.66	56.76	16.90
1983	60.57	43.19	17.38
1984	60.75	48.89	11.86
1985	111.10	82.77	28.33
1986	242.38	230.37	12.01
1987	342.87	308.40	34.48
1988	370.62	295.56	75.06
1989	412.13	287.30	124.83
1990	153.03	88.87	64.17
1991	68.21	26.08	42.13
1992	15.97	−10.90	26.87
1993	20.08	−4.40	24.48
1994	15.09	−5.60	20.69

FIGURE 5-II-2. Performance of the BIA Europe/Pacific Value Index Relative to the BIA Europe/Pacific Growth Index
The indices show divergent trends, but also a large correction in 1986 and 1987.

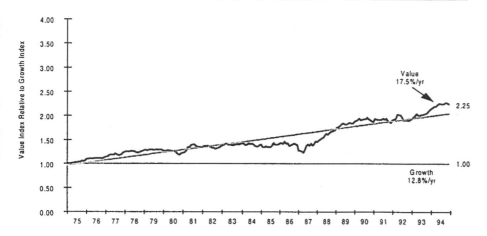

Index. The Growth Index becomes the horizontal axis. The ending value of 2.25 shown on the graph means that a dollar invested in the BIA Europe/Pacific Value Index grew to 2.25 times more than a dollar invested in the BIA Europe/Pacific Growth Index over this period. The 2.25 is simply the ratio of the ending dollar amounts in Figure 5-II-1; i.e., $24.96 divided by $11.11. In Figure 5-II-2 we can easily see the divergent trends for value and growth as well as a large correction in 1986 and 1987. The correction reverses itself fairly quickly which is the reason we do not see much impact in the annual data of Table 5-II-2.

Figure 5-II-3 breaks the graph from Figure 5-II-2 into three regions; Europe, Japan, and Pacific-ex-Japan. This chart makes it clear that the value/growth spread is quite uncorrelated from region to region. It shows that the correction in 1986 and 1987 was a purely Japanese phenomenon. During this period, value continued to outperform growth elsewhere in the Pacific and in Europe. The chart shows that the value/growth spreads in Europe are lower than elsewhere in the world and highlights the fact that the spread in Japan, while volatile, is very large. The ending value of 3.77 for Japan means that the value half of the Japanese market outperformed the growth

**FIGURE 5-II-3.   Performance of the BIA Value Index Relative to the
BIA Growth Index by Region**
*Value/growth spreads are uncorrelated from region to region. Value/growth
spreads tend to be larger in the Pacific than in Europe.*

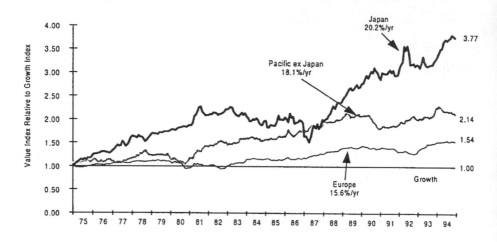

**FIGURE 5-II-4.   Performance of the BIA Value Index Relative to BIA
Growth Index for Each of the 20 Countries in the BIA Europe/Pacific
Index**

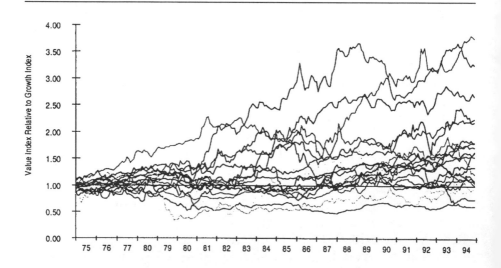

half by nearly four to one. The value half of the Japanese market delivered a return of 20.2% per year over the last 20 years. The growth half produced an annual return of only 12.5%.

Figure 5-II-4 shows the BIA Value Index relative to the BIA Growth Index for each of the 20 countries in the BIA Europe/Pacific Index. We can make a number of interesting observations from this chart:

1. Value beats growth in nearly every country.
2. The value/growth spread is volatile in each country.
3. The spreads are quite uncorrelated from one country to another.

The lack of correlation means that much of the volatility we see when we look at individual countries will disappear when we look at regions. Indeed the proof of this is in Figures 5-II-2 and 5-II-3.

Country Weights

The importance of country diversification in achieving a consistent value/growth spread raises the question of whether capitalization weights are the best way to combine countries. It seems obvious from looking at Figures 5-II-2 and 5-II-3 that the answer is no. Because Japan is such a large market compared to the other 19 markets in the Europe/Pacific Index it should not be surprising that the volatility we see in the value/growth spread for Japan in Figure 5-II-3 shows very prominently in the spread for the Europe/Pacific Index in Figure 5-II-2. This is especially true in the last half of the 1980s when Japan's weight in the index ranged between 50% and 65%.

Table 5-II-4 shows four country weighting-schemes: capitalization weights, GDP weights, BIA weights, and equal weights. Capitalization weights are the weights used in most of the popular international equity-indices. Much has been written about the pros and cons of these weights.[2] The obvious attraction of capitalization weights is that they reflect the aggregate market. The capitalization-weighted aggregation

---

[2] See Ankrim (1993), Ankrim and Gardner (1994), Gillies (1990), and Umstead (1988, 1990).

TABLE 5-II-4. Alternative Country Weights As of December 31, 1994

	CAP	GDP	BIA	EQL
Europe				
Austria	0.4	1.5	2.5	5.0
Belgium	1.0	1.7	2.5	5.0
Denmark	0.7	1.1	2.5	5.0
Finland	0.6	0.9	2.5	5.0
France	5.7	11.0	7.5	5.0
Germany	6.4	14.8	7.5	5.0
Ireland	0.3	0.4	2.5	5.0
Italy	2.2	8.5	2.5	5.0
Netherlands	3.6	2.8	2.5	5.0
Norway	0.3	0.9	2.5	5.0
Spain	1.6	3.8	2.5	5.0
Sweden	1.6	1.7	2.5	5.0
Switzerland	4.6	2.1	2.5	5.0
U.K.	15.6	8.5	7.5	5.0
Europe	44.6	59.8	50.0	70.0
Asia				
Australia	2.7	2.6	6.0	5.0
Hong Kong	2.9	1.1	6.0	5.0
Japan	45.7	34.9	24.0	5.0
Malaysia	2.2	0.6	6.0	5.0
New Zealand	0.4	0.4	2.0	5.0
Singapore	1.5	0.6	6.0	5.0
Asia	55.4	40.2	50.0	30.0

of all individual securities, often called the market portfolio must, after adjustment for cross holdings, equal the asset-weighted aggregation of all investor portfolios. This simple accounting-identity means that the performance of the market portfolio always equals the gross (before costs) performance of investors. The market portfolio therefore provides a very useful performance benchmark and it represents a distillation of the wisdom of the marketplace. One should not bet against the market portfolio without a strong conviction that the collective thinking of millions of investors is wrong. The market portfolio is special for one other reason: it is the only portfolio that all investors can simultaneously hold. If all investors decide to hold the same portfolio, the market portfolio is the only one that can accommodate them.

It is interesting that capitalization weights, in spite of these unique characteristics, are rarely used as the basis for asset allocation decisions. Most investors do not set policy weights for their stock, bond, and real estate allocations to align with the market values of these asset classes. Similarly their allocation to international equities is almost always far below a market weighting. Investors typically define international equities and domestic equities as separate asset classes because they want a home-country bias, and they want to control this allocation. They ordinarily do not want a market exposure to international equities, and they certainly do not want to wake up some morning and find out that their managers have shifted their entire equity-exposure offshore.

Many investors have used this same reasoning to justify carving out Japan, Pacific-ex-Japan, and Europe as separate asset-classes. Some are hiring separate managers for each region; others are hiring one manager but measuring the performance of the manager versus regional weights that are far from capitalization weights. Table 5-II-4 provides three alternatives to capitalization weights.

GDP weights are a popular choice. The rationale here is that a country allocation based on the size of the economy makes more sense than an allocation based on the size of the stock market. The size of the stock market is often a reflection of peculiar historical circumstances. For example, in Table 5-II-4 we see that the German stock market is 6.4% of the total whereas the German economy is 14.8%. There are a number of reasons for this. German companies have historically financed via banks and private equity rather than the stock market. In addition, the German government plays a dominant role in the economy. A healthy portion of GDP is delivered by the government. This is typical in Europe.

We can see in Table 5-II-4 that every one of the small European countries have larger economies than we might expect if we look at the size of their stock markets. Austria, for example is 0.4% of total if we use the stock market as a guide, but 1.5% if we use the economy as a guide. We see the inverse situation in the United Kingdom. Here the stock market represents 15.6% of the total while the economy represents only 8.5%. The only other countries in Europe where the capitalization percentage is larger than the GDP percentage are the Netherlands and Switzerland. In the Pacific, stock markets tend to dominate. Japan's stock market is 45.7% of total—it was as high as 64.8% in 1989—whereas the Japanese economy is only 34.9% of total.

Some argue that GDP is not a good guide because the portion of GDP that is delivered by the government cannot be purchased in the stock market. The entire GDP of North Korea is not available to investors. In the last several years, however, we have seen more and more government enterprise being converted to capitalistic enterprise. We have seen capitalization weights moving towards GDP weights, and we have seen GDP-weighted strategies produce higher returns and lower risk than capitalization-weighted strategies.

Another criticism of GDP weights is that the regional allocation currently works out to approximately 60% Europe and 40% Pacific. Most investors have an intuitive desire to have at least as high a weight in the Pacific as in Europe. This type of reasoning, which reflects a desire for more direct control, opens the door to policy weights for regions and countries. The BIA weights in Table 5-II-4 are one such set of policy weights. The philosophy here is to create weights that are perfectly diversified. By perfect diversification we mean minimum variance in a world where one has no information with which to distinguish the risk of one asset from another. If all assets offer identical covariances, the minimum variance portfolio is an equal-weighted portfolio. The application of this philosophy, in our view, requires two adjustments:

1. Equal-weight the Europe and Pacific regions.
2. Use multiple tiers of equal weights within regions to solve liquidity problems.

In Europe the weights for the United Kingdom, Germany, and France are each weighted 7.5%, with all other European markets weighted 2.5%. We have found this liquidity adjustment to be adequate for European portfolios as large as $200 million. In the Pacific, the weight for Japan is set to 24%, and all other markets are set to 6% except New Zealand, which is reduced to 2%. A small portfolio would not require multiple tiers of equal weights, since liquidity is not an issue.

Figure 5-II-5 compares four BIA Europe/Pacific Value Indices. Country weights are the only differences in these indices. Within each country the indices are identical. The index labeled Cap Weights is our base-case index—the same index shown in Figure 5-II-1. The other three indices correspond to the other weighting schemes shown in Table 5-II-4. We can see that the BIA Europe/Pacific Value Index with GDP weights lagged the capitalization-weighted Value Index in the late 1980s, but caught up quickly when the Japanese bubble burst in 1990. The equal-weighted Value Index, with 70% in Europe, shows a similar pattern. The BIA-weighted Value Index performs well throughout the whole period. A dollar invested in this index on December 31, 1974 grows to $33.06 versus $24.96 for the capitalization-weighted index. The annual rates of return are 19.1% per year for BIA weights versus 17.0% for capitalization weights.

Figure 5-II-6 compares spreads rather than absolute returns. Here we see that cumulative spreads are highest for capitalization

FIGURE 5-II-5.   Performance of BIA Europe/Pacific Value Indices with Alternative Country Weights

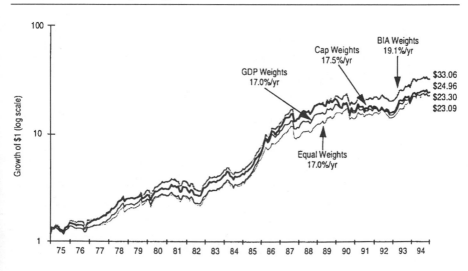

weights, but spread volatility is also highest. GDP and BIA weights offer somewhat lower spreads with considerably lower volatility. The correction in 1986 and 1987, for example, is much smaller for both GDP and BIA weights. Equal weights, because of a 70% allocation to Europe, provided a considerably smaller cumulative-spread.

Table 5-II-5 provides value/growth spread statistics for the four largest individual markets as well as the Europe/Pacific region. These statistics are computed from 240 months of data over the 20-year period from December 31, 1974 to December 31, 1994. There is no compounding in these results. The Average column is the simple average of the monthly performance differences between the various BIA Value and Growth Indices. The Standard Deviation column is the standard deviation of the 240 spreads and the t-statistic is computed from the ratio of the two multiplied by the square root of 240 (the number of observations). The Confidence column provides an assessment of the confidence or likelihood that these results are not due to chance. For example, the BIA Value Index in Japan outperformed the Growth Index by an average of 52 basis points per month with a standard deviation of 305 basis points. The t-statistic of 2.6 tells us that we can be 99.6% confident that this is not a chance occurrence.

FIGURE 5-II-6.   Performance of BIA Europe/Pacific Value Index Relative to Europe/Pacific Growth Index with Alternative Country Weights

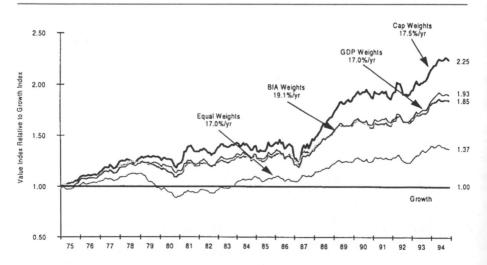

Table 5-II-5 shows that the value/growth spreads in Japan and France are large but volatile. The spreads in the United Kingdom and Germany are smaller but less volatile. The t-statistics in Japan and France are over 2.0 and thus statistically significant by normal scientific standards. The t-statistics are smaller in the United Kingdom and Germany, but still large enough to be interesting. The magic of diversification shows up when we look at the spreads for the Europe/Pacific Indices at the bottom of Table 5-II-5. The standard deviation of the spread for the capitalization-weighted index is 171 basis points with a t-statistic of 3.0. The more diversified BIA-weighted index has a standard deviation of only 117 basis points and t-statistic of 3.5.

These data provide a very convincing argument that international investors can add value by significantly underweighting the growth portion of the market in their passive portfolios. Participation in the growth sector should be primarily confined to aggressive active-managers who can overcome the average underperformance of the group. The style-switching strategies, popular among U.S. investors, are not necessary for highly diversified international or global portfolios. Figure 5-II-4 makes it clear that value/growth spreads are quite uncorrelated from country to country. This allows the volatility of the spread to decline dramatically as more and more country diversification is put into the portfolio.

TABLE 5-II-5.   Value-Growth Spread Statistics for the Europe/Pacific Region and the Four Largest Markets in the Region
Measured over the 240-month period from January 1975 to December 1994. The more country diversification the lower the volatility of the spread.

	Average	Standard Deviation	t-Statistic	Confidence
Japan	52 bps	305 bps	2.6	99.6%
France	44	285	2.4	99.1
U.K.	24	246	1.5	93.6
Germany	21	223	1.5	93.2
Europe-Pacific				
Cap weights	33	171	3.0	99.9
GDP weights	27	130	3.2	99.9
BIA weights	26	117	3.5	100.0
Equal weights	13	111	1.8	96.8

Performance Attribution by Sector

The methodology described in Table 5-II-1 sorts all the stocks in each country by price/book ratio. Stocks in the same economic sector tend to have similar price/book ratios and thus often sort more on one side of the demarcation line or the other. For example, the banks in France often—but not always—cluster in the value half of the French market. The banks in Japan, particularly in the last 10 years, tend to cluster in the growth half of their market. One might expect that this sector clustering is mostly related to accounting differences between one industry and another. Before we can be comfortable buying an index fund to track the value half of the Europe/Pacific markets, we need to know whether these sector concentrations add to or detract from performance relative to the market.

This is an important question because if sector concentrations are counter productive, they can be easily eliminated by changing our methodology to sort within sector. The BIA Value and Growth Indices for France, for example, could be constructed by sorting within sector and splitting the capitalization of each sector into value and growth halves. In this way the BIA Value Index for France would have the same sector weights as the Growth Index for France in the same way that the BIA Value Index for Europe has the same country weights as the Growth Index for Europe. The economic question here is whether the accounting biases across sectors are so large that they eliminate any useful information in the comparison of price/book ratios.

Table 5-II-6 provides the answer. The table shows a performance-attribution summary for the four largest markets in the Europe/Pacific Index.[3] The average monthly performance differential between the BIA Value Index and the BIA Market Index is decom-

---

[3] Value added from sector selection for any month is computed as follows: (1) Sector's weight in the Market Index subtracted from the sector's weight in the Value Index determines the Value Index's active weight in the sector at the beginning of the month. (2) Market Index return subtracted from sector's return in the Market Index determines the active return for the sector during the month. (3) Active weight multiplied by active return determines value-added contribution from sector selection. Value added from stock selection within sector is computed by subtracting the sector's return in the Market Index from the sector's return in the Value Index and multiplying the difference by the sector's weight in the Value Index. Using this method, the interaction between sector selection and stock selection is included in stock selection. For more discussion on this topic, see Carino (1992).

TABLE 5-II-6. Performance Attribution Summary for BIA Value Index versus BIA Market Index

Measured over 240 months of data from January 1975 through December 1994. Performance differential is decomposed into contributions from sector selection and contributions from stock selection within sectors. Return contributions are shown in basis points per month.

Sector	Sector Selection	Stock Selection	Total	Sector Selection	Stock Selection	Total
	Japan			United Kingdom		
Energy	2	1	3	5	0	5
Materials	1	3	4	1	1	2
Capital equipment	1	3	4	1	−1	0
Consumer goods	0	5	5	0	−1	−1
Services	4	4	8	−1	1	0
Finance	−3	6	3	0	1	1
Multi-industry	0	0	0	1	2	3
Total	5	22	27	7	3	10
	Germany			France		
Energy	2	2	4	6	2	8
Materials	−2	1	−1	−1	1	0
Capital equipment	0	3	3	1	3	4
Consumer goods	−1	3	2	1	2	3
Services	1	1	2	0	1	1
Finance	2	−2	0	1	5	6
Multi-industry	0	1	1	0	0	0
Total	2	9	11	8	14	22

posed into two parts; the portion due to sector over- and underweights and the portion due to stock selection within each sector.

In the lower right corner of the panel for Japan in Table 5-II-6 we see that the BIA Japan Value Index outperforms the BIA Market Index by an average of 27 basis points per month.[4] The remainder of the

[4] Note that we have shifted our reference base. We have been comparing the Value Index to the Growth Index. We are now comparing the Value Index to the Market Index. These spreads are therefore half as large as those in Table 5-II-5. We have changed our reference because we want to think about a value index-fund compared to an index fund covering the entire market.

data for Japan show us where this value added came from. We see that 22 of the 27 basis points came from stock selection within sector, but five basis points came from sector selection. This tells us that the inevitable accounting differences between economic sectors do not create biases large enough to destroy the usefulness of price/book ratio as a model for selecting sectors in Japan. We see a similar situation in the other three countries. Sector bets add an average of two basis points per month in Germany, seven basis points per month in the United Kingdom, and eight in France. In Japan we see just one sector, the finance sector, where the average contribution is negative. Over seven sectors in four countries (28 comparisons) we see just five sectors where the average contribution is negative. The consistency of these results is very comforting. This means that when we see that the BIA Value Index is overweighted or underweighted in a sector we should, most of the time, not try to eliminate this bet against the market. We may want to control it if it is extreme, but we should not try to eliminate it.

Aggressive-Value Indices

Given we know that the value half of the Europe/Pacific markets outperform the growth half, it is quite natural to wonder whether more aggressive slices perform even better. If we think back to the methodology in Table 5-II-1, there is no reason why the demarcation line must be drawn at 50% of capitalization. What happens if we slide it up to 20% of capitalization? If value stocks do well, shouldn't high-value stocks perform even better? They do!

Figure 5-II-7 shows value/market spreads for three capitalization-weighted BIA Europe/Pacific Indices; our base-case index with a 50/50 split,[5] a BIA Aggressive Value Index comprising the top 20% of capitalization and a BIA Conservative Value Index comprising all but the 20% highest price/book stocks. This chart makes it very clear that there is a strong positive relationship between value and return. We also see that spread volatility increases as aggressiveness increases, but the tradeoff is highly attractive.

---

[5] Note the Value Index here is shown relative to the Market Index; in Figure 5-II-2 it is shown relative to the Growth Index.

FIGURE 5-II-7. Performance of BIA Europe/Pacific Value Index Relative to BIA Europe/Pacific Market Index Using Various Definitions of Value
The higher the value exposure, the higher the return.

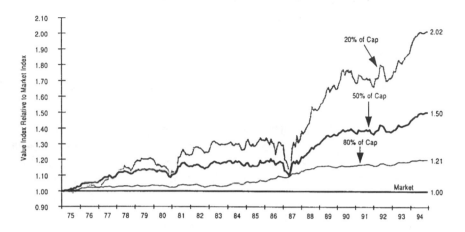

Rebalancing Interval, Transaction Costs, and Performance

All of the BIA indices described so far are rebalanced annually.[6] The methodology illustrated in Table 5-II-1 is repeated at the beginning of each year. The new price/book sort and the new summation of capitalization identifies new constituents for the Value and Growth Indices. Some stocks, categorized as value stocks one year, become growth stocks the next, and vice versa. Anyone considering investing in a value index fund will want to know the turnover engendered by this procedure. We need to compute turnover and assess the transaction costs that an index fund would incur in trying to track the BIA Europe/Pacific Value Index. We also want to see how turnover and performance are affected by rebalance interval. This will help us learn more about why value beats growth and may lead to ways to reduce transaction costs.

---

[6] The indices described in Capaul, Rowley, and Sharpe (1993) are rebalanced semi-annually.

The BIA Europe/Pacific Value Index shown in Figure 5-II-1 has an average annual turnover of 23%.[7] The cost of this turnover has so far been ignored. Our index construction methodology in Table 5-II-1 assumes instantaneous transactions at no cost. Transaction costs are particularly sensitive to the mix of countries and the size of the transaction in relation to the average daily trading-volume for each of the individual securities being purchased. We estimate that a typical institutional investor will spend about 37 basis points per year in transaction costs to track the BIA Europe/Pacific Value Index.

For most of the accounts we manage, we find that it costs about 80 basis points to buy a diversified, capitalization-weighted portfolio of securities in these 20 Europe/Pacific countries. This breaks down to about 20 basis points in commissions, 50 basis points in dealer spreads, and 10 basis points in taxes. To arrive at our estimate of 37 basis points, we multiply the 80 basis points by 23% annual turnover and by 2 to reflect both selling the stocks that have moved out of the Value Index and purchasing the stocks that have moved in. Table 5-II-5 tells us that the capitalization-weighted BIA Europe/Pacific Value Index has historically outperformed the Growth Index by 33 basis points per month or 396 basis points per year.[8] The spread between the Value Index and the Market Index will be half of this or 198 basis points per year. Our 37-basis-point cost estimate is not negligible in comparison to 198 basis points, but it still leaves plenty of room for net value added.

Figure 5-II-8 shows the performance of the BIA Europe/Pacific Value Index relative to the Market Index for four different rebalance intervals. The line labeled 12 Mos is our base-case index (the one shown in Figure 5-II-2).[9] This index is rebalanced every 12 months. The sorting

[7] Turnover for the BIA Europe/Pacific Market Index averages about 7%. The Market Index includes all securities in the market and is therefore not subject to the sorting procedure shown in Table 5-II-1. The 7% turnover arises from rebalancing to accommodate securities coming into and leaving the database. If we net this out, the extra turnover coming from the price/book sort is about 16%.

[8] Note that the spreads in Table 5-II-5 are average monthly differences. The spreads in Figure 5-II-1 and Table 5-II-2 are the differences between the annual compound rates of return. The spreads in Table 5-II-5 ignore the effects of compounding and are therefore "pure" in the sense that they are not distorted by the level of the underlying market returns.

[9] Figure 5-II-2 shows the Value Index relative to the Growth Index. Figure 5-II-8 shows it relative to the Market Index.

FIGURE 5-II-8. Performance of the BIA Europe/Pacific Value Index Relative to the BIA Europe/Pacific Market Index for Four Different Rebalance Intervals
Performance is insensitive to rebalance frequency

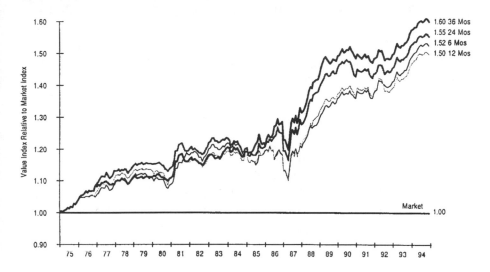

procedure illustrated in Table 5-II-1 is repeated at the first of each year. The three other lines show the effect of varying this rebalance interval.

Figure 5-II-8 makes it clear that the cumulative spreads of these indices are quite insensitive to rebalance interval. One might expect that more frequent rebalancing, especially if we assume cost-free rebalancing as we have done here, would lead to better performance. It does not! The rebalance interval can be relaxed from six months all the way to 36 months without a performance decay—in fact, we actually see a slight improvement in performance. Furthermore, annual turnover is dramatically reduced as rebalance interval is increased. Turnover and estimated transaction costs for the four rebalance-intervals are shown below:

Rebalance Interval	Annual Turnover	Transaction Cost
6 mos	31%	50 bps
12	23	37
24	17	27
36	14	22

These results have important implications for the implementation of a Europe/Pacific value index-fund. Performance will very likely be inversely related to rebalance frequency. There is an approximate 28-basis-point per year cost savings between rebalancing every three years versus every six months. This is a very large potential savings that can easily be thrown away by overmanagement. Sometimes the most difficult part of a portfolio manager's job is to stay out of the trading room. Value investors are contrarian investors. Contrarian investing requires patience.

Why Does Value Beat Growth?

A scientific approach to investing requires theory as well as data. We need to try to understand what behavioral or institutional factors are causing this phenomenon. Are there good reasons for this spread? Are these reasons likely to persist or are they likely to evaporate?

Capaul, Rowley, and Sharpe (1993) suggest two reasons why value beats growth:

> *"A significant number of investors may be concerned with aspects other than before-tax risk and return. If value stocks are inferior to growth stocks in some respect (such as greater taxes owing to higher dividends), one could well expect them to offer greater expected return per unit of risk on a before-tax basis. Moreover, investors may prefer to hold securities of companies with good records and superior growth prospects. For personal and institutional reasons, a portfolio of "household names" may be considered better than one of "fallen angels"— enough so as to offset the prospect that the former may provide less return per unit of risk than the latter."*

Capaul, Rowley, and Sharpe are arguing that it is at least possible that no one is being fooled. They are saying that there are things that matter in addition to before-tax risk and return, and investors may well be willing to pay for these things.

Lakonishok, Shleifer, and Vishny (1994) add two more reasons to the list:

> *"Individual investors might focus on glamour strategies for a variety of reasons. First, they may make judgment errors and extrapolate past growth rates of glamour stocks, such as Wal-Mart or Microsoft, even when such growth rates are highly unlikely to persist in the future.*

Putting excessive weight on recent past history, as opposed to a rational prior, is a common judgment error in psychological experiments, and not just in the stock market. Alternatively, individuals might just equate well-run firms with good investments regardless of price. After all, how can you lose money on Microsoft or Wal-Mart? Indeed, brokers typically recommend 'good' companies, with 'steady' earnings and dividend growth."

Shefrin and Statman (1993) add a fifth:

"In summary, the preference for stocks of good companies begins with a cognitive error that leads most investors to conclude that good stocks are stocks of good companies. The effect of the cognitive error is reinforced through an aversion to regret. Aversion to regret is powerful even when an investor has to answer only to himself. But the effect of aversion to regret is magnified when the investor is a money manager who has to answer to clients."

In summary, we have five good reasons why value beats growth. The first two are consistent with rational behavior and simply allow that investors may be concerned with attributes other than before-tax risk and return.

1. Value stocks have an inferior tax-status. Because of this, taxable investors demand a higher return for value stocks.
2. Value stocks have an inferior comfort-level. This also leads to the need for value stocks to offer a higher return.

The last three relate to various types of behavioral errors that stem from the fact that value stocks tend to be from companies with weak balance sheets and income statements.

3. This leads to pessimistic extrapolations of future earnings and dividends which in turn leads to pleasant earnings surprises.
4. The weak financial statements also lead to the conclusion that the company is a bad company and therefore the stock is a bad investment.
5. And finally, this weak financial record makes value stocks much more susceptible to Monday-morning quarterbacking. It is more difficult to externalize blame if value stocks perform poorly.

A sixth reason is offered by Fama and French (1992). They believe that value stocks outperform because they are riskier.

> *"In fact, if stock prices are rational, BE/ME, the ratio of the book value of a stock to the market's assessment of its value, should be a direct indicator of the relative prospects of firms.[10] For example, we expect that high BE/ME firms have low earnings on assets relative to low BE/ME firms. Our work (in progress) suggests that there is indeed a clean separation between high and low BE/ME firms on various measures of economic fundamentals. Low BE/ME firms are persistently strong performers, while the economic performance of high BE/ME firms is persistently weak."*

Fama and French are in the minority with this opinion for the simple reason that portfolios of value stocks have not been riskier. A rebuttal of Fama and French is offered by Lakonishok, Shleifer, and Vishny (1994).

> *"An alternative explanation of why value strategies have produced superior returns, argued most forcefully by Fama and French (1992), is that they are fundamentally riskier. That is, investors in value stocks, such as high book to market stocks, tend to bear higher fundamental risk of some sort, and their higher average returns are simply compensation for risk.*
>
> *"To be fundamentally riskier, value stocks must underperform glamour stocks with some frequency, and particularly in the states of the world when the marginal utility of wealth is high. This view of risk motivates our tests. We look at the frequency of superior (and inferior) performance of value strategies, as well as at their performance in bad states of the world, such as extreme down markets and economic recessions. We also look at the betas and standard deviations of value and glamour strategies. We find little if any support for the view that value strategies have been fundamentally riskier.*
>
> *"While one can never reject the "metaphysical" version of the risk story, in which securities that earn higher returns must by definition be fundamentally riskier, the weight of evidence suggests a more straightforward model. In this model, out-of-favor (or value) stocks are underpriced relative to their risk and return characteristics, and investing in them indeed earns abnormal returns."*

---

[10] BE/ME stands for book equity to market equity. It is the inverse of the price/book ratio used in Table 5-II-1.

Conclusion

Twenty years of results in 20 markets make it clear that passive investors in the Europe/Pacific region should focus their portfolios on the value end of these markets. The results are profound. The size, consistency, and statistical significance of the value/growth spread is extraordinary. We have found that country diversification is the key to controlling the volatility of the spread. We have decomposed the spread and found that value-added comes from both sector selection and stock selection within sector. We have looked at different levels of aggressiveness and found a clear, direct relationship between value and return. We have assessed turnover and transaction costs and found them to be modest. Finally, we have surveyed the literature and found a number of solid theoretical reasons for the value/growth spread. In summary, we have identified a tremendous opportunity for astute investors to capture higher returns in the passive portion of their international portfolios.

References

Ankrim, E. "The Japanese Weighting Decision in International Equity Portfolios: Measuring the Impact." *Russell Research Commentary,* June 1993.

Ankrim, E., and G. Gardner. "Choosing a Non-U.S. Equity Benchmark: Are There Good Reasons for Underweighting Japan?" *Russell Research Commentary,* December 1994.

Capaul, C., I. Rowley, and W. Sharpe. "International Value and Growth Stock Returns." *Financial Analysts Journal,* January/February 1993.

Carino, David. "Performance Calculations." *Russell Technical Note,* June 1992.

Fama, E., and K. French. "The Cross-Section of Expected Stock Returns." *The Journal of Finance,* 47 (1992).

Gillies, J. "Reflecting Gross Domestic Product in an International Equity Index." *Russell Research Commentary,* November 1990.

Lakonishok, J., A. Shleifer, and R. Vishny. "Contrarian Investment, Extrapolation, and Risk." Working paper presented to The Berkeley Program in Finance, Spring 1994.

Shefrin, H., and M. Statman. "A Behavioral Framework for Expected Stock Returns." Working paper presented to Q Group, Fall 1993.

Umstead, D. "Weighing the Options: Market-Weight Open to One-Country Domination." *Pensions & Investment Age,* May 1988.

Umstead, D. "Current Issues: Benchmarks, Selecting a Benchmark for International Investments." *Financial Analysts Journal,* March–April 1990.

Understanding the Style Benchmarks

Claudia E. Mott, First Vice President
Director of Small-Cap Research
Prudential Securities Inc.

Daniel P. Coker, Assistant Vice President
Prudential Securities Inc.

Growth and value investment styles have been around for decades, but the concept of tailored indices and distinct performance measurement is relatively recent. In the past few years, investment managers, consultants, and plan sponsors have been overwhelmed with the proliferation of style indices across all of the equity size sectors. It is increasingly important to know the characteristics of the various style benchmarks that are commonly used, especially since the styles' characteristics differ not only from growth to value, but also among indices that are presumably benchmarks for the same style.

With the use of style benchmarks by consultants and plan sponsors on the rise, it is now critical for investment managers to know their characteristics. The differences between a portfolio's sector weightings or size distribution and the style benchmark may have more to do with performance variations than the manager's stock-picking abilities. A value manager who chooses not to be as over-weighted in financial services and utilities as some of the style benchmarks may suffer a significant performance shortfall when those two sectors are doing well.

Plan sponsors are increasingly using style benchmarks to measure the performance of their outside managers and performance-based fees are becoming more widely used as well. Therefore, it is essential for plan sponsors to know the idiosyncrasies of the respec-

The authors gratefully acknowledge the help of several people: Melissa Brown, Kevin Condon, Michele Eschert, Susan Levine, and Tara Stergis.

143

tive style indices so that the benchmark they choose for a manager is fair and representative.

Many plans are using style benchmarks to help determine exposures in the asset-allocation process. Because there is so much variation among indices designed to measure the same style, not being aware of these subtleties may result in costly allocation errors. A style allocation model built using a value index heavily weighted in interest-rate sensitive stocks may not give a timing signal that reflects a change in style performance, but rather a shift in rates.

This chapter is a guide to many of the style benchmarks that have been developed to measure the performance of growth and value across the large-, mid-, and small-cap equity classes. At the outset, we provide descriptions of the major style benchmarks which include the construction methodologies and the selection universes. Growth and value are then compared and contrasted by each size category. In all discussions the same seven tables for each category will be referred to (see Appendix A to this chapter for tables). Because the tables aren't individually captioned, we will describe their contents here. Tables 6-1 through 6-7 cover the large-cap style benchmarks, Tables 6-8 through 6-14 are mid-cap, and Tables 6-15 through 6-21 display the small-cap style data. All characteristics described are as of December 30, 1994.

Index Characteristics (Tables 6-1, 6-8, 6-15)

These tables include the number of companies, rebalancing frequency, exchange distribution, average size, and biggest and smallest holdings.

Size Distribution (Tables 6-2, 6-3, 6-9, 6-10, 6-16, 6-17)

Understanding how diverse or concentrated an index is can aid in understanding performance. These tables divide the companies into size categories by percentage of companies and the percentage of market capitalization, because mean and median market-capitalization statistics do not provide a thorough understanding of the size distribution of companies within the indices.

Sector Distribution (Tables 6-4, 6-5, 6-11, 6-12, 6-18, 6-19)

Differences in index performance are frequently attributable to their macroeconomic sector weightings. The first table of each category breaks down sectors by the percentage of companies, and the second distributes the weight based on the percentage of market capitalization.

Fundamental Characteristics (Tables 6-6, 6-13, 6-20)

We have calculated weighted average values for trailing P/E (both with and without negative earnings), forecast P/E using IBES, price/book, price/sales, P/E to growth, historical five-year earnings and sales growth, return on equity, return on assets, debt-to-capital ratios, and average daily volume. We have also included the average yield and the percentage of stocks that are dividend paying.

Performance Statistics (Tables 6-7, 6-14, 6-21)

We look at the annual returns of the indices for the 10 years 1985–1994, and provide 10-year annualized averages if available and the standard deviation of the returns.

Defining the Major Style Indices

There are currently four companies that provide widely used style indices divided into size categories. Standard & Poor's (in conjunction with BARRA) publishes large-cap growth and value indices based on the S&P Composite, and mid-cap indices constructed from the MidCap 400. Frank Russell produces indices for all three size sectors as does Wilshire Associates. Prudential Securities Inc. (PSI) launched their style indices in June 1993 covering all three size sectors as well.

Two Style Index Creation Methodologies Have Evolved

The style indices covered in this chapter are developed using one of two methodologies—a sort by price/book or a screen based on a set of criteria. S&P and Russell use the price/book sort method (with a slight modification for the Russell 2000), while Wilshire and PSI use screening criteria to generate their portfolios. The method of construction, as well as the universe of companies from which the index is formed can lead to substantial differences in the style index characteristics. Although the indices are constructed using different methodologies and universes, indices of the same style tend to move in the same direction as the tables of performance reveal. Below is a brief summary of the construction methodology devised by each index provider.

It is worth mentioning some of the concerns that arise when the different construction methodologies are discussed.

The Value of Book Equity

The simplest and most popular method of discriminating between value and growth stocks is to divide stocks into two mutually exclusive portfolios based on the price/book equity ratios. Recent deterioration of book equity as a result of the vagaries of accrual accounting, FAS (Financial Accounting Statement) 106 and 109, and other accounting changes as well as corporate restructurings call into question the viability of this number as a way to separate the styles. The providers try to place all companies on a comparable basis using various amortization methods to spread out some of the charges.

Mutual Exclusivity

The indices that rely on sorting a universe by price/book ratio require that every company from the main universe fall into one or the other style index. The argument can be made that some companies probably don't belong in either index. In addition, value is often in the eyes of the beholder, therefore some companies may fit both styles.

Lack of Diversification

The standard style indices tend to be overwhelmed by one or two sectors. Existing value indices, for example, tend to extensively overweight financial services and utility sectors to a degree that is unacceptable to most managers. The three sections which detail the style indices by size will delve into this further.

Description of the Indices

The *Prudential Securities Large-Cap Growth and Value Indices* are selected by screening stocks in the top 15 percentiles of market capitalization in the Compustat universe (excluding REITs, ADRs, and limited partnerships) for companies with growth or value characteristics. Mid-cap encompasses percentiles 8 through 25, and the small-cap style indices include the 20th through 45th percentiles. *Growth* stocks have historical sales growth greater than 10%, rank in the top half of their size universe on the IBES forecast growth rate, and have low dividend payouts and debt/capital ratios. *Value* names rank in the bottom 50% of the universe based on a normalized P/E (where the average of the five-year peak earnings and the current year forecast according to IBES is used for the "E"). Additionally, companies that are dividend paying must have sustainable dividend rates, i.e., they have covered their four-quarter dividend for the past three years.

The *Russell Large-Cap Growth and Value Indices* are constructed by sorting the companies in the *Russell 1000* by price/book ratio with the companies at the high end of the sort falling into value and those at the low end comprising growth. The universe is divided so that 50% of the weight of the overall index falls into each style index. This may not mean that 50% of the companies are in each index, however. Combined, the style indices are all-inclusive and mutually exclusive. The *Russell Midcap Growth and Value Indices* are created similarly but are based on the *Russell Midcap Index.*

The *Russell Small-Cap Style Indices* are created in a slightly different fashion than the large-cap indices. The Russell 2000 is sorted once by price/book and secondly by the IBES long-term growth rate. Each series is standardized and then combined for a composite score; breakpoints are determined by the cumulative available market capitalization to create three ranges of securities. The securities in the lower range are 100% Russell Growth while those in the upper range are 100% Russell value. Securities in the middle range are assigned proportionally to both growth and value, based on their value score relative to the median. As a result, many companies are listed in both indices but are not weighted based on their full float-based capitalization.

The *Russell 1000 Universe* represents the largest 1,000 companies (based on total float, not total capitalization) in the *Russell 3000 Index.* The Russell 3000 Index contains the 3,000 largest U.S. domiciled companies, which together represent 98% of the U.S. equity market by market capitalization. Only common stocks of U.S. companies are included in the index; in the case of multiple classes of stock, generally only one is allowed. The *Russell Midcap* comprises the smallest 800 stocks, based on market value, out of the Russell 1000. The *Russell 2000* represents the bottom two-thirds of the Russell 3000.

The *S&P/BARRA Growth and Value Indices* are constructed by sorting the S&P 500 companies based on their price/book ratios, with the low price/book companies comprising the Value Index and high price/book making up the Growth Index. Each S&P 500 company is included in either the Growth or the Value Index, and the two indices are constructed so that they each have approximately the same market value at the semiannual rebalancing. (When new companies are added to the S&P Composite Index, they are placed into the appropriate style index based on the price/book cutoff.) Companies in the Growth Index tend to be bigger; therefore it contains roughly two fifths of the S&P 500 companies. The same methodology is used on the *S&P MidCap 400 Index*.

The *S&P 500*—a.k.a. S&P Composite—is constructed to represent movements in common stocks. Stocks are chosen so that, in aggregate, they represent a broad distribution by industry group comparable to that of stocks traded on the New York Stock Exchange. Decisions about stocks to be included and deleted are made by the S&P Index Committee. The S&P MidCap 400 Index contains companies chosen by committee at Standard & Poor's for their size and industry characteristics. None of the companies in the MidCap Index overlap with those in the S&P Composite. Some companies in the S&P MidCap, however, are larger than those in the S&P Composite, which is a function of the normal drift that takes place in any index as some companies' stock prices appreciate and others depreciate.

Wilshire chooses the stocks for the *Wilshire Growth Indices* and the *Wilshire Value Indices* by using a set of criteria to eliminate names from their large-cap *Top 750, Mid Cap 750,* and small-cap *Next 1750* indices. Elimination criteria for the Growth Index include history of less than five years, high dividend payout, low growth, low price/book, and low ROE. Companies with high relative P/E, low relative dividend yield, and high relative price/book are eliminated from the Value portfolio.

The *Wilshire Top 750 Index* represents the largest 750 companies in the *Wilshire 5000,* which in turn consists of all securities traded in the United States for which price data is available. The Wilshire 5000 actually contains far more than 5,000 companies—over 6,800 as of year-end 1994. The *Wilshire Next 1750* is derived by taking the next 1750 stocks (after the top 750) from the top half of the Wilshire 5000. The *Wilshire Mid Cap 750,* which is quite a bit smaller than either Russell's or Standard & Poor's mid-cap index, uses the smallest 250 names in the Top 750 and the largest 500 names in the Next 1750.

The Growth Style Benchmarks

Growth stock investing has different meanings depending on the size of the stock being purchased. Historically, large-cap growth has focused on the stable growers in the drug, food, and consumer areas while small-cap growth has meant emerging technology and health-care companies and mid-cap growth companies have also tended toward the technology area. In many ways, the style benchmarks reflect these size-related differences.

Large-Cap Growth Focuses on the Consumer

Consumer services and consumer staples rank among the top three sectors in all of the four large-cap growth indices on a market capitalization weighted basis. Combined, these sectors range from 33.9% of the Russell growth index to 40.9% of the Wilshire index. PSI shows a much lower consumer staples weighting at only 10.0%, but has the heaviest technology weighting at 30%. The indices created using a price/book sort (S&P/BARRA and Russell) show heavier weightings in basic industry and lighter weighting in technology. Health care also is well represented in the large-cap growth indices while energy and financial services are underweighted and utilities are almost nonexistent.

Across the four growth indices, there are distinct variations in size. The Wilshire index has the largest company profile, with a weighted average capitalization of $28.8 billion although S&P/BARRA has the heaviest concentration of companies over $10.0 billion in size at 68.2%. The PSI growth index has the smallest size profile, with a weighted average market capitalization of $14.8 billion and only 40.2% of the capitalization in the largest company size category. Much of this difference is due to the placement of one stock: General Electric, which fell into growth in three of the four indices, but landed in PSI's value index.

In most cases, the fundamental characteristics of the four growth indices are comparable, but the construction methodology and selection universe do lead to some differences. Using a definitive screen for growth as PSI does, generates the most "growth-oriented" index. This index has the highest IBES forecast growth rate, as well as the highest historical growth in sales and earnings. The valuation for this index is also higher on both a P/E and price/sales basis.

Mid-Cap Growth Shows Sizable Variations

The size profile is one of the more striking differences of the three mid-cap growth indices. This is one of the major starting points in the choice of style benchmark—choose one that is invested in companies similar in size to the portfolio. As a result of the very different selection universes, the weighted-average market value ranges from $2.3 billion for Russell to $887.8 million for PSI. Over 60% of the weight of the Russell growth index is in companies over $1.5 billion in capitalization, while S&P/BARRA totals 55.2%. PSI and Wilshire have no companies over $3 billion in size.

The stock exchange distribution shows a bias towards NYSE issues, with over 60% weightings for the S&P/BARRA and Russell indices, but only a 44.3% weighting for PSI. It should be noted that in either case, this weighting is quite a bit different from the large-cap growth indices. NASDAQ picks up quite a bit of weight when moving into the mid-cap universe. PSI's growth index is 52.1% NASDAQ issues, while the other indices range from 23.6% to 42.2%.

The initial universe and creation methods generate interesting differences in macroeconomic sector weightings. Health care and basic industry illustrate this. The price/book sort–based Russell index has 14.5% of its weight in basic industry and only 9.7% in health care. The two indices which are screen derived show much heavier weightings in health care—15.9% and 18% for PSI and Wilshire, respectively, compared to 5.2% and 7.8%, respectively, in basic industry. Technology and consumer services are both well represented by all of the mid-cap growth indices ranging from 40.4% of the Russell index to 47.2% of the PSI index. Consumer staples, energy, and utilities play a very small role in the mid-cap growth indices.

Although the valuation criteria, P/E, price/book, and price/ sales for the growth indices are comparable there are some differences worth mentioning. The more industrial orientation of the Russell index creates a higher debt-to-capital ratio as these companies tend to have more leverage than health care and technology names. The net result of the growth-oriented screens are higher historical growth rates for the PSI and Wilshire indices.

Technology Plays a Big Role in Small-Cap Growth

Across the three growth portfolios many characteristics are comparable perhaps more so than in the other two size sectors. Two of the three small-cap growth indices find the heaviest distribution of companies in the medium/small ($250–750 million) grouping and over 50% of the names trade on NASDAQ. PSI has the highest weighting in NASDAQ stocks at 71.7%. Average sizes do vary: Wilshire has the highest weighted-average market capitalization at $692.2 million, PSI's is smallest at $241.8 million.

The screening methodology, with its emphasis on growth rates, tends to weight the indices more heavily in sectors with high growth—for example, technology. PSI is 28.7% technology and Wilshire has a 31% representation in the group, while Russell has a 23.5% weighting. Consumer services is also heavily represented with a 15.3% weighting in the Russell growth index, 17.5% in PSI's and 19.6% in Wilshire's. Russell's index contains 3.7% REITs, which are excluded from the selection universes of the other providers. Like the mid-cap growth indices, consumer staples, energy, and utilities are small components of these style indices.

Fundamentally, a few differences stand out between the small-cap growth indices. The valuations are all comparable whether one looks at P/E, price/book, or price/sales. All have debt-to-capital ratios of over 20%. Russell's index shows the lowest trailing five-year earnings and sales growth rates at 11.9% and 14.2% respectively. Few companies in the growth indices pay dividends and therefore the benchmarks have very low yields.

The Value Style Benchmarks

Value investing tends be more similar across the three size sectors with heavy exposure to financial services and utilities common to all value indices. In addition, the value indices have more issues that trade on the NYSE. Value investors are typically looking for inexpensive stocks or those out-of-favor bargains of little interest to growth mavens. Frequently, P/E or price/book ratios are used to determine a stock's attractiveness and therefore are an integral part to how the value indices are created.

Large-Cap Value Emphasizes Energy, Financial Services, and Utilities

From a sector perspective, large-cap value is heavily concentrated in financial services, utilities, and energy, and the construction process determines which takes on the biggest proportion. By requiring companies to pay a dividend, Wilshire has the heaviest utility weighting at 22.9% while PSI has the lightest at 16.1%. Financial services ranges from 19.4% to 34.5% suggesting that regardless of definition, value means financials. The energy weighting varies from 8.4% for PSI to 28.7% for Wilshire. The price/book sort-based indices show significant representation in basic industry at 13% for Russell and 13.9% for S&P/BARRA. These large differences obviously highlight the importance of knowing your index!

The value indices also show a wide variation in size characteristics. The Russell index has the lowest weighted-average capitalization at $14.3 billion, while the PSI index (with the inclusion of General Electric) has the highest at $17.8 billion. The concentration of companies in the various size categories is a bit more homogeneous in the value indices, all have at least 75% of the capitalization of the indices in companies over $3 billion in size. The value indices have at a minimum 94% of the companies listed on the NYSE as well.

The fundamentals of the value indices point up the differences that definition can create. The heavy utility weighting in the Wilshire index influences many of the valuation parameters, causing the lowest P/E and price/cash flow values, along with the highest yield. It appears that the price/book sort has some impact on the fundamentals as well. The S&P/BARRA and Russell indices have historical earnings growth rates that are actually negative and lower sales growth as compared to the screen-based indices.

Mid-Cap Value's Top Three Sectors Are Basic Industry, Financial Services, and Utilities

As with the large-cap value indices, the lion's share of the companies in the mid-cap value indices trade on the NYSE, but the percentages range from 72.1% for Wilshire to 87.8% for Russell. NASDAQ has the remainder of the companies, with the AMEX accounting for less than 2% of the indices. At $2.3 billion, the weighted average market capitalization for the Russell index is substantially higher than the others, which range from $945 million to $1.6 billion.

The greatest discrepancies in sector weightings are in the utilities and basic industry areas. Wilshire's yield requirement generates a 35.6% weighting for the utility sector and the S&P MidCap Index's heavy exposure to utilities relative to other mid-cap indices causes these issues to fall into their value index as well. PSI has the smallest utility weighting at 13.9%. Russell has the heaviest weighting in basic industry at 19.1% while Wilshire shows the lightest weighting in this sector at 4.3%. Financial services is the largest sector in three of the four indices with the weightings ranging from 23% for S&P/BARRA to 32.2% for Wilshire.

From a valuation perspective, the Russell index has the highest P/E ratios of the three value indices on both a trailing and a forecast basis as a result of its low relative utility weighting. Wilshire, with its yield requirement, has 100% dividend payers and the highest yield of the three indices at 5.1%. In terms of fundamentals, there is little difference in either the historical growth rates or the return on equity/asset values.

Financial Services Loom Large in Small-Cap Value

As size gets smaller, the weighting in NASDAQ gets higher, ranging from 40.2% of the Russell value index's weight to 62% of the Wilshire value index. In terms of stock concentration, over 50% of the Russell and Wilshire indices are stocks of the medium/small category. The Wilshire index has the highest market-capitalization profile with a weighted average of $556.2 million and PSI has the smallest at $247.7 million.

Sector distribution points up the major deviation in the small-cap value portfolios. The low P/E, high-yield screen of Wilshire generates very heavy weightings in the financial services and utilities sectors. As of December 1994, the Wilshire value portfolio had 37.7% in financial services and 31.6% in utilities, or 69.3% of the portfolio. Russell and PSI also contain heavy financial concentrations at 29.9% and 27.8% respectively, but the utilities weighting is only 6.8% and 4.2%. As a result of its concentration in two sectors, Wilshire has almost no weight in technology at 1.4%, compared with 7% for PSI and 7.2% for Russell. Consumer services and basic industry are also well represented in the small-cap value indices (Wilshire excepted). Russell's value index contains 8.3% REITs, because they are not excluded from the selection universe whereas all other index providers remove them.

The yield requirement used by Wilshire shows up in the 99.4% dividend-paying companies compared with 56.3% for Russell and 52.2% for PSI. In addition, the yield is twice as high as the other portfolios at 4.9% compared to 2.5% and 1.7%. Russell has the highest valuation characteristics based on P/E and price/cash flow with the lowest historical EPS growth rate, ROE, and ROA.

Appendix A: Tables of Characteristics of Style Benchmarks

TABLE 6-1. Descriptive Characteristics of Large-Cap Style Benchmarks

	Large-Cap Growth				Large-Cap Value			
	PSI	Russell	S&P/BARRA	Wilshire	PSI	Russell	S&P/BARRA	Wilshire
Number of companies	348	488	182	192	470	499	318	150
First full year of return	1976	1979	1977	1978	1976	1979	1977	1978
Index rebalancing	Semiannually	Annually	Semiannually/ as needed	Quarterly	Semiannually	Annually	Semiannually/ as needed	Quarterly
Weighting method	Market cap	Float*	Market cap	Market cap	Market cap	Float*	Market cap	Market cap
Returns calculation	With income	Principal & with income	With income	With income	With income	Principal & with income	With income	With income
Exchange Distribution								
NASDAQ	25.9%	13.0%	9.2%	11.3%	5.1%	4.0%	1.7%	2.6%
NYSE	71.3	85.8	89.9	88.3	94.5	95.6	98.0	97.2
ASE	2.8	1.3	0.9	0.4	0.4	0.4	0.3	0.2
Total capitalization	$1.1 tril	$1.9 tril	$1.7 tril	$1.4 tril	$2.0 tril	$1.8 tril	$1.6 tril	$705 bil

TABLE 6-1 (continued).

	Large-Cap Growth				Large-Cap Value			
	PSI	Russell	S&P/BARRA	Wilshire	PSI	Russell	S&P/BARRA	Wilshire
Average Size								
Wtd. mean	$14.8 bil	$21.6 bil	$27.1 bil	$28.8 bil	$17.8 bil	$14.3 bil	$17.2 bil	$16.8 bil
Mean	3.1 bil	3.9 bil	9.3 bil	7.2 bil	4.2 bil	3.5 bil	5.2 bil	4.7 bil
Median	1.5 bil	1.4 bil	4.7 bil	2.9 bil	1.9 bil	1.6 bil	2.9 bil	2.5 bil
Size Range								
Largest	$66.3 bil	$87.2 bil	$87.2 bil	$87.2 bil	$87.2 bil	$75.4 bil	$75.4 bil	$75.4 bil
Smallest	695.9 mil	37.0 mil	456.4 mil	804.0 mil	695.6 mil	56.6 mil	122.0 mil	0.9 bil
Concentration								
Largest 10	30.1%	26.2%	30.9%	37.6%	22.4%	20.3%	24.0%	37.8%
Largest 50	57.3	56.4	70.4	74.0	48.9	49.7	55.2	72.2
Largest 100	71.6	71.9	89.0	88.6	64.7	65.2	73.2	90.8

*See section on index construction.
Note: Data are as of December 30, 1994.
Source: Prudential Securities Inc.

TABLE 6-2. Size Distribution of Large-Cap Style Benchmarks

Percentage of companies

	Large-Cap Growth				Large-Cap Value			
	PSI	Russell	S&P/ BARRA	Wilshire	PSI	Russell	S&P/ BARRA	Wilshire
Very Large $10.0 bil & over	5.5	8.4	25.3	15.6	8.1	7.4	11.6	8.7
Large $3.0–10.0 bil	17.2	18.1	43.4	33.9	27.9	22.6	38.1	34.0
Medium-Large $1.5–3.0 bil	25.9	21.8	19.2	34.9	23.0	21.4	22.0	31.3
Medium $750 mil–$1.5 bil	46.3	31.8	8.8	15.6	36.8	31.5	15.1	26.0
Medium-Small $750 mil or less	5.2	19.9	3.3	—	4.3	17.0	13.2	—

Note: Data are as of December 30, 1994.
Source: Prudential Securities Inc.

TABLE 6-3. Size Distribution of Large-Cap Style Benchmarks
Percentage of market cap

	Large-Cap Growth				Large-Cap Value			
	PSI	Russell	S&P/BARRA	Wilshire	PSI	Russell	S&P/BARRA	Wilshire
Very Large								
$10.0 bil & over	40.2	52.1	68.2	62.9	43.6	43.6	48.4	42.2
Large								
$3.0–10.0 bil	26.2	25.0	26.1	24.6	34.7	31.6	37.8	36.7
Medium-Large								
$1.5–3.0 bil	16.9	11.6	4.4	9.8	11.7	12.8	9.4	14.4
Medium								
$750 mil–$1.5 bil	15.4	8.8	1.1	2.7	9.3	9.5	3.2	6.7
Medium-Small								
$750 mil or less	1.2	2.5	0.2	—	0.7	2.5	1.2	—

Note: Data are as of December 30, 1994.
Source: Prudential Securities Inc.

TABLE 6-4. **Macroeconomic Sector Breakdown of Large-Cap Style Benchmarks**
Percentage of companies

	Large-Cap Growth				Large-Cap Value			
	PSI	Russell	S&P/BARRA	Wilshire	PSI	Russell	S&P/BARRA	Wilshire
Basic industry	7.2	12.9	15.9	9.9	13.4	16.6	17.9	4.0
Business services	7.2	7.8	6.0	4.7	2.1	2.6	3.1	0.7
Capital spending	3.7	6.0	7.1	6.8	3.4	3.0	4.4	0.7
Conglomerates	0.3	0.4	1.6	1.0	1.3	1.2	0.9	2.0
Consumer cyclical	4.0	2.5	2.7	2.6	3.6	4.0	7.2	0.7
Consumer services	20.4	21.1	18.1	19.8	6.2	6.6	12.3	2.0
Consumer staples	2.6	7.2	16.5	14.1	4.7	3.2	2.5	1.3
Energy	2.3	4.7	2.7	1.0	6.6	8.4	12.6	10.7
Financial services	11.5	9.2	2.7	10.9	32.8	29.5	17.6	44.0
Health care	12.1	12.1	11.0	13.0	2.6	1.6	2.8	—
Technology	27.3	15.0	14.3	14.6	6.4	6.0	8.8	2.7
Utilities	1.4	1.0	1.1	1.6	17.0	17.2	9.7	31.2

Note: Data are as of December 30, 1994.
Source: Prudential Securities Inc.

TABLE 6-5. Macroeconomic Sector Breakdown of Large-Cap Style Benchmarks

Percentage of market cap

	Large-Cap Growth				Large-Cap Value			
	PSI	Russell	S&P/ BARRA	Wilshire	PSI	Russell	S&P/ BARRA	Wilshire
Basic industry	5.9	7.1	6.0	3.4	8.8	13.0	13.9	3.2
Business services	5.9	9.4	8.0	7.7	1.7	1.1	1.9	0.2
Capital spending	2.1	9.6	9.1	8.9	7.0	1.6	1.3	0.6
Conglomerates	0.1	0.1	1.8	0.2	1.2	1.1	0.9	2.1
Consumer cyclical	1.9	0.8	0.8	0.9	5.6	6.6	6.7	4.0
Consumer services	25.8	15.7	15.3	16.6	4.6	4.2	5.8	0.9
Consumer staples	10.0	18.2	23.0	24.3	7.7	3.1	2.3	1.4
Energy	1.0	2.9	1.9	1.0	8.4	14.6	20.4	28.7
Financial services	7.5	7.0	2.7	6.9	23.9	21.6	19.4	34.5
Health care	8.9	14.4	16.4	14.7	6.7	3.8	1.6	—
Technology	30.0	14.3	13.3	15.0	8.3	8.0	9.0	1.5
Utilities	0.8	0.5	1.8	0.4	16.1	21.2	16.8	22.9

Note: Data are as of December 30, 1994.
Source: Prudential Securities Inc.

TABLE 6-6. Fundamental Characteristics of Large-Cap Style Benchmarks

Market-value-weighted average

	Large-Cap Growth				Large-Cap Value			
	PSI	Russell	S&P/BARRA	Wilshire	PSI	Russell	S&P/BARRA	Wilshire
LTM P/E—without negative earnings	18.8	17.6	17.6	17.2	11.7	12.4	13.1	10.4
P/E—IBES forecast EPS	18.7	16.4	16.2	16.2	10.4	11.5	11.8	10.5
Price/book	3.6	3.8	4.0	3.8	1.4	1.9	1.9	1.6
Price/sales	2.0	1.8	1.8	1.8	1.2	1.0	0.9	1.0
Price/cash flow	17.1	14.4	14.4	14.5	8.1	7.5	7.2	6.3
Debt/capital	27.8	40.4	40.9	36.4	58.1	52.9	50.5	52.2
Yield								
% of companies	48.0	64.7	84.0	81.8	89.3	89.0	88.7	100.0
Weighted average	0.7	1.8	2.0	1.9	2.4	4.0	3.8	4.9
P/E to growth	1.1	1.2	1.3	1.2	1.1	1.6	1.5	1.8
IBES forecast growth	19.1	15.4	14.3	14.6	12.2	9.0	9.5	7.9
Historical five-year EPS growth	18.1	11.8	10.4	14.1	10.8	-0.2	-0.4	4.5
Historical five-year sales growth	18.5	11.6	11.4	13.3	6.9	4.0	3.8	4.2
Return on equity	22.5	23.4	23.5	25.3	12.7	13.4	13.5	15.2
Return on assets	11.2	9.8	10.2	10.6	3.9	4.0	4.0	3.3
Average daily trading volume (thousands)	1123	1055	1240	1284	608	677	711	649

Note: Data are as of December 30, 1994.
Source: Prudential Securities Inc.

TABLE 6-7. Annual Returns of Large-Cap Style Benchmarks
Percent total returns

	Large-Cap Growth				Large-Cap Value			
	PSI	Russell	S&P/BARRA	Wilshire	PSI	Russell	S&P/BARRA	Wilshire
1979	23.7	23.9	15.7	29.5	20.0	20.6	21.1	20.7
1980	44.6	39.6	39.4	41.1	24.1	24.4	23.6	21.9
1981	-16.0	-11.3	-9.8	-10.9	1.1	1.3	0.0	10.5
1982	10.0	20.5	22.0	14.5	19.8	20.0	21.0	15.9
1983	13.7	16.0	16.2	17.4	26.4	28.3	28.9	25.4
1984	-1.2	-1.0	2.3	3.0	5.6	10.1	10.5	19.1
1985	28.6	32.9	33.3	32.9	30.1	31.5	29.7	30.2
1986	7.7	15.4	14.5	15.5	21.0	20.0	21.7	22.2
1987	5.7	5.3	6.5	4.7	2.2	0.5	3.7	4.7
1988	9.3	11.3	11.9	15.4	20.7	23.2	21.7	22.8
1989	29.6	35.9	36.4	35.2	27.7	25.2	26.1	25.1
1990	-0.9	-0.3	0.2	0.3	-5.5	-8.1	-6.8	-7.6
1991	44.8	41.2	38.4	46.6	25.9	24.6	22.6	25.6
1992	4.3	5.0	5.2	5.9	8.7	13.8	10.6	14.4
1993	3.4	2.9	1.5	-0.5	14.4	18.1	18.5	13.5
1994	2.5	2.7	3.0	3.0	0.5	-2.0	-0.6	-4.3
1985–1994 10-Year								
Annualized average	12.6	14.3	14.2	14.9	13.9	13.9	14.1	14.0
Arithmetic average	13.5	15.2	15.1	15.9	14.6	14.7	14.7	14.7
Standard deviation	14.5	14.8	14.4	15.9	11.9	12.7	11.7	12.5

Source: Prudential Securities Inc.

TABLE 6-8. Descriptive Characteristics of Mid-Cap Style Benchmarks

	Mid-Cap Growth				Mid-Cap Value			
	PSI	Russell	S&P/BARRA	Wilshire	PSI	Russell	S&P/BARRA	Wilshire
Number of companies	426	391	172	149	419	400	228	104
First full year of return	1976	1986	1992	1978	1976	1986	1992	1978
Index rebalancing	Semiannually	Annually	As needed	Quarterly	Semiannually	Annually	As needed	Quarterly
Weighting method	Market cap	Float*	Market cap	Market cap	Market cap	Float*	Market cap	Market cap
Returns calculation	With income	Principal & with income	Principal & with income	With income	With income	Principal & with income	Principal & with income	With income
Exchange Distribution								
NASDAQ	52.1%	23.6%	30.7%	42.2%	22.9%	11.1%	19.5%	26.5%
NYSE	44.3	72.1	67.2	55.2	75.6	87.8	78.8	72.1
ASE	3.5	4.3	2.1	2.6	1.6	1.1	1.7	1.4
Total capitalization	$294.6 bil	$567.0 bil	$230.7 bil	$152.8 bil	$320.0 bil	$633.3 bil	$228.1 bil	$93.5 bil

TABLE 6-8 (continued).

	Mid-Cap Growth				Mid-Cap Value			
	PSI	Russell	S&P/BARRA	Wilshire	PSI	Russell	S&P/BARRA	Wilshire
Average Size								
Wtd. mean	$887.8 mil	$2.3 bil	$2.2 bil	$1.2 bil	$945.0 mil	$2.3 bil	$1.6 bil	$1.0 bil
Mean	693.2 mil	1.5 bil	1.3 bil	$1.0 bil	763.7 mil	1.6 bil	1.0 bil	907.5 mil
Median	564.1 mil	1.1 bil	1.1 bil	973.6 mil	692.7 mil	1.2 bil	814.0 mil	874.3 mil
Size Range								
Largest	$1.7 bil	$12.5 bil	$10.3 bil	$2.1 bil	$1.7 bil	$5.2 bil	$5.4 bil	$1.8 bil
Smallest	283.0 mil	37.0 mil	205.5 mil	274.0 mil	283.5 mil	56.6 mil	48.6 mil	415.6 mil
Concentration								
Largest 10	5.5%	8.9%	18.8%	12.7%	5.1%	7.1%	14.9%	17.0%
Largest 50	24.4	31.2	53.2	51.1	22.7	29.6	47.6	64.5
Largest 100	42.6	50.5	80.2	82.8	40.9	49.9	71.9	98.6

*See section on index construction.
Note: Data are as of December 30, 1994.
Source: Prudential Securities Inc.

TABLE 6-9. Size Distribution of Mid-Cap Style Benchmarks
Percentage of companies

	Mid-Cap Growth				Mid-Cap Value			
	PSI	Russell	S&P/BARRA	Wilshire	PSI	Russell	S&P/BARRA	Wilshire
Large								
$3.0–10.0 bil	—	9.0	5.8	—	—	13.5	2.2	—
Medium-Large								
$1.5–3.0 bil	4.5	26.9	25.0	18.1	3.6	26.3	16.2	4.9
Medium								
$750 mil–$1.5 bil	32.2	39.5	41.9	47.0	41.3	39.0	36.4	58.3
Medium-Small								
$250–750 mil	63.4	21.3	25.0	34.9	55.1	18.3	35.1	36.9
Small								
$100–250 mil	—	3.1	2.3	—	—	2.5	10.1	—
Very Small								
Less than $100 mil	—	0.3	—	—	—	0.5	< 0.1	—

Note: Data are as of December 30, 1994.
Source: Prudential Securities Inc.

TABLE 6-10. Size Distribution of Mid-Cap Style Benchmarks
Percentage of market cap

	Mid-Cap Growth				Mid-Cap Value			
	PSI	Russell	S&P/BARRA	Wilshire	PSI	Russell	S&P/BARRA	Wilshire
Large								
$3.0–10.0 bil	—	23.9	18.8	—	—	31.5	8.8	—
Medium-Large								
$1.5–3.0 bil	10.1	38.5	36.4	31.2	7.5	35.1	33.8	9.2
Medium								
$750 mil–$1.5 bil	48.3	29.3	34.2	50.2	58.0	26.3	38.3	68.4
Medium-Small								
$250–750 mil	41.6	7.9	10.2	18.6	34.5	6.7	17.2	22.4
Small								
$100–250 mil	—	0.4	0.4	—	—	0.3	1.9	—
Very Small								
Less than $100 mil	—	< 0.1	—	—	—	< 0.1	< 0.1	—

Note: Data are as of December 30, 1994.
Source: Prudential Securities Inc.

TABLE 6-11. Macroeconomic Sector Breakdown of Mid-Cap Style Benchmarks
Percentage of companies

	Mid-Cap Growth				Mid-Cap Value			
	PSI	Russell	S&P/BARRA	Wilshire	PSI	Russell	S&P/BARRA	Wilshire
Basic industry	6.8	14.4	14.5	8.7	15.5	18.3	17.1	5.8
Business services	6.2	7.7	9.9	4.7	2.1	3.3	4.4	2.9
Capital spending	5.5	5.4	4.1	4.7	4.1	3.3	7.9	1.9
Conglomerates	0.5	0.5	0.6	1.4	0.7	0.8	0.9	1.0
Consumer cyclical	4.2	3.1	5.8	5.4	5.5	4.0	1.3	2.9
Consumer services	18.3	22.3	15.7	22.1	11.0	7.3	10.1	6.8
Consumer staples	2.6	4.4	5.8	2.7	2.9	3.0	5.7	2.9
Energy	3.8	4.6	5.8	4.7	6.4	8.3	6.6	8.7
Financial services	7.3	9.5	2.9	6.7	30.8	28.0	13.6	34.0
Health care	16.0	11.3	11.0	16.1	3.1	0.8	6.1	—
Technology	27.7	15.4	22.1	21.5	5.7	5.8	8.3	1.1
Utilities	1.2	0.8	1.7	1.3	12.2	16.0	18.0	32.0
REITs	—	0.8	—	—	—	1.5	—	—

Note: Data are as of December 30, 1994.
Source: Prudential Securities Inc.

TABLE 6-12. **Macroeconomic Sector Breakdown of Mid-Cap Style Benchmarks**
Percentage of market cap

	Mid-Cap Growth				Mid-Cap Value			
	PSI	Russell	S&P/BARRA	Wilshire	PSI	Russell	S&P/BARRA	Wilshire
Basic industry	5.2	14.5	12.9	7.8	16.0	19.1	13.8	4.3
Business services	6.6	6.7	7.5	4.0	2.0	3.1	4.2	2.5
Capital spending	4.9	4.8	4.3	5.3	4.4	2.8	6.2	2.5
Conglomerates	0.4	0.4	0.4	1.7	0.8	0.4	0.6	1.3
Consumer cyclical	4.4	2.8	4.2	4.3	4.9	5.2	0.9	2.1
Consumer services	18.5	22.4	13.4	18.6	8.8	6.3	6.6	6.5
Consumer staples	2.0	7.1	3.7	3.3	3.2	2.4	5.5	3.1
Energy	3.6	3.9	4.3	2.8	6.8	7.4	5.7	9.3
Financial services	8.5	8.6	5.9	7.9	31.0	26.5	23.0	32.2
Health care	15.9	9.7	11.2	18.0	2.3	1.2	2.8	—
Technology	28.7	18.0	29.9	24.3	5.8	7.7	6.0	0.6
Utilities	1.2	0.7	2.3	2.0	13.9	17.4	24.6	35.6
REITs	—	0.3	—	—	—	0.6	—	—

Note: Data are as of December 30, 1994.
Source: Prudential Securities Inc.

TABLE 6-13. Fundamental Characteristics of Mid-Cap Style Benchmarks

Market-value-weighted average

	Mid-Cap Growth				Mid-Cap Value			
	PSI	Russell	S&P/BARRA	Wilshire	PSI	Russell	S&P/BARRA	Wilshire
LTM P/E—without negative earnings	20.9	17.6	18.4	18.1	11.5	12.6	13.2	11.1
P/E—IBES forecast EPS	18.7	17.5	17.9	18.4	10.9	11.7	12.8	11.1
Price/book	3.5	3.4	3.6	3.5	1.7	1.7	1.6	1.5
Price/sales	1.9	1.7	1.9	1.8	1.0	1.0	1.1	1.0
Price/cash flow	18.0	15.0	17.3	17.5	8.1	8.6	8.8	6.4
Debt/capital	26.2	38.6	32.4	25.6	52.3	51.6	46.6	53.9
Yield								
% of companies	27.3	58.7	57.6	41.2	76.4	86.5	77.6	100.0
Weighted average	0.3	1.0	0.9	0.7	2.9	3.6	3.3	5.1
P/E to growth	1.0	1.2	1.1	1.0	1.4	1.7	1.8	2.2
IBES forecast growth	22.4	17.6	18.1	18.8	10.7	9.4	10.3	7.4
Historical five-year EPS growth	20.7	13.4	16.8	20.0	4.4	1.8	2.9	7.0
Historical five-year sales growth	18.4	12.8	17.6	19.4	5.6	4.3	6.8	4.3
Return on equity	17.0	18.6	19.3	19.2	13.2	11.7	10.7	13.3
Return on assets	9.6	8.6	10.5	10.5	4.4	3.7	3.6	3.2
Average daily trading volume (thousands)	251	376	353	283	129	239	173	82

Note: Data are as of December 30, 1994.
Source: Prudential Securities Inc.

TABLE 6-14. Annual Returns of Mid-Cap Style Benchmarks
Percent total returns

	Mid-Cap Growth				Mid-Cap Value			
	PSI	Russell	S&P/BARRA	Wilshire	PSI	Russell	S&P/BARRA	Wilshire
1979	39.4	—	—	43.8	28.6	—	—	25.7
1980	39.3	—	—	43.6	21.1	—	—	20.1
1981	-0.7	—	—	0.8	11.7	—	—	17.7
1982	22.0	—	—	23.2	27.3	—	—	30.5
1983	26.1	—	—	22.0	31.5	—	—	32.7
1984	-9.3	—	—	-4.6	8.0	—	—	18.3
1985	30.6	—	—	30.2	34.7	—	—	38.7
1986	12.1	17.6	—	14.8	14.6	17.9	—	23.2
1987	-4.9	2.8	—	-5.4	-5.6	-2.2	—	-5.9
1988	13.5	12.9	—	15.1	26.7	24.6	—	23.0
1989	24.7	31.5	—	22.0	20.5	22.7	—	21.5
1990	-7.3	-5.1	—	-12.9	-16.6	-16.1	—	-16.4
1991	56.4	47.0	—	55.4	47.2	37.9	—	48.5
1992	11.7	8.7	6.9	12.3	23.0	21.7	16.0	22.6
1993	14.8	11.2	13.7	15.8	16.6	15.6	13.4	12.8
1994	0.7	-2.2	-7.0	0.9	-0.4	-2.1	-0.6	-2.7
1985–1994 10-Year								
Annualized average	14.0	—	—	13.4	14.6	—	—	14.9
Arithmetic average	15.2	—	—	14.8	16.1	—	—	16.5
Standard deviation	17.8	—	.	18.2	18.2	—	—	19.1

Source: Prudential Securities Inc.

169

TABLE 6-15. Descriptive Characteristics of Small-Cap Style Benchmarks

	Small-Cap Growth			Small-Cap Value		
	PSI	Russell	Wilshire	PSI	Russell	Wilshire
Number of companies	590	1,460	252	465	1,396	180
First full year of return	1976	1984	1978	1976	1984	1978
Index rebalancing	Semiannually	Annually	Quarterly	Seminnually	Annually	Quarterly
Weighting method	Market cap	Float*	Market cap	Market cap	Float*	Market cap
Returns calculation	With income	Principal & with income	With income	With income	Principal & with income	With income
Exchange Distribution						
NASDAQ	71.7%	59.9%	58.4%	46.7%	40.2%	62.0%
NYSE	21.2	35.2	39.3	50.7	56.7	36.7
ASE	7.1	4.9	2.3	2.6	3.1	1.3
Total capitalization	$116.2 bil	$315.5 bil	$124.6 bil	$95.7 bil	$307.5 bil	$74.3 bil

TABLE 6-15 (continued).

	Small-Cap Growth			Small-Cap Value		
	PSI	Russell	Wilshire	PSI	Russell	Wilshire
Average Size						
Wtd. mean	$241.8 mil	$357.7 mil	$692.2 mil	$247.7 mil	$334.7 mil	$556.2 mil
Mean	198.8 mil	217.0 mil	494.4 mil	205.7 mil	221.4 mil	414.8 mil
Median	172.6 mil	159.1 mil	417.0 mil	181.5 mil	168.7 mil	370.9 mil
Size Range						
Largest	$434.6 mil	$1.1 bil	$1.7 bil	$421.8 mil	$1.1 bil	$971.6 mil
Smallest	80.6 mil	6.2 mil	110.5 mil	86.0 mil	10.8 mil	114.8 mil
Concentration						
Largest 10	3.6%	3.4%	10.8%	4.4%	2.4%	12.5%
Largest 50	16.8	12.8	40.2	20.3	9.9	50.0
Largest 100	30.6	22.5	64.6	36.8	19.0	78.2

*See section on index construction.
Note: Data are as of December 30, 1994.
Source: Prudential Securities Inc.

TABLE 6-16. Size Distribution of Small-Cap Style Benchmarks
Percentage of companies

	Small-Cap Growth			Small-Cap Value		
	PSI	Russell	Wilshire	PSI	Russell	Wilshire
Large $3.0 bil & over	—	—	—	—	—	—
Medium-Large $1.5–3.0 bil	—	—	0.8	—	—	—
Medium $750 mil–$1.5 bil	—	1.6	18.7	—	1.2	14.5
Medium-Small $250–750 mil	28.0	29.8	52.8	28.8	31.0	52.5
Small $100–250 mil	61.4	39.4	27.8	62.4	42.3	33.0
Very Small Less than $100 mil	10.7	29.2	—	8.8	25.6	—

Note: Data are as of December 30, 1994.
Source: Prudential Securities Inc.

TABLE 6-17. Size Distribution of Small-Cap Style Benchmarks
Percentage of market cap

	Small-Cap Growth			Small-Cap Value		
	PSI	Russell	Wilshire	PSI	Russell	Wilshire
Large						
$3.0 bil & over	—	—	—	—	—	—
Medium-Large						
$1.5–3.0 bil	—	—	2.6	—	—	—
Medium						
$750 mil–$1.5 bil	—	7.4	37.0	—	3.2	30.0
Medium-Small						
$250–750 mil	45.9	53.5	49.7	46.2	55.4	56.0
Small						
$100–250 mil	49.1	29.4	10.7	49.8	34.2	13.9
Very Small						
Less than $100 mil	5.0	9.7	—	4.0	7.3	—

Note: Data are as of December 30, 1994.
Source: Prudential Securities Inc.

173

TABLE 6-18. Macroeconomic Sector Breakdown of Small-Cap Style Benchmarks
Percentage of companies

	Small-Cap Growth			Small-Cap Value		
	PSI	Russell	Wilshire	PSI	Russell	Wilshire
Basic industry	9.5	11.8	9.6	12.7	12.7	6.7
Business services	5.1	5.2	5.2	2.6	3.7	3.4
Capital spending	7.3	7.1	4.8	6.5	5.6	1.1
Conglomerates	0.4	0.1	0.4	0.4	0.3	—
Consumer cyclical	4.6	4.3	5.6	7.3	5.3	5.0
Consumer services	17.1	16.4	21.3	22.2	14.0	10.1
Consumer staples	1.7	2.5	1.6	3.7	2.8	—
Energy	4.6	5.0	5.6	3.9	5.9	6.1
Financial services	5.4	13.8	7.1	26.5	23.6	36.1
Health care	15.6	10.9	13.2	2.6	5.5	1.1
Technology	27.1	15.7	25.3	8.6	9.6	1.7
Utilities	1.5	2.3	0.4	3.2	4.2	28.7
REITs	—	4.9	—	—	6.8	—

Note: Data are as of December 30, 1994.
Source: Prudential Securities Inc.

TABLE 6-19. Macroeconomic Sector Breakdown of Small-Cap Style Benchmarks

Percentage of market cap

	Small-Cap Growth			Small-Cap Value		
	PSI	Russell	Wilshire	PSI	Russell	Wilshire
Basic industry	8.7	11.0	8.3	13.0	12.6	4.5
Business services	4.9	6.5	4.5	2.1	2.4	4.2
Capital spending	6.9	7.4	3.8	5.7	4.5	1.4
Conglomerates	0.3	0.1	0.3	0.6	0.4	—
Consumer cyclical	4.7	4.0	5.1	8.1	4.9	4.0
Consumer services	17.5	15.3	19.6	21.3	10.3	8.1
Consumer staples	1.8	2.9	1.0	3.5	3.2	—
Energy	4.4	4.1	4.7	3.7	6.4	5.9
Financial services	6.1	6.3	6.6	27.8	29.9	37.7
Health care	14.6	14.0	14.9	3.0	3.2	1.2
Technology	28.7	23.5	31.0	7.0	7.2	1.4
Utilities	1.4	1.2	0.2	4.2	6.8	31.6
REITs	—	3.7	—	—	8.3	—

Note: Data are as of December 30, 1994.
Source: Prudential Securities Inc.

TABLE 6-20. Fundamental Characteristics of Small-Cap Style Benchmarks
Market-value-weighted average

	Small-Cap Growth			Small-Cap Value		
	PSI	Russell	Wilshire	PSI	Russell	Wilshire
LTM P/E—without negative earnings	19.0	16.4	18.7	11.2	13.7	11.8
P/E—IBES forecast EPS	17.5	18.0	19.2	11.3	13.4	10.8
Price/book	3.1	3.2	3.4	1.6	1.6	1.4
Price/sales	1.7	1.7	1.8	0.8	1.1	1.1
Price/cash flow	15.0	14.3	18.3	8.2	8.5	6.3
Debt/capital	22.8	30.3	24.0	38.6	43.3	48.7
Yield						
% of companies	19.2	39.6	26.1	52.2	56.3	99.4
Weighted average	0.2	0.7	0.2	1.7	2.5	4.9
P/E to growth	1.2	1.2	1.0	1.1	1.6	2.0
IBES forecast growth	24.6	21.6	21.1	13.2	12.1	7.5
Historical five-year EPS growth	17.5	11.9	18.3	5.6	1.8	3.5
Historical five-year sales growth	16.3	14.2	19.6	6.5	5.9	5.3
Return on equity	14.3	15.5	18.1	12.2	9.1	13.0
Return on assets	8.3	8.4	10.6	5.0	3.1	3.4
Average daily trading volume (Ths.)	98	132	222	67	62	40

Note: Data are as of December 30, 1994.
Source: Prudential Securities Inc.

TABLE 6-21. Annual Returns of Small-Cap Style Benchmarks
Percent total returns

	Small-Cap Growth			Small-Cap Value		
	PSI	Russell	Wilshire	PSI	Russell	Wilshire
1979	49.1	—	51.7	34.6	—	22.3
1980	43.0	—	52.3	29.5	—	18.6
1981	2.1	—	-1.0	17.9	—	25.0
1982	30.3	—	19.1	37.9	—	35.8
1983	30.0	—	22.6	40.0	—	42.3
1984	-13.0	-15.8	-9.0	6.3	2.3	22.1
1985	28.9	31.0	26.5	34.1	31.1	43.9
1986	3.3	3.6	10.1	11.6	7.4	23.5
1987	-11.7	-10.5	-8.9	-9.9	-7.1	-3.1
1988	17.4	20.4	19.3	32.2	29.5	22.4
1989	21.1	20.2	18.9	16.3	12.4	18.1
1990	-14.3	-17.4	-19.0	-22.3	-21.8	-19.4
1991	54.1	51.2	56.8	51.0	41.7	49.0
1992	9.7	7.8	13.2	25.6	29.1	29.2
1993	14.4	13.4	18.0	18.2	23.8	14.1
1994	-2.6	-2.4	0.6	1.4	-0.5	-2.0
1985–1994 10-Year						
Annualized average	10.4	10.1	11.9	13.9	12.9	15.8
Arithmetic average	12.0	11.7	13.5	15.8	14.6	17.6
Standard deviation	19.3	19.2	19.7	20.7	19.0	20.2

Source: Prudential Securities Inc.

Appendix B: Methodology Used to Calculate Fundamental Characteristics

The calculation of fundamental characteristics for a benchmark can be an onerous task. Many methodologies can be employed and many different measures calculated. We continually try to provide the most accurate and representative calculations.

One of the main problems in calculating benchmark fundamentals is the exclusion of outliers. Outliers are numbers that are so different from the rest of the numbers that they have a distorting effect on measures of central tendency. The meaningfulness of such excessively high or low numbers is questionable. In addition, outliers are often extreme because the calculation of that particular ratio is considered inappropriate due to a particular circumstance, occurrence, or accounting peculiarity. For example, many people exclude all negative earnings in the calculation of P/E or exclude heavily leveraged financial companies when calculating debt to capital.

We chose to use the same interquartile range methodology adopted by the Frank Russell Company in excluding outliers (many thanks to the people at Frank Russell Company for their help). The advantages of this methodology are as follows:

- It does not automatically assume data at the top and bottom of the distribution are outliers.
- It can be applied consistently as a quantitative method for all fundamental characteristics.

Calculating the Critical Points

The upper and lower critical points (that is, the highest and lowest value to be included in the calculation) are calculated for a global universe of stocks that includes both small- and large-cap stocks. The Frank Russell Company uses the Russell 3000 as its universe, while we use the combined Prudential Securities Inc. small-cap and large-cap universes.

The Interquartile Range

The interquartile range, or IQR, is calculated by subtracting the value of the fundamental characteristic of the company at the 75th percentile from the value of the fundamental characteristic of the company at the 25th percentile.

The Critical Values

We multiply the IQR by 3 and add it to the value of the 75th percentile and subtract it from the value of the 25th percentile to form the critical values. All values higher than the upper critical value and lower than the bottom critical value are excluded as outliers.

Notes on Fundamental Data

Fundamental data were taken from Compustat, IBES, or Value Line via Factset as of December 31, 1994. We used latest-12-month earnings for LTM P/E and IBES fiscal-year 1 estimates for forecast EPS; for P/E to growth, we used P/E with forecast EPS and IBES long-term growth estimates. Return on equity and return on assets are for the last 12 months. Debt to capital uses long-term debt, and the average daily volume is for the six months prior to December 31, 1994.

Do We Need Mid-Cap? An Examination of the EAI Database

Elizabeth E. Nevin, Vice President
Director, U.S. Equities, Evaluation Associates, Inc.

Since the introduction of various mid-cap indices, we have had to address several issues concerning mid-cap investing. One of the most important questions, and the focus of this discussion, is, "Do we need mid-cap?" The case for investing in the middle range of the domestic equity-market capitalization spectrum can be compelling for a pension plan with little or no current exposure to that range. However, before creating a separate policy allocation, a pension plan should analyze the overall plan. Based on an examination of our databases, there appears to be little need to add mid-cap managers as most plans already have exposure to this area through their existing manager structures.

The question of "Do we need mid-cap" is not a new one; the discussion formally began in mid-1991 when Standard & Poor's introduced the first mid-cap index. Since that time, many other mid-cap indices have been created. Upon the introduction of the various indices, this pragmatic question arose: "Should we be recommending the inclusion of mid-cap managers in our clients' equity structures?" We listened to the rationales of the creators of mid-cap indices as well as to investment managers seeking to sell their mid-cap products. We were approached by many managers introducing new mid-cap products or "repackaging" existing products (products that they felt never received a fair chance because there was no appropriate performance benchmark), as well as managers who had been offering a mid-cap product for years. As mid-cap has become more popular and is being marketed by investment managers as a separate asset-class in which clients need to have exposure, pension fund administrators and their advisors are faced with addressing the questions: "Do we need mid-cap?" and "Should it be recommended as a separate asset class?"

Rather than issuing a blanket policy advising clients how to handle the mid-cap allocation question, we took the prudent course of analyzing each individual situation. However, now that mid-cap (as a separate asset class) has a few years of history behind it, we decided to take a systematic approach to answering the question by examining the database of domestic equity-advisors who manage assets for our clients.

Definition of Mid-Cap

Currently, the three most widely used benchmarks for mid-cap stocks are the Russell Midcap 800, the S&P MidCap 400 and the Wilshire Mid Cap 750. All of these indices are capitalization-weighted; because all were created relatively recently, historical information is quite limited. Considerable differences exist among these indices as to the exact definition of mid-cap, as shown in Table 7-1.

Just as the most popular mid-cap indices differ from one another, definitions of mid-cap also vary among consulting firms. EAI defines mid-cap by dividing the S&P 500 into quintiles (Table 7-2) and then isolating the third and fourth quintiles as most representative of the opportunities available for mid-cap investing.

TABLE 7-1. Descriptive Characteristics of Mid-Cap Benchmarks

	Russell Midcap	S&P MidCap	Wilshire Mid Cap
Average Size			
Weighted mean	$2.1 bil	$1.8 bil	$1.0 bil
Mean	1.5 bil	1.1 bil	847.7 mil
Median	1.2 bil	881.5 mil	798.3 mil
Size Range			
Largest	$4.7 bil	$9.2 bil	$1.7 bil
Smallest	51.6 mil	56.1 mil	230.8 mil

Note: Data are as of June 30, 1994.
Source: Prudential Securities Inc.

TABLE 7-2.   S&P 500 Stock Index
Quintiles by market ($ millions)

1	Greater than $8,845
2	From $4,649 to $8,845
3	From $2,784 to $4,649
4	From $1,416 to $2,784
5	Less than $1,416

Note: Data are as of September 30, 1994.
Source: Evaluation Associates.

TABLE 7-3.   Mid-Cap Ranges over Time

	Periods Ending					
	12/31/89	12/31/90	12/31/91	12/31/92	12/31/93	9/30/94
Mid-Cap Range						
Largest company	$3,171	$2,398	$3,169	$3,510	$4,407	$4,649
Smallest company	961	689	910	1,080	1,274	1,416

Source: Evaluation Associates.

Obviously, the exact dollar value for quintile breaks can vary from quarter to quarter. Table 7-3 shows the largest and the smallest companies in the third and fourth quintiles at the end of the last five years and the most current period.

Rather than identifying a fixed range for mid-cap, we decided on a definition that is a moving target. We felt it was important for our definition to reflect the realities of a dynamic market.

The EAI Domestic Equity-Manager Database

In order to understand the capitalization patterns of the investment advisors managing our clients' assets, we assembled a database of 109 large-cap domestic-equity portfolios. Considerations constructing the large-cap manager database for our study included the following.

- We eliminated those managers whose styles were small, small/mid, or mid-cap as identified by their statement of a specific range at which they would buy and/or sell stocks in their portfolios. We needed a way to draw the line between those managers who drifted into and out of different capitalization stocks opportunistically, and those who had sell rules that prohibited capitalization drift. As long as the manager was buying stocks according to its stated philosophy and adhering to a set of criteria that remained constant over time, we would expect an active manager to use size opportunistically over time.

- The bogey of all managers in our database was the S&P 500 or some other appropriate large-cap index. The managers were aware that regardless of whether their total-portfolio market capitalization drifted above or below that of the benchmark, their performance benchmark would remain unchanged.

- There was a broad diversity of growth, value, and core managers included in the database. Table 7-4 describes the portfolio characteristics of the group in aggregate, which as one would expect, closely resemble those of the S&P 500.

- Several firms manage separate accounts for several EAI clients in one particular style. Therefore, in an effort to not duplicate the effects of one firm, we used only the most representative portfolio of the manager. More than

TABLE 7-4. Portfolio Characteristics of the Large-Cap Domestic Equity Database

	Database	S&P 500	
		Weighted	Unweighted
P/E ratio (trailing 12 months)	19.9×	22.8×	19.8×
Yield	2.2%	1.9%	2.9%
EPS growth (historic/annual)	8.8%	8.4%	5.6%
Price to book	3.3×	3.7×	3.4×
Debt to equity	83	93	80
5-year ROE	13.8%	14.5%	15.3%
Beta	1.14	1.00	1.00

Note: Data are as of June 30, 1994.

one portfolio from a firm was included only in those cases where the investment advisor was managing port-folios in two or more distinct styles within the same firm.
• For obvious reasons, only active-management styles were included in the database.

What We Found

One question that immediately arises is: "What percentage of the total domestic-equity spectrum should mid-cap occupy?" We felt that the most appropriate allocation to the segment should be similar to the percentage of mid-cap stocks held in a broad index. In order to get a general idea of the size distribution on a market capitalization-weighted basis, we examined the exposure of a few generally accepted broad indices.

Table 7-5 shows three broad-market indices and the size distribu-tion of companies held in each. Because the EAI definition of mid-cap is a moving target, it is difficult to find an exact comparison of mid-cap weights held. However, by looking at the broad-market allocations, there appears to be at least a minimum of 10.8% (companies between

TABLE 7-5.   Size Distribution of Broad-Market Benchmarks
Market-cap weighted

	CRSP 1-10	Russell 3000	Wilshire 5000
Very Large $10.0 bil and over	38.5%	39.9%	38.7%
Large $3.0–10.0 bil	26.9	27.3	27.1
Medium-Large $1.5–3.0 bil	11.0	11.6	10.8
Medium $750–1.5 bil	8.9	8.5	8.7
Medium-Small $750 mil or less	14.7	12.7	14.7

Note: Data are as of June 30, 1994.
Source: Prudential Securities Inc.

$1.5 billion and $3.0 billion) held in mid-cap stocks. Table 7-6, a comparison of EAI large-cap domestic equity managers versus the S&P 500, shows that a total weight of 16% of the S&P 500 (versus 28% for the EAI manager database) is held in what we have defined as mid-cap (companies between $1.4 billion and $4.6 billion). The information gathered from this exercise demonstrates that the managers in the EAI manager database not only hold an adequate exposure, but are clearly overweighted in mid-cap.

Market-Capitalization Correlation with Mid-Cap

The results from the manager database led us to believe that in general, mid-cap exposure was being adequately covered by our clients' existing large-cap domestic equity-managers.

Of the 109 managers in the database (see Figure 7-1), 48 managers (44%) had an allocation of 30% or greater and 43 managers (39%) had between 20% to 29% mid-cap exposure in their portfolios.

Style Correlation with Mid-Cap

We have already seen (see Table 7-4) that the characteristics of the total database closely resemble those of the S&P 500; in addition, we wanted to ascertain whether there were any style biases in the mid-cap universe (e.g., is growth synonymous with mid-cap?). We began by ranking the database by the portfolio weighting held in mid-cap (i.e.,

TABLE 7-6.   Comparison of EAI Large-Cap Domestic Equity Managers versus the S&P 500

	Cap-Weighted Percentage of Total	
Quintile ($ millions)	S&P 500	EAI Manager Database
1 >$8,845	62%	38%
2 From $4,649 to $8,845	19%	18%
3 From $2,784 to $4,649	11%	14%
4 From $1,416 to $2,784	6%	14%
5 <$1,416	2%	15%

Note: Data are as of June 30, 1994.

FIGURE 7-1.   EAI Large-Capitalization Domestic Equity Manager Database

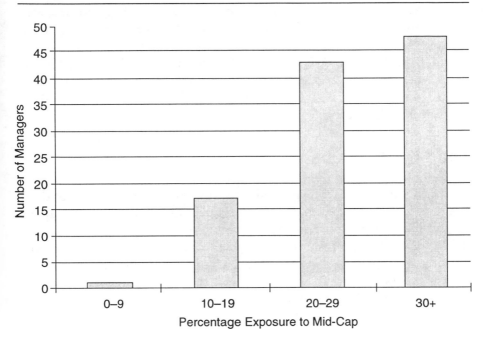

TABLE 7-7.   Correlation between Mid-Cap Exposure and P/E, Price/Book, and EPS Growth

	P/E	Price/Book	EPS Growth
Top half of universe	0.07	0.11	−0.05
Bottom half of universe	−0.25	−0.14	−0.19
Total	−0.08	0.03	−0.01

Note: Data are as of June 30, 1994.

percentage weighting in the third and fourth capitalization quintiles), dividing the group into halves and then running a correlation of P/E, price/book, and EPS growth against mid-cap exposure (see Table 7-7). The conclusion we drew from this exercise is that there is virtually no correlation between a manager's mid-cap exposure and investment-management style.

The EAI Client Database

EAI currently has 100 full-service retainer relationships comprising approximately $100 billion in assets. Our diversified client base includes (percentage of clients): corporations (62%), endowments/ foundations (21%), public retirement plans (13%), and a limited number of Taft-Hartley and personal trust accounts (4%). Client assets range in size from $12 million to $25 billion, the average client account is $723 million.

The Client Database

Having considered the analysis of separate portfolios, we then examined mid-cap exposure from an analysis of total-plan data. We assembled a representative group of EAI client plans eliminating the largest, the smallest, accounts with restrictions, and those with existing specific mid-cap mandates. The sample included 23 clients, whose assets ranged from $31 million to $2.09 billion; the average was $518 million, which for our purposes was close enough to the actual average for our entire client base of $723 million. The breakdown of client type included: 15 corporate plans, three public funds, four endowments/foundations, and one Taft-Hartley account; the percentages are nearly identical to our total-client mix. This exercise demonstrated that our client base fell within an acceptable range for mid-cap exposure. Even if we take into consideration that some of the mid-cap exposure in our client subset came from a few small-cap managers "buying up" in capitalization range, it appears that we are still adequately covered. Table 7-8 shows the actual distribution of clients' market-capitalization exposure broken down by quintile.

Our conclusion, upon examination of the data from both the manager and the client perspective was that there was no compelling reason to pursue separate mid-cap management for our clients.

When Do We Recommend Mid-Cap?

We understand that this is a rather strong statement and while our databases from both the managers and the clients support our case in

TABLE 7-8. EAI Representative Client Database

Client	Total Assets	Total Equity Distribution % in each Quintile				
		1	2	3	4	5
Corporate	$250 mil	42%	18%	16%	13%	10%
Public Fund	2.041 bil	25	16	13	14	32
Corporate	89 mil	27	15	29	21	9
Corporate	75 mil	27	17	21	16	20
Public Fund	155 mil	21	12	14	22	31
Corporate	931 mil	21	17	13	16	33
Corporate	255 mil	33	16	15	20	15
Corporate	31 mil	38	19	15	12	17
Corporate	132 mil	43	24	19	13	2
Corporate	206 mil	35	13	8	15	29
Corporate	629 mil	41	16	18	15	10
Endowment/foundation	40 mil	25	13	10	15	36
Endowment/foundation	684 mil	44	16	14	10	15
Corporate	2.090 bil	36	14	11	10	28
Public Fund	2.011 bil	35	16	11	11	26
Taft Hartley	591 mil	33	22	18	15	12
Corporate	267 mil	33	8	9	6	41
Corporate	976 mil	26	16	8	11	39
Corporate	45 mil	43	21	17	11	8
Endowment/foundation	104 mil	38	17	12	14	18
Corporate	125 mil	26	15	10	14	35
Endowment/foundation	123 mil	32	20	9	9	28
Corporate	59 mil	32	21	16	15	15
Average	$518 mil	33%	17%	14%	14%	22%

Note: Data are as of September 30, 1994.
Source: Evaluation Associates.

general, we recognize that there will still be a need for mid-cap managers in certain specific instances.

- Mid-cap managers could be attractive to a plan that only has very large-cap managers or managers who have little flexibility to buy stocks outside of a set range of market capitalizations. In this situation, we would consider either replacing the manager with one who had the ability to buy both medium and large-cap stocks or complementing the existing manager with one who exclusively buys mid-cap stocks.

- Some clients are uncomfortable with the risk associated with small-cap managers. Although performance data vary depending on the time period examined, we would expect that over time, there is some degree of incremental return offered by small-cap managers over mid-cap managers. However, there is generally more risk associated with the small-cap style. Mid-cap or small/mid-cap managers could serve as a substitute for small-cap managers in this situation.

- Over the past few years, many "top tier" small-cap managers (i.e., those who have had above median returns relative to their benchmarks, a long track record of managing small-cap assets, and have not experienced excessive turnover of investment professionals responsible for the record) have reached their capacity limit in assets under management. We have a choice of going to the "second tier" of managers (i.e., those with weaker relative-performance history, a shorter track-record, and/or portfolio-manager turnover) or buying the mid-cap product of those "top tier" managers whose small-cap product has closed. In this case, we would recommend the more established mid-cap managers whenever we are not satisfied with the available small-cap managers.

Summary

Examination of our manager and client databases leads us to the conclusion that the middle-capitalization sector of the market is being adequately covered on an opportunistic basis as an extension of the large-cap universe by our clients' current managers. We, therefore, feel there is no need to incorporate it as a distinct segment in our overall plan-design. There are some cases, however, where seeking specialized mid-cap managers would be appropriate.

Mid-Cap Investing by Investment Managers

Daniel J. Cardell, CFA, Director of Equities
Bank of America

Any discussion of mid-cap stocks needs to start with the question, "What is a mid-cap stock?" Furthermore, where did this idea of "mid-caps" come from? A search of financial literature before 1991 shows that there is a conspicuous absence of the word "mid-cap."[1] It is only over the fairly recent period that this idea of mid-cap stocks has become popular. It wasn't as if no one invested in medium-capitalization stocks before the 1990s, it was just that the mid-cap area didn't have its own index. Benchmarking had become a national obsession in the investment business and there seemed to be a peculiar lack of a widely accepted index for middle-capitalization stocks. The Standard & Poor's company addressed this deficiency in June of 1991 when it created an index to capture this "underserved" area of the market. This chapter will focus mostly on that index, the S&P MidCap 400.[2]

This chapter will take an in-depth look at the mid-cap phenomenon. After reading this chapter, you should have a better understanding of the mid-cap area of the market and be able to decide for yourself whether mid-caps are going to be a lasting part of the investment landscape or just the latest fad.

---

[1] There remains a difference in agreement even in the proper spelling of the term for middle-capitalization stocks. S&P spells it MidCap, Russell uses Midcap, and Wilshire prefers Mid Cap.

[2] We do not mean to imply in this chapter that the S&P MidCap is the only mid-cap index available or necessarily the "best" one. The Wilshire and Russell mid-cap indices are widely used and have respected companies supporting them. However, for reasons that are discussed extensively throughout the chapter, we view the S&P MidCap as the one that will eventually define the market segment.

After an introduction to the MidCap 400 Index, the second section will discuss the issue of defining a mid-cap stock. The third will review why someone would buy into this class of stocks. The fourth section will take a look at the mid-cap index. The final section will make an attempt to shed some light on adding value to mid-cap stocks through active management.

Introduction to the MidCap 400

Using its clout as the purveyor of the most popular institutional large-cap benchmark, the S&P 500, Standard & Poor's has created a widely followed index that is well on its way to being the industry standard. In its short existence, the MidCap 400 has already gathered approximately $9 billion of passively managed funds and this number continues to grow rapidly. Also, there are already more than a dozen actively managed mid-cap mutual funds that are offered by such fund-family giants as Dreyfus and Fidelity. As a measure of its popularity, there has already been at least one investment industry conference aimed specifically at mid-cap stocks, not to mention chapters in this book as well as several articles in the academic press. All this for a 400-stock index whose total capitalization is less than that of the top seven stocks in the S&P 500: General Electric, AT&T, Wal-Mart, Coca-Cola, Royal Dutch, Exxon, and Philip Morris.

A Short History

The following quote appeared in the *Wall Street Journal* on July 28, 1993:

> *"The whole notion that midsize stocks might be a distinct investment category only surfaced fairly recently. The turning point was the launching of the S&P MidCap 400 Index in 1991."*

This quote also appears in the introduction of S&P's 1993 Mid-Cap 400 Directory. Standard & Poor's is clearly taking credit for creating a new asset class. Why S&P deemed it necessary to create a new asset class is worth exploring further.

Over time institutional investors have made it clear that their desire is for complete exposure to the equity markets. This obviously includes stocks not included in the S&P 500 Index. This desire in many cases was driven by the promise of achieving the excess returns purported to be available in smaller-capitalization stocks. The S&P 500 therefore became the subject of attack by investors that felt that it was an inappropriate all-inclusive equity benchmark.

While the S&P 500 has clearly led the way as the U.S. equity index of choice for institutional investors, it has several shortcomings that make it an incomplete measure of total stock-market return. Aside from being a large-cap index, it is very top-end loaded or skewed toward the first 50 companies. Over 45% of the market capitalization of the entire index is contained in the largest 50 names. Only 2.46% of the capitalization is in the last 100 names. That's less than the capitalization of AT&T on its own. Secondly, returns of the S&P 500 certainly do not reflect the returns of the smaller-stock universe. In short, while the index includes over two-thirds of the market capitalization of U.S. equities, it remains an inadequate proxy for the equity markets as a whole.

The debate regarding the inability of the S&P 500 to reflect the extended market has recently heated up, with a recent study proposing the use of the Russell 3000 as a benchmark for plan sponsors. While this is an important issue for plan sponsors, there are other interested parties involved as well. One of the other driving forces behind the search for better indices comes from investment consulting firms. Consultants are encouraging fund sponsors to use more benchmarking as a way to evaluate managers. The result of this approach to evaluating managers is that each manager must be "pigeonholed" to reflect the proper investment-style or strategy. Consultants find it useful to categorize managers and then compare them to some normal or benchmark portfolio. This helps them to discern luck from skill on the part of active managers. As part of this strategy, consultants need to come up with ever more distinct benchmarks to compare manager expertise. Also, some money managers have for years complained that they are unfairly compared to a large-cap index when they are really investing in mid-sized and smaller companies.[3] In many ways the MidCap 400 was created to

---

[3] A more detailed discussion of the issue of manager segmentation is provided in "Is Style Management Out of Style?" by D. Cardell and J. Miller in the Winter 1994 edition of the *Journal of Applied Corporate Finance.*

meet not only the needs of plan sponsors, but those of consultants and money managers as well.

The Role of Futures

One of the advantages of a widely accepted index such as the S&P 500 is the ability to use derivative securities for asset allocation and handling cash flows, among other things. It is increasingly important to institutional managers to have an easily traded futures contract available.[4] This is especially important for fund managers who have daily inflows and outflows of funds. In constructing the MidCap 400, one of the prime objectives S&P had was the ability to trade a related futures contract. This contract enhances its viability as the preferred index for middle-capitalization stocks.

The MidCap 400 Index has unquestionably achieved its goal of marketplace acceptance as shown by the popularity of its futures contract on the Chicago Mercantile Exchange. Figure 8-1 shows futures volume and open interest of the MidCap 400 since its inception in February 1992.[5] In the span of just over two years, it is already the second most actively traded domestic-market contract behind the S&P 500. At this point, it is highly unlikely that any other index could displace the 400 as the preferred mid-cap contract.

Aside from having its own index, is the mid-cap area really deserving enough to be considered its own asset class? There is a real question as to whether mid-caps serve a legitimate purpose in the portfolio framework. A look at the diversification properties of mid-caps doesn't seem to make a very compelling case for them as a separate asset class. (See Tables 8-1 and 8-2.)

A look at the correlation of the MidCap 400 to the S&P 500 shows a very high association between the two. Despite the seemingly small

---

[4] The S&P 500 has become such a popular contract that it is the de facto standard for U.S. equity exposure. Due to the current acceptance of the contract, as indicated by its daily volume and open interest, it would be nearly impossible for another contract to take its place, no matter how well constructed the new index for that contract might be.

[5] The introduction of the S&P SmallCap 600 Index on October 17, 1994 will probably lead to the trading of an associated futures contract sometime in 1995. There is evidence that the MidCap 400 is being used as a small-cap proxy and the SmallCap 600 may cannibalize trading in the MidCap.

FIGURE 8-1.   S&P MidCap 400 Futures
Monthly volume and month-end open interest, February 1992 through September 1994

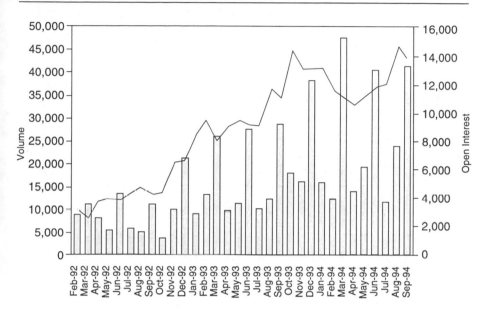

TABLE 8-1.   Correlation Matrix
Daily returns, 1987 through June 1994

	S&P 500	S&P 400 MidCap	DJIA
S&P 500	100.00		
S&P 400 MidCap	82.46	100.00	
DJIA	97.56	79.04	100.00

TABLE 8-2.   Correlation Matrix
Monthly returns, 1987 through June 1994

	S&P 500	S&P 400 MidCap	DJIA
S&P 500	100.00		
S&P 400 MidCap	93.00	100.00	
DJIA	97.00	90.00	100.00

advantage in a diversification sense, many investors are drawn to the middle-capitalization area because of the promise of added returns. Since the MidCap 400 and S&P 500 are not perfectly correlated assets, there is a slight diversification advantage to the combination of the two. If mid-caps can deliver excess returns as an asset class you can make an argument for their inclusion as a complement to the asset mix.

What Is a Mid-Cap Stock?

The answer to this question depends upon whom you ask. Medium-capitalization can mean many things to many people. Generally speaking, we're talking about stocks with a market capitalization of between $200 million and $5 billion. A look at the capitalization statistics from the three major mid-cap indices shows some agreement on the general-size range. (See Table 8-3.)

While there may not be agreement on the exact specifications of a middle-capitalization stock, most people agree that it includes companies that are smaller than the mega-companies in the Fortune 100 but not those that are so small that they suffer severe liquidity problems when buying any meaningful amount of stock. One good way to illustrate the characteristics of mid-cap stocks is to compare the Mid-Cap 400 Index to the most commonly used large-cap index, the S&P 500. Tables 8-4 and 8-5 show the differences between the two indices using various measures of size, risk, institutional following, and sector breakdown.

A look at this table shows us that there are some notable contrasts between the indices aside from the obvious size disparity. The economic-sector makeup has significant differences, with the mid-cap having a larger component of financials and utilities, both interest-sensitive areas. The large-cap index has a relative overweight in

TABLE 8-3.   Capitalization Structure

	High	Low	Weighted Average	Mean	Median
S&P 400 MidCap	$9.2 bil	$56 mil	$1.8 bil	$1.1 bil	$881 mil
Russell Midcap	$4.7 bil	$52 mil	$2.1 bil	$1.5 bil	$1.2 bil
Wilshire Mid Cap	$1.7 bil	$231 mil	$1.0 bil	$874 mil	$798 mil

TABLE 8-4.   Index Characteristics, September 30, 1994

	S&P 500	S&P 400 MidCap
Beta	1.00	1.01
Yield	2.78%	2.12%
% over the counter	3.00%	33.00%
Tracking error	0.00	5.43

Analyst Coverage

	Number of Analysts	
High	47	35
Low	1	1
Average	20	12
Median	19	11

*Risk Characteristics**

	Risk Exposure	
Size	0.35	−1.34
Variability in markets	−0.12	0.39
Success	−0.03	0.01
Trading activity	0.01	0.12
Growth	−0.10	0.23
P/E	0.03	−0.09
Price/book	−0.03	0.12
Earnings variation	−0.06	0.05
Financial leverage	0.03	−0.17
Foreign income	0.16	−0.50
Labor intensity	−0.02	0.01
Yield	0.08	−0.24

Source: BARRA.

TABLE 8-5.   Sector Breakdown

	S&P 500	S&P 400 MidCap
Basic industry	9.09	8.62
Capital goods—other	8.54	7.83
Capital goods—technology	6.92	10.59
Consumer durables	12.01	11.18
Consumer nondurables	16.49	6.59
Energy	9.91	5.19
Finance	11.78	16.65
Health	7.33	5.40
Services	2.94	9.61
Transport	1.63	2.43
Utilities	13.96	16.20

TABLE 8-6.   Performance Attribution
June 1991 through September 1994
Portfolio: MidCap 400 Index
Annualized contribution

Positive		Negative	
Size	2.28	Yield	−0.74
Variability in markets	0.85	Foreign	−0.35
Specific assets	0.79	Telephone	−0.35
Success	0.69	Financial leverage	−0.26
Banks	0.51	Nondrug health care	−0.26

energy and consumer nondurables. Another significant deviation is in the exposure of component companies to foreign income. The larger companies, such as IBM and Coca-Cola, obviously have more overseas exposure. This makes the mid-cap more of a domestic benchmark than the S&P 500. The return patterns of these indices will subsequently differ, sometimes significantly, for reasons other than size. Table 8-6 shows the results from an attribution of MidCap 400 returns between June 1991 and September 1994 relative to the S&P 500. This shows that while most of the excess return came from a size difference, there were also meaningful positive returns from success and variability in markets.[6] The foreign income and yield factors had a negative impact over this period.

Interestingly, the MidCap 400 currently is much more similar to the 500 than when it was first introduced. A measure of tracking error, or annual standard deviation to the 500, has become much smaller since the introduction of the MidCap 400 in 1991. Figure 8-2 shows a history of the tracking error of the MidCap 400 relative to the S&P 500 since its inception. This would indicate that at present, the MidCap 400 could be expected to have an annual return within 5.43% of the S&P 500 in two out of three years. This closer association could be caused by changes in the makeup of the indices, or from a greater acceptance by investors of the MidCap 400.

---

[6] BARRA uses a fundamental factor-allocation approach to attribute performance over past time-periods. The exposures to BARRA factors are in terms of standard deviation to the overall universe of U.S. domestic large-cap stocks as defined by BARRA.

FIGURE 8-2.   Tracking Error
MidCap 400 versus S&P 500

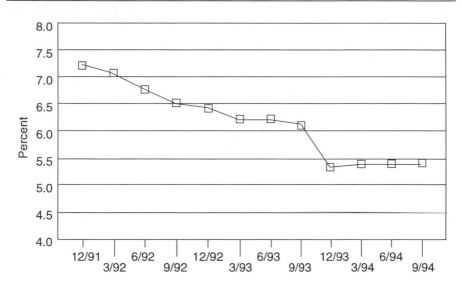

Why Buy Mid-Cap Stocks?

There is no lack of information on how hard it is for professional managers to beat the S&P 500. One of the basic beliefs of many investors is
that the potential to outperform is greater as one moves down the
capitalization spectrum. Small stocks have fewer holders and thus
merit less coverage from Wall Street. Therefore they should fall into a
category of less efficiently priced assets in the capital markets. Several
studies have backed up this premise, a noteworthy one being a paper
by Ho and Michaely published in the *Journal of Quantitative Analysis*
in 1988.[7] Their conclusion was that smaller stocks did indeed behave
differently from large stocks. They showed that the flow of information was incorporated into a smaller-stock price at a slower rate than
that of a well-followed large-cap stock. It makes sense that large companies, with their investor relations staffs and wide contacts on Wall

---

[7] Ho, T., and R. Michaely. "Information Quality and Market Efficiency." *Journal of
Financial and Quantitative Analysis*, March 1988, p. 53.

Street, would have an advantage in disseminating important information.[8]

At some point, this inefficiency is offset with the riskiness and lack of liquidity of smaller stocks. Some would say that if fewer analysts are following a company, the chances are greater of a negative surprise. With less attention paid to a stock, the greater the opportunity for the management to manipulate the earnings or price of a stock. It's not as though this has never occurred with a large company, but the increased attention to the operations of well-followed companies decreases the likelihood.

The idea that small stocks are neglected and thus better candidates for intensive fundamental analysis has been studied at great length. Many of the proponents of the neglected-stock effect have written extensively about the excess returns accruing to stocks that have been neglected by Wall Street and then are "discovered."[9] The problem with this strategy is that for many of the stocks it may take a long time before they are widely followed. In some cases they will never become Wall Street favorites, thus negating any potential discovery effect.

For most investors the lack of liquidity is a much greater concern. The bid-ask spreads on most small stocks make it very expensive for institutional managers to buy or sell stocks with a small number of shares outstanding. This increases their costs considerably and offsets the advantage of superior analysis in many cases.

Mid-Caps As an Alternative to Small Stocks

Mid-caps are attractive in that they have some of the positive attributes of smaller stocks without some of the negatives. Part of the argument for buying mid-caps is the fact that you are able to select stocks in a less-efficient area of the market without the downside of investing in really small companies. The mid-cap companies may be less followed than their larger peers, but these are, in most cases, well-known companies involved in nationally recognized businesses.

---

[8] The literature is full of deliberations on the efficient market hypothesis (EMH), so we will avoid an extended discussion of that controversial subject in this chapter. Alternative views on the EMH will necessarily have a meaningful impact on this argument.

[9] There have been numerous studies done regarding neglected stocks, most notably those by A. Arbel and S. Carvell.

Another key aspect of mid-caps is data availability. As the investment management business gets more and more sophisticated in the use of quantitative techniques, the need for accurate data becomes more critical. The advances in computer power and readily available databases have made it economically feasible for even small investors to utilize advanced quantitative techniques for stock selection. As a rule of thumb, the smaller the company, the more suspect the data that is supplied by the large data-vendors. The companies in the mid-cap area clearly have higher-quality data available when compared to smaller companies. While the data on mid-caps is far from perfect, it does meet the needs of quantitative managers who value data integrity.

The problem of inadequate liquidity does not go away in the mid-cap area. While most companies in the mid-cap area have sufficient liquidity, there are clearly some constraints for large institutional managers. In particular, many mutual funds have grown to a size that precludes them from buying a sizable portfolio-position in all but the largest companies. The consequence for large investors is obvious: mid-caps are better than small-caps but clearly not as good as large-caps when it comes to liquidity.

Table 8-7 summarizes the attributes of mid-caps versus small and large stocks.

The Small-Stock Effect

We surely cannot go any further without addressing the much-ballyhooed small-stock effect. Small-caps outperform large-caps. Everybody knows this. It is so well documented that it is often taken as a fact without debate. At a recent small-cap conference, just about

TABLE 8-7. Attributes of Different Markets

	Liquidity	Coverage	Efficiency	Result
Large-cap	Excellent	Abundant	Very efficient	Less return available in highly competitive S&P stocks
Midcap	Adequate	Sufficient	Less efficient	Potential to outperform in less efficient area
Small-cap	Poor	Sparse	Least efficient	Inadequate data, high risk, large bid-ask spreads

every speaker started his or her presentation with a slide showing the Ibbotson 1926–1993 return-data series showing small-cap outperformance. Several practitioners and academics have made a career of talking about the virtues of small-caps. What does this tell us when there is such universal agreement on something in the investment world? Does this make sense in terms of an efficient market and the principles of risk and return? Doesn't this look like too much of a layup to be true? A closer look at this phenomenon is clearly warranted.

Among the most commonly used reasons why small stocks will continue to outperform large stocks is the theory that small companies can grow faster than large companies. This certainly sounds plausible, as do the many other reasons that are readily put forth justifying the continuation of this phenomenon.

An Alternative View

There is another side to the story. One of the best arguments against the outperformance of small stocks is put forth by William Fouse in his widely discussed article "The Small Stocks Hoax" published in the *Financial Analysts Journal* in 1989. Fouse argues that the small-stock effect is an illusion and it is purely a result of measurement error.[10] He and others cite problems with such issues as migration, bid-ask spreads, equal weighting, and risk adjustment in the major articles supporting the small-stock effect.

There is no shortage of serious academic work addressing the size effect. Some very convincing arguments have been put forth by proponents on both sides. Suffice it to say that the debate will continue with no resolution in sight.

Capacity Issues

Regardless of your view on the small-stock effect, small stocks clearly have capacity issues. A large plan-sponsor is indeed going to encounter difficulties getting a meaningful position in small-cap stocks. Successful small-cap managers have shown that they have difficulty adding value at greater and greater levels of assets under management. This is one of the few areas of the market where the good

---

[10] Fouse, W. "The Small Stocks Hoax." *Financial Analysts Journal*, July/August 1989, p. 12.

players have to take themselves out of the game. The more successful they are at picking good stocks, the more assets they will attract and the more difficult it will become for them to continue to outperform. If they hope to meet the expectations of their existing clients, their best course of action is to refuse to add further assets.

However, if there is a positive excess-return to smaller companies you can probably still get that return in mid-caps and have fewer liquidity and trading constraints. On the other hand, if you don't believe in the small-cap effect, you can still get extended exposure to the marketplace and a slight diversification benefit.

The Mid-Cap Index Effect

Even if you aren't convinced that there is a small-cap effect or that the market is less efficient in smaller stocks, there may be another reason to buy mid-cap stocks—the mid-cap index effect.

Conservative estimates of passively managed mid-cap assets are in the $9 billion range. That only includes indexed assets that are paying a licensing fee to the Standard & Poor's company. There is probably at least another few billion unlicensed by S&P that use the mid-cap as a benchmark. Estimates of total indexed money go as high as $15 billion. This increase in passively managed mid-cap money may be responsible for several interesting anomalies. In large-cap stocks, an anomaly often referred to as the S&P 500 effect has been documented by such researchers as Lakonishok and Chan in the *Journal of Portfolio Management*.[11] Their research showed that during the 1980s, when a large amount of money flowed into passively managed equity funds, the stocks that were included in the S&P 500 enjoyed an excess return to their peers of 2.19% per year. The amount of money flowing into the S&P 500 names caused buyers to bid up the prices of any stocks included in the index. To this day we can still see the effect on stocks when it is announced that they will be added to a popular index. Microsoft was a good example of a stock that enjoyed a surge of passive buying when it was added to the S&P 500 in June of 1994.

The rapid flow from active to passive management has slowed over the past few years, but the existing passively managed funds still hold over $300 billion in assets. While the flow of institutional

---

[11] Chan, L., and J. Lakonishok. "Are the Reports of Beta's Death Premature?" *Journal of Portfolio Management*, Summer 1993, p. 51.

money to passive funds has slowed, index funds seem to be increasingly more accepted by individual investors. The allure of indexed funds makes sense not only to investors in 401(k) plans, but also those plan administrators responsible for overseeing them. A passive approach limits the liability of the company to the employee and keeps costs at a minimum. The future growth of passively managed large-cap funds is increasingly linked to the acceptance of index funds by small investors, especially 401(k) plans and mutual funds. The growth in assets in this sector of the market is undisputed.

Just as we saw an S&P 500 effect in the 1980s, we may experience a MidCap 400 effect in the 1990s. The total market-capitalization of the S&P 500 is $3.45 trillion, and the MidCap 400 is $465 billion. There is approximately $260 billion in passively managed money indexed to the S&P 500. The passively managed assets amount to approximately 7.7% of the total market-capitalization of the S&P 500. By comparison, only about 1.7% of the total market-capitalization of the MidCap 400 is currently indexed. If the passively managed assets invested in the MidCap 400 grow to an equal percentage as that of the S&P 500, that would mean an additional $28 billion of assets flowing into those 400 stocks. It is easy to see how a flow of this magnitude could boost the names in this index to higher levels than that of their peers. It will certainly take some time, maybe many years, but by the end of the 1990s there may well be studies showing that there existed a MidCap 400 effect that could have added excess returns to a portfolio of middle-capitalization stocks.

Aside from the effect of new money flowing into these index stocks, there will also likely be a "migration" effect among the mid-cap names. The mid-cap index has the unique aspect of having companies leave it not only from the bottom, as they become too small or go out of business altogether, but it will lose companies from the top as they become too large. The S&P 500 will never lose one of its main components such as a Wal-Mart or General Electric because it has grown too big. Excluding takeovers, which are rare among the mega-companies, it is unlikely that the makeup of the top companies of the S&P 500 will change. Contrast this to the situation in the MidCap 400. Since the index seeks to capture the returns of middle-capitalization stocks, it is necessary to eliminate companies as they grow too big and distort the index. It becomes awkward when the top companies in the mid-cap index dwarf the bottom names included in the S&P

500. This has a profound effect on the mid-cap index. The largest components of the index are being removed and replaced with much smaller names in most cases.

These larger companies are not removed just because they are too big, but instead because they are the prime candidates for inclusion in the S&P 500 Index. When they are moved to the 500 they usually enjoy the excess returns of the migration effect as passively managed S&P 500 funds are forced to buy them. This creates an interesting dilemma for the actively managed funds that use the Mid-Cap 400 as a benchmark. If managers do not hold the biggest names in the index, not only do they increase their tracking error, but they don't own the very names in the 400 that are likely to enjoy excess returns by inclusion in the 500.

Another aspect of changes in the MidCap 400 also holds true. Predicting which names will be included in the mid-cap index should yield excess returns just as it does in the S&P 500. While these returns will probably be of a lesser magnitude than the returns from those names going into the S&P 500, it nonetheless merits some attention. It will be interesting to see if the names at the top of the new S&P 600 SmallCap become the main candidates for inclusion in the MidCap 400.

A Look at the Mid-Cap Index

Why has S&P prevailed in acceptance of its index for mid-cap stocks? One of the main reasons is the independence of the Standard & Poor's company, but more likely is its association with the S&P 500. S&P has done a very good job of supporting the 500 and has built up credibility in the marketplace as a impartial provider of information. Keep in mind that the mid-cap was the first new index to be proposed by S&P since the 500 was introduced in 1957.

Introduction of this MidCap 400 Index was not taken lightly. It was in development for over five years. Despite the efforts put forth by S&P, there was a chorus of criticism of the index upon its introduction. In particular, the historical performance information provided by S&P was singled out for critique. Even S&P will admit that the performance history provided on mid-caps was very biased. When the index was first introduced, historical return data was provided using the companies that comprised the index in 1991. Unfortunately, fewer than 230 of the those 400 companies were publicly traded and included in the performance calculation for 1981. Obviously, to rely on returns based upon this type of analysis can be very misleading. Having learned their lesson with the MidCap, they were much more careful and did a much better job with the simulated returns of their newly introduced SmallCap 600 Index. For the 600, they used a stratified sampling technique to estimate what companies would have been included in the 600 over the past time-frame and came up with a reconstructed performance history as an approximate. If we reconstruct the MidCap 400 performance using a similar technique, the difference between the S&P 500 and MidCap 400 is less than 0.5% per year, as opposed to over 2% as reported by S&P.[12]

A series of other studies have documented the apparent outperformance of mid-cap stocks using various measures. The most notable of these studies is one by Mott and Eschert published in the Spring 1994 issue of the *Journal of Investing*.[13]

Changes in the Index

One way to look at the mid-cap index is at a given point in time. Another approach is to view it over a certain time span. There are many studies showing the breakdown of the index and comparisons to the Russell and Wilshire and Center for Research in Securities Prices (CRSP) data. Those studies are useful for comparison and they are readily available from numerous sources. Probably the best benchmark comparison is done by Prudential Securities and provides a very detailed look at the indices. Since that information is plentiful elsewhere, we will instead concentrate on looking at the MidCap 400 over different time periods since its inception, and gauge what effect that has had on investors.

Table 8-8 shows the additions and deletions to the 400 since its inception in 1991. There have been 50 changes in the index over the period of October 1991 to September 1994. The turnover of roughly 16

[12] Our numbers are generated using a technique first used by Matt Baker at Sanford Bernstein to analyze the performance of mid-cap stocks. This technique was likely the model for S&P's SmallCap 600 performance calculations.

[13] Mott, C., and M. Eschert. "Performance Numbers Make the Case for Mid-Caps." *Journal of Investing,* Spring 1994, p. 30.

TABLE 8-8. Additions and Deletions to the S&P MidCap 400 Index

Date	Added	Market Cap $ million	Deleted	Added to S&P 500	Market Cap $ million
Oct. 91	Cabot Corp.	$613	Novell	*	$7,409
Nov. 91	Diagnostek	$473	Great Lakes Chemical	*	$3,614
Dec. 91	Granite Construction	$281	Cetus Corp.		$626
Dec. 91	Arnold	$376	Fed. Home Loan Mtge.	*	$8,255
Jan. 92	Paychex	$494	Genetics Institute		$572
Feb. 92	Lancaster Colony	$522	Allergan	*	$1,801
Feb. 92	Giddings & Lewis	$524	Sanford Corp.		$674
Jun. 92	Fisher-Price	$580	Manufacturers National		$1,500
Jun. 92	CML Group	$788	MIPS Computer		$221
Jul. 92	Buffets	$443	Gidding & Lewis	*	$629
Jul. 92	Mark IV Industries	$527	U.S. Surgical	*	$5,396
Jul. 92	FIServ	$575	International Corona		$418
Aug. 92	Ruddick Corp.	$391	Sun Microsystems	*	$2,558
Sep. 92	Dollar General	$633	Critical Care America		$832
Sep. 92	Medical Care America	$1,964	Medical Care International		$1,122
Sep. 92	Phillips-Van Heusen	$628	Durr-Fillauer Medical		$393
Oct. 92	American Power Conversion	$873	INB Financial		$837
Oct. 92	Dibrell Brothers	$471	Interpublic Group	*	$2,553
Dec. 92	LDDS Communications	$1,317	Advanced Telecomm.		$717
Mar. 93	IBP	$849	Colonial Cos		$608
Apr. 93	Arrow Electronics	$949	Leslie Fay		$103
Jun. 93	El Paso Natural Gas	$1,447	Immunex		$716
Jun. 93	York International	$1,234	McCaw Cellular	*	$9,889
Sep. 93	Nextel Communications	$3,604	Wachovia	*	$6,773
Oct. 93	AES Corp.	$1,552	Affiliated Publications		$1,056
Oct. 93	Hannaford Bros.	$959	MNC Financial		$1,356
Oct. 93	Cabletron Systems	$2,613	Pioneer Hi-Bred	*	$2,974
Oct. 93	Fingerhut	$1,337	A&W Brands		$337
Oct. 93	P.H. Glatfelter	$727	Costco Wholesale		$2,140
Nov. 93	National Health Labs	$1,108	American Barrick	*	$7,697
Nov. 93	Perrigo Co.	$2,239	Medco Containment		$5,799
Nov. 93	Informix	$1,178	Burlington Resources	*	$6,022
Nov. 93	Staples Inc.	$890	Fisher-Price		$1,179
Dec. 93	Alumax	$948	Cisco Systems	*	$6,942
Jan. 94	EMC Corp.	$3,814	Merry-Go-Round		$181
Jan. 94	Parker & Parsley	$720	Baroid Corp.		$763
Feb. 94	Hunt Transport	$844	Keycorp	*	$3,819

TABLE 8-8 (continued).

Date	Added	Market Cap $ million	Deleted	Added to S&P 500	Market Cap $ million
Apr. 94	Hubbell	$1,871	U.S. Healthcare	*	$6,634
Jun. 94	Value Health	$1,723	United Healthcare	*	$7,576
Jul. 94	Coram Healthcare	$441	T2 Medical		$424
Jul. 94	Litton Industries	$1,697	Southwest Airlines	*	$3,729
Aug. 94	Tecumseh Products	$1,072	Liberty National Bancorp		$798
Aug. 94	Olsten	$1,491	Dreyfus		$1,809
Aug. 94	Callaway Golf	$1,176	Continental Bank		$1,935
Aug. 94	Ethyl	$1,347	Aldus		$412
Sep. 94	Rayonier	$843	Medical Care America		$1,082
Sep. 94	Superior Industries	$866	LAC Minerals		$1,734
Sep. 94	Albemarle Corp.	$983	Sigma-Aldrich	*	$1,806
Sep. 94	Lee Enterprises	$736	Neutrogena		$901
Sep. 94	Kohl's Corp.	$1,652	Micron Technology	*	$4,000

companies per year is close to that of the average for the S&P 500. However, while only 4% of the names have changed each year, approximately 10% of the market capitalization of the index has been removed annually. This compares to an annual rate of approximately 5% of market capitalization for the S&P 500. A closer examination of the changes yields some interesting insights. One thing that comes across clearly is the size difference between names added and deleted. The average market-capitalization for stocks deleted is $2.6 billion compared to $1.1 billion for stocks that were added. Another item worth noting is the economic-sector differences between added and deleted stocks.

Of the changes that involved companies of quite different size, the most pronounced are those involving companies moving out to join the S&P 500. Over the past three-year period, 20 companies have been deleted from the MidCap 400 and added to the S&P 500. The companies removed from the index had a total market-capitalization of over $100 billion. These stocks made up over 75% of the total market-capitalization that was removed from the index.

One interesting case is that of U.S. Surgical. In June 1992, it made up 1.4% of the MidCap 400 Index. The stock sold at $100 per share after a spectacular run over the previous few years. It was added to the S&P 500 on July 7, 1992 and had a market capitalization of $5.4 billion.

Shortly afterward its fortunes reversed and it fell to $25, had a market capitalization of $1.4 billion, and now was only 0.04% of the S&P 500. Here was a case where the increase in the stock price was represented in the MidCap 400 performance, but it was taken out before the slide back down. The net effect was that the MidCap 400 got the added boost from U.S. Surgical as it rose to over $100 per share and became a large part of the index. Yet the negative performance had little impact on the much larger S&P 500 Index where it was located when it skidded back down to $25. The final result is, in this case, a slightly exaggerated performance record for the MidCap 400.

This brings to mind the issue of when and how changes are made to the index. S&P has a special index-committee that makes these decisions based upon a variety of criteria. Companies that meet the selection criteria of the committee are voted on and added to a replacement pool. When a company in the index is removed a new name is selected from the pool based upon its appropriateness. In the S&P 500, companies are removed for four reasons—mergers, restructuring, financial operating failure, or lack of representation. Lack of representation involves companies where size has diminished to such a point that their inclusion doesn't contribute much to the price performance of the index. This usually has to persist for an extended period to be invoked as a reason for removal. As mentioned previously however, in the MidCap 400 there is an additional reason for removal: becoming too big. The S&P committee has decided that before a company will be removed, the increase in size must appear permanent.

One way to see which stocks don't belong in the index is a simple bar chart of companies ranked by capitalization and grouped in sectors. Figures 8-3, 8-4, and 8-5 reflect the MidCap 400 in October 1993. By mid-1994, the stocks that obviously stood out by capitalization were all gone from the MidCap 400 and added to the S&P 500. This included Southwest Airlines (LUV), American Barrick (ABX), and Burlington Resources (BR).

Along with the changes in the individual names in the index comes a transformation in its overall makeup. Economic sectors' differences over time can be quite pronounced. Quite often when a company leaves the index, it is not replaced by a stock from a similar industry or sector. For example, Wachovia Bank, a $6.1 billion market capitalization financial company that made up 1.2% of the index, was

FIGURE 8-3. Market Cap: Transportation

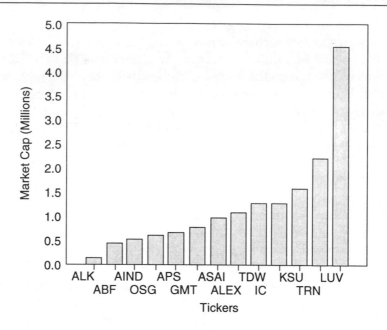

FIGURE 8-4. Market Cap: Basics

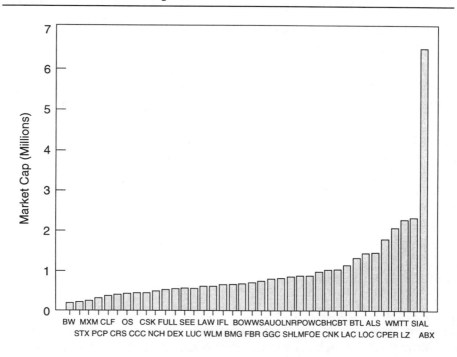

FIGURE 8-5.   Market Cap: Energy

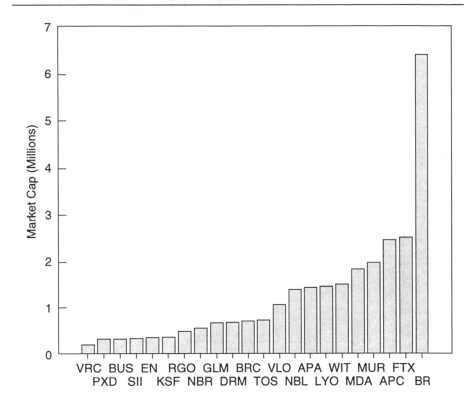

removed and replaced by Nextel, a communications company that became 0.61% of the index. In an even bigger change in the index, McCaw Cellular, a $9.9 billion company that composed 2.0% of the index, was replaced with York International, a $1.2 billion industrial products company that is only 0.26% of the index.

These changes show up in a look at the difference in sector allocation of the index over time. While much of the difference is due to price changes of the companies involved, a comparison of 1991 to 1994 in Table 8-9 also reflects changes in the makeup of the index. It is normal for the industry percentages to change over time as groups go in and out of favor and this is usually not a problem for managers because their portfolios should change by roughly the same magnitude. However, when a large component of the index is removed and replaced with a stock from another sector, a manager may suddenly

TABLE 8-9. S&P MidCap 400 Index—Sector Breakdown

	Dec. 31, 1991	Sep. 30, 1994
Basic industry	9.47%	8.62%
Capital goods—other	5.16%	7.83%
Capital goods—technology	5.74%	10.59%
Consumer durables	8.76%	11.18%
Consumer nondurables	7.87%	6.59%
Energy	5.21%	5.19%
Finance	19.11%	16.65%
Health	10.98%	5.40%
Services	9.65%	9.61%
Transportation	1.96%	2.43%
Utilities	16.09%	16.20%

be out of balance on a sector basis. Not paying attention to changes in the index can thus bring about an added level of risk for the active manager.

Adding Value to Mid-Cap Stocks

There are obviously as many ways to actively manage mid-cap stocks as there are to manage large-cap stocks. The idea that there is one best way to manage mid-caps doesn't make much sense, just as it doesn't make much sense to say there is only one surefire way to outperform the market. The marketplace is made up of countless people implementing diverse strategies and all attempting to add some value above and beyond a passive approach. History shows that much of this effort fails to achieve its desired result. This does not deter investors from trying however. As investors pursue their different strategies, they often respond differently to the same information. This makes for a marketplace where many strategies can be justified by rational decision makers. This holds true in the mid-cap area as well, where there are a lot of ways to do things that make sense. However, while there are many strategies that can be employed to outperform in the mid-cap area, they are not necessarily the identical strategies that are being practiced in large and small stocks. The process of constructing a strategy to apply to the mid-cap area should be care-

FIGURE 8-6.   Universe Selection

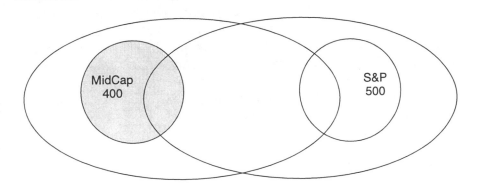

fully thought out with regard to the particular area of the market to which it is being applied. An investment strategy dedicated to the mid-cap area of the market should be tailored specifically to the middle-capitalization universe of stocks.

The Mid-Cap Universe

Figure 8-6 shows a graphical depiction of the stocks that fall into the mid-cap universe. This universe includes not only the companies in the MidCap 400, but also companies outside the index along with names that are included in the S&P 500. Identification of this universe is an important starting point when developing a mid-cap strategy. The universe of stocks will ideally have the same characteristics as the benchmark that is being used.

Value Added

There are many strategies to pick from. An investor can choose from growth or value; fundamental, quantitative, or technical; top down or bottom up; sector rotation or industry neutral. Or they can choose some combination or variation of these and other strategies. Whichever approach is taken, it is selected with the idea of being able to add some value to the investment process. One of the questions that investors must ask themselves is whether the value added is coming from some type of expertise or just the expectation that mid-caps will outperform as an asset class. Indeed, many investment professionals have focused on the idea of selling mid-cap stocks as an asset class to clients. The discussion has been focused on giving investors reasons to be in the mid-cap area of the market. Instead, the focus of this discussion should be on how to add value to an index of mid-cap stocks. In most cases, the job of deciding whether to include mid-cap stocks is an asset-allocation decision that should be handled by the plan sponsor or its consultant. If mid-cap stocks are chosen, the active manager then needs to show some ability in creating value above and beyond a low-fee index fund.

Return Factors

Over any universe of stocks, we can identify certain return generating factors. It is useful to recognize the contribution to return that can be attributed to these factors. Some examples of commonly used factors are low P/E, low price/book, and earnings growth. An analysis of factor returns over different capitalization-spectrums will tell us something about how factors behave within different areas of the market. A key question is whether these factors behave differently in midsized stocks versus large stocks.

To answer that question, an analysis was performed using two segments of the market, which we'll call large-cap and mid-cap. To generate these two segments, a universe of 900 buyable institutional stocks was split into four parts. The large-cap universe is composed of the top two quartiles and the mid-cap universe is made up of the middle two. A look at three basic factors can then be used to illustrate the difference between factor returns across these different capitalization spectrums.[14] Figure 8-7 shows the cumulative excess-returns from price/book over the period from 1980 to 1994. Figure 8-8 shows P/E and Figure 8-9 shows consensus earnings increases on a one-month basis. In each case it is clear that the factor behaves differently over different capitalization segments of the market. These differences obviously have implications for developing a strategy to add active return to a mid-cap index.

---

[14] The data shown in Figures 8-7, 8-8, and 8-9 are cumulative excess-returns to the individual factors based upon a one standard-deviation exposure to that factor. The coefficients are based upon a capitalization-weighted, sector-neutral regression using residual return as the dependent variable.

FIGURE 8-7. Universe Comparison Price/Book

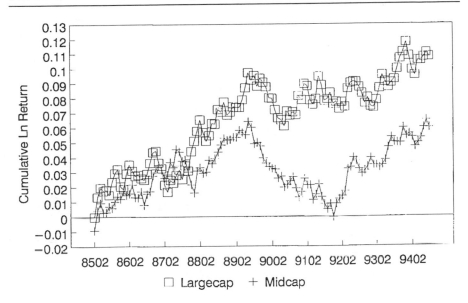

FIGURE 8-8. Universe Comparison Price/Earnings

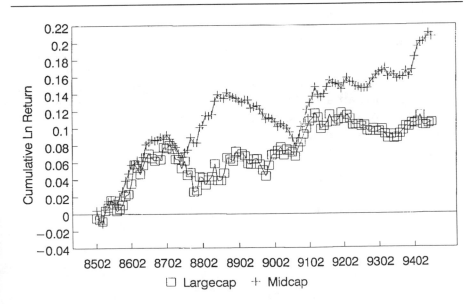

FIGURE 8-9. Universe Comparison Earnings Growth

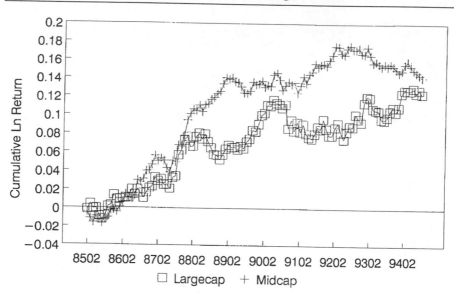

Summary

This chapter is meant to be an introductory review of middle-capitalization stocks as represented by the S&P 400 MidCap Index. By all indications, the MidCap 400 is on its way to becoming a permanent and meaningful part of the investment business. Through time, more and more institutional managers will find themselves using the MidCap 400 as a performance benchmark. Those managers who understand the nuances of the index will be best positioned to outperform it.

Exploring the Cycles of Small-Cap Style Performance

Claudia E. Mott, First Vice President
Director of Small-Cap Research
Prudential Securities Inc.

Kevin C. Condon, Associate Vice President
Prudential Securities, Inc.

Small-cap growth and value investors should be aware of the performance cycles that their chosen investment style's experience. Small-cap value can outperform small-cap growth, and vice versa, for multiyear periods depending on which investment style is in or out of favor with investors.

In this chapter we will examine these style cycles, small-cap value's long-term performance advantage over growth, and some of the reasons for this relative performance differential.

All references to style performance in this analysis are drawn from the total rates of return of the Prudential Securities Small-Cap Style Indices from December 31, 1975 to December 31, 1994. A brief summary of how these indices are constructed is noted in Appendix A to this chapter.

Investment Styles Can Fall In and Out of Favor

Each of the Prudential Securities' Small-Cap Style Indices have experienced extended periods of relative strength and weakness. Figure 9-1 details the growth of $1.00 invested in a portfolio which generated a monthly return equal to the spread between small-cap value's and small-cap growth's monthly total-return. In this relative-performance analysis, small-cap value is considered to be out of favor when the line is trending down and in favor when the line is rising. Clear and distinct style-cycles are depicted in this exhibit.

217

FIGURE 9-1. Small-Cap Growth and Value Outperform in Cycles
Cumulative relative growth of $1 invested (value relative to growth)

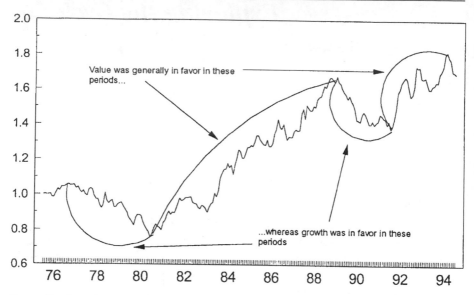

Source: Prudential Securities, Inc.

Small-cap growth stocks were generally in favor from 1976 to 1980. Small-cap growth investors enjoyed a 22.3% cumulative performance advantage versus small-cap value during this time frame. In 1981, the leadership torch was passed to small-cap value. Small-cap value stocks were largely in favor from 1981 to 1988, outperforming small-cap growth by 107.6% over this eight-year period.

In 1989, small-cap growth again began outperforming small-cap value. Growth would remain in favor through the end of 1991, outperforming value by 14.6% over the three years. Finally the pendulum swung back to value as small-cap value outperformed small-cap growth by 23.1% over the 1992 to 1994 time frame.

Style Cycles Can Be Volatile But Rewarding

Investors should note that "being in favor" does not mean a particular style will outperform in every month or quarter of the style cycle.

FIGURE 9-2. Cycles Can Last for Many Years
Rolling 12-month performance of value relative to growth

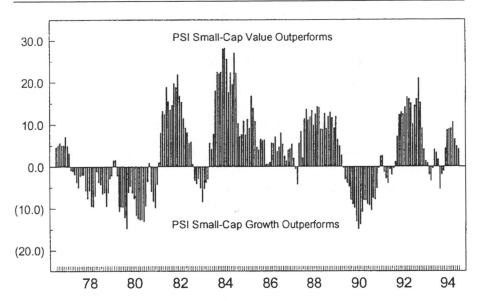

Source: Prudential Securities, Inc.

There are many intracycle corrections which can be quite lengthy and painful for the style manager on the wrong end of market sentiment. One-month relative returns between the small-cap styles exhibit only a small degree of first-order autocorrelation. This implies that the relative style-performance in a particular month contains little information with respect to forecasting which style will out perform in the following month. However, Figure 9-2 indicates that a particular style does tend to stay in favor for extended periods of time.

Overall, Small-Cap Value Outperforms Small-Cap Growth

The Prudential Securities Small-Cap Style Indices were developed in the summer of 1993. The indices' holdings, macroeconomic sector-weights, and total monthly returns were recreated historically starting in December 1975 and continue to be maintained today.

From inception through the end of 1994, small-cap value rose at an annualized rate of 19.9%, while small-cap growth experienced total returns of 16.6% per year.

Growth Stocks May Outperform When the Market Is Up . . .

The small-cap core index (growth and value are subsets of this core index) increased in 142 of the 228 months in our 19-year study or in 62.3% of the months. Small-cap growth stocks appreciated at an annualized rate of 85.1% while small-cap value increased by 69.2% per year during these months of positive small-cap returns.

. . . But They Give It Back and Then Some in a Down Market

Virtually all of small-cap value's relative-return advantage is gained in down markets. Small-cap value stocks experienced annualized declines of 32.1% while small-cap growth stocks declined at an annualized rate of 45.6% in down markets. Small-cap growth's relatively poor showing in down markets more than offset the performance advantage it tended to garner in up markets.

Small-Cap Value Investors Are Rewarded over the Long Term . . .

We started with the simplest of hypothesesas to why value outperforms growth: that the time period we studied was too short and that value was simply in favor for much of this time frame. In fact, value was in favor more often than growth over the life of our study. Using our broadly defined style-cycles, we see that value outperformed growth in 11 of the 19 years in our study.

However, we dismiss the notion that small-cap value's outperformance is simply a function of the time period we focused on in our study. We believe this for a couple of reasons. First, for simplicity's sake, we designated style cycles into calendar years even though these cycles obviously didn't begin and end at the stroke of midnight on New Year's Eve. Of the 228 months in our study, small-cap value only outperformed growth 115 times or 50.4% of the months in the study. So it's safe to say we didn't select a time period unfairly dominated by value. We also believe that the study was sufficiently long (19 years, or 228 months), and covered enough economic cycles (three recessions) to be valid.

... And Value Investing Is a Time-Tested Strategy

Second, the merits of value investing have been espoused for years starting with Graham and Dodd's 1934 publication, *Security Analysis*. A later study championing value investing covered a longer period of time than our study (1962 to 1990) but drew the same conclusions— that value stocks are a superior long-term investment.

Growth- and Value-Style Index Sector-Weights Differ ...

Could small-cap value's relative-performance advantage over growth be a function of different macroeconomic sector-weights? Sector bets, or the under- or overweighting of a sector relative to a core universe, is an inevitable by-product of style investing (Tables 9-1, 9-2, and 9-3). For example, small-cap value has a much heavier focus on financial services (22.8%) than does growth (8.6%), whereas the growth index places more emphasis on technology (21.8%) than the value index (7.2%).

The weight, or the proportion of each index that is comprised of a particular macroeconomic sector, can change over time (Table 9-4). To a certain degree, a sector's weight can be influenced by the sector's relative rate of return. But the relationship between relative return and sector weight is not as strong as one might think because of the tendency for really successful small-cap stocks to jump up into the mid-cap indices. Figure 9-3 details the sector weights and relative performance of two sectors in each of our small-cap style indices. It is clear that healthcare's weight in the growth index is partly a function

TABLE 9-1. Small-Cap Value Index Performance by Sector
1976 through 1994

Sector	Average Weight	Annualized Return	Standard Deviation	Reward/ Risk*	Attribution†
Basic industry	18.2%	18.8%	22.2%	0.8	19.9
Business services	4.0	18.7	22.2	0.8	4.2
Capital spending	5.1	17.6	23.4	0.8	5.5
Consumer cyclical	7.5	18.1	28.3	0.6	7.4
Consumer services	15.5	17.4	25.7	0.7	13.9
Consumer staples	4.2	21.3	20.1	1.1	4.6
Energy	5.3	12.6	22.9	0.6	3.6
Financial services	22.8	20.3	22.6	0.9	24.6
Health care	2.2	31.2	33.5	0.9	3.3
Technology	7.2	18.1	28.4	0.6	5.7
Utilities	8.1	17.2	12.9	1.3	7.3
PSI Small-Cap Value	100.0%	19.9%	20.7%	1.0	100.0

* Return per unit of risk (annualized return divided by annualized standard deviation of return).
† Percentage of the PSI Small-Cap Value Index's return attributed to each sector.
Source: Prudential Securities Inc.

TABLE 9-2. Small-Cap Growth Index Performance by Sector
1976 through 1994

Sector	Average Weight	Annualized Return	Standard Deviation	Reward/ Risk*	Attribution†
Basic industry	13.4%	15.3%	22.5%	0.7	14.6
Business services	6.8	17.2	24.0	0.7	7.4
Capital spending	6.8	10.9	25.0	0.4	5.7
Consumer cyclical	4.8	15.4	31.4	0.5	5.0
Consumer services	17.1	15.3	26.7	0.6	15.7
Consumer staples	3.2	17.6	22.4	0.8	3.5
Energy	5.7	10.3	29.5	0.3	5.4
Financial services	8.6	18.3	24.7	0.7	10.7
Health care	10.6	23.7	31.3	0.8	11.0
Technology	21.8	17.5	30.7	0.6	20.5
Utilities	1.1	7.7	36.6	0.2	0.5
PSI Small-Cap Growth	100.0%	16.6%	24.9%	0.7	100.0

* Return per unit of risk (annualized return divided by annualized standard deviation of return).
† Percentage of the PSI Small-Cap Growth Index's return attributed to each sector.
Source: Prudential Securities Inc.

TABLE 9-3. **Value Has Outperformed Growth in Each Macroeconomic Sector**

Sector	Average Weight	Annualized Return	Relative Standard Deviation	Reward/ Risk*	Attribution†
Basic industry	4.8	3.0	−0.3	N/A	5.3
Business services	−2.7	1.3	−1.8	N/A	−3.2
Capital spending	−1.7	6.1	−1.6	N/A	−0.2
Consumer cyclical	2.6	2.3	−3.1	N/A	2.4
Consumer services	−1.7	1.8	−1.0	N/A	−1.8
Consumer staples	1.0	3.1	−2.3	N/A	1.0
Energy	−0.4	2.1	−6.7	N/A	−1.8
Financial services	14.2	1.7	−2.1	N/A	13.9
Health care	−8.4	6.1	2.2	N/A	−7.7
Technology	−14.6	0.5	−2.3	N/A	−14.8
Utilities	7.0	8.9	−23.7	N/A	6.8
Value relative to growth	0.0	2.8	−4.3	N/A	0.0

† Percentage of the PSI Small-Cap Value Index's return attributed to each sector relative to * Return per unit of risk (annualized return divided by annualized standard deviation of return).
growth.
Source: Prudential Securities Inc.

of the group's positive relative return. This relationship is less apparent in value's financial services group.

We do not believe, however, that the success of small-cap value's sector bets, relative to small-cap growth's sector bets, is the primary reason for value's long-term outperformance but rather a smaller secondary reason for value's higher long-term total returns.

. . . But Sector Bets Don't Fully Explain Relative Style-Performance

We drew this conclusion by quantifying through regression analysis what proportion of value's relative-performance advantage can be explained by value and growth's different sector weights and different sector returns (Appendix B). The regression output in Table 9-5 indicates that 84% of the variation in value's quarterly relative-return

TABLE 9-4.   Style Index Sector-Weights Have Changed Dramatically over Time

	PSI Small-Cap Value Index Historical Sector-Weights			PSI Small-Cap Growth Index Historical Sector-Weights		
	Maximum	Average	Minimum	Maximum	Average	Minimum
Basic industry	24.3%	18.2%	11.1%	26.9%	13.4%	5.2%
Business services	5.8	4.0	2.5	10.1	6.8	3.4
Capital spending	8.6	5.1	2.6	11.5	6.8	3.0
Consumer cyclical	12.0	7.5	3.4	8.8	4.8	1.5
Consumer services	23.3	15.5	10.7	23.9	17.1	11.0
Consumer staples	6.9	4.2	1.6	6.6	3.2	0.8
Energy	9.7	5.3	2.0	15.4	5.7	1.3
Financial services	29.4	22.8	17.1	19.0	8.6	2.9
Health care	6.3	2.2	0.4	26.3	10.6	2.4
Technology	15.1	7.2	1.1	37.9	21.8	6.4
Utilities	15.0	8.1	2.6	2.5	1.1	0.4

Source: Prudential Securities Inc. (PSI).

advantage can be explained by differences in the style's sector weights and sector returns. Based on the value of the independent variable's beta coefficients and the relatively low correlation between these two factors, we estimate that relative returns have approximately twice the explanatory power of relative sector-weights.

Over the past 19 years, each and every value sector has outperformed its growth counterpart (Figure 9-4 and Table 9-3). So we are not surprised that sector weights play a smaller role in value's outperformance than sector returns. Over shorter periods of time however, we believe that sector weights play a more important role in relative performance. Value sectors are not universally successful over shorter periods of time. Figure 9-5 details sector performance of value rela-

FIGURE 9-3.   Sector Weights Are Influenced by Relative Performance

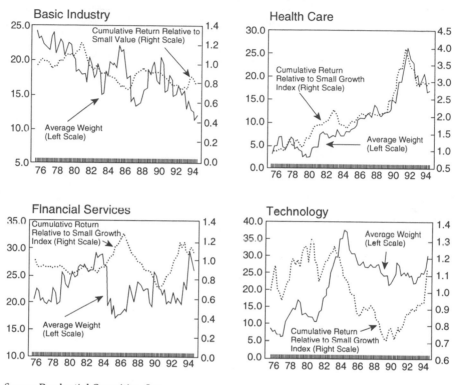

Source: Prudential Securities, Inc.

tive to growth during growth and value cycles. Some growth sectors did outperform value when growth was in favor, most notably, the heavily weighted technology sector.

Factor Exposure Is Responsible for Most of Value's Performance Advantage

So if returns, not sector weights, are responsible for much of value's success, then what is driving returns? We strongly believe that the majority of the performance differential between growth and value

TABLE 9-5. Value's Performance Advantage Is in Part a Function of Relative Sector Weights and Relative Sector Returns

Coefficient of determination—R-square	0.840
Adjusted R-square	0.836
F-statistic	192.761

Independent Variables	Beta Coefficient	t-Statistic
Variable X1: Relative performance due to sector return differential	1.07	15.50
Variable X2: Relative performance due to sector weight differential	0.61	5.95
Constant:	0.42	

Dependent Variable

Variable Y: Value's quarterly performance relative to growth

Correlation Matrix

	X1	X2	Y
X1	1	0.35	0.87
X2		1	0.56
Y			1

Source: Prudential Securities Inc.

can be explained by factor exposure. Factor exposure refers to a stock's, or in this case a portfolio's, characteristics, such as its P/E ratio, financial leverage, market capitalization, and responsiveness to macroeconomic events, like unanticipated changes in inflation or the price of oil.

Growth stocks are expected to grow their earnings at greater-than-average growth-rates. Very often, these glamorous-growth stocks experience spectacular earnings per share growth and many securities analysts extrapolate this strong historical growth well into the future. Investors often reward companies with these high growth-expectations by bidding up the price of those stocks giving them high valuation-multiples (P/E, price/book). Companies have an incentive to encourage a higher rather than a lower valuation-multiple because a high multiple reduces a company's cost of equity capital thereby improving its competitive position.

FIGURE 9-4.   Small-Cap Value Outperformed Growth in Each Macroeconomic Sector

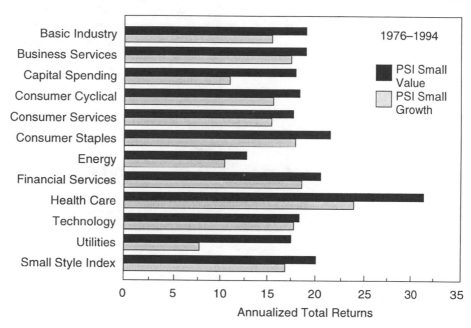

Source: Prudential Securities, Inc.

At year-end 1994, the Prudential Securities Small-Cap Growth Index carried a P/E ratio, based on next year's estimated earnings, of 17.1, versus small growth's P/E multiple of 11.2.

The Market Has Little Patience for Small-Cap Growth Stocks That Disappoint

Unfortunately for growth-stock investors, their lofty expectations for earnings growth are all too often overly optimistic. When an expensive stock with a high valuation-multiple announces lower-than-expected earnings, the market unmercifully pummels these once-high-flying glamour stocks into submission.

It is our belief that the small-cap growth index's high exposure to these expensive, high multiple and ultimately disappointing stocks

FIGURE 9-5. When Growth Is in Favor, Value Sectors Often Lag
Relative performance of value versus growth

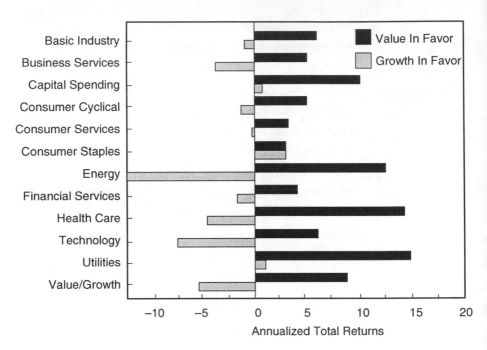

Source: Prudential Securities, Inc.

is the primary reason that, over the long term, small-cap value out-performed small-cap growth.

Style Cycles May Be Tied to the Economic Cycle

One of the most cognizant and intuitive explanations for style cycles is related to the ebbs and flows of the economy. This explanation argues that when the stock market begins to anticipate a slowdown in the economic cycle, the market will begin to favor growth stocks. The reason being, that growth stocks are generally less cyclical than value stocks so these growth stocks should be able to maintain reasonable earnings-growth despite the economic downturn. The market rewards this earning growth "stamina" by bidding up the price of growth stocks.

The value cycle is said to begin when the market starts to anticipate an upturn in the economy. Value stocks are more cyclical than growth and may experience higher earnings-growth rates during an economic boom than their growth counterparts.

Unfortunately, this strategy of forecasting style-cycles by forecasting economic activity works better in theory than in reality. Part of the reason for this is that shifts in the economy are notoriously difficult to predict. Stock markets and economists alike often fail to predict economic downturns or upswings. And even if one could correctly time a shift in the economy, style-cycle shifts do not lead or lag the economic shift by a consistent amount of time, and that makes it difficult to decide when to alter your investment style.

Growth Stocks Are Not Obsolete

Long-term investors will be better off allocating a larger proportion of their asset to small-cap value stocks than to small-cap growth stocks. Growth stocks, however, remain a necessary investment vehicle due to the cyclical nature of the style cycles and of the importance of diversification.

Appendix A: Prudential Securities Small-Cap Style Indices

The Prudential Securities Small-Cap Style Indices are subsets of a universe of securities that comprise the 20th through 45th percentiles of stocks based on market capitalization of all the stocks followed by Compustat. We also eliminated ADRs, REITs, and limited partnerships.

The Value Indices

This group comprises stocks with low normalized P/E multiples and high sustainable dividend yields. These are defined below.

- If a stock's normalized P/E ratio is in the bottom 40th percentile of the small-cap universe then it is included in the value index. Earnings are normalized by taking the average of a stock's forecast earnings per share and trailing peak earnings per share over a maximum of the past five years. The normalization process allows us to consistently categorize deep-cyclical stocks as value stocks.
- If a stock pays a dividend, its sustainable dividend yield must be high enough to place it in the top 40th percentile of the large-cap universe in order for it to be included in the value index. We consider a dividend to be sustainable if the aggregate trailing four quarters of dividends did not exceed the trailing four quarters of next income at any time in the past three years. We use the large-cap universe to determine the relative strength of the dividend because of the large number of companies in the small-cap universe that do not pay a dividend.

The Growth Indices

Growth, not valuation, is the issue for the growth-stocks criteria. Our growth indices seek companies with traditional growth characteristics. Our indices include stocks that are expected to grow earnings faster than the market average, have a history of strong sales growth, possess very little debt, and retain virtually all of their earnings to fuel growth. In general, to be included in our growth index, a stock must possess at least three of the four following characteristics.

- The IBES long-term earnings-growth estimate must be greater than the universe average. If the stock is not covered by the street, we substitute trend-line growth for the IBES estimate.
- Last three-year top-line growth rate greater than 10%
- Debt less than 35% of market capitalization
- Dividend-payout ratio less than 20%

Appendix B: Methodology

The following is a description of the methodology used to create the two independent variables for the regression analysis included in this study. Our goal is to measure how much of value's performance-differential versus growth's is driven by the first independent variable (X1), the relative performance due to sector-return differentials, and the second independent variable (X2), the relative performance due to sector-weight differential.

The quarterly total-return of the value index (V) can be calculated by multiplying each value sector's return (V-return) by the beginning of the period sector-weight (V-weight) and then summing these products for each sector. The growth index's quarterly return (G) is the sum of the product of its sector returns (G-return) and sector weights (G-weight). This common practice is often employed by investors performing attribution analysis.

In order to more clearly explain this next step, we will imply that each index has only one sector, but the following transpositions were actually employed across all 11 macroeconomic sectors.

As we noted earlier:

V = V-return × V-weight

G = G-return × G-weight

$X1$ = (V-return × V-weight) − (G-return × V-weight)

Variable X1 is a function of the return differential between value and growth because each of the returns (V-return and G-return) were multiplied by the value's weight (V-weight); that is, the only difference between the left and right side of the equation is the returns.

$X2$ = (V-return × V-weight) − (V-return × G-weight)

The variable X2 is a function of the sector-weight differential between value and growth because each of the weights (V-weight and G-weight) were multiplied by the value's return (V-return).

Independent variables X1 and X2 were calculated for each quarter in our study and regressed against relative style-performance (V less G). The regression output was shown in Table 9-5. The detailed analysis in Table 9-6 shows the exact steps taken to create our independent variable for the third quarter of 1994.

TABLE 9-6. An Example of How the Independent Variables Were Created

Sector	Small-Cap Style Sectors				Value Return Attribution	Value-Weighted Growth Return	Growth-Weighted Value Return
	Value Weight	Value Return	Growth Weight	Growth Return	V-weight × V-return	V-weight × G-return	G-weight × V-return
Basic industry	12.6	3.5	6.5	6.3	0.4	0.8	0.2
Business services	2.5	7.8	4.4	11.3	0.2	0.3	0.3
Capital spending	4.4	12.0	3.4	6.8	0.5	0.3	0.4
Consumer cyclical	4.9	6.0	2.3	2.9	0.3	0.1	0.1
Consumer services	18.0	5.5	17.7	5.1	1.0	0.9	1.0
Consumer staples	3.6	8.9	1.8	5.8	0.3	0.2	0.2
Energy	5.2	6.4	5.9	-2.7	0.3	-0.1	0.4
Financial services	29.4	7.7	11.0	7.3	2.3	2.2	0.9
Health care	5.6	26.9	19.8	13.3	1.5	0.7	5.3
Technology	9.6	19.0	25.0	21.6	1.8	2.1	4.7
Utilities	4.2	4.6	2.2	11.8	0.2	0.5	0.1
Sum					8.9	8.0	13.6

X1 = a function of the style return differential
associated with relative returns.   = (8.9 − 8) = 0.9

X2 = a function of the style return differential
associated with relative weights.   = (8.9 − 13.6) = −4.7

The Presence of Value in Small-Cap Equities

Satya Dev Pradhuman, Vice President
Merrill Lynch & Co.

Suzanne M. Crosby, Ph.D., Analyst
Standard & Poor's

Investment managers have long recognized the size segmentation within the equity market. More recently, equities have become delineated by style, i.e., growth and value. If we were to examine the feasible region of investments, the size and style factor would lead to a style-by-size matrix, as shown below.

	Growth	Value
Large-cap		
Small-cap		?

This grid implies that four distinct size and style relationships exist—large-cap growth, large-cap value, small-cap growth, and small-cap value. While large-cap growth and value are commonly accepted style vehicles, it is less clear whether these style distinctions exist among smaller stocks.

The growing interest in style management is evidenced by the recent explosion in the number of style oriented mutual funds. For example, according to Morningstar, the mutual-fund databank, at year-end 1994, there were approximately 726 funds classified as growth and an additional 256 funds specializing in small-capitalization stocks. This compares with 285 growth and 92 small-cap funds only five years ago.

Growth and value styles have been defined in large-cap equities using a variety of valuation measures. The most common of these are P/E, price/book, price/cash flow, and price/sales ratios. In seminal papers, Sharpe[1] and Fama and French[2] discovered that the price/book ratio, together with market capitalization, explains the variability in average stock-returns over time. As a result, the price/book ratio is commonly used to define growth and value in stocks.

Our findings suggest that small-cap value not only exists as a theoretical entity, but also exists as a practical investment vehicle. Furthermore, a close look at several common fundamental and financial factors points out that small-cap value and large-cap value profiles have much in common. The comparison of small-cap value to large-cap value indicates that the value theme may be more extreme within smaller-tier firms. A few of the key supporting factors are neglect, leverage, and the large number of small companies that trade in the secondary markets. Our results support a finding by Fisher that style segmentation may be more extreme among smaller stocks.[3] Because our work suggests that value traits may be more extreme among small stocks, it follows that the small-cap growth and value tradeoff may be similarly more dramatic. We tested for the value-based relationship in two ways: first, by using a quantitative break of small-cap value verses large-cap value, and second, by looking at active managers and their portfolio holdings.

[1] Sharpe, William F. "Asset Allocation: Management Style and Performance Measurement." *The Journal of Portfolio Management*, Winter 1990, pp. 7–19.

[2] Fama, Eugene F., and Kenneth R. French. "The Cross-Section of Expected Stock Returns." *The Journal of Finance*, June 1992, pp. 427–465.

[3] Fisher, Kenneth L., and Joseph L. Toms. "Value and Growth Cycles in Small Cap Investing." *Small Cap Stocks*, eds. Robert A. Klein and Jess Lederman, 1993, Probus Publishing, pp. 345–378.

Methodology

We used a sampling of stocks and actual market participants, mutual funds, to determine the relationship between value and size. We selected eight small-cap value and eight large-cap value mutual funds to determine the value characteristics of small stocks, and to gain insights into the distinction from large stocks. Initially, we compared the valuation characteristics of the composite of small-cap value portfolios to an average small-cap benchmark. Because we wanted to normalize for some of the size differences, we examined the relative relationships. For example, small-cap price/book ratios tend to be at a discount to large-cap ratios. Therefore, by removing the bias relative to a small-cap benchmark, we are better able to make small-style versus large-style comparisons.

In order to determine the appropriate factors in which to gauge the small-cap groups, we focused on four ratios commonly used to identify a value approach: P/E, price/book, price/sales, and price/cash flow.

While a number of approaches could be used to formulate a value proxy, we chose a simple and more tangible method. Instead of defining theoretical portfolios, we chose a sample of actual existing portfolios supplied by the Morningstar database. Our resulting sample of value-style mutual funds is derived in part by their description and in part by the categorization used by Morningstar. In addition to being described as value, the funds had to be well known, actively managed, and dedicated to U.S. equities.

Consideration was also given to the age of the fund. To qualify, funds had to have at least 10 years of trading history. Given that all managers can sometimes find opportunities outside their stated goals, we looked to funds that had some history to confirm that a value orientation exists. Furthermore, newer funds may experience changes in management, marketing, or investment style, which can drastically alter the investment characteristics of a fund. While such factors can also potentially affect longstanding funds, they are less likely to face such challenges.

The fundamental and financial factors we focused on are P/E, price/cash flow, price/sales, price/book, dividend yield, and leverage on the industrial segments (debt to total capitalization and short-term debt to total capitalization). A few of the factors that relate to forecast information are projected five-year earnings growth and analyst coverage, used as a proxy for information flow.

Once the funds were selected, we gathered the issues and their respective weights into a single small-cap value composite portfolio. The holdings are share-weighted, such that the securities with larger dollar exposures within the fund get a similarly large weighting. The portfolio holding of each of the funds and the financial statements used are based as of June 30, 1994. All pricing data are as of September 30, 1994. Although a more rigorous approach would look at holdings over time, a snapshot, as shown here, may present some insight into the changing nature of value investing.

Value in Small-Cap Stocks

Table 10-1 presents the summary statistics of the small-cap value funds compared to the Merrill Lynch Small Cap composite. The comparative P/E, price/cash flow, price/sales, and price/book ratios suggest that the small-cap value portfolio is more conservatively priced. The composite P/E ratio is 19.8 versus the average small-stock

TABLE 10-1. Small-Cap Value Is Considerably Cheaper than the Average Small Stock

	Small-Cap Value Portfolio	MLQA Small Stocks	Prem/Discount to Benchmark
Valuation			
P/E	19.8	55.2	−64%
Price/cash flow	8.67×	12.78×	−32%
Price/sales	0.55×	0.74×	−27%
Price/book	1.64×	1.90×	−13%
Yield	1.6%	1.4%	14%
Leverage			
Long-term debt/total capital	26.5%	43.1%	−38%
Short-term debt/total capital	5.0%	5.2%	−4%
Expectational			
Projected five-year EPS growth	13.7%	17.9%	−23%
Average number of analysts	5	4	31%

level of 55.2. Though the overall composite suggests a fairly high multiple, we believe that some of this is due not only to faster growing companies in the small-stock segment, but also to lower quality companies that have depressed earnings. After all, a higher multiple may be due to deserving companies, or to companies that are "beaten down" and barely turning a profit.

Because of the scarcity of earnings within the small-cap arena, small-stock analysis is often based on fundamental data other than reported earnings. Comparisons become even more valid when more of the universe of stocks have valid data. Other factors such as price/cash flow, and even those further up the income statement such as price/sales, permit valuation comparisons.

The price/cash flow level of the small-cap value portfolio also suggests that the composite is decidedly value compared to the universe. The price/cash relationship is approximately discounted 32% to the small-cap universe. The price/sales relationship is similarly conservative in that the small-cap value portfolio appears to sell at a 27% discount to the average small stock.

Due to the changes in accounting in recent years, the meaning of book value has come into question. While objections to using price/book remain at a fundamental level, some research has pointed out the usefulness of this ratio in security selection. The price/book ratio of the value composite is at a 13% discount to the average small stock, again suggesting a value tilt.

Income or dividend yield can also be a signal to the overall value bias of a stock or portfolio. One method of enticing investors without a higher promised growth rate is to offer some form of income. This factor also supports the value tilt of the composite. The small-cap value portfolio offers a 1.6% dividend yield compared to the 1.4% composite yield, suggesting that the value composite offers a 14% premium in income.

In addition to conservative valuation, value investing leads to a pool of stocks with lower earnings-expectations. Generally, a higher multiple or a lower dividend-yield implies that the future earnings outlook is superior to a security with a typically lower earnings-multiple and a higher dividend-yield. In other words, earnings expectations of value stocks should be inferior to an average set of stocks. Our results appear to reflect this position. The level of projected five-year earnings growth is approximately 13.7% versus a 17.9% average for the small-stock universe. This is approximately a 23% discount in expected growth.

Bear in mind that the average sample of small stocks is based on companies with at least three analyst estimates. Our work suggests that while 100% of the large-company universe has some level of analyst coverage, only 70% has similar coverage at the small-company level. This implies that the 18% expected five-year earnings growth-rate is based on those with coverage. The remaining 30% of the universe is unaccounted for.[4]

The leverage of the industrial segment of the small-cap value group appears to be below that of the typical small stock. The small-cap value portfolio has an average debt-to-capital ratio of 27% compared to an average of 43% for the small-cap aggregate. If smaller-value issues tend to be more "beaten down," and we suspect they are, financing for such companies is less likely to be available. While smaller companies, in general, tend to be at a disadvantage when it comes to financing, the small-cap value stocks may be a more extreme example of this situation. They have little or no access to the commercial-paper market and issuing a bond is similarly unrealistic. The only alternative is through the traditional financing arrangement, usually bank borrowing. If a company falls on tough times, a bank is unlikely to come to its rescue. To some extent, equity financing has been its only source of sizable financing.

If the source of new financing is questionable, the prospects for the company may indeed be limited. This further causes the firm to remain a low-expectation candidate. Because smaller stocks have fewer sources of financing, a small-cap value firm is more likely to remain a value candidate longer than its large-capitalization counterpart.

This result, however, differs from that found in a Standard & Poor's internal study, where value stocks in the S&P SmallCap 600 Index carry a debt-to-capital ratio of approximately 25%, substantially more than the 17.4% carried by the average stock in the SmallCap 600.[5]

Our results indicate that from a sample of small-cap funds, a value orientation does appear to exist. The data suggest that man-

---

[4] Pradhuman, Satya, and Richard Bernstein. "The Small-Cap Perspective." January 1994, Merrill Lynch research publication.

[5] Crosby, Suzanne M. "Value in the S&P SmallCap 600 Index." Standard & Poor's Index Products and Services Working Paper, January 1995.

agers who claim to buy more lower-expectation, conservatively priced securities do appear to be doing exactly that. All the factors we compared appear to support the value bias among the mutual funds selected. To formalize the segmentation of growth and value along a size comparison, a further test not undertaken here would be to compare and contrast the similar characteristics of the small-cap value pool to a set of mutual funds that claim to be small emerging growth.

Value in Large-Cap Stocks

The following discussion takes a detailed look at large-cap versus small-cap value investing. Is the small-cap value portfolio previously discussed any different from a large-cap value portfolio? To address this question, we developed a framework for the large-cap segment similar to the small-cap value portfolio. Using the same requirements as the pool of small-cap mutual funds, we selected eight large-capitalization funds with a value bias.

The results in Table 10-2 suggest that the large-cap value portfolio is cheaper than the large-cap benchmark. The portfolio has smaller P/E, price/cash flow, price/sales, and price/book ratio. Furthermore, the large-cap value group also offers a dividend yield above that of

TABLE 10-2. Large-Cap Value Also Appears Conservatively Priced

	Large-Cap Value Portfolio	MLQA Small Stocks	Prem/Discount to Benchmark
Valuation			
P/E	17.3	17.4	0%
Price/cash flow	8.06×	8.60×	–6%
Price/sales	0.85%	0.99%	–15%
Price/book	2.05%	2.49%	–17%
Yield	3.3%	2.9%	14%
Leverage			
Long-term debt/total capital	42.2%	53.7%	–22%
Short-term debt/total capital	10.6%	15.1%	–30%
Expectational			
Projected five-year EPS growth	10.7%	11.9%	–10%
Average number of analysts	17	22	–21%

the large-cap benchmark. Expectation factors, such as projected earnings growth, also offer confirming evidence of a decided value tilt.

While the P/E ratio of the large-cap value group appears in line with the average large-cap stock, the remainder of the descriptive factors appear to support the value bias of the large-cap proxy. The P/E ratio of the large-cap value portfolio is nearly identical to the average large stock. The price/cash flow is at a 6% discount to the overall universe. The price/sales ratio is at a 15% discount, and the price/book is at a 17% discount. Furthermore, the value composite offers a 14% premium in dividend yield.

Economic-Sector Exposures of Large-Cap and Small-Cap Value Stocks

While the sector exposures of value and growth can be distinct, so can those of large-cap and small-cap value. Figure 10-1 shows the sector exposure of the small-cap value group compared to the small-cap benchmark. The results suggest that the average small-cap value investor holds a significant consumer-cyclical overweight, almost 10% compared to the benchmark. The small-cap value sector-holdings also point to a significant overweight among the capital-goods issues. The value-style portfolio also appears to hold a larger share of basic industrial stocks, while the significant overweight in consumer-cyclical issues may partly reflect the particular cyclical bias among small-cap managers.

The value-biased portfolio is noticeably underweight in technology stocks. This falls in line with popular reasoning that value investors are less likely to hold high-expectation stocks such as technology-related issues. It is also underweight in financial and utility issues. Because of the sheer bulk of small financial-stocks that make up the small stock universe, it may not be too surprising that the active-value portfolio is underweight in financial stocks. After all, if managers were to hold a sector-neutral exposure in financials, they would be holding an excess of 20% in financial stocks. The absolute level of financial-sector exposure still remains high at 17.1%. While the traditional value-style theme tends to look more towards income or dividend yield as a part of total return, the utility underweight may represent a bias of active managers steering away from the utility issues.

FIGURE 10-1.   Small Value Appears Underweight, Not Overweight, in the Financial Sector
Economic-sector comparisons, small versus small value

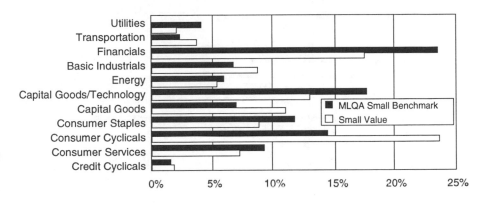

Figure 10-2 shows the style comparison for large stocks. The data suggest that large-cap value managers hold a significant overweight in the financial sector. The active large-cap value portfolio holds an excess of 23% in the financial sector compared to the benchmark holding of 14%, creating a 10% overweight. The large-cap value group also has an overweight in energy stocks. This may be related to the above-average dividend yield that typically accompanies energy stocks. The large-cap value segment also has some distinct underweights. The group is underweight in consumer cyclicals, consumer staples, capital goods, and utility stocks. The consumer-cyclical underweight appears to stem from a below-average holding in autos and retail issues. The underweight in utilities again may simply be part of the tendency of active managers.

Small-Cap versus Large-Cap Value: A Comparison

While a number of the sector exposures appear to be similar for the value-style portfolios, there are a few sectors that are significantly different. Figure 10-3 presents the benchmark-adjusted sector exposures

FIGURE 10-2.   Large Value Appears Overweight in the Financial and Energy Sectors
Economic-sector comparisons, large versus large value

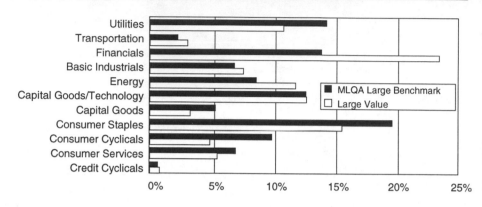

of the large-cap and small-cap value portfolios. Except in the financial, consumer-cyclical, technology, energy, and capital-goods groups, the remaining sector-exposures are fairly similar. That is, the respective under- and overweights among large-cap value and small-cap value tend to be similar.

The more surprising of the sector differences relate to the financial and consumer-cyclical holdings. While the small-cap value portfolio holds approximately a 6% underweight in the financial sector, the large-cap value portfolio has an overweight of almost 10%. Small stocks, as a composite, constitute a significant percentage of financial stocks or, more specifically, regional banks. This difference may represent a positive view of money centers among large-cap managers and conversely, a weak outlook of regional banks among small-cap managers. The data further suggest that managers of smaller stocks currently hold a significant proportion of their assets in the consumer-cyclical sector. While this segment has fared well during the 1994 economic rebound, the large holdings of consumer-cyclical shares indicate a belief that the economic environment will remain favorable.

The data also suggest that smaller-capitalization managers seem to hold a lower-than-average technology weighting. This may be indica-

FIGURE 10-3.   Small Value Appears to Be Significantly Different from Large Value with Respect to the Financial and Consumer-Cyclical Sectors
Economic-sector comparisons, large versus small value

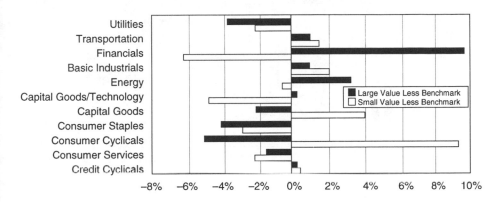

tive of the traditional value-investor who avoids high-expectation issues. The expected earnings-growth data further supports this point.

Figure 10-4 presents the relative exposure to factors that may contribute to a portfolio being more or less value-based. For the most part, our results suggest that value characteristics appear to be more extreme in small-caps than in large-caps. Additionally, it does appear that value themes tend to be more abundant among the secondary stocks.

Because of the depressed level of earnings in small-stock averages, the P/E ratio may be less of an appropriate yardstick. However, factors such as price/cash flow, price/sales, and dividend yield appear to consistently support a more extreme value-bias among smaller stocks. The smaller issues also have lower expectations, and are comprised of companies that are less leveraged. The exception to our results is the price/book value. In this instance, the size-adjusted, large-cap value portfolio appears cheaper than the adjusted small-cap value proxy. One possible explanation for this effect may be the extremely low price/book value of the small-cap segment. The significant weight of financial stocks within the small-cap arena may account for the low price/book ratio. Because of this, few active

FIGURE 10-4.   Many Factors Suggest That Smaller Stocks Offer a More Extreme Value-Style

Small versus large value, premium/discount to benchmark

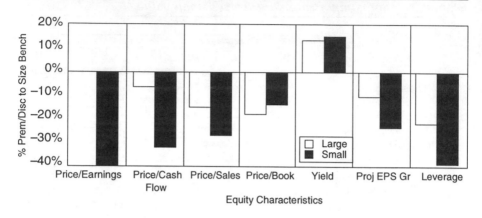

small-cap value portfolios are likely to exhibit a portfolio price/book below that of the small-cap composite.

Conclusion

There are several reasons that may support the extreme small-cap style results. First, the pool of small-cap value stocks may be greater than the pool of large-cap value companies. As a result, small-cap managers may have greater access to value candidates. Of the 5,000 to 6,000 issues that make up the U.S. equity market, only 400 or so companies are above a market capitalization of $2.4 billion.[6] The remaining 90% are effectively small stocks.

Second, limited access to finance may also suggest that a small company with dim prospects is likely to see its stock price remain depressed. After all, a large company has more access to financing,

[6] Pradhuman, Satya, and Richard Bernstein. "The Small-Cap Perspective." January 1994, Merrill Lynch research publication.

and therefore is better capable of offering projects which may return superior growth. This is less likely for smaller firms, especially smaller value-firms. This may be analogous to a large, low-expectation company versus a large, fast-growing company. The large-cap growth stock may have an advantage in financing which allows it to pursue more aggressive projects. While a large-cap value firm may have access to capital, the cost of such capital may be significantly higher than its large-cap growth counterpart. Access to capital may alter the prospects enough, such that a large-cap value firm changes from being a company of low or no expectation to a firm with some prospects.

Third, firms that have a greater value-bent are unlikely to be the topic of discussion at cocktail parties. These "beaten-down" firms tend to be more the backwater rather than at the forefront of the investment spectrum. While the neglect factor may be operating among all value stocks, it is more dramatic at the small-cap value level. Avner Arbel and Paul Strebel[7] have pointed to neglect as an operating factor to account for risk among equities. They also suggest that the neglect of securities is linked to the small-cap effect. Smaller stocks in general tend to be an underfollowed set of stocks. The average number of analysts that cover a large stock is approximately 22 compared to an average of four for a small stock.

The indication that smaller stocks tend to be underfollowed suggests that smaller stocks are less efficiently priced. While the small-cap value portfolio coverage is not lower than the average small stock, the smaller number of analysts that cover smaller companies strongly suggests that neglect as a value factor may be much more significant at the small-stock level. The small-cap value portfolio reflects a slightly higher-than-average analyst coverage partly because of a manager's need for information. An active manager is more likely to look at an idea if there is some form of research information. Because of a manager's preference for coverage, the average active portfolio is more likely to contain issues with greater analyst-coverage. The coverage figure is likely to be well below that of an active manager's level because of the many issues that trade within the small-stock universe.

[7] Arbel, Avner, and Paul Strebel. "The Neglected and Small Firm Effects." *Financial Review*, November 1982, pp. 201–218.

Finally, our results suggest that an investor searching for a "pure" value investment-vehicle is more likely to find such a theme among small-cap stocks rather than in the large-cap segment. Furthermore, the nature of small stocks suggests that an abundance of value candidates exists, and because of factors such as neglect and lack of financing, such traits are likely to perpetuate. We believe that such unique small-stock traits are likely to have a strong value influence on the security-selection efforts of small-cap investment managers.

PART III

The Different Approaches to the Investment Process

The Evolution of Equity Indexation in the U.S. Market

Arlene M. Rockefeller, CFA, Managing Director
State Street Global Advisors

Anne B. Eisenberg, Vice President
State Street Global Advisors

Possibly the most significant innovation to take place in the era of modern-day investing was the birth of modern portfolio theory (MPT) back in the early 1950s. Although much of Harry Markowitz's original theory has been challenged or revised in recent years, MPT's contribution to investment theory has been enormous in that it presented a new methodology for the analysis of portfolio risk and led, ultimately, to the birth of indexation as an investment methodology.

MPT contends that efficient investors construct portfolios of assets which, in the aggregate, maximize return for an accepted level of risk. Investment risk and expected returns can be quantifiably measured and optimal portfolios can be mathematically determined from all possible combinations of available assets.

This theory has been reexamined many times over the years since 1952. Some of the offshoots of MPT such as the capital asset pricing model (CAPM) have been strenuously challenged. However, other offshoots of MPT such as the efficient market hypotheses (EMH) remain very much in use today. The EMH states that current stock prices reflect all available information. Since there are no mispriced assets, it is not possible to add value by trading mispriced assets and, therefore, wise investors will adopt a passive investment approach in which a well-diversified portfolio is established and held for the long term. EMH is, clearly, a direct challenge to traditional active-style investment management where investors search for and trade temporarily over- and undervalued securities. By arguing that securities are fairly priced—given available information—followers of EMH believe that a passive management approach is preferable to an active approach because, first, no value is added by frequently trading in a portfolio, and, second, passive management involves less portfolio turnover and trading costs, and, in the real world, trading costs must be considered since they negatively impact performance.

One of the most common methods of passive management involve index funds which replicate the performance of a broad-based index of stocks. Indexers wishing to receive the return of the overall U.S. equity market found in the S&P 500 Index a convenient vehicle to accomplish their goals. Thoroughly established as a credible composite consisting of a broad range of industries, and recognized as the leading benchmark against which active manager performance is measured, the index was, and is, ideally suited to meet the needs of this new generation of investors. Covering over 88 different industry groups and representing approximately 70–75% of the capitalization of the U.S. equity market, the S&P 500 serves as an excellent proxy for the market. Current estimates of the total dollars indexed to the S&P 500 range between $300–400 billion.

Interestingly enough, this estimate reflects a recent decrease in assets indexed to the S&P 500. In 1991, the top 10 U.S. equity money managers were running over $148 billion in U.S. index funds with roughly $113 billion (76%) indexed to the S&P 500. Only two years later, while the total dollars indexed in the United States had increased to $221.9 billion, the dollars run against the S&P 500 had increased only to $148.6 billion (67%) (****S&P 1993 Bulletin). One explanation for this trend is that the practice of equity indexation in the United States is a constantly evolving one and, in recent years, there has been increased investor interest in indexing beyond the S&P 500. During the 1980s and early 1990s many new indices appeared. While some have failed to incite investor interest, others have attracted quite a lot of attention. In addition, the market has spawned new derivative instruments based on many of these new indices. Finally, there has been strong investor interest in customized indexation, style management, and enhanced strategies. U.S. equity indexing no longer implies only the S&P 500.

Table 11-1 lists just some of the indices established over the last decade or so. While some of these are not actually new, many have experienced a surge of interest from investors.

TABLE 11-1.   U.S. Equity Indices

Index	Description
S&P MidCap	Medium capitalization—non-S&P 500 securities
S&P/BARRA Growth	S&P 500 securities with high P/B ratios
S&P/BARRA Value	S&P 500 securities with low P/B ratios
Russell 1000	The 1000 largest U.S. companies
Russell 2000	The next largest 2000 U.S. companies
Russell 3000	The Russell 1000 plus the Russell 2000
Russell 2500	The Russell 3000 minus the largest 500 companies
Russell Special Small Company	The Russell 3000 minus the S&P 500 companies
Russell 1000 Value	Russell 1000 stocks with low P/B ratios
Russell 1000 Growth	Russell 1000 stocks with high P/B ratios
Russell 2000 Value	Russell 2000 stocks with low P/B ratios
Russell 2000 Growth	Russell 2000 stocks with high P/B ratios

The S&P 500 Index has a large-cap bias relative to the entire U.S. equity market (although not nearly as much of a bias as that found in the most widely quoted index, the Dow Jones Industrial Average.) For the most part, the S&P 500 consists of the largest, most liquid U.S. securities. During periods when large-cap stocks are strong performers, the S&P 500 will do well relative to other market-capitalization segments. On the other hand, when small-cap companies as a class outperform their larger-cap cousins, the S&P 500 will not perform as well as indices representing the mid- and small-cap sections of the market. Year by year there can be huge differences in the returns offered by the different indices. An investor seeking the returns offered by small-cap stocks should not be invested in the S&P 500 Index. Table 11-2 compares the historical total returns of the S&P 500 to those of the Russell 2000 Index for the last 10 years.

In addition to expanding their investment horizons beyond the large-cap sector, many investors seek to capture the returns of different segments within indices. For example, those interested in large-cap value opportunities should prefer the Russell 1000 Value Index to the Russell 1000 Index. Style management permits investors to customize their portfolios to almost any degree desired.

Investors need to know exactly what each of the different indices represents. The indices are very different from one another in their

TABLE 11-2.   Comparative Returns

	Russell 2000	S&P 500
1979	43.08%	18.94%
1980	38.60	32.57
1981	2.04	–5.34
1982	24.95	21.08
1983	29.13	22.39
1984	–7.28	6.11
1985	31.04	31.73
1986	5.67	18.55
1987	–8.77	5.23
1988	24.89	16.83
1989	16.24	31.52
1990	–19.51	–3.18
1991	46.05	30.57
1992	18.41	7.61
1993	18.91	10.08
Period return	818.92%	887.47%
Annualized return	15.94%	16.49%

characteristics. For example, the S&P 500 as of December 31, 1993 had an annual dividend-yield of 2.71%. The Russell 1000 Growth Index's yield was 1.92% and that of the Russell 2000 Index was 1.20%. An investor seeking to maximize dividend yield may not wish to invest in small-cap or growth companies. The increase in popularity of many of the non–S&P 500 indices in recent years reflects a growing awareness that the S&P 500 is not the index of choice for every investor.

It is also possible to manage a portfolio in a manner that falls somewhere between a traditional active approach and a purely passive one. These strategies "enhanced" seek to add a small amount of incremental value through the assumption of a small amount of additional risk.

Equal-Weighting—A Form of Enhancement

The securities held by some of the small-cap indices, such as the Russell 2000, can be very illiquid and costly to trade. This illiquidity has provided a dilemma to investors who desire small-cap exposure but are unwilling to sacrifice the liquidity offered by the S&P 500. One option for these investors is an equal-weighted S&P 500 portfolio.

Instead of owning each security in the index in its market-capitalization weight, the assets in an equal-weighted portfolio are each assigned a weight of 0.2% (100% divided by 500 securities). This methodology results in a portfolio with a significantly lower average capitalization—$7.0 billion instead of $25.0 billion for a capitalization-weighted S&P 500 portfolio.

Equal weighting requires a disciplined, systematic management and trading approach. A certain amount of portfolio rebalancing is required in order to maintain each security at a weight of 0.2%. Each day, shares of those assets whose price has appreciated relative to the market must be sold and, likewise, assets that have underperformed must have their portfolio weight increased with the purchase of additional shares.

Equal weighting provides two very significant benefits: (1) increased small-cap exposure without the loss of liquidity, and (2) historical outperformance of 3% to 3.5% over the capitalization-weighted S&P 500.

Performance

Studies over the past 40 years show that the equal-weighted S&P 500 strategy has outperformed the capitalization-weighted strategy by 3.5% before transaction costs. The equal-weighted S&P 500 portfolio managed by State Street Global Advisors over the last four years has produced an annualized return of 3.24% outperformance above the capitalization-weighted S&P 500 Index *after* transaction costs. This performance comes from two sources: exposure to better performing small-cap stocks and the mean-reversion effect (see Figure 11-1).

In an equal-weighted portfolio, each S&P 500 company is held at the same weight of 0.2%. In comparison, the capitalization-weighted S&P 500 Index has 130 companies with a weight greater than 20 basis points and 370 companies with a weight less than 20 basis points. That means that compared with the capitalization-weighted index, the smallest 370 companies are "overweighted." Equal weighting eliminates this bias toward a few companies. The increased small-cap exposure is accomplished without sacrificing liquidity and incurring high transaction-costs associated with trading non–S&P 500 names.

FIGURE 11-1.   Growth of $10,000,000, 1979 through 1993

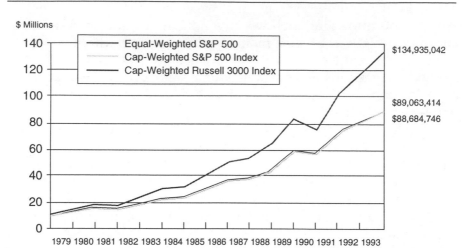

The natural rebalancing which is part of this strategy makes it a perfect portfolio-substitute for investors looking for a more enhanced approach. The disciplined "buy low, sell high" strategy translates price fluctuations into real gains. The tendency of stocks to be over-bought and oversold results in stock-price extremes which eventually move back toward more market-like performance. It is this tendency, called *mean reversion*, which is captured by the equal-weighted strategy. Capturing this reversion has allowed the equal-weighted S&P 500 to outperform the capitalization-weighted index even in years such as 1987 when small-cap stocks did poorly.

Figure 11-2 shows that although the capitalization-weighted and equal-weighted S&P 500 portfolios are both on or near the efficient frontier of portfolios (the optimal portfolio that investors will choose in order to maximize return for a given level of risk), the equal-weighted portfolio does add a small amount of incremental return through the assumption of a small amount of additional risk (as measured by the portfolio's standard deviation of return).

An equal-weighed benchmark often provides a more appropriate benchmark for active managers then a capitalization-weighted one since equal weighting of assets in active portfolios frequently account for a large part of active-manager returns. The equal-weighted S&P 500 strategy captures equal-weighting benefits at

FIGURE 11-2. Efficient Frontier

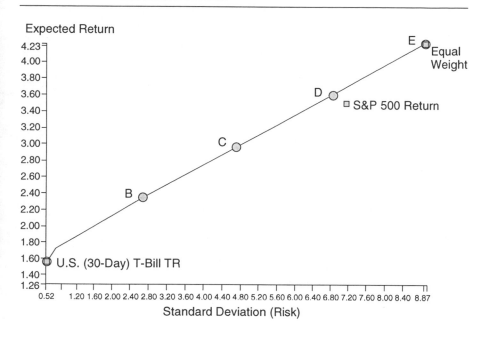

lower management-fees than those for active management. This strategy is the perfect substitute for active management or it can serve as a temporary investment while an investor is engaged in an active manager search.

Conclusion

As investor sophistication and technological capabilities have expanded, so have investment options proliferated. In their quest to replicate the return of the equity "market," investors may, today, define the market in a multitude of ways or they may choose to hone in on a particular segment of their market. In addition, the edges are blurring between active and passive management styles. The word "passive" connotes something sedentary or dormant. This has not been the case with passive equity-investing in the United States over the last 20 years.

Historical Tendencies of Equity Style Returns and the Prospects for Tactical Style Allocation

Douglas W. Case, CFA, Director of Equity Portfolio Management
LBS Capital Management

Steven Cusimano, CFA, Senior Portfolio Manager
Florida State Board of Administration

When one thinks of asset allocation, typically what comes to mind is investing a fund across unique investment alternatives: stocks, bonds, cash, and real estate. This allocation is frequently cited as the most important decision an investor can make and is likely to dominate all lower-level decisions. But is this necessarily true?

A study by the authors compared the returns of perfect asset-class selection to the returns of perfect economic-sector selection within the S&P 500 for the period 1982 through 1993 (see Figure 12-1).

A $1 investment with the asset-class selector (selecting monthly between the S&P 500, long-term U.S. Treasury bonds, and three-month U.S. Treasury bills) would have grown to $85, while the same investment with the sector selector (choosing monthly between the 10 S&P 500 economic-sector groups) would have grown to $4,170. Clearly the sector selection dominated the asset-class decision, while both outperformed a buy-and-hold investment in the S&P 500, which would have grown to $5.90.

In addition, a study performed by investment advisor Balch, Hardy examined the differences between the best and worst perform-

The authors would like to thank Susan Reigel, an assistant portfolio manager with the Florida State Board of Administration, for her valuable assistance in preparing this paper.

FIGURE 12-1.   Perfect Asset-Class Selection versus Perfect Sector-Selection

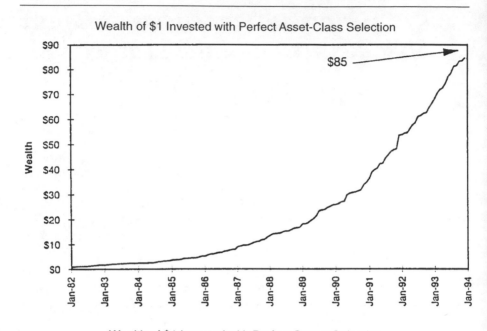

Wealth of $1 Invested with Perfect Asset-Class Selection

Wealth of $1 Invested with Perfect Sector-Selection

Source: Asset-class returns courtesy of Ibbotson & Associates. S&P 500 sector-returns courtesy of Smith Barney.

TABLE 12-1.   Attributions to Monthly Variations in Returns
January 1985 through December 1989

	Attribution	
	Style %	Selection %
161 growth equity funds	89.9	10.1
118 growth and income funds	90.9	9.1
34 small-stock funds	87.6	12.4
Fidelity Magellan Fund	97.3	2.7
Average	90.1	9.9

Source: William F. Sharpe, "Asset Allocation: Management Style and Performance Measurement." *The Journal of Portfolio Management,* Vol. 18, No. 2, Winter 1992, pp. 7–19.

ing asset class (i.e., stocks, bonds, cash, and real estate) and the best and worst performing equity style (i.e., large-cap value, large-cap growth, small-cap value, and small-cap growth) for the period 1978 through 1991.[1] The average differential between asset classes was 20.2% annually versus 23.5% annually for the equity styles. Thus return differentials were greater within the four equity styles than within the four broad asset-classes.

Further support of the relative importance of style in determining portfolio performance was advanced by Nobel laureate William Sharpe.[2] Sharpe created a two-dimensional definition of domestic-equity characteristics: size and style. These definitions led to four domestic-equity intra-asset classes: large-cap value stocks, large-cap growth stocks, mid-cap stocks, and small-cap stocks. Using these definitions of equity style, Sharpe measured the variability in returns attributable to style exposures versus the variability in returns attributable to security selection for a large sample of mutual funds over the period 1985 through 1989. Some of the attribution findings are summarized in Table 12-1. On average, approximately 90% of a portfolio's return variability was explained by its exposures to the intra-asset classes (i.e., style) with the remaining 10% arising from individ-

[1] Balch, Hardy, Scheinman & Winston, "Asset Allocation Is Not the Most Important Decision You Will Ever Make." *Seventh Asset Allocation Conference for the Institute for International Research,* February 22, 1993.

[2] Sharpe, William F. "Asset Allocation: Management Style and Performance Measurement." *The Journal of Portfolio Management,* Vol. 18, No. 2, Winter 1992, pp. 7–19.

ual stock selection. This is a dramatic statement regarding the need for understanding the importance of equity intra-asset-class style allocation.

Clearly large subsequent decisions loom below the surface of broad asset-class allocations taking the form of intra-asset class allocations. This chapter will explore the opportunities available from intra-asset-class style allocation. Specifically, the return behavior of three popular domestic equity large-cap style products will be evaluated for their potential use in a tactical intra-asset-class allocation framework. The three style-products are the BARRA/S&P Value and Growth Indices, the Salomon Brothers Large Value and Large Growth Indices, and the Wilshire Associates Large Value and Large Growth Indices.

Defining Equity Style

Three different equity-style products were chosen for analysis in order to demonstrate that there is a great deal of variation, and even some debate in how to define style. The three style-index creation methodologies are similar because they utilize measures of valuation to segregate growth stocks from value stocks. However, the three methodologies differ significantly in the type and number of factors used, as well as the methods employed to measure the sensitivity of each stock to such factors. Obviously, the various techniques will result in considerable differences between the indices with respect to holdings and returns, and there may be certain implications from these differences for deciding on an appropriate tactical intra-asset-class style allocation procedure.

In general, stylistic definitions have appeared to polarize along a univariate versus multivariate criteria. The univariate definition follows the research findings of Sharpe as well as work done by Eugene Fama and Kenneth French.[3] Under both research efforts, the ratio of book value per share to market price per share (book/price) was found to classify stocks efficiently as either growth or value. These studies found that this univariate criterion was better at isolating

---

[3] Fama, Eugene F., and Kenneth R. French. "The Cross-Section of Expected Stock Returns." *The Journal of Finance*, Vol. 47, No. 2, June, 1992, pp. 427-465.

pure style-effects within a broad universe of stocks than multivariate criteria that included factors such as dividend yield and the ratio of earnings per share to price per share (E/P). Thus, Sharpe's procedure for defining value and growth stocks was to rank the stocks in the S&P 500 by the book/price ratio and divide the universe such that half of the total market-capitalization was on either side of the break point. Those stocks with the higher book/price ratios were considered value stocks, while those with the lower book/price ratios were considered growth stocks. The S&P/BARRA Value and Growth Indices are created using this methodology. This definition assumes that a stock is a member of a mutually exclusive and exhaustive definition of value or growth. This either/or style criterion is where the multivariate proponents find their greatest fault with the univariate style-definition.

The multivariate position, represented by Wilshire Associates and Salomon Brothers, finds that value and growth are not an either/or characterization.[4] Their premise is to create more concentrated definitions of value and growth by utilizing multiple selection-criteria such as dividend yield per share, earnings yield per share, and forecasted earnings-per-share growth rates, in addition to the book/price ratio. This multivariate characterization of value and growth leads to more extreme style-definitions and avoids the forced either/or style characterization of every stock in a universe. Therefore, using the multivariate definition of style, a significant number of stocks are found to possess profiles that are insufficiently value or growth, and are left *unstyled.*

It can be seen in Table 12-2 that the returns to the respective style-index products do vary considerably. In fact, over the period examined (1982 through 1993), both the Wilshire and S&P/BARRA style indices showed annualized returns that favored the value style, while the Salomon style indices showed that the growth style had outperformed. While it is difficult to make definitive judgments as to which style-index construction methodology is best, or whether one investment style dominates the other over the long run, it does make sense to examine which one(s) might work best within the context of a tactical intra-asset-class allocation scheme.

---

[4] Bienstock, Sergio, and Eric H. Sorensen. "Segregating Growth from Value: It's Not Always Either/Or." *Quantitative Equity Strategies*, Derivative Research Group, Salomon Brothers, July, 1992.

TABLE 12-2. Relative Style-Return Comparison
January 1982 through December 1993

Year	Wilshire			Salomon			BARRA/S&P		
	LV	LG	LV – LG	LV	LG	LV – LG	LV	LG	LV – LG
1982	15.87	14.83	1.34	16.54	25.56	–9.02	21.04	22.03	–0.99
1983	25.40	17.41	7.99	27.20	7.90	19.30	28.89	16.24	12.65
1984	19.12	2.96	16.16	7.28	1.77	5.51	10.52	2.33	8.19
1985	30.21	32.95	–2.74	29.02	33.32	–4.30	29.68	33.31	–3.63
1986	22.22	15.46	6.76	12.70	25.16	–12.46	21.67	14.50	7.17
1987	3.59	4.74	–1.15	7.76	5.91	1.85	3.68	6.50	–2.82
1988	22.79	15.20	7.59	18.15	14.11	4.04	21.67	11.95	9.72
1989	25.14	35.21	–10.07	26.94	44.70	–17.76	26.13	36.40	–10.27
1990	–7.59	0.34	–7.93	–4.48	6.58	–11.06	–6.85	0.20	–7.05
1991	25.64	46.62	–20.98	13.40	71.73	–58.33	22.56	38.37	–15.81
1992	14.39	5.93	8.46	8.23	–4.19	12.42	10.59	5.14	5.45
1993	13.45	–0.54	13.99	20.73	–3.50	24.22	18.57	1.65	16.92
Annualized									
	17.04	15.07	1.97	14.89	17.33	–2.44	16.85	14.98	1.87

Source: FSBA, Salomon Brothers, Wilshire Associates, BARRA.

One of the driving considerations in evaluating alternative equity-style classification methods is the size of the separation in relative returns, or the spread between value and growth. A wider absolute spread between value and growth implies that there is greater potential for return enhancement from actively managing the style allocation of the equity portfolio. While narrower absolute spreads between value and growth imply that actively switching between the styles may not offer substantial excess rewards, particularly when transaction costs are considered. Table 12-3 illustrates the absolute-average return difference between the large-cap value and large-cap growth indices for the three style-index products in our study. The two multivariate style-classification methods demonstrate wider, more distinct absolute-average return differentials than the univariate book-to-market price-classification scheme. This is consistent with the Wilshire and Salomon objective to offer more concentrated value and growth exposures in their style indices. These higher levels of style concentration offer greater potential rewards in a style timing-strategy because of the wider value and growth return-spreads. The more concentrated style exposure also allows more flexibility to core-type portfolios to tactically allocate portions of the portfolio dollar-

TABLE 12-3. Differences in Equity Style Returns
Large-cap value versus large-cap growth, January 1982 through December 1993

	Absolute Average Difference in Style Returns	Median of Absolute Differences	Range of Style-Return Differences	
			Max	Min
Monthly Returns				
Wilshire	1.96	1.53	7.47	−7.90
Salomon	3.04	2.48	8.17	−9.57
BARRA/S&P	1.54	1.14	5.47	−5.58
Quarterly Returns				
Wilshire	3.88	3.37	12.24	−9.48
Salomon	6.44	4.89	13.83	−18.09
BARRA/S&P	3.29	2.70	10.28	−8.59
Semiannual Returns				
Wilshire	5.95	5.53	16.02	−9.54
Salomon	10.43	7.92	20.93	−31.39
BARRA/S&P	5.00	4.08	14.85	−11.20

Source: FSBA, Salomon Brothers, Wilshire Associates, BARRA.

value towards a particular style because a smaller percentage of the fund would be required to gain the desired style tilt.[5] These reasons are why a multivariate style-classification approach may be better suited for tactical style-allocation than the univariate method.

Let's evaluate the demonstrated time-series behavior of the separate style-index products' return patterns in order to formulate a basic construct for tactical style-allocation.

Seasonality of Equity Style Returns

Numerous seasonal anomalies in the financial markets have been thoroughly researched and documented in the financial literature.

[5] See Sorensen, Eric H., et al. "Equity Style Management—Implementing Salomon Brothers's Growth/Value: Part 1." *Derivatives Research*, Salomon Brothers, April 6, 1993.

TABLE 12-4.   Seasonal Effects in Equity Style Returns
January 1982 through December 1993

Month	Wilshire LV – LG Mean	Wilshire LV – LG t-Stat	Salomon LV – LG Mean	Salomon LV – LG t-Stat	BARRA/S&P LV – LG Mean	BARRA/S&P LV – LG t-Stat
January	1.28	1.45[1]	0.23	0.21	1.87	3.06[3]
February	0.11	0.11	–0.50	–0.41	0.42	0.59
March	0.05	0.07	0.78	0.82	0.11	0.23
April	0.52	0.69	1.09	0.85	0.50	0.75
May	–0.59	–1.08	–1.74	–2.84[3]	–0.31	–0.82
June	–0.12	–0.17	–0.49	–0.45	–0.58	–1.28
July	0.19	0.23	–0.47	–0.36	–0.13	–0.20
August	0.98	1.88[2]	–0.15	–0.18	1.09	1.77[1]
September	0.55	0.88	1.19	1.10	0.63	1.33
October	0.15	0.16	–0.56	–0.50	–0.57	–1.15
November	–0.80	–1.10	–2.15	–1.86[2]	–0.75	–1.48[1]
December	–1.11	–1.28	–0.42	–0.41	–0.95	–1.73[1]

Quarter	Wilshire LV – LG Mean	Wilshire LV – LG t-Stat	Salomon LV – LG Mean	Salomon LV – LG t-Stat	BARRA/S&P LV – LG Mean	BARRA/S&P LV – LG t-Stat
1st	1.32	0.85	0.21	0.08	2.37	1.84[2]
2nd	–0.20	–0.15	–1.13	–0.56	–0.38	–0.39
3rd	1.69	1.18	0.31	0.11	1.50	1.21
4th	–1.81	–1.33	–3.30	–1.70[1]	–2.38	–2.47[2]

Note: (1) Indicates significance at the 10% level, (2) indicates significance at the 5% level,
(3) indicates significance at the 1% level.
Source: FSBA, Salomon Brothers, Wilshire Associates, BARRA.

However, most of the studies have dealt with single-factor phenomena and/or return behavior at particular calendar turning-points.[6] Is it possible that broader definitions such as value- and growth-style classifications could exhibit significant calendar return patterns? To test for significant seasonal behavior in our three representative style-index products, t-statistics were calculated on the average-return spread between large value and large growth for each month and for each calendar quarter. As can be seen in Table 12-4, there were some

[6] See Jacobs, Bruce I., and Kenneth N. Levy. "Calendar Anomalies: Abnormal Returns at Calendar Turning Points." *Financial Analysts Journal*, November/December 1988.

significant effects observed. The S&P/BARRA return series exhibited significant average returns favoring the value style in the month of January. On a calendar-quarter basis, the S&P/BARRA return series exhibited significant average returns favoring the growth style in the fourth quarter. It would appear that there are some year-end phenomena impacting the S&P/BARRA style-index return series.

There were various significant calendar observations for both of the multivariate style-index products. The most significant of which were that the Salomon Brothers style returns exhibited significant average returns favoring the growth style in the months of May and November. The Wilshire style-returns exhibited significant value outperformance in the month of August. It is difficult to determine what economic or financial influences may be driving this observed return behavior. These results are simply historical observations. We will make no attempt to identify what, if any, causal factors may be responsible for the observed calendar-biased return patterns, but they are interesting to note nonetheless.

An additional method to test for significant patterns in the return data is to test for the presence of autocorrelation in the time series of returns. Autocorrelation measures the direction and strength of the statistical relationship between ordered pairs of observations.[7] In this case we are measuring the relationship between one-period-lagged return observations and subsequent returns. In other words, is the relative style-return (value minus growth) at time $t - 1$ significantly related to the relative style return at time t? The value-minus-growth return time-series was tested across all three style products using monthly, quarterly, and semiannual return-spreads. The one-month-lagged autocorrelation in the undifferenced series is displayed in Table 12-5. Only the Salomon Brothers monthly relative style-return series exhibited significant autocorrelation.

Cyclicality of Equity Style Returns

The differential behavior of the styled intra-asset classes can be further evaluated by measuring the return correlations within and between the paired styles. Table 12-6 provides correlations for the

---

[7] Pankratz, Alan. *Forecasting with Univariate Box-Jenkins Models* (New York: John Wiley and Sons, 1983).

TABLE 12-5. Relative Style-Return Series
Autocorrelations: one-period lag with no differencing, January 1982 through December 1993

	Monthly LV – LG	Quarterly LV – LG	Semiannual LV – LG
Wilshire	0.090	–0.079	–0.011
Salomon	0.154[1]	0.130	–0.197
BARRA/S&P	0.111	–0.048	–0.147

Note: (1) Indicates significance at the 5% level.
Source: FSBA, Salomon Brothers, Wilshire Associates, BARRA.

TABLE 12-6. Paired-Style Return Correlations—Ex Universe Returns
January 1982 through December 1993

Return Horizon	Wilshire	Salomon	BARRA/S&P
Monthly	–0.690	–0.701	–0.776
Quarterly	–0.745	–0.850	–0.998
Semiannual	–0.701	–0.907	–0.998

Universes: Wilshire Top 750—Wilshire & Salomon
                S&P 500—BARRA/S&P

Source: FSBA, Salomon Brothers, Wilshire Associates, BARRA.

Wilshire, Salomon, and S&P/BARRA paired-style returns, ex the respective universe[8] return for monthly, quarterly, and semiannual return-horizons. For each return horizon, considerable negative correlations are observed between value and growth returns for each of the paired styles. Obviously, the style-index creation methodology will impact this analysis; however, the fact that all three style-index products exhibited strong negative correlations between value and growth fosters an interest in determining what is potentially driving this relative-return distinctiveness. This distinctiveness can be seen in Figure 12-2: when one component of a paired style is outperforming its universe, the other component is typically underperforming.

---

[8] The S&P/BARRA style indices are derived from the S&P 500 index. The Wilshire Large Value and Large Growth indices are derived from the Wilshire Top 750 index. The Wilshire Top 750 was chosen as a representative large-cap index for use as the Salomon Brothers universe return.

FIGURE 12-2.   Quarterly Ex-Universe Value/Growth Return Comparison

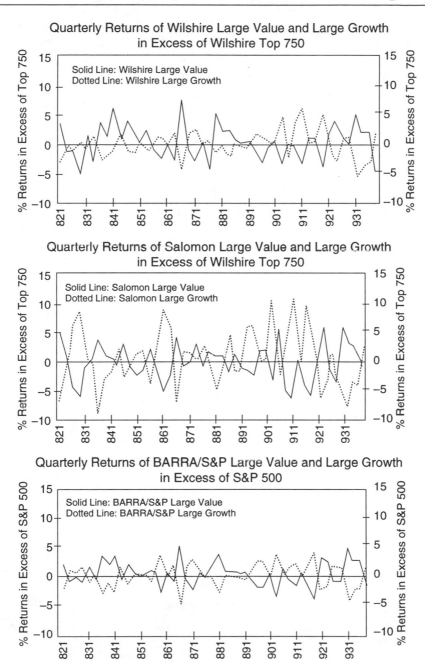

Source: FSBA, Salomon Brothers, Wilshire Associates, BARRA.

FIGURE 12-3.   Cyclicality of Relative Style-Returns

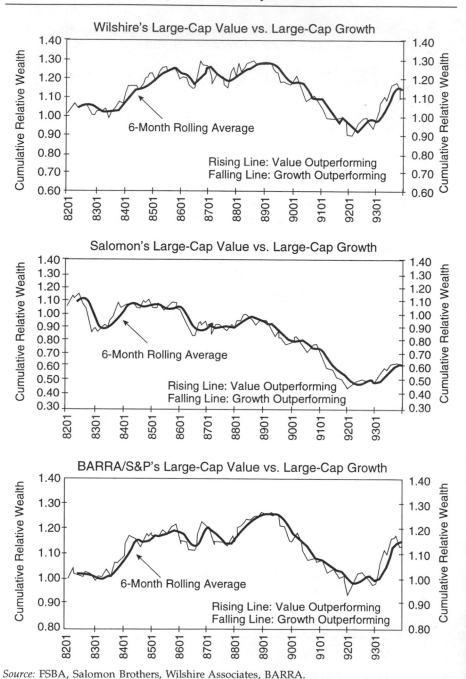

Source: FSBA, Salomon Brothers, Wilshire Associates, BARRA.

In addition to the mirror-image nature of paired-style returns, the relative returns between the paired styles appear to exhibit cyclical patterns through time. The relative style-returns for the three pairs of style indices are plotted in Figure 12-3.

While the behavior of the monthly relative returns tends to be rather choppy, there appears to exist a smoother cyclical behavior to the relative return series. The paired styles appear to follow cyclical runs where one style exhibits consistently strong relative performance only to be followed by a cyclical run of relative underperformance. The question one must then ask is, *are the cyclical runs occurring by sheer chance alone, or not?*

A procedure for evaluating the randomness of runs can be employed to provide us with the desired insights regarding the nature of the cyclical movements in the paired styles.[9] Defining a run as one or more sequential increases or decreases in the relative-return series, one can determine the randomness of the runs using the following formula:

$$K = [3R - (2N + 2.5)] / [(16N - 29)/10]^{1/2}$$

where R is the number of runs, N is the total number of observations, and K is a standard normal variable. If K is calculated to be between +1.96 and −1.96, then the runs could have occurred by chance. If the K value lies outside the specified range, then the runs probably did not occur by chance alone. Table 12-7 provides the calculated K values for

[9] This technique is discussed in Sherry, Clifford J. *The Mathematics of Technical Analysis* (Chicago: Probus Publishing Company, 1992).

TABLE 12-7. Randomness of Paired-Style Relative Returns
January 1982 through December 1993

Return Horizon	Calculated K Values		
	Wilshire	Salomon	BARRA/S&P
Monthly	−5.93	−5.85	−5.34
Quarterly	0.99[1]	−2.38	−1.67[1]

Note: (1) Indicates that the runs are probably occurring by chance alone. Since the other calculated K values fall outside of +1.96 to −1.96, the runs in relative performance are probably not occurring by chance alone.
Source: FSBA, Salomon Brothers, Wilshire Associates, BARRA.

TABLE 12-8.   Predominance of Paired-Style Relative Returns
January 1982 through December 1993

Return Horizon	Calculated J Values		
	Wilshire	Salomon	BARRA/S&P
Monthly	0.29	0.58	0.58
Quarterly	—[1]	0.00	—[1]

Note: (1) Indicates no predominance test was necessary. Since all calculated J values fall inside the range of +1.96 to –1.96, there is probably no predominance of one component of a paired style over its counterpart.
Source: FSBA, Salomon Brothers, Wilshire Associates, BARRA.

each paired style for monthly and quarterly runs in relative style-performance. The runs in monthly relative style-returns tested to be nonrandom across all three paired styles. So, based on these calculated *K* values, *it is probable that the runs in paired style relative performance are not occurring by chance alone, and that a deterministic process may be at work driving the runs in relative performance.* The results were less conclusive for quarterly return runs, with only the Salomon relative style-return series appearing to be nonrandom.

A closely related technique allows one to evaluate if a predominance exists of one component of a paired style over its counterpart.[10] This test makes use of the formula detailed below:

$$J = [N - 2(S + 1)]/[(N + 1)/3]^{1/2}$$

where *N* is the total number of observations, *S* is the lesser of the number of times a component outperformed its paired-style counterpart (and vice versa), and *J* is a standard normal variable. Table 12-8 contains the calculated *J* values for the paired styles. For each relative style-return series that tested to be nonrandom, *no predominance of one style over the other was found to exist.* Therefore you would not expect to be tactically favoring any one component (i.e., value or growth) of these specific paired styles any more frequently than its counterpart.

[10] Ibid.

In general, it would appear that the cyclical patterns we have observed in relative style-returns are likely being generated by a deterministic process. What remains unclear however, is if the deterministic process is relatively stable, or if it changes through time? This process stability is referred to as *stationarity*. For time-series data, stationarity usually implies a constant mean and standard deviation through time. If a time series is stationary, it suggests that the rules that generate the time series do not change over time.

To test for stationarity, a simple test is utilized that compares the cumulative-probability density functions of the relative-return series for significant mean differences.[11] First, the 144 monthly relative-return observations were split into two halves, each with 72 months. Next, the cumulative-probability density functions were calculated separately for each half of the data. These are depicted graphically in Figure 12-4.

The x-axis shows the range of relative style-return outcomes, and is broken into 50 basis-point increments, or bins, for each of the three representative paired-style return series. The solid lines in the graphs simply show the cumulative percentage of observations in each bin for the first half of the data, while the dashed line shows the same for the second half of the data. The difference between the solid line and the dashed line is determined at each bin, and a Z-score is calculated based on the mean and standard deviation of these differences. If the Z-score is significant, then the differences between the two halves of the data are significant, and we can conclude that the time series of relative style-returns is not stationary. It would appear from this simple test that all three of the relative style-return series examined were stationary over the 1982 to 1993 time period.

What does all of this mean when it comes to making tactical intra-asset-class style allocation decisions? The seemingly nonrandom runs in the time series of relative style-returns, that exhibit no predominance of style outperformance, and that behave in an apparently stationary manner imply that from a statistical standpoint it may be possible to develop a deterministic algorithm to generate expected outcomes of relative style-performance.

---

[11] An example can be found in Sherry, C. J., and W. R. Klemm. "Stationarity, Randomness, and Serial Dependence in Neuronal Spike Trains." *J. Electrophysiol. Tech.*, Vol. 10, pp. 59-73, 1983.

FIGURE 12-4. Tests for Stationarity

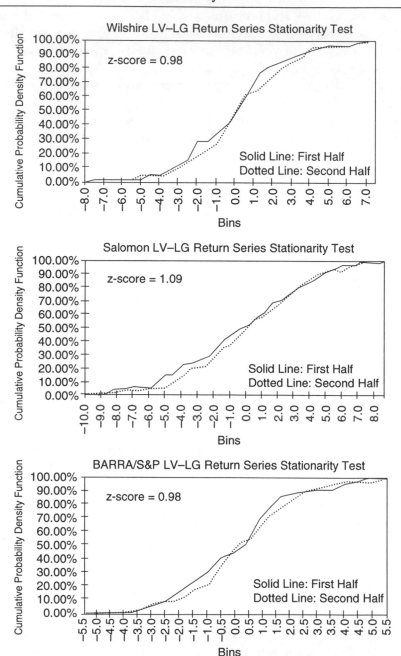

Source: FSBA, Salomon Brothers, Wilshire Associates, BARRA.

Developing a Style Prediction Theorem

One of the distinguishing features of value/growth paired styles is their differential industrial composition. Value styles tend to be dominated by banks, utilities, basic industrials, and, to a lesser extent, energy. Growth styles are typically dominated by consumer non-durables and, to a lesser degree, technology. The demand for each industry's output has a certain sensitivity to overall economic growth. Table 12-9 shows the results from a study that attempted to

TABLE 12-9. Industrial Sensitivity to Overall Economic Activity

Most Economically Sensitive

Industry	Coefficient of Percent Change in Real GDP
1 Coal mining	11.08
2 Autos	8.85
3 Trucks & buses	7.37
4 Iron, steel	5.60
5 Motor vehicle parts	4.68
6 Metal mining	4.44
7 TV and radios	3.58
8 Synthetic materials	3.14
9 Nonferrous metals	3.00
10 Railroad & misc. equip.	2.62

Least Economically Sensitive

Industry	Coefficient of Percent Change in Real GDP
1 Agriculture	0.06
2 Drugs, medicine	0.19
3 Services	0.25
4 Oil well drilling	0.30
5 Food	0.31
6 Electric, gas, sanitary services	0.39
7 Communications	0.42
8 Finance, insurance, real estate	0.44
9 Tobacco	0.49
10 Soaps	0.57

Estimated equation was:

% change (real industrial output) = [coefficient] × % change (real GNP)

Period of estimation was 1955:QI–1986:QIV.

Source: Rosanne Cahn, "Economic Prospects." *Equity Research,* First Boston, March 30, 1988.

determine which industries were the most, and least sensitive to overall economic growth.[12] While this study did not include utilities and banks, one can observe the heavy consumer-nondurable representation among those industries that are the least sensitive to economic activity.

Industrial sensitivities to economic growth are important considerations when developing style-return expectations. This is because when an investment is made, ownership in the growth of future earnings is actually being purchased. Therefore, a crucial evaluation is the nature of an investment's earnings growth. From Table 12-9 we see that industries tend to have widely varying degrees of sensitivity to overall economic growth. Given that economic growth tends to follow observable cycles of expansion and contraction, those companies with greater economic sensitivities will have their earnings growth tending to mirror cycles in overall economic activity. Companies with little sensitivity to the general economy must be able to create demand for their output in a self-sustained manner. These notions have given rise to the classic differential stock-categories of cyclical and consumer stocks whose industrial representations have tended to map favorably into value and growth stocks, respectively. Therefore, the belief is that *by being able to determine the current location in, and future progression through, the general economic growth cycle (or business cycle), this should provide useful information with respect to value/growth paired style return expectations.*

A Brief Overview of U.S. Business Cycles

A business cycle is characterized by fluctuating growth in aggregate output which coincides with procyclical movements in employment, inflation rates, and increases in real interest-rates. The cycle is found to be recurrent yet nonperiodic such that if the cycle was periodic, then down-trends and up-trends would be perfectly predictable. In length, business cycles vary considerably and are not divisible into shorter subcycles of similar characteristics. Figure 12-5

---

[12] Cahn, Rosanne. "Economic Prospects." *Equity Research,* First Boston, March 30, 1988.

FIGURE 12-5.   Average Length of Business Cycles

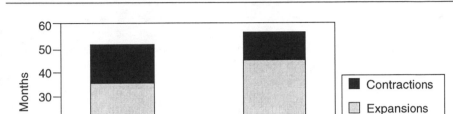

Source: Adapted from Dore, Mohammed H. I. *The Macrodynamics of Business Cycles* (Cambridge, MA: Blackwell Publishers, 1993).

summarizes statistics which provide a profile for business cycles within the U.S.[13]

During the 1945 to 1982 time period, the typical business cycle averaged 56 months in duration, where the expansionary phase tended to last 45 months while the contraction was 11 months long. Cycles have been observed to vary considerably during this time period. Expansions are found to vary typically between 17 months and 73 months while contractions have tended to vary between seven months and 15 months. Therefore we find that the broad economy tends to be in an expansionary phase more frequently than a contracting phase.

It is perhaps more instructive to examine business-cycle behavior in the more modern era. More recent cycles over the 1961 to 1991 time period vary considerably in length from the long-term average cycle behavior that incorporates data back to 1854. In fact, modern business-cycle expansions have averaged over twice the length of the average expansion dating back to the mid-1850s (see Figure 12-6).

[13] Adapted from Dore, Mohammed H. I. *The Macrodynamics of Business Cycles* (Cambridge, MA: Blackwell Publishers, 1993).

FIGURE 12-6.   Average Length of Business Cycles

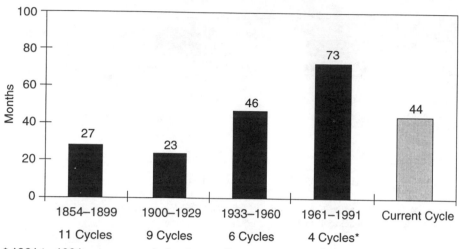

* 1961 to 1991 average excludes the credit-controls-induced 1980–81 cycle.

Source: Stephen S. Roach of Morgan Stanley. *Economics: Business Cycle Myths,* National Bureau of Economic Research.

There is considerable debate about what drives the length of business-cycle expansion. However, one popular belief is that the one key factor determining the length of a business cycle is inflation.[14] Inflationary pressures trigger subsequent shifts in monetary policy and interest rates that may bring a cycle to its ultimate conclusion.

Developing a Style Prediction Algorithm

Our style prediction theorem states that the industry compositions of value and growth (as determined by the respective style-classification schemes) have significantly different sensitivities to the economic cycle. Given that the dominant characteristics of business cycles are changes in output, employment, and prices along with procyclical movements in real interest-rates, two priors are established. The first

[14] Roach, Stephen S. "Economics: Business Cycle Myths." *U.S. Investment Perspectives,* Morgan Stanley Research, November 28, 1994.

is that value investing would be relatively better suited for an economy characterized by troughing and/or expanding output and employment, plus rising prices and real interest-rates due to increased demand for goods and credit. The second is that growth-investing is better suited in an economy where output and employment growth are peaking and/or contracting, where growth characteristics are scarce in general.

It is important to determine the exact nature of the linkages between economic conditions and the value/growth cycle. Do business-cycle movements lead subsequent relative style-returns, or do the style cycles discount future economic activity?

In order to answer this question, the sensitivity of relative style-returns to economic measures was estimated over the 1982 to 1993 time period. To do this in a realistic fashion a custom database composed of original-release economic data was constructed by the authors. Several measures of economic activity are subject to large revisions subsequent to the preliminary release information. These revisions were tracked for trailing 12-month periods and incorporated into the data transformations. It is the authors' opinion that any data revisions made after the 12-month trailing period were much less likely to impact investor behavior, but that revisions within this time frame would most likely be incorporated into investment strategy. This methodology would help eliminate the impact of revisions that occurred well after market participants were able to act on the information.

Several measures of economic output, prices, and real interest-rates were evaluated for their relationship with the value/growth cycle. Table 12-10 summarizes these findings. In general, it would appear that movements in the business-cycle characteristics have tended to lead subsequent relative returns between styles, as illustrated by the higher correlations between economic activity prior to observed returns than correlations measured coincident and subsequent to the observed return periods. It would also appear that having perfect forecasts regarding the movements of key economic characteristics offer inferior insights to style performance versus simply acting upon available historic economic information. This is illustrated by the generally lower coincident correlations compared to the leading economic data correlations with the relative style-returns. This is a rather dramatic statement since it implies some form of market inefficiency has been found to exist historically.

TABLE 12-10. Correlations between Relative Style-Returns and Economic Indicators

	Real GDP Growth	Industrial Production	Employment Growth	Expected GDP	Real T-Bond Changes	Real T-Bill Changes
12 Months Prior						
Wilshire	0.290	0.377	0.527	N.M.	0.329	0.173
Salomon	0.302	0.288	0.414	N.M.	0.243	0.210
BARRA/S&P	0.201	0.251	0.383	N.M.	0.332	0.255
6 Months Prior						
Wilshire	0.438	0.416	0.578	N.M.	0.086	-0.055
Salomon	0.288	0.379	0.571	N.M.	0.036	-0.165
BARRA/S&P	0.371	0.381	0.519	N.M.	0.057	0.032
3 Months Prior						
Wilshire	0.358	0.274	0.354	N.M.	0.302	-0.072
Salomon	0.216	0.212	0.359	N.M.	0.263	0.018
BARRA/S&P	0.410	0.167	0.355	N.M.	0.226	0.059
Coincident						
Wilshire	0.110	0.167	0.362	0.275	-0.130	0.038
Salomon	0.309	0.296	0.105	0.108	0.013	0.213
BARRA/S&P	0.089	0.255	0.387	0.238	-0.016	0.166
Coincident + 6 Months						
Wilshire	0.353	0.211	-0.056	0.371	-0.085	0.088
Salomon	0.396	0.133	-0.241	0.233	0.009	0.137
BARRA/S&P	0.430	0.292	0.073	0.337	0.006	0.199

Note: N.M. indicates not meaningful.
Source: FSBA, Salomon Brothers, Wilshire Associates, BARRA.

Let's assume that the above mentioned inefficiency is truly exploitable—in other words, that it is possible to profit from tactically allocating assets between the large-cap style segments of the market. Figure 12-7 illustrates what the potential rewards would have been from making perfect large-cap style allocations relative to holding a broad-market index such as the S&P 500.

Perfect allocation within all three of the style products would have provided significant returns in excess of the S&P 500. At the extreme, perfect switching within the Salomon style-product would have provided nearly 10 times the return of the S&P 500. (If smaller-cap style products were included in the study then perfect style-allocation would have provided twice the excess returns observed in only the large-cap market segment.)

The excess-return potential from actively managing the style bias of a portfolio certainly appears enticing. However, real market-considerations and constraints would be a factor in implementing such a strategy. The next section deals with some of these considerations and offers some implementation insights.

FIGURE 12-7.   Rewards from Perfect Monthly Large-Cap Style Selection

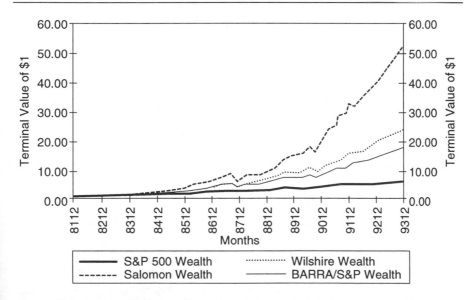

Source: FSBA, Salomon Brothers, Wilshire Associates, BARRA. Returns are from 8201-9312.

Implementing Tactical Intra-Asset-Class Style Allocations

Accurate expectations regarding the prospective relative performance between large-cap styles can potentially provide useful investment enhancements at the individual portfolio level as well as at the aggregate plan-sponsor level. This section will consider each potential usage separately so that operational considerations and constraints can be individually addressed.

Individual Portfolio Usage

Figure 12-7 provided a perspective into the maximum cumulative-benefits accrued to tactical style-allocation decisions. However, return differences between large-cap styles are not material for each monthly or quarterly evaluation period. Table 12-11 details the relative-return observations in a tabular histogram format. Assuming a style-allocation transaction cost of 1%, round trip, we find that the monthly returns for the Wilshire, Salomon, and S&P/BARRA fall within the "spread cost" 36.8%, 17.4%, and 45.8% of the time, respectively. Once again we are able to observe the tactical benefits of using a more concentrated style definition (i.e., Salomon) as the monthly S&P/BARRA returns exceed the costs of transacting only 54.2% of the time. When one evaluates quarterly return-differences, we find the occurrence of neutral separations dropping to 25% for Wilshire, 8.3% for Salomon, and 20.8% for the S&P/BARRA products. Therefore you would expect to realize larger style-allocation benefits as you extend your investment holding-period.

Not all of the neutral return-occurrences would have resulted in an unprofitable allocation trade where transaction costs exceed the benefit of a correct allocation decision. Unprofitable trades would have been realized only if a switch from the alternative style was required, say from growth one month into value the next month. A neutral style-return difference that occurred as a continuation of a particular style's outperformance would in fact remain profitable. This distinction between unprofitable and profitable neutral return-observations is displayed in Table 12-12. On a monthly basis, while continuing to assume a 1% transaction cost, we now find that tactical trades within the Wilshire product would have been unprofitable

TABLE 12-11. Style Return Frequency Distributions

Monthly Large-Value/Large-Growth Returns from 8201–9312

	Wilshire Monthly Frequency		Salomon Monthly Frequency		BARRA/S&P Monthly Frequency	
	Count	Percent	Count	Percent	Count	Percent
Rtn < −5.0	4	2.8%	15	10.4%	2	1.4%
−5.0 < Rtn < −4.0	2	1.4%	12	8.3%	0	0.0%
−4.0 < Rtn < −3.0	10	6.9%	7	4.9%	7	4.9%
−3.0 < Rtn < −2.0	17	11.8%	11	7.6%	9	6.3%
−2.0 < Rtn < −1.0	10	6.9%	16	11.1%	19	13.2%
−1.0 < Rtn < 1.0	53	36.8%	25	17.4%	66	45.8%
1.0 < Rtn < 2.0	18	12.5%	16	11.1%	21	14.6%
2.0 < Rtn < 3.0	11	7.6%	12	8.3%	7	4.9%
3.0 < Rtn < 4.0	10	6.9%	12	8.3%	7	4.9%
4.0 < Rtn < 5.0	4	2.8%	8	5.6%	4	2.8%
5.0 < Rtn	5	3.5%	10	6.9%	2	1.4%
Totals	144	100%	144	100%	144	100%

Quarterly Large-Value/Large-Growth Returns from 8201–9312

	Wilshire Quarterly Frequency		Salomon Quarterly Frequency		BARRA/S&P Quarterly Frequency	
	Count	Percent	Count	Percent	Count	Percent
Rtn < −5.0	8	16.7%	12	25.0%	4	8.3%
−5.0 < Rtn < −4.0	3	6.3%	1	2.1%	2	4.2%
−4.0 < Rtn < 3.0	2	4.2%	6	12.5%	3	6.3%
−3.0 < Rtn < −2.0	1	2.1%	1	2.1%	6	12.5%
−2.0 < Rtn < −1.0	4	8.3%	3	6.3%	4	8.3%
−1.0 < Rtn < 1.0	12	25.0%	4	8.3%	10	20.8%
1.0 < Rtn < 2.0	0	0.0%	1	2.1%	5	10.4%
2.0 < Rtn < 3.0	5	10.4%	6	12.5%	2	4.2%
3.0 < Rtn < 4.0	2	4.2%	2	4.2%	2	4.2%
4.0 < Rtn < 5.0	1	2.1%	0	0.0%	3	6.3%
5.0 < Rtn	10	20.8%	12	25.0%	7	14.6%
Totals	48	100%	48	100%	48	100%

Source: FSBA, Salomon Brothers, Wilshire Associates, BARRA.

TABLE 12-12.   Unprofitable Switches

Monthly Returns from 8201–9312

	Wilshire Monthly Frequency		Salomon Monthly Frequency		BARRA/S&P Monthly Frequency	
	Count	Percent	Count	Percent	Count	Percent
–1.0 < Rtn < 1.0	53	36.8%	25	17.4%	66	45.8%
Unprofitable switch	29	20.1%	13	9.0%	35	24.3%
Profitable nonswitch	24	16.7%	12	8.4%	31	21.5%

Quarterly Returns from 8201–9312

	Wilshire Quarterly Frequency		Salomon Quarterly Frequency		BARRA/S&P Quarterly Frequency	
	Count	Percent	Count	Percent	Count	Percent
–1.0 < Rtn < 1.0	12	25.0%	4	8.4%	10	20.8%
Unprofitable switch	7	14.6%	2	4.2%	6	12.5%
Profitable nonswitch	5	10.4%	2	4.2%	4	8.3%
1-month %/3-month %		1.4×		2.1×		1.9×

20.1% of the time with 16.7% representing a modestly profitable continuation of a style's outperformance. For the others we observe 9% of the Salomon tactical trades being unprofitable and 24.3% for S&P/BARRA. As before, we find lower percentages for the quarterly differences, 14.6% for Wilshire, 4.2% for Salomon, and 12.5% for S&P/BARRA.

Table 12-13 demonstrates the maximum annualized benefits accrued from tactically allocating between growth and value styles within each product on a gross and net basis. Turnover within each product was estimated on a monthly and quarterly basis and was assessed a 1% cost to arrive at a maximum net-benefit estimate. Table 12-13 reveals that considerable annualized benefits are present on a gross and net basis, but that it may require levels of turnover that can be considered rather high. For both monthly and quarterly return-horizons, the multivariate style-products yield the greater tactical opportunities which drop off materially when moving from a

TABLE 12-13.   Maximum Annualized Style Allocation Benefits

Perfect Monthly Allocations

	Wilshire	Salomon	BARRA/S&P
Strategy annualized return	30.38%	38.94%	27.20%
S&P 500 annualized return	15.94%	15.94%	15.94%
Annual excess return	14.44%	23.00%	11.08%
Strategy annualized turnover	550%	533%	517%
Transaction costs at 1.0% round trip	5.50%	5.33%	5.17%
Annual net excess return	8.94%	17.67%	5.91%

Perfect Quarterly Allocations

	Wilshire	Salomon	BARRA/S&P
Strategy annualized return	25.10%	31.32%	23.52%
S&P 500 annualized return	15.94%	15.94%	15.94%
Annual excess return	9.16%	15.38%	7.58%
Strategy annualized turnover	250%	217%	233%
Transaction costs at 1.0% round trip	2.50%	2.17%	2.33%
Annual net excess return	6.66%	13.21%	5.25%

Source: FSBA, Salomon Brothers, Wilshire Associates, BARRA.

monthly to quarterly investment horizon. Net tactical opportunities within the S&P/BARRA products change very little when one extends the investment horizon.

While net annualized excess returns are clearly superior for the multivariate products, potential product-capacity is an issue that also needs to be considered. Simplistically, the larger the basket of stocks included in a style product, the greater the potential strategy-capacity. This greater capacity will translate into ease of tactical execution. Here we find the S&P/BARRA style-products tending to offer, on average, the larger baskets in terms of the number of stocks, while Salomon's are the smallest, and Wilshire's falling in between. Thus there appears to exist an inverse relationship between tactical opportunities and strategic capacity for the multivariate and univariate style-products.

Aggregate Plan-Sponsor Usage

A plan sponsor's opportunity set for enhancing domestic equity-returns includes funding superior active managers, tactically influencing overall systematic market exposure through the aggregate portfolio beta, or tactically managing the active stylistic biases within the aggregate portfolio's risk profile. At a minimum, each plan sponsor is presented with the potential to capitalize on such opportunities as positive or negative cash flows are experienced within the aggregate portfolio. Let's focus on methods for managing active stylistic biases relative to the aggregate portfolio's target portfolio.

For a plan sponsor with a multimanager aggregate portfolio, the optimal risk-configuration of the aggregate is to have the weighted combination of all manager benchmarks providing a risk profile equivalent to the equity target, say the Wilshire 5000. Differences between the aggregation of manager benchmarks and the equity target provide sources of risk to the plan sponsor. One method to provide positive return-expectations to this source of risk is to utilize tactical style-allocations that result in controlled active departures of the aggregated benchmark from the target. The management of this active style-allocation can be accomplished through incremental cash-flow decisions and/or tactical movement of funded assets between existing managers based upon each manager's benchmark style-bias with the relative stylistic return expectations.

A plan sponsor's ability to accrue benefits from tactical style-allocation depends on: (1) how well the roster of manager benchmarks correspond to the underlying style products being used to generate the allocation discipline, (2) how well each manager actively performs relative to his or her benchmark, and (3) how costly the implementation of tactical style-allocation proves to be for the plan sponsor. For instance, the plan sponsor could tactically fund a manager whose benchmark return falls short of the pure style-product return. This shortfall could be exacerbated if the manager in turn actively underperforms his or her benchmark. A possible solution to such a problem would be to use passive portfolio-products that are constructed to mimic the behavior of the pure style-products. This alternative could limit both sources of implementation slippage.

The costs to the plan sponsor for implementing such a tactical style-allocation strategy would include the individual security-level transaction costs of defunding one manager to fund another and the resulting business risk such allocations create for each manager. Presumably such funding decisions would be an assessment of the relative attractiveness of a manager's inherent style-strategy biases and have little to do with a manager's active performance. Thus the manager would experience potentially material revenue-fluctuations as a result of issues beyond his or her influence and, taken to the extreme, managers whose style was expected to be out of favor would be completely defunded only to be rehired when their style came back into favor. Of course the use of derivative instruments could also lessen the implementation slippage identified above.

Summary

The previous sections have illustrated the dominant impact of style on domestic equity large-cap returns. Based on the statistical evidence that a deterministic process linked to the economic cycle was prevalent in historical relative style-return behavior, it would appear that opportunities may exist to develop an intra-asset-class style allocation strategy. As illustrated, this strategy may take various forms, both at the individual portfolio level and at the sponsor level. Whatever form such a strategy takes, it is imperative that the user continue to monitor the linkage between the business cycle and relative style-return behavior.

How Does Stock Selection Criteria Performance Vary across Investment Style Universes?

Gregory J. Forsythe, CFA, President
Chicago Investment Analytics, Inc.

In recent years, performance measurement consultants have made equity managers very aware of "investment style" or how portfolios deviate on average from broad market benchmarks in terms of market capitalization, valuation multiples, growth rates, etc. Policy constraints, stock-selection methodology, and portfolio construction all interact to determine portfolio characteristics. For many equity managers, investment style is simply a by-product of the investment process. However, other equity managers make a conscious effort to utilize a specific investment style for their portfolios.

Proliferation of style-specific equity products has been a direct outgrowth of greater investment style awareness. Increasingly, equity managers see providing style-specific portfolio options as key to controlling a greater proportion of client assets. Risk control through style diversification is the usual investment motivation for spreading assets across investment styles. But with so much focus on risk, style differentiation, and product positioning, stock selection is often an afterthought in the product development process. This is unfortunate since specific stock selection can be a value-added element within any equity style portfolio.

This study focuses strictly on stock-selection issues within the context of equity style portfolios. From a stock selection point of view, how should style-specific products be developed? Which equity styles lend themselves to value-added stock selection? Do stock-selection criteria that are effective within diversified portfolios perform equally as well within common investment-style universe restrictions? Or should stock-selection criteria be customized for each style-specific portfolio?

Research Methodology

Investment-style benchmarks are generally created by segregating a large universe of stocks into smaller subsets. Since the most common style distinctions among institutional equity managers are the large-cap versus small-cap dimension and the growth versus value dimension, we decided to examine how various stock-selection criteria performed within and across these two style dimensions. Our research approach was quantitative in order to objectively measure performance differences. However, most of our conclusions can be generalized to nonquantitative stock-selection methods as well.

Our research database contained the 1,500 largest companies by market capitalization (including nonsurvivors) each quarter over the 12-year period from September 1982 to June 1994. Each quarter, we split the 1,500 companies into style subsets based upon size and growth profiles. The large-cap style universe was simply defined as containing the largest 750 companies; the remaining 750 companies were placed in the small-cap style universe. For a second set of tests, we used *consensus* five-year expected EPS growth to divide stocks into growth and value style universes of 750 companies each.

To study stock-selection performance within and across style universes, we employed a "survey" approach. We selected a sample of 13 variables representing value, growth, earnings expectation, risk adversity, and technical approaches to stock selection. Each of these selection criteria has historically been effective in discriminating future performance over a broad cross-section of stocks. The 13 test variables are defined in Table 13-1.

All stocks were ranked quarterly into quintile groupings by each criteria within each investment-style universe. Subsequent quarterly total returns were aggregated on an equal weighted basis without transaction costs. Excess returns were calculated relative to the equal weighted average of all stocks within the style universe. The Spearman Rank Correlation Coefficient, also known as the information coefficient (IC), was used to gauge cross-sectional predictive power. In these tests, positive ICs were desirable and IC values exceeding +0.03 can be interpreted as economically significant (i.e., the test criteria would be capable of providing excess returns in actual portfolio trading).

TABLE 13-1.   Selection Criteria Definitions

	Prefer	Definition
Value Criteria		
Est EPS/Price	High	Consensus fiscal year estimated EPS/stock price
Price/book	Low	Stock price/book value per share
P/E/Est EPS Gth	Low	Estimated P/E/consensus estimated five-year annual EPS growth rate
Growth Criteria		
3Y EPS Gth	High	Actual reported EPS growth rate last three years
1Y EPS Gth	High	Actual reported EPS growth rate last four quarters
ROE	High	Reported EPS last four quarters/book value per share
EPS Expectation Criteria		
Qtrly EPS Surprise	High	(Reported EPS – Consensus estimated EPS)/Consensus estimated EPS
3M EPS Est Chg	High	Change in current year consensus estimated EPS over last three months
Risk Adversity Criteria		
Est EPS Coef Variation	Low	Standard deviation of current year EPS estimates/Consensus EPS estimate
R-sq 3Y EPS Gth	High	R-square value from regression through reported EPS last three years
Beta	Low	Covariance of monthly stock returns with S&P 500 Index
Technical Criteria		
12M Price Momentum	High	Stock price change last 12 months
1M Price Reversal	Low	Stock price change last month

Market-Capitalization Style Universe Results

Tables 13-2 and 13-3 summarize stock-selection factor predictive power within the large-cap and small-cap style universes.

Note first the large difference in overall stock-selection effectiveness within the two capitalization style universes (line 19 in each table).

TABLE 13-2. Stock Selection within Large-Cap Universe

Selection Criteria	Avg IC	Std Dev IC	Qn 1 Exc Ret	Qn 2 Exc Ret	Qn 3 Exc Ret	Qn 4 Exc Ret	Qn 5 Exc Ret
1 Est EPS/Price	0.059	0.155	1.01	0.19	−0.05	−0.32	−0.81
2 Price/book	0.034	0.172	0.88	−0.16	−0.21	−0.30	−0.22
3 P/E/Est EPS Gth	0.029	0.158	0.15	0.72	0.27	−0.44	−0.68
4 *Value Average*	0.041	0.162	0.68	0.25	0.00	−0.36	−0.57
5 3Y EPS Gth	0.020	0.123	0.24	0.03	0.22	0.12	−0.60
6 1Y EPS Gth	0.019	0.115	0.54	0.48	0.08	−0.70	−0.42
7 ROE	0.017	0.136	0.35	0.05	0.09	−0.25	−0.24
8 *Growth Average*	0.019	0.125	0.38	0.19	0.13	−0.28	−0.42
9 Qtrly EPS Surprise	0.033	0.073	0.56	0.78	−0.11	−0.24	−0.99
10 3M EPS Est Chg	0.050	0.124	1.12	0.39	0.02	−0.48	−1.03
11 *EPS Expectations Average*	0.042	0.099	0.84	0.58	−0.05	−0.36	−1.01
12 Est EPS Coef Variation	0.038	0.142	0.54	0.13	0.00	0.11	−0.77
13 R-sq 3Y EPS Gth	0.008	0.109	0.33	−0.03	−0.13	0.01	−0.18
14 Beta	0.028	0.207	−0.07	0.37	0.21	−0.16	−0.37
15 *Risk Adversity Average*	0.025	0.153	0.27	0.16	0.03	−0.01	−0.44
16 12M Price Momentum	0.024	0.162	0.78	0.28	−0.15	−0.08	−0.82
17 1M Price Reversal	0.020	0.117	−0.09	0.34	0.32	0.17	−0.76
18 *Technical Average*	0.022	0.140	0.35	0.31	0.09	0.05	−0.79
19 *Large-Cap Univ Average*	0.029	0.138	0.49	0.27	0.04	−0.20	−0.61

Average ICs and quintile excess returns were about twice as great in the small-cap universe.[1] Predictive performance consistency was significantly better as well. The small-cap universe IC standard deviation was only 0.109 versus 0.138 in the large-cap universe. These results are not really surprising since we might expect small-cap stocks to be less efficiently priced than large-caps. Unfortunately, greater transaction costs within the small-cap universe would eat up some or all of these return differences in "real-world" portfolio trading.

Relative stock-selection performance was stronger within the small-cap universe for each of our five selection criteria groups as

[1] Simple averages across criteria groups and universes are used to show performance tendencies; the performance of multivariate model constructions using the same factors would surely differ.

TABLE 13-3.   Stock Selection within Small-Cap Universe

Selection Criteria	Avg IC	Std Dev IC	Qn 1 Exc Ret	Qn 2 Exc Ret	Qn 3 Exc Ret	Qn 4 Exc Ret	Qn 5 Exc Ret
1 Est EPS/Price	0.073	0.147	1.79	0.22	−0.20	−0.82	−1.01
2 Price/book	0.038	0.155	1.25	0.06	−0.49	−0.89	0.09
3 P/E/Est EPS Gth	0.028	0.127	0.69	0.56	−0.04	−0.27	−0.96
4 *Value Average*	0.046	0.143	1.24	0.28	−0.24	−0.66	−0.63
5 3Y EPS Gth	0.045	0.102	0.99	0.46	−0.07	−0.53	−0.85
6 1Y EPS Gth	0.067	0.076	1.90	0.68	−0.03	−0.91	−1.62
7 ROE	0.030	0.094	0.63	0.28	−0.08	−0.31	−0.50
8 *Growth Average*	0.047	0.091	1.17	0.47	−0.06	−0.59	−0.99
9 Qtrly EPS Surprise	0.055	0.089	1.04	1.06	−0.17	−0.69	−1.22
10 3M EPS Est Chg	0.107	0.099	2.55	1.22	−0.15	−1.18	−2.44
11 *EPS Expectations Average*	0.081	0.094	1.79	1.14	−0.16	−0.94	−1.83
12 Est EPS Coef Variation	0.055	0.092	1.05	0.66	0.13	−0.75	−1.11
13 R-sq 3Y EPS Gth	0.019	0.080	0.70	−0.09	−0.31	0.23	−0.51
14 Beta	0.050	0.193	0.31	0.26	0.23	−0.44	−0.37
15 *Risk Adversity Average*	0.041	0.122	0.69	0.28	0.02	−0.32	−0.66
16 12M Price Momentum	0.062	0.132	1.98	0.27	−0.17	−0.33	−1.76
17 1M Price Reversal	0.012	0.079	−0.06	0.03	0.91	−0.03	−0.86
18 *Technical Average*	0.037	0.106	0.96	0.15	0.37	−0.18	−1.31
19 *Small-Cap Univ Average*	0.052	0.109	1.10	0.50	0.07	−0.46	−1.21

well (see lines 4, 8, 11, 15, and 18 in Tables 13-2 and 13-3). Only the value criteria group showed similar performance within the large-cap and small-cap style universes. Growth and EPS expectations group performances were much stronger within the small-cap universe.

Similar relationships held at the individual selection criteria level. Only the price/book, "PEG," and price reversal criteria (lines 2, 3, and 17) performed similarly within both capitalization-style universes. One-year EPS growth, three-month EPS estimate change, and 12-month price momentum (lines 6, 10, and 16) were significantly stronger within the small-cap universe.

In summary, these results suggest that a single set of stock-selection criteria would *not* be optimal for separate large-cap and small-cap style portfolios. If possible, large-cap specialists should emphasize value over growth criteria and also pay attention to earnings expectations for best stock-selection performance. Small-cap specialists may employ either a fundamental value or growth approach, but should give very strong consideration to earnings expectations and other momentum-oriented criteria in their stock selection processes.

Growth/Value Style Universe Results

Our growth- and value-style universe tests provided much more disparate results. Tables 13-4 and 13-5 summarize predictive power within the growth and value universes.

Though overall stock-selection criteria performance was similar across both universes, excess returns were larger and predictive con-

TABLE 13-4.   Stock Selection within Growth Universe

Selection Criteria	Avg IC	Std Dev IC	Qn 1 Exc Ret	Qn 2 Exc Ret	Qn 3 Exc Ret	Qn 4 Exc Ret	Qn 5 Exc Ret
1 Est EPS/Price	0.039	0.115	0.82	0.36	−0.07	−0.51	−0.62
2 Price/book	−0.001	0.140	0.46	−0.28	−0.45	−0.34	0.63
3 P/E/Est EPS Gth	0.023	0.122	0.55	−0.01	0.16	0.43	−1.12
4 *Value Average*	0.020	0.126	0.61	0.02	−0.12	−0.14	−0.37
5 3Y EPS Gth	0.007	0.096	0.18	0.12	−0.15	0.24	−0.41
6 1Y EPS Gth	0.057	0.081	1.51	0.80	0.12	−1.11	−1.33
7 ROE	0.029	0.098	0.83	0.23	−0.27	−0.50	−0.30
8 *Growth Average*	0.031	0.092	0.84	0.39	−0.10	−0.45	−0.68
9 Qtrly EPS Surprise	0.066	0.064	1.76	0.96	−0.30	−0.98	−1.45
10 3M EPS Est Chg	0.101	0.096	2.67	1.00	−0.30	−0.95	−2.42
11 *EPS Expectations Average*	0.084	0.080	2.22	0.98	−0.30	−0.96	−1.93
12 Est EPS Coef Variation	0.052	0.104	0.81	0.66	−0.05	−0.31	−1.11
13 R-sq 3Y EPS Gth	0.025	0.100	0.38	0.40	−0.24	−0.13	−0.42
14 Beta	0.038	0.153	0.36	0.18	−0.05	−0.10	−0.40
15 *Risk Adversity Average*	0.038	0.119	0.52	0.41	−0.11	−0.18	−0.64
16 12M Price Momentum	0.070	0.134	1.93	0.73	0.08	−0.88	−1.85
17 1M Price Reversal	0.008	0.091	−0.54	0.64	0.55	0.18	−0.83
18 *Technical Average*	0.039	0.113	0.69	0.68	0.31	−0.35	−1.34
19 *Growth Universe Average*	0.040	0.107	0.90	0.45	−0.07	−0.38	−0.89

sistency a bit better within the growth-style universe (see line 19 in both tables). However, many interesting differences emerged at the level of the five selection-criteria groups (lines 4, 8, 11, 15, and 18), with only the growth criteria performing somewhat similarly within both style universes. Interestingly, growth criteria had slightly greater predictive power within the value-stock universe than within the growth-stock universe. However, the value criteria group did not conform to the same pattern. Value-criteria performance was far better within the value universe than within the growth universe. EPS expectations, risk adversity, and technical criteria all performed much better within the growth universe.

Several additional divergences arose among the individual stock selection criteria. While the price/book criteria (line 2) worked quite

TABLE 13-5. Stock Selection within Value Universe

Selection Criteria	Avg IC	Std Dev IC	Qn 1 Exc Ret	Qn 2 Exc Ret	Qn 3 Exc Ret	Qn 4 Exc Ret	Qn 5 Exc Ret
1 Est EPS/Price	0.082	0.172	1.37	0.54	−0.28	−0.40	−1.25
2 Price/book	0.056	0.136	0.89	0.60	−0.18	−0.53	−0.77
3 P/E/Est EPS Gth	0.057	0.166	1.03	0.54	0.06	−0.74	−0.88
4 *Value Average*	0.065	0.158	1.10	0.56	−0.13	−0.56	−0.97
5 3Y EPS Gth	0.052	0.141	1.06	0.18	0.01	−0.60	−0.66
6 1Y EPS Gth	0.030	0.107	0.79	0.21	0.04	−0.36	−0.68
7 ROE	0.025	0.152	0.26	−0.17	0.49	−0.14	−0.46
8 *Growth Average*	0.036	0.133	0.71	0.08	0.18	−0.36	−0.60
9 Qtrly EPS Surprise	0.032	0.080	0.53	0.37	−0.16	0.15	−0.89
10 3M EPS Est Chg	0.057	0.138	1.12	0.32	0.13	−0.46	−1.13
11 *EPS Expectations Average*	0.045	0.109	0.83	0.35	−0.01	−0.15	−1.01
12 Est EPS Coef Variation	0.037	0.142	0.39	0.25	0.06	−0.02	−0.66
13 R-sq 3Y EPS Gth	0.015	0.074	0.34	−0.03	−0.08	−0.03	−0.19
14 Beta	0.020	0.225	−0.11	0.02	0.25	0.11	−0.29
15 *Risk Adversity Average*	0.024	0.147	0.21	0.08	0.08	0.02	−0.38
16 12M Price Momentum	0.014	0.155	0.64	−0.20	0.10	−0.01	−0.51
17 1M Price Reversal	0.030	0.109	0.34	0.11	0.11	0.13	−0.70
18 *Technical Average*	0.022	0.132	0.49	−0.05	0.10	0.06	−0.61
19 *Value Universe Average*	0.039	0.138	0.67	0.21	0.04	−0.22	−0.70

well within the value universe, price/book actually performed per-versely within the growth universe. The three-year EPS growth crite-ria (line 5) showed a similar pattern. By contrast, the momentum-ori-ented one-year EPS growth, quarterly EPS surprise, three-month EPS estimate change, and 12-month price strength criteria (lines 6, 9, 10, and 16) all performed much better within the growth-style universe than within the value universe.

In summary, these results again suggest that a single set of stock-selection criteria would not be optimal for both growth- and value-style portfolios. Growth-stock specialists should focus on earnings expectations and other momentum-oriented criteria and pay little attention to value (or even additional growth factors!) for best stock-selection performance. Value specialists should emphasize basic value in their stock selection, but also give some consideration to short- and long-term earnings growth prospects in their stock-selection processes.

Conclusions

This research survey clearly indicates that stock-selection criteria per-formance varies within and across market subsets, sometimes signifi-cantly. Therefore, investors who have been successful using a given stock-selection approach within either a broad stock universe or a particular market subset should not blindly apply the same selection strategy within a different selection universe. Before creating new equity-investment style products or implementing style-rotation strategies, proposed stock-selection criteria should be carefully tested to ensure optimal future performance within constrained selection universes.

Equity Style Timing and Allocation

Stephen C. Fan, Ph.D., Vice President
Vestek Systems, Inc.

Equity style investment has been around for years. The most prominent equity investment styles are the "value" investment style and the "growth" investment styles. These two investment-styles are the result of century-old investment philosophies. The value investment-style philosophy is based on the assumption that some stocks are underpriced relative to the value of their current assets or current cash flows. These underpriced stocks tend to be the stocks that are oversold by investors due to negative news or less-glamorous stocks that are neglected by general investors. The growth investment-style philosophy is based on the optimistic expectation of the future cash flows of fast-growing companies. Such companies tend to be overpriced if measured against the value of their current assets or current cash flows.

Derived from different investment philosophies, the value and growth equity-style portfolios represent different segments of the overall equity market. Historically, these two segments of the equity market have performed quite differently. As a consequence, equity style management is an important part of an equity portfolio manager's job. For passive-portfolio managers, a neutralized style exposure is essential to minimize the tracking error against any equity benchmark. For active-portfolio managers, the style segments provide an excellent opportunity to enhance portfolio returns through active equity style timing.

However, under the efficient market hypothesis, is active equity style timing and allocation an illusive fantasy or a reality? Using the Standard & Poor's 500 Value and Growth Indices as an example, this chapter explores various techniques for equity style timing and allocation. It shows that skillful equity style timing can be quite profitable. Assuming monthly rebalance, a perfect equity style timing skill could have produced an annual gross excess-return of 10.16% in the last 10 years (January 1985 to December 1994). The average annual turnover was about 530%. This assumes a 100% turnover at each monthly style-trend change. However, equity style allocation can also be dangerous. At the extreme, the worst equity style timing skill would have incurred a gross annual excess-loss of 9.41%.

This research introduces three hypotheses for equity style timing: the economic-cycle hypothesis, the stock-valuation hypothesis and the mean-reversion hypothesis. The economic-cycle hypothesis is based upon the assumption that the style trend reflects the economic cycles. The stock-valuation hypothesis is based upon the assumption that the style trend reflects the fundamental value of individual stocks in each style pool. The mean-reversion hypothesis is based upon the assumption that the style trend reflects the mean reversion of the overvalued and the undervalued stocks. Four successful equity-style timing models were subsequently derived from these three hypotheses; namely, the forecast real GDP model, the earning-revision spread model, the forecast P/E spread model, and the residual-risk spread model.

This chapter shows that any one of these four models can produce a profitable investment strategy. Nevertheless, it also demonstrates that a properly structured multifactor style timing-model can enhance the effectiveness of the single-factor models. Several multifactor equity-style timing-model construction techniques are presented in this chapter. The multifactor style timing-model introduced in this chapter would have generated about 5.29% annual gross excess-return during the last 10 years with an average annual turnover of 260%. The style timing-models introduced here were constructed at the end of October, 1993. Since then, these style timing-models have experienced about 14 months of real-time simulation, during which time the multifactor style timing-model generated a gross excess return of 4.52% with a turnover of 200%.

These style-timing models can be tailored into a variety of investment strategies. They can be easily modified to meet various risk tolerance and turnover-constraint mandates. Possible applications of these style timing-models range from plan sponsors' total fund-allocation and cash-flow management, active portfolio-management strategies, to proprietary trading strategies. Given the polarized nature of equity style performance, the style timing-models are ideal for market-neutral strategies which would double the potential of alphas.

Equity Style Definition

Even though we can conceptually identify the value and the growth investment-styles, there is no unique definition for them. The most convenient and natural way to define value and growth equity-styles is to use the ratio of each stock's price to its current asset-value or cash flows. Standard & Poor's equity style indices are based on the price-to-book (P/B) ratio of each stock. Frank Russell's equity style indices are based on the price-to-adjusted-book-value ratio. Using the price-to-book ratio is better than using the price-to-current-cash-flow ratio, because the latter is a less stable number.

However, using the P/B ratio seems to oversimplify the definition of the investment styles. First of all, reported accounting book-value versus the true economic value of corporate assets is controversial. Second, basic economics suggests that not all companies with high P/B ratios are growth companies. Some companies have low book-value due to poor corporate management. Such companies are understressed (sometimes shrinking) companies rather than growing companies. Of course, one could argue that the understressed companies are qualified as growth companies. That argument suggests that if these companies emerge from the lows of their recent performance, the improvement could be a drastic growth from their poor past. However, that is a big "if" to assume, since it is more likely that these companies could go under. Third, both the Standard & Poor's and the Frank Russell's style indices (except the more recent Russell 2000 style indices) split the whole equity-universe in the middle based on the cumulative capitalization. It is not convincing that a company with a P/B ratio of 2 is a value company while a company with a P/B ratio of 2.1 is a growth company. Companies with a market-like P/B ratio are usually neither a growth nor a value company. Including them in either equity style index is misleading.

The current trend of the value- and growth-index construction is to allow a market-like section to prevent stocks with market-like characteristics from getting into either the value or the growth universe. In addition, multifactor models beyond the P/B ratio are proposed to identify the true (or more true) value- and growth-oriented stocks.

Since none of the improved indices are commercially available, this study uses the Standard & Poor's 500 style indices as the equity style surrogates. Figure 14-1 shows the similar performance pattern of two of the most popular sets of equity style indices: S&P 500 style

FIGURE 14-1. Normalized Cumulative Excess-Return
Value and growth

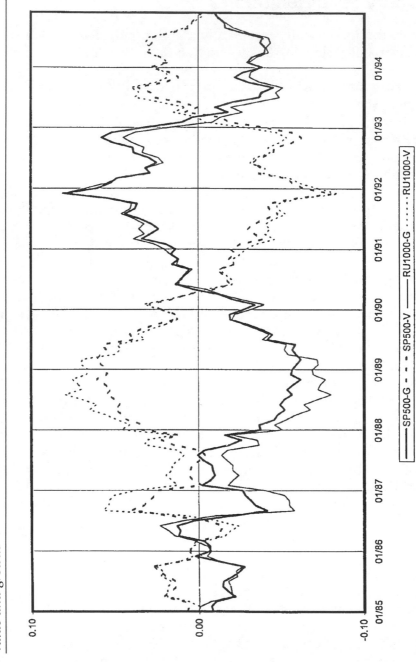

indices and Russell 1000 style indices. In the exhibit, the equity style trends can be easily identified. For instance, from mid-1987 to the end of 1988, the value investment-style outperformed the growth investment-style. After that, the style trend reversed to favor the growth investment-style for three years until the end of 1991. From that time, the value investment-style dominated the growth investment-style up to mid 1994. These equity style trends do not seem to be random aberrations of market volatility. Each of the afore-mentioned style trends protracted for more than one year. Another noticeable observation is that the equity style trend seems to be a mean-reverting phenomenon. After a period of out- or underperformance, both equity styles' performance revert to the market mean-performance, i.e., S&P 500 Index or Russell 1000 Index performance.

Economic-Sector Composition of Style Indices

One intuitive explanation of the equity style trends is that they result from different economic-sector compositions. Each national economy has matured and burgeoning economic sectors. One would expect that the value-style index is more pronounced in the matured economic sectors and the growth-style index is more pronounced in the growing economic sectors. Figure 14-2 shows the over- and underexposures of economic sectors of the S&P 500 Value Index relative to the S&P 500 index over last 10 years.

In general, the value universe is overweighted in the more matured economic sectors such as consumer durables, energy, financial services, raw materials, shelter, transportation, and utilities. On the other hand, the growth-style universe is overweighted in the less matured or still growing economic sectors such as business equipment and services, capital goods, consumer nondurables, consumer services, healthcare, and retail. This economic-sector dominance is quite intuitive. More interestingly, the economic-sector domination is not a static phenomenon. The technology sector began as a growth sector and ended up as a value sector. At the end of 1994, the technology sector seemed to be heading toward the growth sector. This reflects the economic history of the U.S. high-tech industry very well. In the early 1980s, the technology sector was dominated by fast growing, computer-hardware-related startup companies. In the late 1980s,

FIGURE 14-2. Sector-Exposure Difference
S&P 500 Value Index versus S&P 500 Index

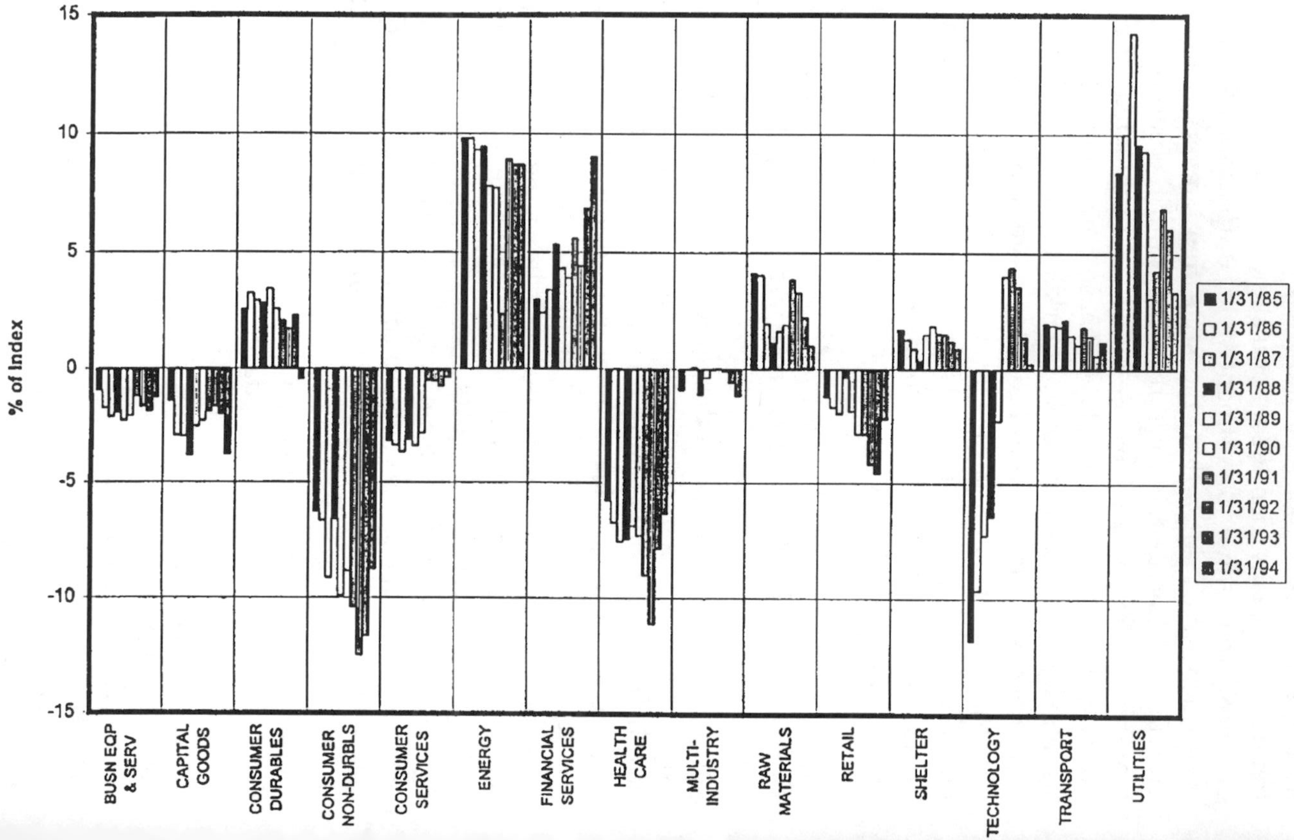

these companies matured as the first generation of computing technology matured. Then, in the early 1990s, a new wave of computing and software technology started to emerge in the area of computer networking, telecommunication, and multimedia application. Not surprisingly, the technology sector became a growth-oriented sector again. Another noticeable trend is that the consumer service-industry gradually matured since the U.S. economy transformed into a service economy in the early 1980s.

Observing the characteristics of economic-sector concentration, one would expect that the style trend is related to economic cycles. In general, the value-style index should do well during strong economic cycles because the matured economic sectors tend to expand and shrink with the general economy. On the other hand, the growth-style index should do better during weaker economic cycles because only the growing companies can defy the force of a shrinking economy.

The Return and Risk Nature of Equity Style Allocations

Before introducing any equity style timing-model, it is important to examine the risk and return characteristics of equity style allocation. Figure 14-3 shows the cumulative performance of extremely successful and unsuccessful style-allocation strategies against the cumulative performance of the S&P 500 Index, the S&P 500 Value Index, and the S&P 500 Growth Index.

Due to the mean-reversion nature (see Figure 14-1) of equity style performance, the S&P 500 Index, the S&P 500 Value Index, and the S&P 500 Growth Index have more or less equal performance in the long run. However, assuming monthly rebalance, the best style allocation skill (correct style allocation every month) would lead to 523% gross excess return relative to the S&P 500 Index, while the worst style allocation skill (incorrect style allocation every month) would lead to 224% gross underperformance relative to the S&P 500 Index over the 10-year period (1985–1994). Table 14-1 presents the annual excess returns and turnovers of these extreme cases.

Assuming an average five cents per share commission cost and an average $40 share price for the stocks in the S&P 500 universe, the one-way trading cost in terms of fund performance is about 12.5 basis

FIGURE 14-3. Cumulative Returns

Best allocation, worst allocation, and indices

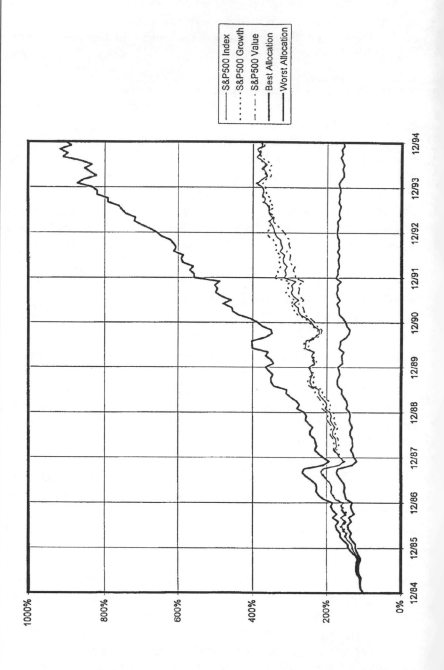

TABLE 14-1. Potential of Style Timing

	Best Allocation		Worst Allocation		
	Gross	Net	Gross	Net	Turnover
1985	7.91%	6.11%	−7.59%	−9.39%	300%
1986	12.11%	8.51%	−11.49%	−15.09%	600%
1987	9.05%	6.65%	−8.40%	−10.80%	400%
1988	8.22%	3.42%	−7.56%	−12.36%	800%
1989	7.96%	4.36%	−8.22%	−11.82%	600%
1990	9.08%	5.48%	−8.72%	−12.32%	600%
1991	13.25%	9.65%	−12.66%	−16.26%	600%
1992	10.52%	7.52%	−9.59%	−12.59%	500%
1993	16.54%	14.14%	−14.73%	−17.13%	400%
1994	6.99%	3.99%	−5.12%	−8.12%	500%
Average	10.16%	6.98%	−9.41%	−12.59%	530%
Standard deviation	2.99%	2.14%	2.81%	1.96%	142%

points. The round-trip cost on the performance is about 25 basis points. Allowing other factors in the trading events such as price impact, a conservative 60 basis-point round-trip turnover cost (or 12 cents per share one-way trading cost) is assumed in the calculation of the net excess-returns.

On an annual basis, the best style-allocation skill generated a positive gross excess-return of 10.16% and net excess-return of 6.98%. The worst style-allocation skill generated a gross excess-return of −9.41% and net excess-return of −12.59%. The average annual turnover is 530%.

Foundations for Style Timing-Models

There are many ways to construct a style timing-model. Four style timing-models are introduced. They are based on the three different hypotheses discussed earlier; namely, the economic-cycle hypothesis, the stock-valuation hypothesis, and the mean-reversion hypothesis. The first of these models, the real GDP forecast model, is based on the economic-cycle hypothesis. Under this hypothesis, the strong economy favors the investment of value style and vice versa. The second model, the forecast P/E spread model, is based on the mean-reversion hypothesis. Under this hypothesis, the trend of the narrowing forecast P/E ratio between the value index and the growth index should favor the value-style investment. The third model, the earning-revision spread model, is based on the stock-valuation hypothesis. Under this hypothesis, when the earning-revision score of the value-style index is higher than that of the growth index, the value index should outperform the growth index and vice versa. The fourth model, the residual-risk spread model, is also based on the mean-reversion model. When a stock's residual risk increases, it indicates that the stock is either falling out of market fad or is being neglected by investors. Under this hypothesis, when the residual risk of the value-style index is higher than that of the growth index, the value index is underperforming the growth index, and vice versa.

Style Trend and Real GDP Growth Forecast

Given the sector bias in the style universes, one would expect the forecast economic-performances to signal the style trend. Figure 14-4 shows the relationship between the consensus real GDP growth forecast (provided by the Blue Chip Economic Indicator Service, which includes about 60 economists from various blue-chip companies) and the relative cumulative return of S&P 500 Value Index relative to the S&P 500 Growth Index.

As expected, the value-style index did well when the economy was expected to do well, and vice versa.

Style Trend and Forecast P/E Spread

In general, the growth index has a higher P/E ratio than the value index. This reflects the higher growth-potential of stocks in the growth index. This model assumes that the P/E spread between the growth index and the value index maintains an equilibrium level in the long run. Hence, when the forecast P/E narrows, the value index should do well. Figure 14-5 shows the relationship between the forecast P/E spread (the forecast P/E is calculated based on the IBES year-one earnings forecast versus the current stock-price) and the relative cumulative return of S&P 500 Value Index against the S&P 500 Growth Index.

As expected, the value index did well when the forecast P/E spread was low (smaller negative value), and vice versa.

FIGURE 14-4. Value-Growth Relative Return versus Real GDP Growth Forecast

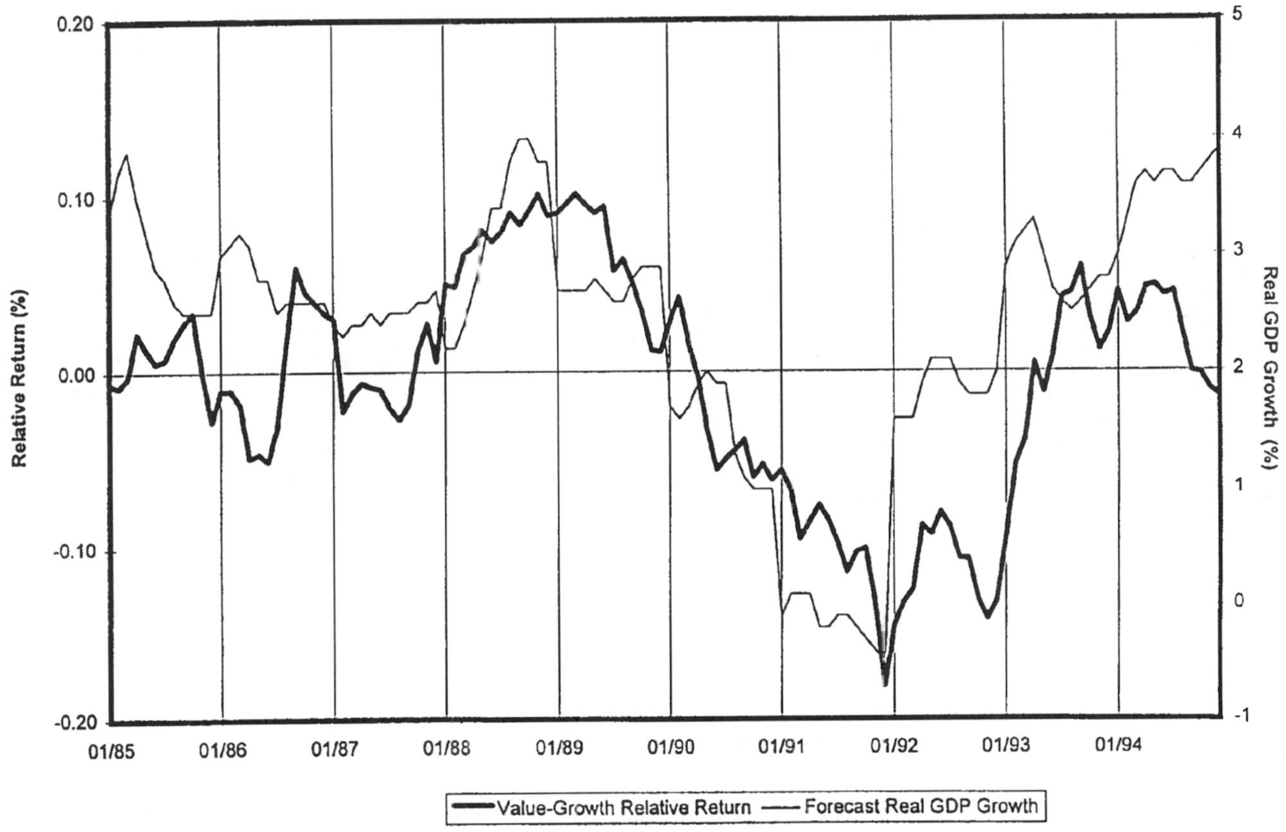

FIGURE 14-5. Value-Growth Relative Return versus Forecast P/E Spread

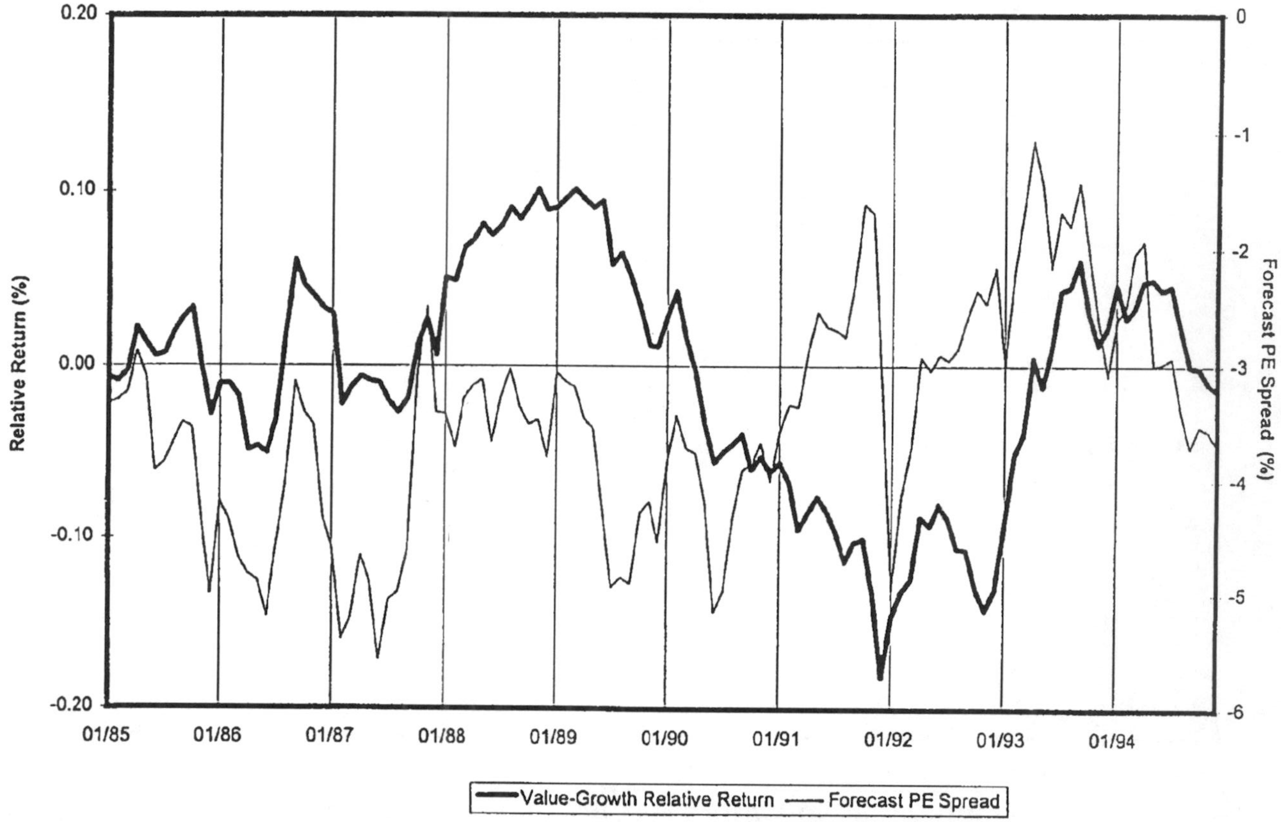

308

Style Trend and Earning-Revision Model

The earning-revision model has been a successful model for individual stock ranking in the past. One would expect that the bottom-up earning-revision score of style indices would shed some light on the style trend. The earning-revision model used here is the weighted-average five-month earning forecast (the IBES FY1 consensus forecast) changes. Figure 14-6 shows the close relationship between the earning-revision model score-spread and the relative cumulative return between S&P 500 Value Index relative to the S&P 500 Growth Index.

Style Trend and Residual-Risk Spread

When a stock's residual risk increases, it indicates that the stock is either falling behind the general market fad or is being neglected by the investors. Given the mean-reversion nature of the style trend, one would expect that the bottom-up specific-risk spread between the style indices would shed some light on the style trend. Figure 14-7 shows the relationship between the spread of residual risk between the value-style index and the growth index and the relative cumulative return of S&P 500 Value Index against the S&P 500 Growth Index.

Style Timing-Model Construction

Figures 14-4 through 14-7 graphically show the potential of four single-factor style timing-models (the forecast real GDP model, the forecast P/E spread, the earning-revision spread model, and the residual-risk spread model). This section more rigorously examines the forecast capability of each model.

Basic Statistics of Single-Factor Style Timing-Models

Tables 14-2 through 14-5 show five simple statistics—the rank correlation, the value correlation, the hit ratio, the cumulative alpha, and the annual alpha—for each of the four single-factor style timing-models. The rank correlation is the correlation between the ex post equity-style rank and the predicted style rank. The rank of the value style is set to 1 and the rank of the growth style is set to −1. The value correlation is the correlation between the value of the predictor and

FIGURE 14-6. Value-Growth Relative Return versus Earning-Revision Score Spread

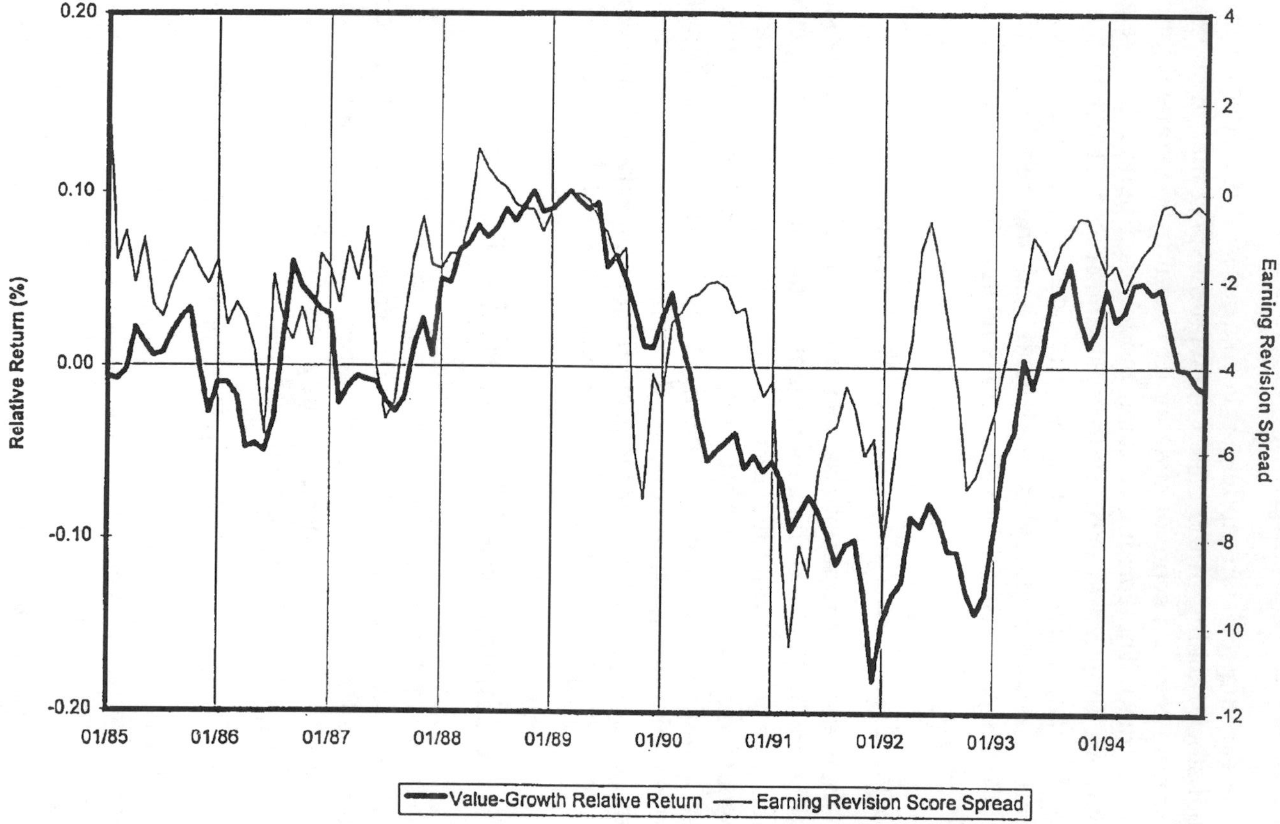

310

FIGURE 14-7. Value-Growth Relative Return versus Residual-Risk Spread

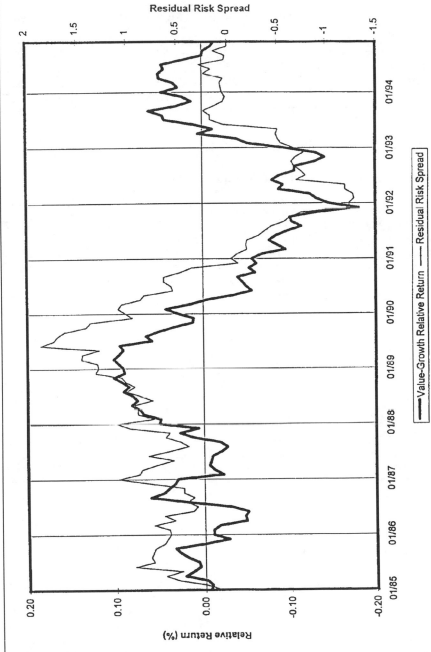

311

TABLE 14-2. Forecast Real GDP Model

	Concurrent	Lag-1	Mov-3	Mov-4	Mov-5	Mov-6
Correlation—rank	−0.06	0.04	0.10	0.09	0.11	0.11
Correlation—value	−0.11	−0.09	−0.09	−0.08	−0.06	−0.03
Hit ratio	46.67%	51.26%	54.24%	53.85%	55.17%	54.78%
Cumulative	59.94%	15.22%	57.29%	84.42%	70.29%	63.22%
Annual	1.77%	0.48%	1.73%	2.62%	2.26%	2.07%

TABLE 14-3. Forecast P/E Spread Model

	Concurrent	Lag-1	Mov-3	Mov-4	Mov-5	Mov-6
Correlation—rank	0.45	0.08	−0.09	−0.19	−0.06	−0.07
Correlation—value	0.03	0.02	0.04	0.03	0.03	0.01
Hit ratio	72.50%	53.78%	44.92%	40.17%	46.55%	46.09%
Cumulative	276.83%	11.55%	22.66%	−0.57%	30.38%	−35.60%
Annual	6.70%	0.36%	0.71%	−0.02%	1.03%	−1.32%

TABLE 14-4. Earning-Revision Spread Model

	Concurrent	Lag-1	Mov-3	Mov-4	Mov-5	Mov-6
Correlation—rank	0.23	0.11	−0.06	−0.03	−0.04	−0.04
Correlation—value	0.02	0.09	0.12	0.11	0.10	0.09
Hit ratio	59.17%	53.78%	46.61%	47.86%	47.41%	46.96%
Cumulative	106.11%	101.58%	−2.65%	34.93%	13.07%	−1.91%
Annual	2.99%	2.90%	−0.09%	1.15%	0.45%	−0.07%

TABLE 14-5. Residual-Risk Spread Model

	Concurrent	Lag-1	Mov-3	Mov-4	Mov-5	Mov-6
Correlation—rank	0.39	−0.05	−0.09	−0.02	0.03	−0.15
Correlation—value	0.22	0.21	0.35	0.37	0.40	0.00
Hit ratio	69.17%	47.06%	44.92%	48.72%	50.86%	42.61%
Cumulative	235.71%	17.97%	−31.99%	9.94%	7.56%	−45.04%
Annual	5.89%	0.56%	−1.08%	0.34%	0.26%	−1.70%

the value of the ex post return of the predicted equity style relative to the other equity style. The hit ratio is the percentage of time, the equity style predictor predicts the right equity style. The cumulative excess return is the cumulative return of each model performance relative to the S&P 500 Index performance. The annual excess return is the average annual excess model-performance relative to the S&P 500 Index. Each single-factor model has six model-structures: the concurrent model, the Lag-1 model, the Mov-3 model, the Mov-4 model, the Mov-5 model, and the Mov-6 model. The concurrent model uses the concurrent signal. The concurrent signal is the change of each factor score between the point of forecast t and the end of the following time-period $t + 1$, i.e., $(x_{t+1} - x_t)$. A strong concurrent model indicates the model is a lagging indicator rather than a leading indicator. The Lag-1 model uses the trailing one-month signal. It is the change of each variable between the point of forecast t and the end of previous period $t - 1$, i.e., $(x_t - x_{t-1})$. The Mov-3, Mov-4, Mov-5 and Mov-6 models are the moving average models using three to six months of *ex ante* information.

For the forecast real GDP models, the moving-average models seem to have a lot of potential. The *ex ante* rank correlation is around 0.1; however, the value correlations are negative. The hit ratios are low, but the models seem to be able to generate positive alphas. The forecast P/E spread model seems to be more of a lagging indicator than a leading indicator for equity style trends (huge rank-correlation and alphas for the concurrent model form). However, the Lag 1 model seems to have some *ex ante* equity style trend-forecast power. Interestingly enough, the value correlations are positive throughout the model forms of the forecast P/E spread model. The earning-revision spread model seems to work better in the Lag-1 form. In this form, both the rank and value correlations are positive and a sizable alpha was generated. The residual-risk spread model seems to be more a lagging indicator than a leading indicator. However, the positive value-correlations indicate that there is information content in the model.

The Ideal Style Timing-Model

Tables 14-2 through 14-5 show that there are two aspects of style timing: the style indicator, which correctly predicts the monthly style-trends, and the return associated with the style-trend forecast. A clairvoyant style-indicator would forecast each monthly style-trend correctly and capture the full benefits of 10.16% per annum alpha mentioned earlier. When this is not possible, capturing the longer-term trend (the return associated with the style-trend forecast) is more important than correctly predicting some of the monthly style-trends that have little excess return associated with them. Figure 14-8 demonstrates these two aspects of equity style timing. The longer-term style trend can be identified by the normalized cumulative excess return of the style indices. The short-term monthly style-trends are represented by the bars at the bottom of the exhibit. Each lower bar reflects a growth month and each upper bar indicates a value month. As can be seen, during the longer-term growth trend, there are large numbers of value months and vice versa. This explains why it is possible to have a low hit-ratio and the positive alphas at the same time as shown in Tables 14-2 through 14-5.

To balance the importance of monthly style-trends and the returns associated with them, a generalized regression process is suggested for constructing an ideal style timing-model. The first step is to identify the *ex post* monthly style-trend. The next step is to distinguish the significance of each monthly style-trend. An ad hoc way to approach this is to assign higher-rank significance to the monthly trends that are consistent with the longer-term style-trend. A less-involved way is to use each monthly relative-return as the indicator of the relative importance of each monthly style-trend. Figure 14-9 shows the relationship between the cumulative relative style-index return and the monthly style-trends. The curve is the cumulative relative return of the value index against the growth index. The bars at the bottom indicate the monthly style-trend. The upper bars, again, indicate the value months and the lower bars indicate the growth months.

The following model-specification is recommended for the generalized regression.

$$S_t = \alpha 0 + \beta_1 x_{t-1} + \beta_2 x_{t-2} + \beta_3 x_{t-3} + \beta_4 x_{t-4} + \beta_5 x_{t-5}$$

where S_t is the *ex post* style-trend with a rank value of either 1 or −1, i.e.,

$$\begin{cases} S_t = 1, \text{ if Value trend} \\ S_t = -1, \text{ if Growth trend} \end{cases}$$

FIGURE 14-8. Normalized Cumulative Excess Returns and Monthly Style-Trends

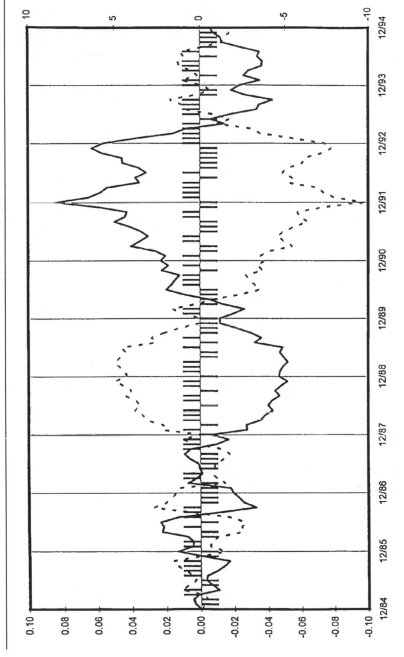

315

316

FIGURE 14-9. Value-Growth Relative Returns versus Monthly Style-Trend

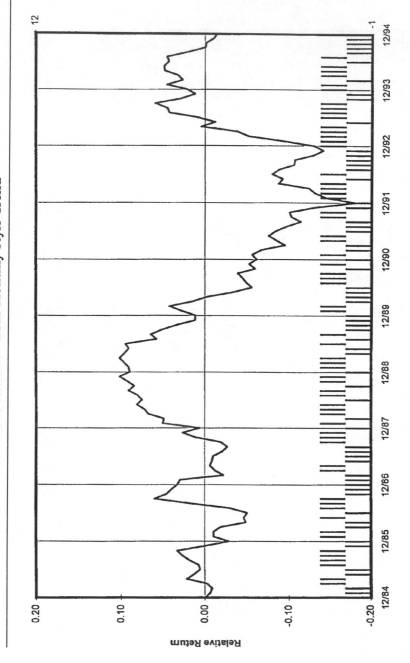

The Concept of Model Strength

Besides the significance of each monthly style-trend, there is the issue of model strength. For instance, when the forecast real GDP growth is at its normal range (say from 2% to 3%), any minor GDP change is usually a nonevent to the market. Figure 14-10 illustrates the arguments.

The lower bars indicate the months that the forecast GDP model forecast the equity style wrong when the model is used to forecast for all months. The upper bars indicate the error months when the same forecast GDP model is only used to forecast months when the forecast real GDP growth rate is greater than 3% or less than 2%. The hit ratio was improved from 59% to 74%.

Examples of Single-Factor Style Timing-Models

A set of heuristic single-factor style timing-models were constructed using spreadsheet models. Instead of the rigorous generalized regression, the trial-and-error method in the spirit of the generalized regression is used. Since these models are not constructed by the rigorous generalized regression, they are suboptimal. Nevertheless, they all demonstrate good style-trend forecast capability with sizable net excess-return over the S&P 500 Index. To minimize the aspect of data mining, only nicely rounded numbers were tried for model parameters.

The forecast real GDP model:

$$\hat{S}_t = 0.95 + 2x_{t-1} + 1.5x_{t-2} + x_{t-3} + x_{t-4} + x_{t-5}$$

The forecast P/E spread model:

$$\hat{S}_t = -0.3 + x_{t-1} + x_{t-2} + x_{t-3} + x_{t-4} + x_{t-5}$$

The earning-revision spread model:

$$\hat{S}_t = 0.6 + x_{t-1}$$

The residual-risk spread model:

$$\hat{S}_t = x_{t-1} + 1.5x_{t-3} - 0.5x_{t-5}$$

FIGURE 14-10. Forecast Error
All-period versus subperiod

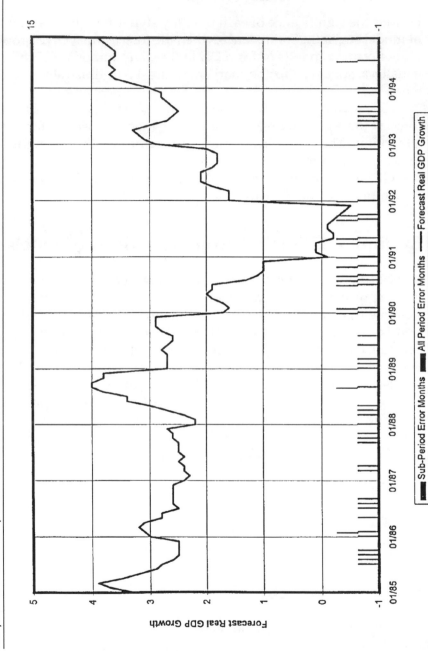

Single-Factor Model Performance

Tables 14-6 and 14-7 summarize the performance of the four single-factor style timing-models. Table 14-6 shows the results when the models were used to forecast style trends for the whole study-period. Table 14-7 shows the results when the models were used to forecast style-trends for appropriate subperiods. There are many ways to decide the appropriate subperiods for each model. For instance, one can use a neural network to pick appropriate subperiods for each model. To avoid data mining, the subperiods heuristically based on the forecast economic strength were chosen. The hypothesis is that during extreme economic condition, the forecast real GDP model would have the most information about the style trends and during normal economic conditions, other models have more information. The subperiod definition for each model is shown in the last column of Table 14-7. The residual-risk spread model is chosen to predict the style trends during the period of extraordinary GDP growth based on the intention to have two models for each economic condition.

Comparing Table 14-7 with Table 14-6, the subperiod method has higher excess-return and higher hit-ratios. The turnover cost,

TABLE 14-6.   All-Period Forecast

	Gross	Net	Turnover	Hit Ratio
Forecast GDP model	2.53%	1.93%	100%	59%
Forecast P/E spread model	1.39%	0.07%	220%	48%
Earning revision spread model	3.02%	0.06%	410%	55%
Residual risk spread model	1.35%	–2.31%	610%	54%

TABLE 14-7.   Subperiod Forecast

	Gross	Net	Turnover	Hit Ratio	GDP Growth Range
Forecast GDP model	2.84%	1.58%	210%	74%	>3.0% and <2.0%
Forecast P/E spread model	3.06%	1.68%	230%	55%	<3.5% and >2.0%
Earning revision spread model	3.11%	0.06%	420%	56%	<3.5% and >–1.5%
Residual risk spread model	1.45%	0.19%	210%	67%	>3.5% and <1.5%

again, is conservatively assumed at 12 cents per share one-way trading.

Figures 14-11 through 14-14 show two cumulative excess returns of each model, one for the all-period and one for the subperiod. The bars on the bottom of each figure indicate the subperiods defined in Table 14-7.

Multifactor Style Timing-Model

Modern portfolio theory teaches that diversification is a virtue. Just as experts can make mistakes, so can good models. A well-structured multifactor model should be able to diversify away some of the individual model's forecast errors. Given the concept of model strength introduced in Table 14-7, the multifactor-model approach can also enhance single-factor models' forecast capability through their complementary model strength.

Conceptual Multifactor Style Timing-Models

There are many ways to implement a multifactor style timing-model. First of all, the multifactor model can be intuitively put together based on the GARCH concept. The main spirit of the GARCH approach is to capture the major information-shocks from the market events. For instance, if there is a drastic change in the real GDP growth forecast, the forecast real GDP model should play the central role in the style-trend forecast. The implementation steps of a GARCH model could look like this. First, one can create a general multifactor style timing-model through a multivariate time-series regression. The model weighting can then be adjusted by refitting the model through various different historical market-events.

The second approach for constructing a multifactor style timing-model is to use Bayesian statistics. The first step is to construct Bayesian statistics for each single-factor model. These models are then dynamically adjusted based on Bayesian statistics.

The third approach for constructing a multifactor style timing-model is to use the principal-component analysis to find the canonical weights for each single-factor model.

The fourth approach is to use the Markowitz mean-variance optimization. The optimal weights are the weights that generate the

FIGURE 14-11. **Cumulative Excess Return**
Forecast real GDP model

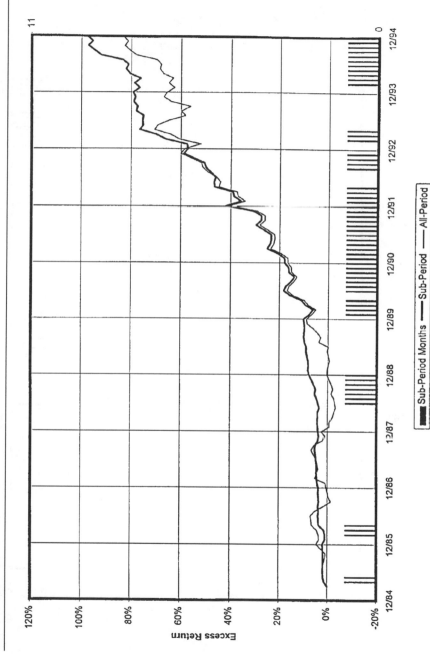

FIGURE 14-12. Cumulative Excess Return
Forecast P/E model

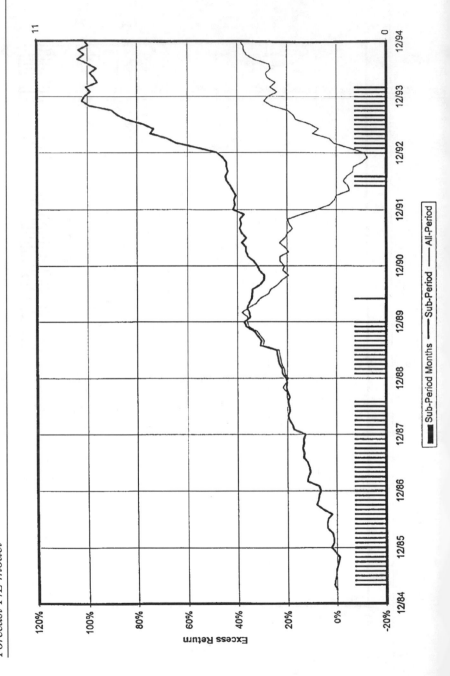

FIGURE 14-13. Cumulative Excess Return

Earning-revision model

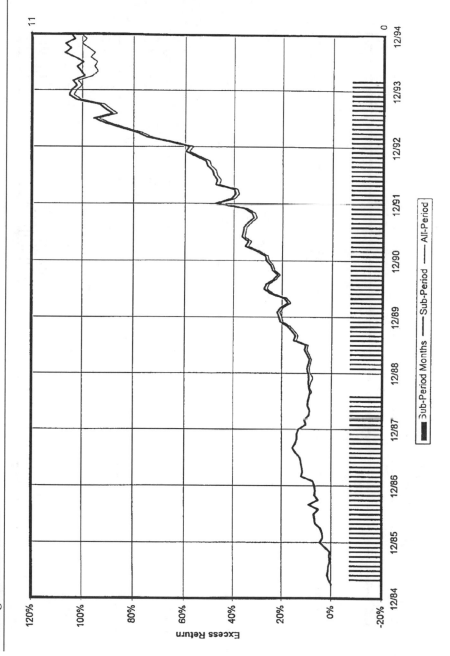

323

FIGURE 14-14.   Cumulative Excess Return
Residual-risk spread model

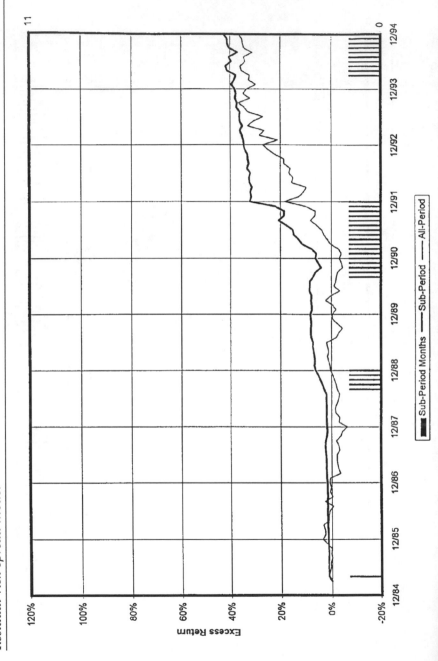

maximum expected return (expected alpha of the combined model) and minimum uncertainty (model forecast-error).

An Example of Multifactor Style Timing-Model

A heuristic multifactor style timing-model consisting of the four single-factor style timing-models was constructed using a spreadsheet. The trial-and-error approach was used to maximize the model return and minimize the model forecast-error (maximize the hit ratio). Again, only nicely rounded numbers were tried for the model weights. Table 14-8 lists the model weights for each single-factor style timing-model. Since this is not a rigorous optimization process, the model is assumed to be suboptimal.

Using the same conservative trading-cost assumption, Table 14-9 shows the model performance-summary. This multifactor style timing-model shows tremendous improvement over the individual single-factor models.

Figure 14-15 shows the individual annual excess-returns of the model. The 1985 excess return reflects a nine-month result due to the lagging of variables. Among the 10-year study period, the model was able to generate positive gross excess-return every year and only 1990 has a small negative net excess-return (keep in mind that a relatively-

TABLE 14-8.   Multifactor-Model Weights

	Weights
Forecast real GDP model	4.0
Forecast P/E model	2.0
Earning-revision model	1.0
Residual-risk reversal model	1.0

TABLE 14-9.   Multifactor-Model Performance (1985–1994)

	Mean	Standard Deviation
Gross annual excess-return	5.29%	3.43%
Net annual excess-return	3.73%	3.93%
Average annual turnover	260%	143%
Hit ratio	62%	

FIGURE 14-15. Annual Performance of Multifactor Style Timing-Model

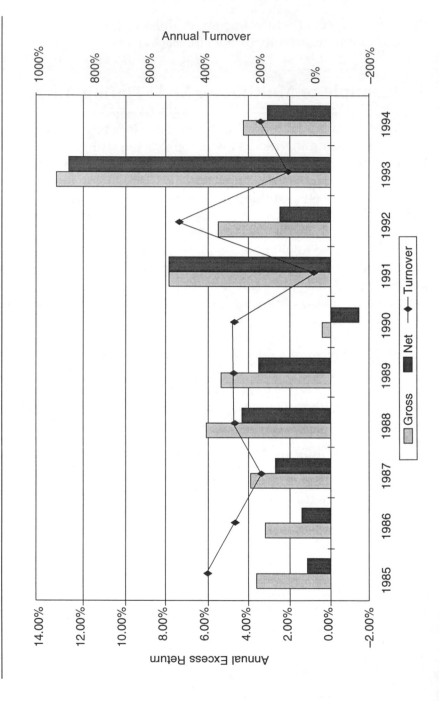

TABLE 14-10.   Out-of-Sample Model Performance

	1993 (2 months)	1994 (12 months)	Total (14 months)
Gross excess return	0.34%	4.15%	4.52%
Net excess return	0.34%	2.95%	3.32%
Turnover	0%	200%	200%
Hit ratio	50%	83%	78%

high transaction cost is assumed). The actual annual turnover ranges from the high of 500% in 1992 and the low of 0% in 1991.

This heuristic model was constructed at the end of October 1993. Table 14-10 shows the out-of-sample results.

Figure 14-16 shows the cumulative excess return of the multifactor style timing-model and that of each individual style timing-model. It shows that the multifactor model has about 70% more alpha than the best single-factor model.

Application of Style Timing-Models

Equity style is the main element of equity portfolio management. Fund managers usually have to identify themselves in terms of their investment styles (nonstyle-specific managers will be classified as style neutral or core style). The fund sponsors usually design their total fund-structure along the line of equity styles and then hire managers specialized in each style.

Style Allocation for Sponsors

Plan sponsors can use the style timing-models to develop their style-allocation policies. The study here assumes a full swing (i.e., 100% turnover) of fund allocation when the style timing-model forecasts a different style trend. For plan sponsors, it will be more meaningful to develop style-allocation policies to over- or underweight each equity style by an amount that is less than 100%. Conservative plan-sponsors may limit their active equity style exposure to 5%, while an aggressive plan-sponsor may tolerate a 10% to 20% active exposure. Table 14-11 shows the potential annual alpha for various style-allocation policies.

FIGURE 14-16. Cumulative Excess Returns
Model comparison

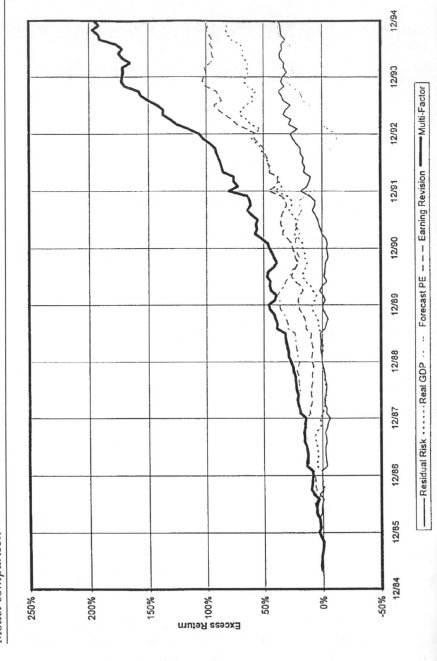

TABLE 14-11. Plan Sponsors' Style-Allocation Policies

Active Style Policy	Gross Alpha	Net Alpha
5%	0.263%	0.187%
10%	0.529%	0.373%
15%	0.792%	0.560%
20%	1.052%	0.746%

Another way plan sponsors can use these style timing-models is to create alphas in the cash contribution and cash withdrawal process. When there is a cash contribution, the cash can be allocated to good managers in the right equity style. When there is a cash withdrawal, the cash can be withdrawn from bad managers in the disfavored equity style.

Style Allocation for Money Managers or Proprietary Traders

For money managers, the style timing-model can be used in many different ways. For instance, an active fund with S&P 500 index as the benchmark can use the style timing-model as the sole alpha-generating engine or in conjunction with other alpha-generating machines. Fund mangers can control their fund risk through establishing a proper active equity-style exposure policy. For proprietary traders, the style timing provides excellent monthly arbitrage-opportunities. Recent news indicates that derivatives of the S&P 500 style indices are coming to markets in 1995. The trading cost of derivatives will be only a fraction of the physical positions. Given the polarized nature of equity style performance, the style timing-models are perfect for market-neutral strategies which would double the potential of alphas. Table 14-12 shows the benefits of a market-neutral strategy using the multifactor style timing-model.

TABLE 14-12. Market-Neutral Strategy Performance (1985–1994)

	Mean	Standard Deviation
Gross annual excess return	10.58%	7.85%
Net annual excess return	7.46%	7.86%
Average annual turnover	520%	286%
Hit ratio	62%	

Using Style Timing-Models to Enhance the Stock-Selection Process

Many money managers already apply sector-specific stock-selection models in their stock-selection processes. An extension of this research found that the stock-selection process is style dependent (Fan, working paper, 1995). Table 14-13 summarizes some of the findings. This is a nonexhaustive list. In sum, investors are willing to take more risk during the value periods. Hence, risky stocks (in terms of beta, EPS dispersion, price volatility, etc.) tend to do well. The opposite tends to be true during the growth periods. To avoid doubling the risk of style-trend forecast error, it is important to balance the style dependent stock-selection models with style independent stock-ranking models such as the earning revision models.

Conclusion

This research introduces three hypotheses for equity style timing; namely, the economic-cycle hypothesis, the stock-valuation hypothesis and the mean-reversion hypothesis. The economic-cycle hypothesis assumes that the style trend reflects the economic cycles. The stock-valuation hypothesis assumes that the style trend reflects the fundamental value of individual stocks in each style pool. The mean-reversion hypothesis assumes that the style trend reflects the mean

TABLE 14-13. Stock-Selection Model and Style Trends

	Value Universe	Growth Universe
Value Periods	High earning-revision	High earning-revision
	High P/B	High P/B
	High volatility	High debt-to-capital
	High EPS-dispersion	High EPS-dispersion
	High expected-return	Low P/E
Growth Periods	High earning-revision	High earning-revision
	Low volatility	Low dividend-yield
	Low beta	High beta
	High ROE	Low P/B
	Low EPS-dispersion	Low EPS-dispersion

reversion of the overvalued and the undervalued stocks. Four successful equity style timing-models were subsequently derived from these three hypotheses, namely the forecast real GDP model, the earning-revision spread model, the forecast P/E spread model, and the residual-risk spread model. The chapter shows that each of these four models can produced a profitable investment strategy.

In addition, a multifactor style timing-model was introduced which generated about 5.29% annual gross excess-return during the past 10 years with an annual turnover of 260%. The model has about 14 months' worth of real-time simulation. During that period, the model generated a gross excess-return of 4.52% with a turnover of 200%.

These results contradict the efficient market hypothesis. However, the efficient market hypothesis assumes that the future events are random in nature. By betting on style trends, the investor is betting on the random future events and assumes the nonmarket risk.

Country-Selection Style

Rosemary Macedo, Senior Vice President, Quantitative Research
Bailard, Biehl & Kaiser

Just as in equity selection, country selection reflects distinct investment styles. For example, many stock pickers focus on undervalued stocks or stocks with high prospective earnings-growth; similarly, many international equity managers focus on undervalued markets or markets likely to experience the strongest economic growth. Although a considerable literature addresses various styles used for stock selection, relatively little has been published regarding the application of style to country selection. Keppler [1990a, 1990b] has documented the benefits of value tilts applied to country selection using dividend yield and cash flow/price. Keppler and Traub [1993] have documented the benefits of tilting towards smaller markets. Macedo [1995] has compared value and relative-strength strategies, testing four value-indicators—book value/price, earnings/price (E/P), cash flow/price, and dividend yield—and various measurement periods of relative strength.

This chapter expands on the previous research on style tilts for country selection using value and relative strength. Part I evaluates value and relative-strength tilts for different, longer investment-horizons and assesses the impact of currency movements. Both styles are found to work for investment horizons up to a year. Value tilts work equally well over shorter and longer horizons; they are less effective when measured in U.S. dollar terms. Relative-strength tilts, in contrast, decline in predictive power as the investment horizon lengthens and they are more effective when measured in U.S. dollar returns.

Thanks to Forrest Berkley, Arjun Divecha, W. Van Harlow III, and Meir Statman for their comments.

No single investment-style works all the time, whether it is applied to stock picking or market selection. A discipline that indicates when to use which style could help investors avoid the dry spells inherent in any scheme that values assets according to fixed criteria regardless of changing market conditions. Value and relative strength are obvious candidates for a style-rotation strategy. They are strongly negatively correlated; when one of these two styles is out of favor, the other is likely to be in favor.

Research on domestic stock-selection has found that volatility is a powerful *ex ante* indicator of the subsequent performance of investment styles, both for stock selection and for portfolio selection [Arnott et al. 1989, Arnott et al. 1992, Macedo 1993]. After periods of high volatility, growth tends to outperform value, small-cap stocks to outperform large-cap stocks, leveraged stocks tend to be rewarded, and previously successful stocks tend to be penalized.

The explanation posited for this link between volatility and style performance comes from behavioral finance. When the market is turbulent, the prospective reward for holding assets perceived to be riskier increases as nervous investors' risk tolerance decreases and they pay a premium for comfort and oversell assets they believe to be riskier.

If this explanation is valid, then the same pattern ought to be evident for country-selection strategies. During volatile periods, when investors are more comfortable holding winners, they will be more comfortable holding markets with high relative-strength. Accordingly, a premium should be paid to those who instead invest in markets that are out of favor. Macedo [1995] found just such a pattern using monthly data. Relative value tends to outperform relative strength after periods of high volatility. This study expands on the previous country style-timing research by testing it over different, longer investment-horizons and also assesses the impact of currency movements. Furthermore, it shows how style timing can be used not just for style rotation, but also to enhance performance within a single investment-style.

Data

Morgan Stanley Capital International provided the following month-end valuation ratios for the 20 years from December 1974 through

November 1994: book/price, E/P, cash flow/price, and dividend yield. Returns with net dividends were calculated through December 1994 using MSCI national indices both in U.S. dollars and in local currencies. "Free" indices, which exclude stocks restricted from foreign ownership, were used where and when available. This study comprised 18 markets up to 1990: Australia, Austria, Belgium, Canada, Denmark, France, Germany, Hong Kong, Italy, Japan, Malaysia/Singapore, Netherlands, Norway, Spain, Sweden, Switzerland, the United Kingdom, and the United States. From January 1990 there were 19 markets, including Finland.

Methodology

Part I of the chapter investigates fixed style-tilts. We test several indicators for each of the two country-selection styles, relative value and relative strength. Book/price, E/P, cash flow/price, and dividend yield are all measures of value, with book/price being the most prevalent. Relative strength, or momentum, is just the percentage change in local price; typically it is measured over one year. In order to find the measure that most successfully predicts the next period's relative return, we test relative strength calculated over the following intervals: one, three, six, nine, 12, 15, 18, 21, and 24 months.

For each indicator, four equal-weighted portfolios were created based on the value of the indicator as of the end of the previous period:

QI: Four most attractive countries

QII: Five next most attractive countries

QIII: Five next least attractive countries

QIV: Four least attractive countries (five post-1990)

Each indicator's ability to discriminate between attractive and unattractive markets is gauged by the significance of the average difference in returns between portfolios QI and QIV, for monthly, quarterly, semiannual, and annual investment-horizons.

Part II of the chapter addresses style timing. We examine the relationship between relative value and relative strength, then combine them in a single, simple style-rotation discipline. Again using only the data that would have been available at the end of the previous period, four equal-weighted portfolios are created. The model's ability to discriminate between attractive and unattractive markets is tested, and the investment results for the strategy are evaluated in terms of added value, consistency of added value, and significance after transaction costs.[1]

We next demonstrate that this style timing-model also can be used as a valuable trading signal to enhance a tilt strategy. As in Part I, we create four equal-weighted portfolios based on a single style. This time, though, rather than rebalancing the portfolios continuously we rebalance only when the specified investment style is attractive according to the style timing-model. If the style is not attractive, the composition of the portfolios continues unchanged from the preceding period.

Part I: Style Tilts

Relative Value

The idea behind value investing is to buy assets that are cheap relative to some underlying value, such as the book value, earnings, or dividend stream. Tilts toward these characteristics have been found to add value for stock selection in Australia, Canada, France, Germany, Japan, Sweden, Switzerland, the United Kingdom, and the United States [see, for example, Capaul et al. 1993 and Meier 1992]. Why value works, and why it should continue to work, are questions that so far have eluded definitive answers.

The evidence to date does not support the idea that these ratios are proxies for fundamental risk that must be compensated for with higher returns [Lakonishok et al. 1992]. Instead, the anomalous returns seem to stem from investors' tendency to overreact, that is, to

[1] Commissions, trading taxes, custody, and the bid-offer spread make international equities more expensive to trade than domestic equities. This 2% estimate for round-trip total cost was for EAFE + 1/2Japan, from Grantham [1990]. Derivatives might be used as a cheaper alternative. Currently, derivatives are available for 15 out of the 19 markets studied. Of these, eight out of the nine larger markets had a higher average daily volume in futures and options than in the underlying stocks, and five of the six smaller markets exceeded 50% of the stock volume in futures and options volume. Averages are for 1993. Source: Goldman Sachs.

have excessively high expectations for "glamour" stocks—those of successful or well-run companies—and excessively low expectations for those with recently poor results [Solt and Statman 1989 and Shefrin and Statman 1995]. Aversion to regret reinforces this preference for glamour stocks. The inclination to believe that a good stock is the stock of a good company arises from representativeness, a cognitive error. Cognitive errors by definition are resistant to learning. Hence, despite widespread awareness of the value anomaly, according to this line of reasoning one can expect value-investing to continue to work due to this persistent personal and institutional preference for stocks of perceived winners.

Value tilts also work for country selection. Is this because global investors make representativeness errors, by assuming that a good equity-market is the market of a successful or well-run country? This conjecture is intuitively appealing but difficult to prove. Certainly the other two cognitive errors, aversion to regret and excessive expectations at the extremes, should apply equally to country selection and stock selection.

Or do value tilts work for country selection simply because these markets are fundamentally riskier? Actually, markets in the high-value portfolio were slightly less volatile than average.

Table 15-1 presents the outcomes for tilts using the various valuation measures. Four investment-horizons were tested, with portfolio rebalancing occurring every one, three, six, or 12 months. All performance data is reported annualized, in order to facilitate comparisons of the results for different holding periods. The spread between the top and bottom quartiles, QI–QIV, is the return advantage for holding high-value markets instead of low-value markets. Information ratios are reported before and after transaction costs, and * and ** indicate statistical significance at the 90% and 95% level, respectively.

Book/price discriminated between attractive and unattractive markets best, with significant spreads between the top and bottom quartiles, QI–QIV, for all four investment-horizons, even after transaction costs. The spread between markets with high book/price and low was about 10% per annum after transaction costs, depending on the frequency of rebalancing (local currencies). In U.S. dollar terms, however, the results were only half as good.

Dividend yield was the next strongest indicator, also generating statistically significant spreads between QI and QIV. The E/P tilt

TABLE 15-1. Value Tilts for Country Selection

Average spreads, QI–QIV, net dividends   7501–9412

		Monthly Rebalancing					Quarterly Rebalancing				
		QI–QIV (annual %)	Info Ratio (annualized)	Turnover (annualized)	QI–QIV (net turnover)	Info Ratio (net turnover)	QI–QIV (annual %)	Info Ratio (annualized)	Turnover (annualized)	QI–QIV (net turnover)	Info Ratio (net turnover)
Book/price	Lcl	9.78	0.64*	96%	7.86	0.52**	9.54	0.65**	52%	8.50	0.58**
Book/price	US$	5.57	0.35	96%	3.65	0.23	4.80	0.31	52%	3.76	0.25
Cash flow/price	Lcl	-1.11	-0.07	84%	-2.79	-0.18	0.27	0.02	48%	-0.69	-0.04
Cash flow/price	US$	-3.43	-0.21	84%	-5.11	-0.32	-1.99	-0.11	48%	-2.95	-0.17
Dividend yield	Lcl	9.05	0.64**	84%	7.37	0.52**	6.91	0.47**	44%	6.03	0.41*
Dividend yield	US$	3.95	0.26	84%	2.27	0.15	1.81	0.11	44%	0.93	0.06
E/P	Lcl	6.07	0.41*	108%	3.91	0.27	4.83	0.32	64%	3.55	0.23
E/P	US$	4.11	0.26	108%	1.95	0.12	2.59	0.16	64%	1.31	0.08

TABLE 15-1 (continued).

		Semiannual Rebalancing					Annual Rebalancing				
		QI–QIV (annual %)	Info Ratio (annualized)	Turnover (annualized)	QI–QIV (net turnover)	Info Ratio (net turnover)	QI–QIV (annual %)	Info Ratio (annualized)	Turnover (annualized)	QI–QIV (net turnover)	Info Ratio (net turnover)
Book/price	Lcl	9.40	0.59**	36%	8.68	0.55**	12.35	0.63**	26%	11.83	0.61**
Book/price	US$	4.16	0.25	36%	3.44	0.21	6.80	0.34	26%	6.28	0.32
Cash flow/price	Lcl	1.28	0.07	34%	0.60	0.03	2.91	0.14	24%	2.43	0.12
Cash flow/price	US$	-1.25	-0.07	34%	-1.93	-0.10	-0.02	0.00	24%	-0.50	-0.02
Dividend yield	Lcl	7.21	0.45**	30%	6.61	0.42*	9.52	0.48**	21%	9.10	0.46**
Dividend yield	US$	2.15	0.12	30%	1.55	0.09	4.26	0.20	21%	3.84	0.18
E/P	Lcl	5.21	0.33	46%	4.29	0.27	5.30	0.27	34%	4.62	0.24
E/P	US$	2.56	0.16	46%	1.64	0.10	1.31	0.07	34%	0.63	0.03

Notes: Transaction costs estimated as 2% round trip. Local currencies' returns are *not* net of any hedging costs.
* Indicates significance at 90% level.
** Indicates significance at 95% level.

strategy added value, as well. The spreads for E/P were not significant, however, perhaps because this test employs trailing E/P, not
forecast E/P. For both, results were superior in local currencies.

Cash flow/price was the sole value indicator for which there
was not a statistically significant difference in the mean returns to
portfolios QI and QIV. Although a cash flow/price tilt worked in the
1970s, results have been poor for the last decade.

The strength of valuation measures in explaining returns across
countries may surprise many investors. Evidently, the differences in
accounting standards from country to country either are not so large
as to undermine completely such naive comparisons, or else investors
simply ignore these differences. Anecdotal evidence, when individual
companies have restated their accounts, supports the latter explanation. In the absence of actual restatements from one country's
accounting standards to another's, the markets do not appear to
make allowances for such differences in accounting practices.

Relative Strength

An investor who focuses on relative strength, or price momentum,
simply overweights the markets whose prices have risen the most,
and underweights those whose prices have fallen the most. The idea
is to buy markets with improving prospects, which are assumed to
have been fairly reflected in price movements. If market performance
is driven by economic activity, and if economic cycles are not syn-
chronized across countries and are relatively slow compared with the
forecast horizon, then relative strength might be a proxy for countries' relative positions within the economic cycle. Relative strength is
also a proxy for popularity or demand.

Table 15-2 presents the outcomes for tilts using the various measures of relative strength, using the same format as in Table 15-1.

Referring to Table 15-2, we see that relative strength's ability to
distinguish between attractive and unattractive markets peaks at a 12-
month measurement period.[2] Compared with other measurement
periods, tilts based on 12-month price change generated the highest
added value, significant over the greatest number of investment hori-

---

[2] The superiority of 12-month relative strength for country selection, versus longer
and shorter measurement intervals, is consistent with Engerman's findings for stock
selection in the United States, United Kingdom, and Japan [1993].

TABLE 15-2. Relative-Strength Tilts for Country Selection

Average spreads, QI–QIV, net dividends

		Monthly Rebalancing					Quarterly Rebalancing				
		QI-QIV (annual %)	Info Ratio (annualized)	Turnover (annualized)	QI-QIV (net turnover)	Info Ratio (net turnover)	QI-QIV (annual %)	Info Ratio (annualized)	Turnover (annualized)	QI-QIV (net turnover)	Info Ratio (net turnover)
Rel. strength 1 mo	Lcl	7.87	0.53**	660%	−5.33	−0.36	2.77	0.16	220%	−1.63	−0.09
Rel. strength 1 mo	US$	8.04	0.52**	660%	−5.16	−0.33	4.06	0.23	220%	−0.34	−0.02
Rel. strength 3 mo	Lcl	1.39	0.08	432%	−7.25	−0.44*	4.44	0.25	216%	0.12	0.01
Rel. strength 3 mo	US$	3.26	0.19	432%	−5.38	−0.31	5.65	0.31	216%	1.33	0.07
Rel. strength 6 mo	Lcl	7.75	0.42*	312%	1.51	0.08	8.84	0.47**	168%	5.48	0.29
Rel. strength 6 mo	US$	9.88	0.53**	312%	3.64	0.19	10.45	0.55**	168%	7.09	0.37*
Rel. strength 9 mo	Lcl	8.55	0.46**	264%	3.27	0.18	11.77	0.67**	132%	9.13	0.52**
Rel. strength 9 mo	US$	11.04	0.57**	264%	5.76	0.30	14.14	0.75**	132%	11.50	0.61**
Rel. strength 12 mo	Lcl	13.43	0.74**	216%	9.11	0.50**	11.37	0.64**	120%	8.97	0.51**
Rel. strength 12 mo	US$	17.22	0.91**	216%	12.90	0.68**	15.09	0.79**	120%	12.69	0.67**
Rel. strength 15 mo	Lcl	6.92	0.37*	192%	3.08	0.17	7.11	0.40*	108%	4.95	0.28
Rel. strength 15 mo	US$	9.82	0.50**	192%	5.98	0.31	10.56	0.56**	108%	8.40	0.44**
Rel. strength 18 mo	Lcl	6.69	0.38*	168%	3.33	0.19	5.46	0.30	96%	3.54	0.19
Rel. strength 18 mo	US$	9.93	0.54**	168%	6.57	0.36	9.04	0.47**	96%	7.12	0.37
Rel. strength 21 mo	Lcl	2.01	0.11	168%	−1.35	−0.07	4.16	0.23	92%	2.32	0.13
Rel. strength 21 mo	US$	5.11	0.26	168%	1.75	0.09	7.26	0.37	92%	5.42	0.28
Rel. strength 24 mo	Lcl	4.20	0.24	144%	1.32	0.07	2.60	0.14	88%	0.84	0.05
Rel. strength 24 mo	US$	6.38	0.33	144%	3.50	0.18	5.78	0.30	88%	4.02	0.21

TABLE 15-2 (continued).

		Semiannual Rebalancing					Annual Rebalancing				
		QI–QIV (annual %)	Info Ratio (annualized)	Turnover (annualized)	QI–QIV (net turnover)	Info Ratio (net turnover)	QI–QIV (annual %)	Info Ratio (annualized)	Turnover (annualized)	QI–QIV (net turnover)	Info Ratio (net turnover)
Rel. strength 1 mo	Lcl	4.54	0.25	110%	2.34	0.13	5.04	0.25	55%	3.94	0.20
Rel. strength 1 mo	US$	4.94	0.27	110%	2.74	0.15	6.51	0.30	55%	5.41	0.25
Rel. strength 3 mo	Lcl	6.29	0.35	110%	4.09	0.23	7.38	0.35	54%	6.30	0.30
Rel. strength 3 mo	US$	7.36	0.39*	110%	5.16	0.28	9.54	0.47**	54%	8.46	0.42*
Rel. strength 6 mo	Lcl	10.57	0.60**	106%	8.45	0.48**	7.31	0.38	56%	6.19	0.32
Rel. strength 6 mo	US$	12.76	0.69**	106%	10.64	0.58**	10.36	0.53**	56%	9.24	0.48**
Rel. strength 9 mo	Lcl	12.29	0.74**	88%	10.53	0.63**	6.86	0.37	55%	5.76	0.31
Rel. strength 9 mo	US$	15.18	0.85**	88%	13.42	0.75**	10.60	0.55**	55%	9.50	0.49**
Rel. strength 12 mo	Lcl	8.61	0.48**	80%	7.01	0.39*	4.47	0.22	53%	3.41	0.16
Rel. strength 12 mo	US$	12.25	0.65**	80%	10.65	0.56**	8.94	0.42*	53%	7.88	0.37
Rel. strength 15 mo	Lcl	6.56	0.36	74%	5.08	0.28	3.24	0.15	49%	2.26	0.10
Rel. strength 15 mo	US$	10.47	0.53**	74%	8.99	0.46**	7.98	0.36	49%	7.00	0.31
Rel. strength 18 mo	Lcl	4.54	0.25	68%	3.18	0.18	1.29	0.06	48%	0.33	0.02
Rel. strength 18 mo	US$	8.53	0.44*	68%	7.17	0.37	5.83	0.26	48%	4.87	0.22
Rel. strength 21 mo	Lcl	3.84	0.20	62%	2.60	0.14	0.01	0.00	46%	-0.91	-0.04
Rel. strength 21 mo	US$	7.54	0.37	62%	6.30	0.31	4.18	0.18	46%	3.26	0.14
Rel. strength 24 mo	Lcl	1.25	0.07	62%	0.01	0.00	-1.40	-0.06	44%	-2.28	-0.10
Rel. strength 24 mo	US$	5.25	0.27	62%	4.01	0.21	3.20	0.14	44%	2.32	0.10

Notes: Transaction costs estimated as 2% round trip. Local currencies' returns are *not* net of any hedging costs.
* Indicates significance at 90% level.
** Indicates significant at 95% level.

zons, before and after transaction costs. Short-term relative strength was a good near-term indicator, but colossal turnover eliminates it as a viable strategy. Indeed, all the relative-strength indicators generated high levels of turnover. Going to longer holding-periods reduced turnover, but at the cost of substantially lower added value. Relative-strength tilts looked better in U.S. dollar terms than in local currencies.

Is a relative-strength strategy equivalent to merely buying markets as they become more volatile? The average volatility rank for countries in the top quartile of relative strength was about the same as for the bottom quartile. Constructing portfolios based on quartiles of volatility and comparing their performance, measured by the QI–QIV spread, with the portfolios based on relative strength gave a negligible correlation.

Comparison: Value and Relative Strength

Tilts toward either style worked for investment horizons up to a year. Value tilts performed equally well over shorter and longer horizons, but were less effective when measured in U.S. dollar terms. The performance of relative-strength tilts declined as the investment horizon lengthened. Relative-strength tilts looked better in U.S. dollar returns than in local currencies.

Relative value and relative strength are complementary strategies: the markets with the highest relative-value ranks tend to have the lowest relative-strength ranks. How could both value and relative strength work? The answer is that the market rewards these styles at different times for different reasons. A discipline that indicates when to use which style could offer higher added value and, moreover, higher consistency than either style alone.

Part II: Style Timing

The most prevalent approach to style timing, whether for stock selection, manager selection, or country selection, is to favor whichever style has performed best recently. This rearview-mirror strategy proved a poor guide, however. Prior performance-differences between relative-value and relative-strength strategies over trailing one-, three-, six-, and 12-month periods did not forecast subsequent performance. The likelihood that one style would outperform the other was virtually the same regardless of their recent relative perfor-mance. Thus, capturing any of the potential reward for style timing requires a forward-looking approach.

How is an investor to know which style to use when? Shefrin and Statman [1995] provide direct evidence that investment style is linked to investors' perceptions of quality and risk. Their "Behavioral Capital Asset Pricing Theory" [1994] provides the theoretical founda-tion for differentials in the returns to various investment styles—in other words, risk premiums for investment styles. And market equi-librium and mean-variance portfolio theory prescribe that a decrease in risk tolerance results in an increase in risk premium. If investors' risk tolerance decreases, the premium to those styles perceived to be riskier must increase.

Neither the risk premium nor societal risk-aversion can be mea-sured directly, but we can approximate. The return spread between Quartiles I and IV will serve as a proxy for the risk premium associ-ated with style. As proxies for risk aversion, Sharpe [1989] has used measures of investor wealth, noting several studies that demonstrate the link between whether investors feel rich or poor and their level of aggressiveness in their investment portfolios. The "flight to quality" phenomenon suggests an alternative proxy for risk aversion, one that is more closely coupled with investment style.

The urge to "play it safe" is strongest when investors are most nervous or uncertain. Since market volatility reflects—and perhaps even amplifies—investor uncertainty, a "flight to quality" is often observed during periods of high volatility. During such times, investors' risk aversion increases, they bid up "quality," and they oversell assets perceived to be riskier. The consequence is a higher premium for bearing risk. Style characteristics are strongly linked to perceptions of quality. Therefore, the premium for uncomfortable or contrarian styles should be especially high after a period of high volatility.

A global-market volatility was calculated for each month as the standard deviation of monthly returns to each country over the most recent six months. This measure captures both the volatility of returns over time and, to a lesser extent, the dispersion of returns among countries. When volatility was higher than its prior average, investors were presumed to have been nervous, and the "risk aversion proxy" variable was defined to be "high." When volatility was lower, investors were presumed to have been less nervous, and the "risk aversion proxy" variable was defined to be "low" (refer to Figure 15-1). Note that no look-ahead bias is introduced, since each month's volatility level is compared to an average of previous months only.

This risk-aversion proxy indicates when markets have been volatile. We hypothesize the following relationship between market volatility and subsequent style returns: the premium for value should increase after a period of high volatility and the premium for relative strength should be negative. (Were we able to forecast periods of volatility, we would know in advance when a "flight to quality" was coming. Relative strength would be preferred over value at such times.)

Figure 15-2 illustrates the dramatic differences in the performance of book/price and relative-strength tilts after periods of high and low volatility, our proxy for risk aversion. As expected, the contrarian style, book/price, worked substantially better—much larger QI–QIV spreads—when volatility had been high and investors are presumed to have been risk averse. The comfortable style, relative strength, worked better when the risk-aversion proxy was low.

Detailed results for all the indicators during periods of low and high presumed risk-aversion are presented in Table 15-3. For

FIGURE 15-1.   Risk-Aversion Proxy
Global volatility

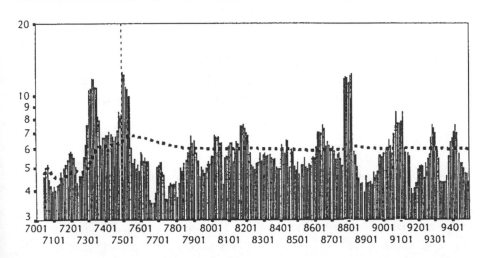

**FIGURE 15-2.   Country Selection Style Performance versus Risk
Aversion Proxy**

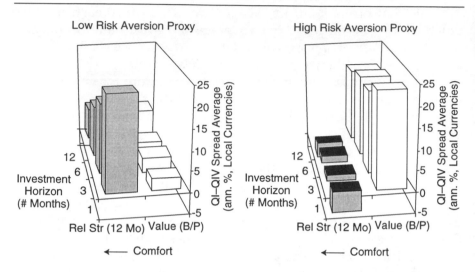

book/price, the spread between QI and QIV was not significantly different from zero when the risk-aversion proxy was low. When the risk-aversion proxy (RAP) was high, however, the premium was highly significant, even for long holding-periods. More rigorously, there was a statistically significant difference in the premium when RAP was high versus when it was not.

The premium for relative strength also responded as expected. Looking at 12-month relative strength, the risk premium was negative after periods of high volatility, though not significantly so. There was, however, a statistically significant difference in the premium when RAP was high versus when it was not.

These results provide substantial evidence that the hypothesized relation between volatility and the performance of country-selection styles exists.

Style Rotation

The results above suggest a simple model for style rotation: relative value when volatility is above average, relative strength when below. As before, four portfolios were created for each period from January 1975 through December 1994, with QI containing the markets with the highest forecast each period, QIV containing the markets with the

TABLE 15-3. Country-Selection Style Performance versus Risk-Aversion Proxy

Average spreads, QI–QIV, net dividends

		Monthly Rebalancing				Quarterly Rebalancing			
		QI–QIV Spread (Annualized %)		Difference (High – Low)		QI–QIV Spread (Annualized %)		Difference (High – Low)	
		Low RAP	High RAP	Annual %	t-Stat	Low RAP	High RAP	Annual %	t-Stat
Book/price	Lcl	3.00	23.60**	20.60	2.8**	4.28	20.13**	15.85	2.4**
Book/price	US$	-1.18	19.32**	20.50	2.6**	-0.80	16.08**	16.87	2.4**
Cash flow/price	Lcl	-3.00	2.75	5.75	0.8	0.67	-0.54	-1.21	-0.2
Cash flow/price	US$	-4.71	-0.82	3.90	0.5	-0.42	-5.16	-4.74	-0.6
Dividend yield	Lcl	3.44	20.50**	17.06	2.5**	3.57	13.61**	10.04	1.3
Dividend yield	US$	-2.00	16.06**	18.06	2.4**	-2.12	9.70	11.82	1.4
E/P	Lcl	3.68	10.96	7.28	1.0	3.27	7.97	4.71	0.6
E/P	US$	2.11	8.20	6.09	0.7	1.44	4.90	3.46	

Notes: Gross return spreads: No transaction or hedging costs deducted.
* Indicates significance at 90 level.
** Indicates significance at 95% level.

347

TABLE 15-3 (continued).

		Monthly Rebalancing				Quarterly Rebalancing			
		QI–QIV Spread (Annualized %)		Difference (High – Low)		QI–QIV Spread (Annualized %)		Difference (High – Low)	
		Low RAP	High RAP	Annual %	t-Stat	Low RAP	High RAP	Annual %	t-Stat
Rel. strength 1 mo	Lcl	9.91**	3.70	−6.21	−0.8	2.69	2.93	0.24	0.0
Rel. strength 1 mo	US$	10.83**	2.35	−8.48	−1.1	5.27	1.62	−3.65	−0.4
Rel. strength 3 mo	Lcl	5.89	−7.77	−13.66	−1.6	5.69	1.93	−3.76	−0.4
Rel. strength 3 mo	US$	9.78**	−10.02	−19.80	−2.3**	8.65*	−0.41	−9.06	−1.0
Rel. strength 6 mo	Lcl	12.85**	−2.67	−15.52	−1.6	10.55**	5.39	−5.16	−0.5
Rel. strength 6 mo	US$	16.28**	−3.18	−19.46	−2.0**	13.00**	5.34	−7.66	−0.8
Rel. strength 9 mo	Lcl	15.30**	−5.19	−20.49	−2.1**	15.49**	4.29	−11.20	−1.3
Rel. strength 9 mo	US$	18.11**	−3.35	−21.46	−2.2**	18.04**	6.30	−11.74	−1.3
Rel. strength 12 mo	Lcl	23.08**	−6.23	−29.31	−3.1**	17.85**	−1.67	−19.53	−2.3**
Rel. strength 12 mo	US$	27.93**	−4.61	−32.54	−3.5**	22.48**	−0.22	−22.26	−2.5**
Rel. strength 15 mo	Lcl	16.11**	−11.81	−27.91	−2.9**	12.93**	−4.60	−17.54	−2.0**
Rel. strength 15 mo	US$	19.93**	−10.78	−30.70	−3.1**	16.97**	−2.35	−19.32	−2.1**
Rel. strength 18 mo	Lcl	13.70**	−7.58	−21.28	−2.3**	11.20**	−6.09	−17.28	−2.0*
Rel. strength 18 mo	US$	17.83**	−6.18	−24.01	−2.5**	15.44**	−3.83	−19.26	−2.1**
Rel. strength 21 mo	Lcl	11.41**	−17.14**	−28.56	−3.0**	10.98**	−9.56	−20.53	−2.3**
Rel. strength 21 mo	US$	15.39**	−15.84*	−31.23	−3.1**	14.62**	−7.57	−22.19	−2.3**
Rel. strength 24 mo	Lcl	12.07**	−11.85	−23.93	−2.6**	8.86*	−10.01	−18.87	−2.1**
Rel. strength 24 mo	US$	15.29**	−11.79	−27.08	−2.7**	12.57**	−7.88	−20.45	−2.2**

TABLE 15-3 (continued).

		Semiannual Rebalancing				Annual Rebalancing			
		QI-QIV Spread (Annualized %)		Difference (High – Low)		QI-QIV Spread (Annualized %)		Difference (High – Low)	
		Low RAP	High RAP	Annual %	t-Stat	Low RAP	High RAP	Annual %	t-Stat
Book/price	Lcl	3.67	20.70**	17.03	2.6**	8.83	19.73**	10.91	1.3
Book/price	US$	-1.38	15.10**	16.47	2.4**	3.71	13.27**	9.56	1.1
Cash flow/price	Lcl	0.48	2.88	2.40	0.3	3.16	2.38	-0.78	-0.1
Cash flow/price	US$	0.04	-3.79	-3.83	-0.4	1.95	-4.13	-6.08	-0.6
Dividend Yield	Lcl	3.80	13.95**	10.15	1.3	7.48	13.80	6.32	0.6
Dividend Yield	US$	-1.49	9.35	10.84	1.2	1.54	9.97	8.42	0.7
E/P	Lcl	3.18	9.22	6.04	0.8	4.25	7.48	3.23	0.3
E/P	US$	1.16	5.33	4.17	0.6	0.58	2.84	2.27	0.3

Notes: Gross return spreads: No transaction or hedging costs deducted.
*Indicates significance at 90% level.
**Indicates significance at 95% level.

TABLE 15-3 (continued).

		Semiannual Rebalancing				Annual Rebalancing			
		QI–QIV Spread (Annualized %)		Difference (High – Low)		QI–QIV Spread (Annualized %)		Difference (High – Low)	
		Low RAP	High RAP	Annual %	t-Stat	Low RAP	High RAP	Annual %	t-Stat
Rel. strength 1 mo	Lcl	4.06	5.49	1.43	0.2	3.72	7.81	4.09	0.4
Rel. strength 1 mo	US$	5.18	4.46	−0.72	−0.1	6.18	7.21	1.03	0.1
Rel. strength 3 mo	Lcl	6.90	5.08	−1.82	−0.2	5.66	10.97	5.31	0.5
Rel. strength 3 mo	US$	9.25*	3.64	−5.62	−0.7	9.37	9.90	0.53	0.1
Rel. strength 6 mo	Lcl	11.33**	9.08	−2.24	−0.3	6.46	9.09	2.63	0.3
Rel. strength 6 mo	US$	14.13**	10.05	−4.08	−0.4	10.63**	9.79	−0.84	−0.1
Rel. strength 9 mo	Lcl	14.79**	7.37	−7.42	−0.9	7.54	5.44	−2.10	−0.2
Rel. strength 9 mo	US$	17.69**	10.24	−7.45	−0.9	11.87**	7.93	−3.94	−0.4
Rel. strength 12 mo	Lcl	13.57**	−1.19	−14.76	−1.8*	8.47	−3.90	−12.37	−1.3
Rel. strength 12 mo	US$	17.54**	1.81	−15.73	−1.8*	13.39**	−0.39	−13.77	−1.4
Rel. strength 15 mo	Lcl	13.01**	−6.18	−19.19	−2.3**	8.78	−8.36	−17.14	−1.8*
Rel. strength 15 mo	US$	17.05**	−2.55	−19.60	−2.2**	13.78**	−4.18	−17.95	−1.8*
Rel. strength 18 mo	Lcl	11.32**	−8.83	−20.14	−2.5**	7.30	−11.32	−18.62	−1.9*
Rel. strength 18 mo	US$	15.49**	−5.22	−20.71	−2.4**	12.15**	−7.42	−19.58	−2.0**
Rel. strength 21 mo	Lcl	10.78**	−9.86	−20.64	−2.4**	6.51	−13.61	−20.12	−2.0**
Rel. strength 21 mo	US$	14.55**	−6.30	−20.86	−2.2**	10.98*	−10.07	−21.05	−2.1**
Rel. strength 24 mo	Lcl	7.86	−11.82*	−19.69	−2.4**	5.01	−14.82*	−19.83	−2.0*
Rel. strength 24 mo	US$	12.20**	−8.49	−20.70	−2.4**	9.79	−10.60	−20.40	−2.0**

Notes: Gross return spreads: No transaction or hedging costs deducted.
* Indicates significance at 90% level.
** Indicates significance at 95% level.

TABLE 15-4. Style Rotation

Rebalancing Frequency		QI–QIV (annual %)	Info Ratio (annualized)	Turnover (annualized)	QI–QIV (net turnover)	Info Ratio (net turnover)
Monthly	Lcl	23.25	1.46**	228%	18.69	1.17**
	US$	25.10	1.46**	228%	20.54	1.20**
Quarterly	Lcl	18.61	1.20**	132%	15.97	1.03**
	US$	20.36	1.19**	132%	17.72	1.03**
Semiannual	Lcl	15.97	1.01**	88%	14.21	0.90**
	US$	16.72	0.99**	88%	14.96	0.88**
Annual	Lcl	12.11	0.63**	52%	11.07	0.58**
	US$	13.35	0.71**	52%	12.31	0.66**

Notes: Local currencies returns are *not* net of any hedging costs.
** Indicates significance at 95% level.

worst forecast. Table 15-4 shows that, after transaction costs, the average spread between the top and bottom quartiles ranged from 11% to 19% per annum, depending on the investment horizon. The spread was significant for all four rebalancing schemes and for U.S. dollar or local-currency returns after transaction costs.

Style Timing

Finally, not every investor is able—or even willing—to change or reverse style. Nonetheless, knowing when a given style is likely to work best can improve investment results by signaling when to rebalance one's portfolio. As an example, consider the value-tilt strategy once again. When value is not expected to perform well, there is no point in rebalancing the portfolio, incurring transaction costs with no expectation of added value from the changes. What if we use the style timing-model to postpone rebalancing when value is not attractive, letting the composition of the portfolio continue unchanged until the next signal favoring value? An example of this rebalancing scheme is provided in Table 15-5. Effectively, this strategy varies the aggressiveness of a portfolio's tilt toward value in accordance with expectations. The result will certainly be lower turnover and should also include higher added value, over and above the saved transaction costs.

TABLE 15-5.   Style-Timing Example

	Highest Book/Price Market	Risk Aversion Proxy	Is Value Attractive?	Rebalance?	New Portfolio
January	Australia	High	Yes	Yes	Australia
February	Belgium	Low	No	No	Australia
March	Canada	High	Yes	Yes	Canada
April	France	High	Yes	Yes	France
May	Germany	Low	No	No	France

Table 15-6 verifies that, indeed, turnover was reduced and the reward to the strategy increased substantially, well above the saved transaction costs alone. This discipline for timing value produced significant spreads of about 13% per annum, despite rather modest levels of turnover. What's more, the gap between U.S. dollar and local-currency returns was much smaller than for a continuously rebalanced value tilt. In U.S. dollar terms the spread was still 10% per annum, which was statistically significant.

Implementation Note: Mileage May Vary

A key consideration is how much of the value added by this model comes from shorting or underweighting smaller, illiquid markets. This question is important for three reasons. First, the larger the portfolio, the less one can overweight smaller markets due to liquidity constraints. Second, for any portfolio that has a capitalization-weighted benchmark, one cannot underweight these markets materially since they are such a small portion of the benchmark. Last, transaction costs are considerably higher when you can implement at all. Between one third and one half of back-test results is a reasonable estimate for what actual investment-results over this period might have been, once adjustments are made for smaller markets.

Conclusion

These results provide substantial evidence that the hypothesized relation between volatility and the performance of country-selection styles exists. By knowing when to use them, value and relative

TABLE 15-6. Book Value/Price

		Tilt					Timing				
		QI–QIV (annual %)	Info Ratio (annualized)	Turnover (annualized)	QI–QIV (net turnover)	Info Ratio (net turnover)	QI–QIV (annual %)	Info Ratio (annualized)	Turnover (annualized)	QI–QIV (net turnover)	Info Ratio (net turnover)
Monthly	Lcl	9.78	0.64**	96%	7.86	0.52**	13.73	0.97**	36%	13.01	0.92**
	US$	5.57	0.35	96%	3.65	0.23	10.62	0.69**	36%	9.90	0.64**
Quarterly	Lcl	9.54	0.65**	52%	8.50	0.58**	13.55	0.91**	28%	12.99	0.87**
	US$	4.80	0.31	52%	3.76	0.25	10.48	0.65**	28%	9.92	0.61**
Semiannual	Lcl	9.40	0.59**	36%	8.68	0.55**	13.72	0.87**	22%	13.28	0.84**
	US$	4.16	0.25	36%	3.44	0.21	10.34	0.60**	22%	9.90	0.58**
Annual	Lcl	12.35	0.63**	26%	11.83	0.61**	14.39	0.78**	19%	14.01	0.76**
	US$	6.80	0.34	26%	6.28	0.32	10.88	0.54**	19%	10.50	0.52**

Notes: Local currency returns are *not* net of any hedging costs.
** Indicates significance at 95% level.

strength can be more effective components in any country-selection discipline. Furthermore, the relations described here are consistent with investment theory and they can exist even if everyone knows about them.

References

Arnott, Robert D., Charles M. Kelso Jr., Stephan Kiscadden, and Rosemary Macedo. "Forecasting Factor Returns: An Intriguing Possibility." *Journal of Portfolio Management,* Fall 1989.

Arnott, Robert D., John L. Dorian, and Rosemary Macedo. "Style Management: The Missing Element in Equity Portfolios." *Journal of Investing,* Summer 1992.

Capaul, Carlo, Ian Rowley, and William F. Sharpe. "International Value and Growth Stock Returns." *Financial Analysts Journal,* January–February 1993.

Clarke, Roger, and Meir Statman. "Growth, Value, Good, and Bad." *Financial Analysts Journal,* November–December 1994.

Engerman, Mark. "Reversal and Momentum Strategies." BARRA Equity Research Conference, Pebble Beach, Calif., June 1993.

Grantham, R. Jeremy. "Dirty Secrets of International Investing." In *Investing Worldwide,* Association for Investment Management and Research, 1990.

Keppler, Michael. "Further Evidence on the Predictability of International Equity Returns." *Journal of Portfolio Management,* Fall 1990.

Keppler, Michael. "The Importance of Dividend Yields in Country Selection." *Journal of Portfolio Management,* Winter 1990.

Keppler, Michael, and Heydon Traub. "The Small Country Effect." In *Small Cap Stocks,* Robert A. Klein and Jess Lederman, eds. Probus Publishing, Chicago, 1993.

Lakonishok, Josef, Andrei Schleifer, and Robert Vishny. "Contrarian Investment, Extrapolation, and Stock Returns." Working Paper, University of Illinois, 1992.

Macedo, Rosemary. "Value, Relative Strength and Volatility in Global Equity Country Selection." *Financial Analysts Journal,* March–April 1995.

Macedo, Rosemary. "Tactical Style Allocation Using Small Cap Strategies." In *Small Cap Stocks,* Robert A. Klein and Jess Lederman, eds. Probus Publishing, Chicago, 1993.

Meier, John. "Do Styles Make Sense Globally? Growth vs. Value." BARRA International Research Conference, Berkeley, Calif., May 1992.

Sharpe, William F. "Investor Wealth and Expected Return." In *Quantifying the Market Risk Premium Phenomenon for Investment Decision Making*, William F. Sharpe and Katrina F. Sherrerd, eds. Institute of Chartered Financial Analysts, New York, September 26–27, 1989.

Shefrin, Hersh, and Meir Statman. "Behavioral Capital Asset Pricing Theory." *The Journal of Financial and Quantitative Analysis*, September 1994.

Shefrin, Hersh, and Meir Statman. "Making Sense of Beta, Size and Book-to-Market." *Journal of Portfolio Management*, 1995.

Solt, Michael E., and Meir Statman. "Good Companies, Bad Stocks." *Journal of Portfolio Management*, Summer 1989.

CHAPTER 16

Don't Leave Excess Return on the Table: The Case for Active Style-Management

Lawrence J. Marks, CFA, Managing Director
Harbor Capital Management Company, Inc.

Style, at least in the investment world, came of age in the 1980s. To be sure, our yellowing copy of the 1969 membership directory of the Financial Analysts Federation listed several specialized investment boutiques. As we recall, most of those firms trafficked in the "story" stocks that made and unmade the "gunslingers" of the 1960s. Despite the industry's indebtedness to Ben Graham, the legendary value investor, value investing (apart from certain income-oriented strategies) didn't begin to catch on until the 1970s. Nor did institutional investors pay much attention to the ebb and flow of excess returns associated with market capitalization. Capitalization was a by-product of the serious business of picking stocks. Stock selection, in turn, was often keyed to market sectors, e.g., transportation, utilities, capital goods. This interplay among sectors, generally in response to unfolding economic cycles, was recognized nearly a century ago with the creation of the Dow Jones Averages and its constituent subindices, initially rails and industrials. The utility average was added in 1929.

In the 1980s, thanks in part to the research of James L. Farrell, Jr., William Breed, and others, style as a performance discriminator came into its own. Today, we have "buy side" style specialists, style benchmarks, and style peer-group comparisons.

From the identification and measurement of returns attributable to style, it is a logical step to the next level of sophistication: *active style-management*. It is well and good to say that there are times when one is better off in growth stocks and times when it is value's turn to lead. It is important to know when smaller-cap stocks are in favor and when they are not. It is even useful to know that, over time, small stocks outperform large stocks (albeit with more risk) and that value indices tend to outperform growth indices. But a portfolio with fixed style-allocations, or even one that is periodically rebalanced, cannot capture the full impact of changes in style leadership. If the style allocation is not actively managed, too much money is left on the table. If the wheel of fortune is favoring growth, sooner or later the wise investor must put his or her chips on value, or risk losing whatever excess return has been earned by betting on growth.

The schematic set of stairs depicted in Figure 16-1 illustrates where active style-management and active style-management together with active stock-selection fit on a continuum of portfolio-management alternatives. Active style-management can be implemented by the use of passive style-indices or by active stock-selection within each style. For our purposes, active style-management refers to "growth" and "value" concepts, although a similar case could be made for large-cap and small-cap or, perhaps, high quality complemented by speculative holdings.

FIGURE 16-1.   Stepping Up in Style

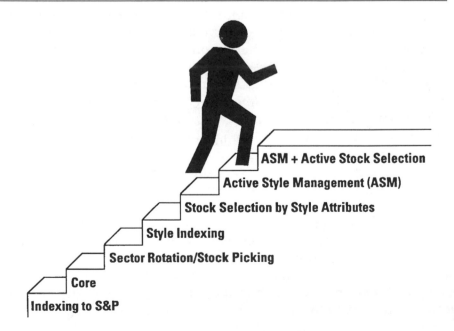

ASM + Active Stock Selection

Active Style Management (ASM)

Stock Selection by Style Attributes

Style Indexing

Sector Rotation/Stock Picking

Core

Indexing to S&P

Two Winning Strategies

Over a "reasonable" period of time, both growth managers and value managers are capable of outperforming a broad-based passive market-portfolio such as the Standard & Poor's 500. Value managers outperform by purchasing securities for less than their intrinsic value. Growth managers outperform by investing in companies that grow faster than the overall economy. As Figure 16-2 illustrates, since the beginning of the 1980s, a well-known consulting firm's universe of growth managers and value managers each added value over and above the S&P 500 return. Amazingly, for the entire 17-year period, value-style managers and growth-style managers produced almost identical returns, although volatility characteristics differed.

Can we conclude, then, that all a plan sponsor has to do is hire a

FIGURE 16-2.   Growth and Value Managers versus the S&P 500
Median annualized returns (1978–1994)

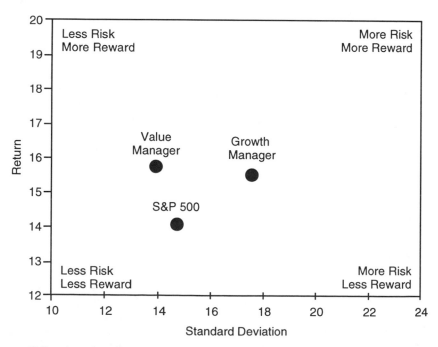

Source: Callan Associates Inc.

good growth-manager, a good value-manager, and sit back and enjoy the fruits of his or her manager selection? Not so fast! Few plan sponsors have the fortitude to hang in there when results appear to disprove the theory. For the five-year period ending mid-1989, according to Callan Associates, both the median value-manager and the median growth-manager underperformed the S&P 500. Readers may recall that this period favored the large companies that dominated the market averages; indexing was in vogue. Active stock-selection and style-based strategies couldn't keep up the pace. For a while it appeared as if indexing, with its low cost and superior performance, would relegate style investing to a footnote in investment texts. Fortunately for the practitioners of style, the large-cap growth stocks that came to dominate the S&P 500 began to fade. For the last five years, indexing has been on the defensive.

FIGURE 16-3.   Growth and Value Index versus the S&P 500

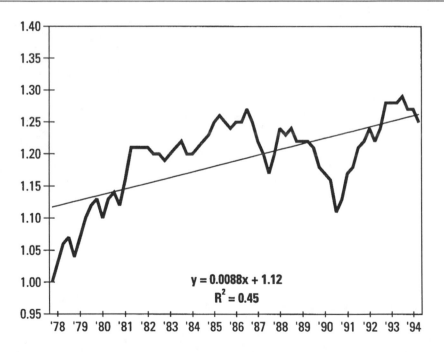

Data source: Wilshire Associates Incorporated.
Calculations: Harbor Capital Management Co., Inc.

Fortunately, style managers are working with a universe of stocks that has a slight edge over the S&P 500. Figure 16-3 uses Wilshire Associates' large-cap and mid-cap growth and value indices (with a double weighting for large-cap) to represent a passive portfolio equally weighted between growth and value. In broad terms, this portfolio outperformed the market from 1978 to 1986 and again during 1990–1993. It underperformed in 1987–1990. For the entire period, growth- and value-style investing performed better than the market by almost 0.9% annually. The inclusion of a one-third weighting in mid-cap stocks contributed less than half of the outperformance. These results provide an indication that style investing adds value. In a business of eighths and quarters, 0.9% a year is, indeed, meaningful.

We also know that there are times when growth stocks do well, and there are times when value stocks outperform. Figure 16-4 isolates the major waves of relative performance between growth and

FIGURE 16-4. **Performance of Growth Stocks Relative to Value Stocks**

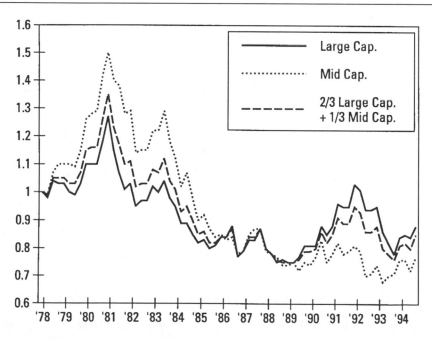

Data source: Wilshire Associates Incorporated.

value since 1978, as measured by Wilshire Associates' large-cap and mid-cap indices, as well as our blended mix.

It does not take a rocket scientist to figure out that if one were clever enough to be wholly in growth stocks during 1978–1980 and 1989–1991, and value stocks in 1981–1988 and 1992–1993, results would have been extraordinary. For the record, being wholly on the right side of the major style-trends (requiring only four decisions in 16 years) would have produced a compound annual return of 20.5%. For comparison, the S&P 500 compounded at 15.1% during the same period.

Of course, the prudent investor must consider the penalty for being wrong. If an unlucky investor were always on the wrong side of the style bet, results would have underperformed the S&P 500, 11.3% versus 15.1%. Or suppose a cautious investor waited until a new style-trend was firmly in place for a year before making a switch. It is much better, in this case, to be late than wrong. This tactic still beat the market handily, 17.9% to 15.1%. Being on the right side of style leadership is, indeed, a powerful tool for enhancing performance.

For most of us, betting the ranch on one style is not a prudent alternative. Just as a balanced account comprising stocks and bonds is never entirely out of either asset class, so should a style-oriented equity portfolio never be concentrated in just one style. The prudent solution is "active style-management," that is, tilting the equity portfolio toward either growth stocks or value stocks in order to capture more of the superior return generated by the in-favor style. Such a tilt could be modest (55%–45%), aggressive (75%–25%), or some place in between, depending upon the risk tolerance of the plan sponsor and the confidence level of the manager.

The Seven Advantages of Active Style-Management

Active style-management has many positive attributes. Not all will apply in every case, but most plan sponsors will find several advantages that are relevant to their own situation. The advantages are as follows.

Active Style Management Locks in Excess Returns

Of greatest importance is the ability to capture and lock in the excess returns generated by the outperforming style. If money is not taken off the table, i.e., if the allocation to winning style is not reduced, sooner or later that style will underperform and portfolio returns will revert to average. Active style-management can be implemented in three different ways: first, in a proactive, judgmental fashion; second, by a set of "black box" rules based upon historic regression models; or third, through automatic rebalancing, e.g., when either style reaches 55% of the equity portfolio, it will be reduced back to a neutral 50/50 mix. Each method has its advantages and disadvantages.

Active Style-Management Provides Diversification

A portfolio consisting of both growth stocks and value stocks in roughly similar proportion is automatically diversified by sector. Diversification smooths out the volatility inherent in either style. Interestingly, the natural diversification advantages of active style-management enable the active stock-picker to concentrate bets within each style if it is advantageous to do so. If financial stocks, for example, are attractive to the value manager, the style tilter could make a much larger bet on financials than the pure value-manager, knowing that there is a complement of growth stocks on the other side of the portfolio to provide the diversification.

Active Style-Management Eliminates the Single-Style Tendency Toward Style Drift

When stock selection is actively managed, the active style-manager can afford to be very choosy in his or her stock picks. After all, one needs to assemble only half a portfolio for each style. It also eliminates the tendency for the out-of-favor manager to engage in "style drift," buying stocks whose characteristics more closely resemble those of the in-favor style.

Active Style-Management Provides a Safety Net to Cushion Sudden Style Shifts

Active style-management is prudent. There have been times when intermediate-term (six months) style leadership has changed overnight in response to an unexpected economic report or a surprising move in interest rates. Active style-management—and the luxury of holding a portion of the equity assets in an out-of-favor style—provides a safety net to cushion sudden style shifts. In addition, changing portfolio emphasis is relatively simple: all one has to do is switch 5% or 10% of the portfolio from one side to the other and *voilá*, the portfolio has a new look.

Active Style-Management Contributes to a More Consistent Performance Pattern

Active style-management may also mean more consistent performance when compared with separate value and growth managers. A growth-stock picker can shoot the lights out when growth stocks are in favor. But how the clients suffer when it is value's turn. The reverse also holds true. In contrast, when one manager is pulling the trigger for both growth and value, the result is a more consistent approach to stock selection. Active style-management eliminates the tendency of a single-style manager to take on more risk when returns start to slip relative to a peer group.

Active Style-Management Stands Alone or Complements Other Portfolio-Management Techniques

Active style-management is flexible. It can function as the "swing" portfolio in a multimanager setting similar to the way that tactical asset allocation can alter a portfolio's weighting of stocks, bonds, and cash. Thus, an active style-manager can complement a core manager, add a flexible dimension to existing growth and value managers, or even serve as the core manager if market capitalization and beta are controlled.

Active Style-Management Saves Plan Sponsor Time and Fees

For a plan sponsor, hiring one active style-manager can be more cost efficient and time efficient then hiring separate style-managers. Most managers offer price discounts as portfolio size increases. When one manager can take the place of two, the "breakpoint" in fees is more quickly reached. Time is also saved if there are fewer managers with whom the plan sponsor must contend. Not only are there fewer meetings, but the plan sponsor does not have to listen to "my-style-was-out-of-favor" excuses for poor performance. The active style-manager has no excuse.

The Drawbacks

If active style-management offers so many advantages, why isn't it more widely used? There must be a catch. Indeed, there are several. First, active style-management reduces the plan sponsor's absolute control of the equity asset-mix. Many plan sponsors believe that they can control their risk by setting stock-bond-cash allocations and, within equities, the proportion going into domestic, international, emerging markets, large-cap, small-cap, long and short, growth and value, etc. Active style-management may upset the equation.

Second, active style-management is very difficult to market. Its very nature challenges one of the roles of a consultant who has no incentive to take the lead. For them, two managers are better than one, requiring more reporting, more data analysis, and more manager searches. Nevertheless, plan sponsors are just beginning to embrace the concept and instruct their consultants to conduct an active style-manager search. Several firms now hold themselves out as style managers. If several more join the fold, active style-management may achieve sufficient critical mass to merit its own "pigeonhole" in the consultant's aviary.

Third, active style-management, especially when combined with active stock-selection, complicates the tasks of research and portfolio management. The culture of a growth-oriented firm or portfolio manager is very different from that of a dyed-in-the-wool value investor. Growth-stock managers are optimistic risk takers; the value buyer is risk averse. The professional who traffics in growth stocks finds value stocks dull; hard-core growth-stock aficionados seldom have the patience needed for successful value-stock investing. It takes a great deal of discipline for these two different cultures to exist side by side.

The last drawback concerns those times when both growth stocks and value stocks underperform the S&P 500. If we look at the 17-year period beginning in 178, both Wilshire's large-cap growth and large-cap value indices underperformed the S&P 500 in 11 quarters, one-sixth of the time. Not surprisingly, both indices simultaneously outperformed the S&P 500 during a similar dozen quarters out of the last 68. But a moment's reflection suggests that these win-win or lose-lose quarters occur when there is not much disparity in performance among growth, value, and the overall market. However, it is in those quarters when there is a significant difference between growth results and value results that active style-management pays off. We don't advocate portfolio style-timing on a quarterly basis, but we note that there were 25 quarters in the last 17 years (37% of the total) when the performance differential between growth and value was greater than five percentage points. There were 13 quarters in which one style recorded a gain while the other posted a loss.

Conclusion

Active portfolio-management combines both science and art. As academia expands the frontiers of investment knowledge, money managers, plan sponsors, and consultants gradually become familiar with and slowly adopt these new ideas. Option theory is a recent example of new insights that have made the transition from theory to practice. Equity style management, too, now has its advocates in the real world of professional investors. Active style-management, on the other hand, has been slow to emerge from its ivory tower because it is arduous to implement and difficult to market. But the potential for enhanced performance is well worth the struggle. Active style-management is logical in concept and elegant in structure. There are now several sources of style benchmarks to facilitate the measurement of value added. A handful of firms, including this author's, have embraced the concept and implemented the strategy. Harbor Capital Management, in fact, has achieved a successful 15-year track record using active style-management and active stock-selection.

Victor Hugo wrote that "an invasion of armies can be resisted, but not an idea whose time has come." Active style-management, we believe, is such an idea. To avoid the active style decision is to knowingly leave excess return on the table.

Style Trends in Institutional Investment

Michael Markov, President
Markov Processes, Inc.

It is intuitively clear that certain fashions exist in the investment industry: at times we witness "technology fashion" or "emerging markets fashion." In this chapter we describe a methodology that allows us to diagnose and measure these style trends or fashions in institutional investment management. Using readily available manager-performance databases and a return-based style-analysis technique introduced by William F. Sharpe, we were able to identify style cycles for U.S. domestic-equity money managers.

Our approach can be used to measure deficiencies and biases in the managers' performance databases. It can be used by money managers to design their marketing strategies. It can be applied to fixed income and international markets, and used as a basis for arbitrage and style-rotation strategies.

The goal of this study is to identify certain trends or cycles which exist in the institutional investment industry. If we consider the U.S. equity market, it is reasonable to assume that growth stocks are fashionable in some periods, and value stocks during other periods. Very often this fashion is driven by the past performance, while sometimes it is just marketing hype. Securities-fashion drives the demand for new investment-products and we witness an increased money flow into the fashionable products—either mutual funds or institutional accounts.

One way to identify this fashion would seem to be to measure account *cash flows*. Unfortunately, these data are not available for

Copyright 1994 Michael Markov.

The author would like to thank Professor William F. Sharpe of Stanford University, Professor Brian Shay of Hunter College CUNY, and Steven Hardy of Zephyr Associates for their helpful comments.

most accounts; some accounts represent mixture of styles, and some money managers tend to misrepresent their style in order to move to a favorable style category. The best way to overcome these problems would be to analyze the *actual portfolios* historically for all accounts. This would be a large-scale project and, again, the portfolios will not be available for the majority of small accounts.

We will use a different approach, comparing the dynamic of *style allocations* of managed portfolios to the market. The increased demand for, say, value management would increase the supply of value money-managers and/or assets in value portfolios. In this case the portion of value stocks in institutional portfolios will be higher than in the market as a whole. In this case, we say that there is a value trend. In the same way we can describe growth and size trends.

We will derive these style allocations by using only portfolio performance-data (total returns) and historical assets under management, figures which are available from numerous manager-database providers.

One would expect that the fashion trends are driven by style performance—that some of the managers are "trend followers" who would sell the worst performing assets and buy the best performing, other managers would overreact to the bad or good performance of the style, and so on. In our study, we will link this behavior with the investment-style performance.

All data manipulation procedures were performed in Microsoft Access Database using Access Basic language. For data analysis, we used Zephyr Associates' Style Advisor performance analysis and visualization software.

Data Selection

The selection of managers' historical performance and asset data was crucial for our research.

We examined several manager-performance databases that are available on the market: PSN from Effron Enterprises, M-Search from Mobius Group, NELSON from Nelson Publications, PIPER from Rogers, Casey & Associates. All of them, except PIPER, have survivorship bias—they don't keep managers or products that went out of business in the database. This gap is quite understandable because the vendors provide data to the consultants who perform manager searches and who are concerned with the products that are available at the time of search.

Only two data providers, Mobius and Nelson, have historical asset data. For each product, they provide year-end assets together with quarterly returns. Mobius covers a longer time-period, with the data starting in 1978. Nelson data start in 1982, but Nelson's universe is much broader, at least in the U.S. domestic-equity market. They have data for more than 2,000 managers in 1994 while Mobius covers only 1,423 managers.

We have selected Nelson Publications' Manager Performance Database as a comprehensive and apparently reliable source of both asset and return data.

Figure 17-1 shows the distribution of assets under management of the U.S. equity products at the end of 1993. Note that the x-axis is intentionally made logarithmic because of the "lognormal" nature of capitalization figures. The line graph represents cumulative assets under management.

Evidently, about 50% of all assets are concentrated in less than 4% of all products, offered by those money managers with the assets greater than $2.5 billion.

In this chapter we will examine the distribution of style between these large and small products.

FIGURE 17-1.   The U.S. Domestic Equity Products as of 1993

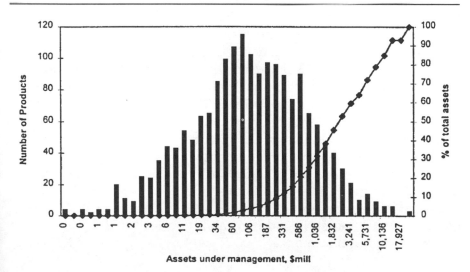

Building a Composite Index

Our first step was to test the reliability of performance and asset data. About 80% of all managers, in compliance with AIMR reporting standards, report the performance of all their assets, while the rest of the managers would report, on average, about 50% of their accounts' performance—apparently the best-performing portfolios. One would expect that the composite index of all managers would significantly outperform a broad U.S. market index.

In order to test that hypothesis, we created a composite index for the U.S. domestic-equity managers. We started the index at the end of 1983 with the assets given at the year end. We continued this index in 1984 compounding quarterly returns (buy-and-hold). At the end of 1984, we rebalanced to the assets given in the database. Note that the number of managers can increase (it cannot decrease because this database has only survivors). This process is very similar to the creation of any capitalization-weighted index. We continued this process up to the June 1994 rebalancing to the provided asset weights at every year-end. We will call the resulting index the *institutional index*.

In addition to the total composite index we have created in like manner two indices that represent the top 50% and the bottom 50% of the cumulative product capitalization. We constructed these indices to have exactly one-half of the total assets at the end of each year.

We compared performance of the institutional indices thus created to the market benchmark selected for this study, the Russell 3000 Index. The choice of a market benchmark is very important. In their study, Lakonishok, Shleifer, and Vishny [1992] compared equal-weighted and value-weighted composite returns of 769 managed portfolios to the S&P 500 Index. They observed the managers' annual average return for the 1983–1989 period to be 17.7%, compared to 19% for the S&P 500; based on the 1.3% difference, they concluded that "active money management subtracted rather than added value." The S&P 500 Index was selected as a benchmark in their study because they assumed that plan sponsors were hiring money managers primarily to beat the S&P 500 Index. We think this approach to the manager selection process is oversimplified. There are plenty of small-cap, value, and growth money managers that are valued for the consistency of their style and their ability to beat their style-specific benchmarks, not just the S&P 500. Therefore, a broad-market index would be more appropriate for this and similar studies. Interestingly, the average annual return of the Russell 3000 Index for 1983–1989 was 17.7%, which matches the performance of the managers in the Lakonishok study! The only conclusion one can make is that the managers in the study had pretty good coverage of the U.S. equity market.

The performance of our institutional indices compared to the Russell 3000 is given in Tables 17-1 and 17-2. During the whole 10-year period, the tracking numbers look very good.

The performance numbers in Tables 17-1 and 17-2 show the average superiority of the 4% of equity portfolios with the largest assets under management. One would expect quite the opposite: managers with less money under management should have higher

TABLE 17-1. Institutional Indices Compared to Russell 3000
January 1984 through June 1994

	Annualized Excess Return (%)	Cumulative Excess Return (%)	Tracking Error (%)	Correlation	Beta versus R3000	Annualized Alpha (%)
Institutional Index	0.05	1.60	1.82	0.9963	0.92	0.46
Institutional 50% top cap	0.67	23.00	1.77	0.9964	0.93	0.84
Institutional 50% bottom cap	−0.29	−9.61	2.09	0.9948	0.91	0.04

TABLE 17-2. Annualized Performance
January 1984–June 1994

	Annualized Return (%)	Cumulative Return (%)	Standard Deviation (%)	Sharpe Ratio
Russell 3000 Index	13.14	265.58	15.93	0.42
Russell 1000 Index	13.48	277.29	15.66	0.45
Russell 2000 Index	9.66	163.32	21.47	0.15
Institutional Index	13.19	267.18	14.67	0.46
Institutional 50% top cap	13.65	283.37	14.81	0.49
Institutional 50% bottom cap	12.70	250.76	14.62	0.43

volatility of their performance numbers which should be rewarded (on average) by higher returns. Here we observe that these managers have lower returns and lower standard deviations. Note that the composite institutional index has a superior Sharpe ratio (0.46) than the broad-market index (0.42), but all superiority comes from the managers with the largest assets (0.49). As it follows from Table 17-1, smaller accounts have lower historical beta and lower Jensen's alpha. While the total composite index has superior risk-adjusted performance ($\alpha = 0.46\%$), all outperformance comes from the top 4% of equity products.

It is intuitively clear that small account-managers should have greater exposure to small-cap stocks, which significantly underperformed large-caps in the past decade (compare the Russell 1000 and Russell 2000 in Table 17-2). This clearly could degrade the performance of these managers. It is also possible that smaller accounts have proportionally more cash than larger accounts—this can also make their performance and volatility lower.

We will show in the following sections that both assumptions hold: smaller accounts have proportionally more cash and more small-cap stocks.

The line graph in Figure 17-2 shows how the institutional index compares to the Russell 3000 index. The bar graph shows quarterly excess return of the institutional index versus the Russell 3000. Note the unusually stable outperformance for the last several quarters. It could be due to managers, on average, reporting results for the best recently performing portfolios.

The 3% spike in the last quarter of 1987 is apparently due to the cash position in managers' portfolios during the market crash in October 1987. The Russell 3000 Index contains equity returns only. Most of the managers' return data in the performance databases includes cash position, which means that we had to extract the equity-only portion from the manager's data before reasonably comparing it to market data.

The above results suggest that the quality of the data is high and also show that active managers, on average, do not add much value (about 0.05% per year) when compared to a broad-market index or, to put it differently, do not misrepresent their performance by much. All excess performance generated in the past decade came from the top 4% of the managers with the most assets under management.

FIGURE 17-2. Institutional Index versus Russell 3000 Broad-Market Index

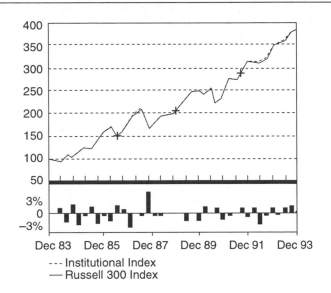

--- Institutional Index
— Russell 300 Index

Style Analysis

For each year in the 1984–1994 period, we will identify four style-components—large-cap growth, small-cap growth, large-cap value, and small-cap value—in the U.S. equity market (Russell 3000 universe) and in the institutional portfolio (Nelson Manager Database).

In each year we will find a combination of generic style-portfolios that minimizes tracking error to each of the two. We decided to use Russell's style indices, the 1000 Value, 1000 Growth, 2000 Value, and 2000 Growth, because they are exhaustive and add up to the Russell 3000 Index. The portfolio weights to be found have to be non-negative and have to add up to 100%.

This process is usually called *style analysis* and requires quadratic optimization where the objective function is a sample variance of the difference between portfolio return and the style combination return for a certain period, which we call *estimation window*. In this study the estimation window was two years or eight quarters. Because managers' return data in databases is quarterly, we had eight data-points for each estimation. We used Salomon Brothers' three-month T-bill total return index as our fifth index to account for cash in managers' portfolios.

Style analysis can be considered as an extension of the *single index* CAPM and has much higher explanatory power when applied to the managed portfolios. The standard *beta regression* model can be written in the following form:

$$R_p - R_f = \alpha + \beta(R_m - R_f) + \varepsilon$$

or

$$R_p = \alpha + \beta R_m + (1 - \beta)R_f + \varepsilon$$

where R_p is the rate of return of a managed portfolio, R_f is the risk-free rate, and R_m is return on the market.

Or in the matrix form:

$$R_p = \alpha + R'\beta + \varepsilon$$

where

$$\beta' = (\beta, (1 - \beta))$$
$$R' = (R_m, R_f)$$

In some sense we are looking for a portfolio with two assets—Treasury bills and the market portfolio—that has the best tracking of a manager. One of the major deficiencies of this model, when applied to managed portfolios, is that we are not using some of the *a priori* available information, say, that managers on average don't have short positions. In the above model we can short either T-bills ($\beta > 1$) or market portfolio ($\beta < 0$). Unfortunately, if we introduce non-negativity constraints in this single-index model we will have, on average, a much lower explanation of the manager's returns than with an unconstrained model.

Usually the generic dimensions of investment for a manager are known in advance: for a domestic U.S. equity-manager these could be value, growth, size, and cash; for an international-equity manager, country indices and cash; for a domestic fixed-income manager, quality, duration, and cash. Including generic style indices in the model and imposing non-negativity constraints will greatly improve the explanation of the manager's performance and will give the insight in his or her management style. This method was introduced by William Sharpe and described in detail in Sharpe [1992].

The modified model will now have the following form:

$$R_p = \alpha + R'\beta + \varepsilon \tag{1}$$

subject to

$$\beta \geq 0$$

$$\beta'1 = 1$$

where

$\beta' = (\beta_1,...,\beta_n)$ are style "weights"

$R' = (R_1,...,R_n)$ are style index returns

Note that higher explanatory power of the model can be attributed to the Bayesian nature of the estimation (we are using "prior knowledge" of the manager's return distribution in constraints).

Modified Style-Analysis

To estimate parameters of Equation (1) one would need to solve the following linearly constrained quadratic problem:

$$\min (R_p - \alpha - R'\beta)'(R_p - \alpha - R'\beta) \tag{2}$$

$$\alpha, \beta$$

$$\text{s.t. } \beta \geq 0$$

$$\beta'1 = 1$$

where R is the matrix of historical returns on the generic style indices included in the model, and R_p is the vector of historical returns of the portfolio for the same period of time, which we called the estimation window above.

Style betas obtained in this manner give us an estimation of the style allocation of the manager during the estimation period. If we are interested in the style allocation at the end of the period (or current style) we would have to take the shortest possible period—but long enough to have the covariance matrix of Equation (2) to be of full rank and have a unique solution, i.e., we would need the number of observations to be greater than the number of style indices.

Instead of analyzing the style of individual managers, in this study we analyzed the composite index of all U.S. equity-managers. If our goal was to identify the style allocation of this composite index and catch the dynamic of style allocations, we would be always behind in identifying these changes. Consider the following example.

Let's assume there are only two money managers in the United States: a value manager and a growth manager. For the previous year, growth fashion prevailed and most (say 90%) of the funds were managed by the growth manager. This year things have changed, and during the first quarter, the value manager captured 90% of the market. If we analyze the composite index of two managers using their historical asset numbers in order to identify *current* style allocation of the institutional portfolios, we would be getting wrong answers, because the composite index is dominated by the growth returns except for the last quarter.

One solution to this problem is (a) to assume that the managers' style has not changed much during the estimation period, and (b) to use *constant current assets* in calculating composite instead of the real, time-varying asset figures. In our case the style regression of Equation (2) would produce correct style-allocation of 10% growth, 90% value with this approach.

For the U.S. equity market, the assumption (a) seems reasonable on average, because money managers are valued by plan sponsors and individual investors for the consistency of their style. In the international-equity market this is not true; managers shift their country loadings frequently. In this case, it's worth getting monthly performance numbers to make the estimation time-window shorter and to work with the composite index.

Another solution is to use an *equal-weighted* composite instead of capitalization (asset) weighted, i.e., to use average return among all money managers for each time period. These indices for mutual funds are readily available from Morningstar and are called *invest-*

ment objectives. The asset allocation derived from the equal-weighted index is actually a "number of products" allocation, and shows the dynamic of the number of available products in each style rather than the actual style-assets allocated. While this could be considered a very useful number, the detailed analysis of this dynamic is beyond the scope of this chapter and can be a subject of further research (see the section on "Further Research").

We used the first approach to derive the style allocations among the U.S. institutional portfolios. For each year, we calculated a separate composite using asset weights at the end of the year. The results of the analysis are shown in Figures 17-3 through 17-6. Each graph reflects the history of loadings on each of the style components. Note that we rescaled the noncash portion of the institutional index, so that it would add to 100% without cash. We observed about 7% cash loading on average in the institutional index, and the above rescaling

FIGURE 17-3.   Large-Cap Growth Holdings versus Style Excess Performance

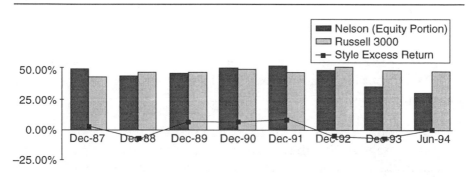

FIGURE 17-4.   Large-Cap Value Holdings versus Style Excess Performance

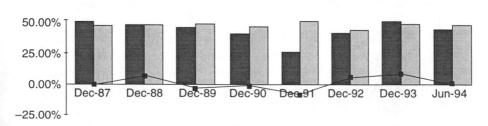

FIGURE 17-5.   Small-Cap Growth Holdings versus Style Excess Performance

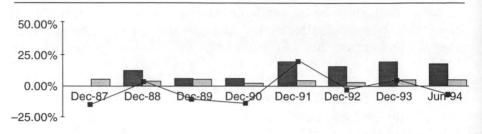

FIGURE 17-6.   Small-cap Value Holdings versus Style Excess Performance

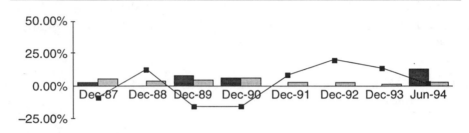

allowed us to compare equity-only positions in both indices (the Russell 3000 didn't load cash, as expected). The R-squareds for the regressions were in the range of 99.8–99.9%.

The line on each graph shows the return of the corresponding style portfolio in excess of the market (Russell 3000).

It is noteworthy that small-cap growth stocks are overrepresented in the institutional portfolios, compared to the market.

Several observations can be made from these graphs without any further exploratory analysis:

- Large-cap managers, whether growth or value, are "trend-followers."
- Small-cap growth managers "overreact" to the performance of the managed portfolios—two small boosts in performance in 1988 and 1991 were sufficient to keep money in this sector despite its poor performance in the following years.

- Small-cap value managers are very cautious and slow—it takes years of good style-performance for them to jump into the style, and years of bad performance to jump out. It is interesting that the highest loadings in small-cap value portfolios coincide with the worst performance of the sector.

So far we haven't discussed *causality*, i.e., whether the past performance drives the fashion or the fashion drives style performance. Implicitly we assumed the former while it is possible that the latter is true. The dynamic of the small-cap growth loadings/performance graph indicates that dramatic increase in small-cap growth holdings could have caused their superior performance during this drive and, as a result, overpricing and the degrade of performance in the two to three following years.

Figure 17-7 shows style allocation for the two Nelson subindices at the end of 1993. In one of the previous sections, we suggested that the performance of smaller accounts had been degraded by larger-than-average cash and small-cap holdings. Note that the difference in style allocation is not as dramatic as one would expect. Smaller stocks have higher representation in smaller accounts, which at the same time hold 50% more cash than bigger accounts.

FIGURE 17-7. Allocation of Style between Large and Small Accounts
Asset allocation analysis, December 1993

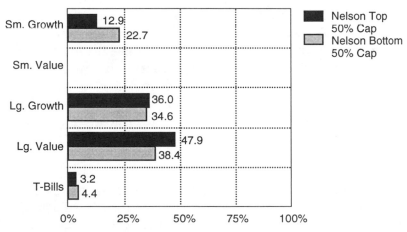

Style Advisor: Markov Processes, Inc.

Further Research

In this section we will outline several directions for further research based on the methodology described in the previous sections.

Style-Allocation Strategies

Once the causality issue in style performance versus style allocation is tested, it could lead to an obvious style-rotation strategy. If, for example, for a certain style higher than the market average, style-loading degrades the style performance in the next few years, then a good strategy would be buying a generic complement to this style in the market portfolio.

We believe that using monthly returns instead of quarterly will make the asset-allocation figures more reliable and suitable for creating a sensible style-allocation strategy.

Small Accounts versus Large Accounts

We have briefly compared the performance of the two composites: small and large accounts. We used style-analysis technique here just to estimate the parameters of return-generating process (we call it style allocation) for both composites. If we could demonstrate that larger accounts are better managed and produce superior performance, this could have serious implications for the money-manager selection process for a plan sponsor, because when hiring smaller money-managers the plan sponsor is taking higher risks.

In Table 17-3 we show sample cross-sectional statistics of the 1993 annual return distribution of the domestic-equity products sorted and grouped by the end of 1992 assets under management figure. We used 1992 year-end asset figures in order not to introduce a performance bias in the groups that we have created.

While the confidence interval for the mean return of small accounts is obviously narrower than for the large accounts, the standard deviation is still 50% higher, and in hiring a smaller manager, the plan sponsor is taking 50% higher risk.

We think that eliminating survivorship bias, taking historical data for 15 to 20 years, and using the simulated style-adjusted benchmark [Sharpe 1992] could be the right framework for this study.

**TABLE 17-3. Cross-Sectional Sample Statistics of Managers'
Performance**
1993 annual returns

	Standard Deviation of Return	Mean (Equal-Weighted) Return	Asset-Weighted Mean Return	Median Return	Number of Accounts in the Group
Large: 50% of total assets	6.12%	12.90%	13.06%	12.67%	60
Core: next 40% of total assets	6.84%	13.07%	13.13%	13.36%	460
Small: 10% of total assets	9.96%	13.79%	13.80%	12.86%	1000

International/Global Accounts

We applied the same technique to the composite performance index of the international/global equity money-managers in the Nelson database (International Institutional Index). We used the asset-weighted composite index instead of year-end composites with the year-end weights for the reasons that we mentioned in the previous section. For the palette of indices, we selected the following Salomon Brothers Global Equity indices:

- Canada Broad Index (SICAB)
- Japan Broad Index (SIJAB)
- Asia-Pacific excluding Japan Broad Index (SIAPXJAB)
- European Broad Index (SIEUB)

We added Baring Securities' Emerging Market Index (BEMI), three Russell U.S. style indices (R1000, R2VALUE, R2GROWTH), and Salomon Brothers' Three-month T-bill index to account for other areas of international equity investment.[1] Each index represents total returns in U.S. dollars. The results of the analysis are shown in Figure 17-8. In order to compare the asset allocation in managed portfolios to

---

[1] Unfortunately, there exists a small "overlap" between Baring Emerging Market Index and Salomon Brothers Asia-Pacific Broad Index. We were not able to obtain Salomon Brothers emerging markets index for our study.

FIGURE 17-8.   Style Allocation of Global Money Managers
Nelson Global Composite asset allocation analysis, June 1994

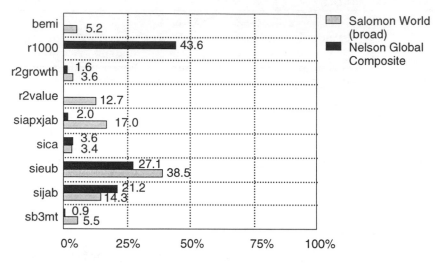

Style Advisor: Markov Processes, Inc.

the one of the market, we have run the same analysis on the Salomon Global Broad Index.

Interestingly, when it comes to the U.S. equity portion of their portfolios, global money managers prefer to invest in smaller equities (12.7% in R2VALUE, the Russell Small Value Index). The reason is quite obvious: international managers can attain higher degree of diversification than domestic managers by investing in the assets with low correlation. That's why they can "afford" to take assets with higher risk (and higher return) small-cap domestic equities. Note that U.S. small-cap value stocks dominate U.S. small-cap growth stocks in portfolios of global money managers—quite the opposite of what we observed for the domestic managers!

One of the possible applications of this analysis is that the asset weights obtained during style analysis of the International Institutional Index can be used to create an overall benchmark for an international money manager. For example, instead of looking at his or her peers (which are hard to find sometimes) or some capitalization-weighted benchmark like MSCI EAFE index, a plan sponsor should compare the manager's results to a combination of indices weighted according to the style allocation of the institutional composite index and not to the

FIGURE 17-9.   Style Allocation of the Morningstar World Stock Equal-Weighted Index

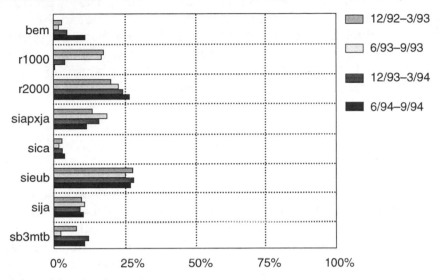

Style Advisor: Markov Processes, Inc.

capitalization-weighted global index. The logic behind this is that this combination of assets represents the plan sponsor's "opportunity mix."

A similar analysis can be done using country indices instead of region indices. A MSCI EAFE country index subset weighted proportionately to the weights obtained by the style analysis of the International Institutional Index can be a viable alternative to the market capitalization-weighted or GDP-weighted indices. By definition, this benchmark would consider all investment restrictions, pricing inefficiencies, and illiquidities of international markets.[2]

As we have mentioned in one of the previous sections, the same analysis can be done with the equal-weighted indices. The asset allocation will show the dynamic of the number of products rather than the assets under management. In Figure 17-9, we show the results of the analysis of the Morningstar World Stock Index,

[2] Zephyr Associates plans to provide quarterly country weights of the "Invested EAFE" index thus created, as a part of their Style Advisor subscription services. The International Institutional Index will also be provided so that the country weights can be easily reproduced.

which is just an equal-weighted average of the mutual funds in this style category.

Note an increased representation of emerging-markets products during the last four years. The same is true, while not to the same extent, for the U.S. small-cap equities. On the other hand the portion of large-cap U.S. stocks in global products (on average) decreased.

We think that an obvious application for analysis of equal-weighted composite indices would be measurement of deficiencies of performance databases.

Conclusions

Return-based style analysis is a valuable tool. It gives you insight into a manager's strategy when no exact holdings information is available. When applied to the composite indices—either equal-weighted or asset-weighted—derived from the manager-performance database, style analysis permits the identification of trends in allocation of institutional assets and products. Linking the dynamics of style allocation with style performance can explain changes in both.

Just using a generic personal computer and one of the widely available manager-performance databases and data analysis tools we were able to follow style trends in institutional investment and identify the reaction of money managers to style performance.

Our approach can be used to measure the deficiencies and biases in manager-performance databases. It can be used by money managers to design their marketing strategies. When applied to international markets, it allows for the creation of a valuable benchmark that considers all pricing inefficiencies of these markets.

Reference

Sharpe, William. "Asset Allocation: Management Style and Performance Measurement." *The Journal of Portfolio Management,* Winter 1992, pp. 7–19.
Lakonishok, Josef, Andrei Shleifer, and Robert W. Vishny. "The Structure and Performance of the Money Management Industry," Brookings Papers on Economic Activity: Microeconomics, 1992, pp. 339–391.

CHAPTER 18

Portfolio Applications Using Synthetic Convertible Bonds

Daniel J. Bukowski, Director of Quantitative Research
Kemper Financial Services

William M. Knapp, Ph.D., Vice President and Quantitative Analyst
Kemper Financial Services

This chapter deals with convertible bonds and synthetic convertible bonds. Our principal concern will be a generic structure, where the bonds are fixed-income obligations of a corporate (XYZ Corporation) or a third-party issuer. The instrument pays a coupon, but this coupon will be less than a similarly rated straight bond, since a portion of the bond's coupon goes toward the purchase of a long-dated call option, or warrant. The holder has the option to convert the bond into a fixed number of shares (at a set, or struck, price) of XYZ's common equity at maturity.

With synthetic convertible bonds, the bond issuer and the firm(s) represented in the option are different. In this case a third party (typically a broker-dealer) creates a bond whose return is linked to the performance of an outstanding common equity (XYZ). Note that the underlying credit of the bond, in this case, the broker-dealer, is different than the credit of the underlying equity. In the case of a generic convertible of XYZ, the two are the same; the equity underlying the option is XYZ, as is the credit underlying the bond.

Wall Street brokers have already begun to issue various types of convertible bonds linked to the common-stock performance of publicly traded companies, where the underlying credit is not the company whose equity is represented in the issue. These are synthetic convertibles and go by a variety of names: ELKS, PERCS, DECS, etc.

The creation and management of synthetic convertible bonds combines quantitative disciplines in stock selection, option valuation, and portfolio construction. The following describes the process where we create synthetic convertible bonds to meet portfolio requirements unavailable from original issuer convertibles.

For brevity, we are omitting issues such as forced conversions or more exotic convertible structures containing different option structures. In terms of the analysis described, these can be handled quite readily with just a few modifications to the models. While it is beyond the scope of the chapter, we note some of the recent research analyzing convertibles by simultaneously modeling both interest-rate and stock-price moves (the "quadro tree" approach). This removes some of the biases encountered when convertible bonds are approximated by a combination of a bond plus a warrant. Synthetic converts, where we explicitly attach a warrant to a straight noncallable debt-obligation, avoid many of these pitfalls.

Motivation for Creating Synthetic Convertible Bonds

When running a convertible bond portfolio, one is faced with a limited universe of issuers, limited to a far greater degree than the universe of issuers of common equity. Requirements such as restricting holdings to be of investment grade and above further diminish the available universe of issuers. Synthetic convertible bonds allow the portfolio manager to create exposure to names previously unavailable in the standard-issue market.

Synthetics are also useful when structural requirements force a manager to hold fixed-income or principal-protected investments but an equity return is desired. Synthetic convertible bonds permit the manager to customize the equity as well as the debt exposure to conform to nearly any externally imposed limitations.

Concept Review

Options

At this point, it may be useful to review some concepts regarding options. As noted above, we will be dealing with a long-dated call option. This option will be of the European variety, which means it may not be exercised prior to maturity.

The value of an option depends upon several factors, the most important are: stock price, strike (exercise price of the call), time to maturity, and volatility of the underlying stock (since an option has a nonsymmetrical payoff distribution). Since we are dealing with a call, the value of the option is positively related to the stock price, the time remaining to maturity, and the stock volatility. Conversely, the value is negatively related to the strike price.

Another important concept is the option delta, or hedge ratio. The option delta measures the sensitivity of the option value to a move in the underlying stock price. This is the first derivative of the option price with respect to the stock price. It will range from zero to one. For instance a delta of 0.4 implies that a $1 move in the stock price causes the option price to change 40 cents.

A delta of zero typically arises when the stock price is far beneath the strike price and there is a short time to maturity. Thus, the likelihood of the stock price exceeding the strike price, which would allow the call to be exercised and thus have value, is infinitesimally small. A delta of one generally means that the stock price has far exceeded the strike price, so that the likelihood of the option being exercised is close to one. The value of the call option will then change dollar for dollar with the value of the equity since, with near certainty, it will be converted into the equity.

Delta can also be thought of as measuring the equity exposure within the option. We call this the "hedge ratio" in that by owning the number of shares of stock equal to the delta, one can dynamically replicate the performance of the call option. This is typically how a broker-dealer hedges his derivative related exposure. For instance, a call option on two shares of stock with a delta of 0.5 may be hedged with one share of stock.

The instantaneous measurement of delta gives rise to gamma, which is the sensitivity of delta to a change in the underlying stock price. Recall that, as the stock price increases (decreases), not only does the value of the call option increase (decrease), but so does its delta, or sensitivity to further changes in the stock price. While the delta is the first derivative of the option value with respect to the stock price, the gamma is the second derivative.

Finally the leverage, or gearing, represents how many units of the underlying which the option represents. For instance, if a note were purchased which had two calls embedded in it, it would have a gearing of two. Clearly, this directly impacts the sensitivity of the option to the underlying price.

Portfolio-Risk Measurement

The first concept is tracking error. This is the expected deviation in performance between two portfolios. It is measured in percent, and represents a standard deviation. In short, the smaller the number, the closer the portfolios behave, or the more they look like one another. Tracking error is typically broken into "factor," or macroeconomic risk and residual, or stock-specific risk.

The CAPM beta, which represents an individual stock's sensitivity to broad market moves, is an example of a factor-risk sensitivity. In this case, the macroeconomic factor would be the broad market. Stock-specific risk, meanwhile, is unique to the individual issue.

Uses for Synthetic Convertible Bonds

Overcoming Institutional Restrictions

Consider the case of an investor wishing to receive U.S. equity-market exposure but, due to some institutional restriction, needs to do so in a fixed income instrument. The investor is required to hold a note whose return of initial principal is only a function of the underlying credit risk.

One of the most cost effective means of accomplishing this objective is to purchase a bond whose payoff is linked to the performance of the S&P 500 Index. In effect, the dealer designing the note would use its own balance sheet and would use some of the coupon payments inherent in a bond issuance to purchase long-dated calls on the index. Most likely, the dealer would enter the futures market and would dynamically, or delta, hedge the long-dated call option. Having a liquid futures market to utilize for the hedge is a major reason why the use of the S&P 500 to represent the equity exposure is cost effective.

Once the investor has decided to use this instrument, there are still several choices to make in determining the actual structure. Since the investor has a set dollar-value to spend, as represented by the present value of coupons foregone, the investor must still decide on time to maturity, strike price, leverage (gearing), and amount of coupon desired, if any.

For instance, the lower the strike price, the more likely the option will have value at expiration ("in the money"). However, the lower the strike price, the more expensive the option and, thus, the investor may need to settle for a lower level of gearing, a lower coupon, or both.

Customizing a Note to Meet Specific Needs

An S&P 500-linked note is certainly not appropriate to all situations. The portfolio manager's benchmark may be unrelated to the S&P 500, so an S&P 500 instrument may contain risks relative to the benchmark that the manager may find disquieting. Therefore, exposure to an alternate index may be desirable. Indeed, the manager may wish to construct a customized index of stocks to meet a unique set of risks and/or capture a perceived alpha.

As an example of a more customized note, the following offers a comparison of an S&P 500 note and a note linked to the S&P/BARRA Growth Index. Here we assume the manager has an inherent growth stock orientation (growth is his or her benchmark) or believes the growth style will outperform over the term of the note.

The Growth Index is a slightly more volatile subset of the S&P 500. This is demonstrated through its estimated beta of 1.04 versus the S&P 500 (where we use the forecast beta produced by the BARRA IPORCH system, which is also where all tracking error estimates are derived). Its tracking error versus the S&P 500 is approximately 3%.

Using the above scenario, a broker-dealer offers the following prices. An A-rated issuer will sell us an at-the-money, five-year instrument tied to the S&P 500 with a coupon of 2.71%. With current five-year, A-rated paper yielding 8.82%, this implies an option cost of $23.65 for a $100 face-value bond. The implied volatility is 17.8% per annum. In short, we have a five-year bond in which we have foregone 6.11% of coupon (8.82% − 2.71%), which equates to a present value of $24.39 on a par value of $100. We have used the foregone coupon to purchase a five-year call option tied to the S&P 500 Index with a strike price set at the current index level (at the money).

If the manager would rather purchase a note tied to the Growth Index, the quoted coupon falls to 1.71%. The increase in price reflects not only the difference in volatility between the indices, but also the fact that it is more difficult to hedge this note. The S&P 500 has a fairly liquid futures market available to aid in hedging the S&P 500-linked note. Growth/value style futures will start trading in early 1995. If these contracts become liquid, their presence may reduce the cost of hedging this type of instrument.

The implied volatility for the Growth note comes to 18.8% per annum, and an option cost of $28.38 for a $100-face bond. With both bonds the option delta is approximately 0.74. This means that for a 1% change in the underlying index, the relevant bond will change roughly 0.74%. In other words, within a $100-face bond, we are gaining $74 in equivalent equity exposure.

If the manager purchases the S&P 500-linked note, he or she will receive an extra 101 basis points in coupon annually over the Growth-linked note. The price for this choice is the 3% annual tracking error between the indices. If the manager is bullish on the S&P 500 over the Growth Index, or simply desires equity exposure as represented by the S&P 500, it would make sense to purchase the S&P 500-linked vehicle. However, if the manager is bullish on the Growth Index over the S&P 500, or if the manager is benchmarked versus the Growth Index and wishes this instrument to neither add to nor subtract from excess performance (the manager will achieve "alpha" elsewhere and wishes this instrument to merely mimic the benchmark), he or she may wish to forego the 101 basis-point yield enhancement and purchase the growth-linked instrument.

Since the Growth Index has an estimated beta of 1.04 versus the S&P 500, we have some natural gearing within the Growth-linked vehicle versus the S&P 500-linked vehicle. While we noted that the Growth-linked instrument was 16% more expensive than the S&P 500-linked instrument ($28.38 versus $24.39), a large part of this can be attributed to the beta risk. In effect, owing to the 14% discount in the price of the S&P 500-linked note, the manager could choose to embed 1.15 times the S&P 500's price return into his or her note and keep the equivalent 1.70% coupon. Yet, as measured by beta, the Growth note has a natural 1.04 times leverage.

Realize that there are many other choice variables at the manager's disposal. As the manager feels bullish (bearish) towards rates, the manager may extend (shorten) the maturity of the instrument. As the manager feels bullish (bearish) towards the equity market, the manager may forego more (less) coupon for a greater (lesser) equity exposure. If the manager only feels comfortable about the equity market over a longer-term horizon, the manager may wish to purchase only a longer-dated call. Clearly, the introduction of more complex bond and option structures allows an infinite variety of views regarding the equity and fixed-income markets.

Forming Completion Funds

Now turn to a second case. Here the manager holds convertible bonds in an actively managed portfolio. Because of some limitation the manager can purchase bonds on only a portion of the index he or she is benchmarked against. Moreover, the manager wishes to purchase bonds on other specific names but none are available with convertibles.

As an example, we will take the case of a manager who is again attempting to replicate the Growth Index. To illustrate, we assume the manager holds convertibles on the 10 largest names in the index, but wishes to construct his or her portfolio so that the entire portfolio will behave like the Growth portfolio, save for a leverage factor.

Assume that the manager has a $100 million portfolio, of which $66 million is invested in the 10 largest names in the index, weighted according to their market capitalization of common equity. For simplicity, assume that the bonds are all identical in terms of their equity exposure (delta, gamma) so they move 60% relative to the underlying equity (a delta of 0.60). Thus, in equity terms, the manager has a portfolio that has an effective equity exposure of $40 million invested in the 10 largest names of the Growth Index.

Now we create a "completion" fund. In this case, we take the universe of stocks within the Growth Index (although we need not limit ourselves to this universe) and construct a portfolio so, when added to the active portfolio, the overall portfolio mimics the Growth Index. We limit ourselves to 10 names, since the manager would likely have a short list of names he or she feels are likely to outperform.

When we consider the list of 10 names already in the portfolio, we can detect several biases. The first, and most obvious bias, is firm size. These 10 issues were chosen solely due to their weight in the index. Since the index is capitalization-weighted, it becomes apparent that this list would have a bias toward large firms. When we measure the list analytically within the IPORCH system, we note an excess exposure toward large size when compared to the Growth Index, as expected.

The existing large-cap portfolio is also more volatile than the Growth Index. Again using IPORCH, we estimate this list to have a volatility of 16.8% per annum, versus 15.5% for the Growth Index. Recall that the pricing of the option depends crucially upon this number. The beta is estimated at 1.02, and the tracking error is estimated to be 5.4% versus the index. Over half the estimated volatility is stock-specific risk. This is not surprising since we are comparing a portfolio of 10 stocks to an index of 191 issues. Although these 10 stocks represent over one-quarter the weight of the index, we are exposed to a great deal of issue-specific risk.

We then construct our completion portfolio of 10 issues so that, in aggregate (20 holdings), we attempt to mimic the index. Recall that the manager has $66 million in his or her 10-issue portfolio, and wishes to place the remaining $34 million into this structure. The manager is free to choose the names he or she wishes to put within the basket. In this case, we are choosing names for a completion fund.

When we construct our completion fund, we select issues so that the fund provides a counterbalance to the actively managed portfolio. Since the 10-bond portfolio has a large-cap bias, for instance, this portfolio will have a small-cap bias relative to both the 10-bond portfolio as well as the index. As we noted, the 10-bond portfolio has an estimated beta of 1.02 versus the index. This portfolio is constructed so that it has a beta of 0.93; therefore, in the aggregate (the 10-bond portfolio holds a 2:1 weight advantage), the portfolio has an average beta of 0.99 versus the index. Using portfolio optimization, we attempt to achieve such averaging over a variety of industry weights and macroeconomic and other risk factors.

We obtain a 0.77% quoted coupon on a five-year, at-the-money bond with an option tied to our 10-stock completion basket. This prices out to an option value of $32.14 for a $100-face bond with a 8.82% coupon (the current A-rate). The implied volatility is 19.40%, which is higher than the IPORCH estimate of 16.0%. We note, however, that this price incorporates the increased cost of hedging this instrument, which uses issues that are less liquid than S&P 500 futures. Also recall that we were deliberately choosing relatively smaller issues, which tend to be even less liquid.

The main point, however, is that we can build a structure containing issues reflecting the manager's desired exposure in a fashion which allows maximum participation. Not only does this structure allow exposure to names that otherwise are not available in the marketplace, but the structure can be modified to incorporate many different investment views and to meet many different restrictions. Furthermore, we are also able to monitor the overall portfolio in terms of its fixed-income, equity, and option exposure, both on the basis of individual issues and on a portfolio basis.

Summary

There are innumerable permutations in the construction of synthetic convertible bonds. With proper consideration these bonds can be a powerful tool for any money manager. Traditional convertible-fund managers can achieve diversification unattainable through company issued convertibles. Managers limited to fixed-income investments may access equity related returns while maintaining investment restrictions. And, in a permutation not discussed here, traditional equity managers may find synthetic convertibles useful in enhancing a fund's yield, even with stocks not paying dividends.

Managers may enter synthetic convertible investing either through broker-dealer general issues (PERCS, DECS, ELKS, etc.), or by customizing their own bonds. In both cases the portfolio manager needs to first set forth an investment objective (e.g., match the returns of a existing index, track an industry or a particular stock, or perhaps target a specific factor risk like interest-rate sensitivity). Secondly, attention must be paid to the pricing structure (coupon, maturity, gearing, and implied volatility). Finally, as with all fixed-income investing, credit risk, either the broker-dealer's or third party, must be noted.

Appendix: Issues Regarding Option Deltas

We have performed the previous analyses assuming equivalent deltas between the active portfolio and the synthetic. The structure could easily account for differing deltas between the portfolios. For instance, the synthetic could be leveraged to achieve a higher delta to increase the equivalent equity exposure using the same amount of underlying assets.

Realize that we have been considering the equivalent equity exposure in terms of the option deltas. Thus, we note that, with a delta of 0.60, for instance, a 1% rise in the underlying translates into an instantaneous $0.60 increase in the value of the note. The options were struck at the money so, if held to maturity, with no further change in the underlying, the note will be worth $101. The option does not instantaneously reflect the entire $1 since there is a probability of further price change in the underlying.

Finally, we wish to note several differences between a portfolio option and a portfolio of options. In our completion-fund example, the synthetic convertible represents a portfolio option (an option on a portfolio), while the portfolio of individual issues represents a portfolio of options. First, the portfolio option tends to be less expensive since, all other things being equal, due to diversification, the portfolio will have a lower estimated volatility than an individual name. By purchasing an option on a portfolio, we retain this cost advantage.

At maturity, however, the option on the portfolio will tend to be worth less than the portfolio of options. To illustrate why, if two stocks are equally represented in a portfolio and the first increases by 10% while the second decreases by 10%, their impact will cancel on the overall portfolio. Thus, an option purchased on the portfolio will show no change in value. However, if one owned two individual options on the securities, both struck at the money, the first will increase in value to reflect the 10% price rise, while the second will expire out of the money (worthless). Thus, the overall option-portfolio will show a net increase. This situation reflects an implicit cost in purchasing an option on a basket of securities.

Additionally, with individual options, the deltas of the options change to reflect movements in the price of the underlying equity. As noted previously, the delta increases (decreases) as the equity's price rises (declines). Thus, as the equity rises (declines), the delta changes so that the equivalent exposure to the issue rises (declines) as well.

When analyzing the index option, however, the situation becomes a bit more complicated. The delta of the option will change in accordance with the level of the index. However, the delta for an individual issue within the index is determined by the level of the index and the weight of the individual issue within the index. Since the synthetic convertible is structured to maintain exposure to specific names, it is this two-stage process to calculate individual stock deltas that becomes relevant.

In general, the delta for the individual stock will increase (decrease) along with the individual stock's price, as in the case of the individual option. As the individual stock's price rises, all other things being equal, so will the index price (increasing the overall delta) as well as the stock's weight within the index (increasing the stock's delta). Thus, the delta of the instrument will increase (decrease) along with the level of the individual equity, but the relationship is not as straightforward as in the case with convertibles on individual issues.

PART IV

Aggregate Fund (Sponsor) Issues

Reversing Manager-Selection Failure: Using Style Allocation to Improve Fund Returns

David J. Kudish, President
Stratford Advisory Group, Inc.

Fund Sponsors Seek Enhanced Returns . . .

Government statistics suggest there is $10 trillion in the United States invested by institutional investors in stocks and bonds. This includes corporate, union, and municipal pension-funds, profit-sharing funds, endowments, and foundations. These funds all have a singular objective: they seek enhanced returns.

If the stewards of these funds representing just 5% of the assets could improve their funds' returns by only one percentage point per year, the result would be an annual wealth redistribution of $5 billion.

From the fiduciaries' perspective, it is clear the payoff is large enough to justify spending tens of millions of dollars and millions of hours to seek enhanced returns. The problem is that this enormous resource-commitment by fund sponsors is focused on finding the "best" investment-management-firms. This is the wrong focus.

At the individual-fund level, the payoff for achieving enhanced performance is substantial. For example, if a typical pension fund could achieve a one percentage point higher rate of return each year—11% versus 10%—this could reduce the corporate sponsor's contribution to that plan by as much as 25%. For an endowment or foundation with a typical spending policy of 5% per year, a one percentage point increase in return is a substantial addition to the institution's philanthropic mission.

399

... But Are Chronically Disappointed

Fiduciaries may seek the best managers. But, they are not achieving success. Evidence demonstrates that most investment managers' returns disappoint fund sponsors. Otherwise, why would so many successful business people who serve as fiduciaries be hiring and firing managers so frequently?

Examine a copy of *Institutional Investor* or *Pensions and Investments*. Each contains several pages featuring the names of investment managers that were terminated and the firms replacing them. Why would institutional funds go through this costly turnover process— shifting around billions of dollars each year—if they weren't disappointed with their existing managers?

Fund Sponsors Chase Past Performance

Why do investment managers chronically disappoint fund sponsors? The fundamental answer is that fund sponsors select managers based on past performance. They tend to choose today's "hot" managers. Unfortunately, these are yesterday's "winners"—not tomorrow's leaders.

Prudential Securities conducted a survey of the most popular managers listed each year in *Institutional Investor* magazine's *Pension Olympics.*[1] The *Pension Olympics* survey lists the investment-management firms gaining or losing the most accounts from the large Fortune 1000 corporations. Prudential wanted to examine whether there were any common characteristics among the managers gaining the most accounts that would lead to a better understanding of how fund sponsors select investment managers. One criterion stood out among all others: past performance.

Prudential conducted this study for seven years (five rolling three-year periods). For each year, it examined the performance achieved by these popular managers. The managers that gained the most new accounts—during each prior three-year period—achieved spectacularly good investment performance. The consistency of past excellent performance was the singular variable that emerged from the analysis. Table 19-1 demonstrates that, on average, the managers

[1] "The 1992 Pension Olympics." *Institutional Investor,* February 1992, p. 61.

TABLE 19-1.   Evidence: Fund Sponsors Chase Past Performance

	Managers Who Gained the Most Large Accounts	
	Performance *Before* Becoming Popular	Performance *After* Becoming Popular
1982	+10.6%	(1.9%)
1983	+8.8%	(3.4%)
1984	+11.2%	(1.9%)
1985	+5.7%	(0.1%)
1986	+5.5%	(1.5%)
Average value added	+8.4%	(1.8%)

Source: Institutional Investor magazine survey ("Pension Olympics").
Analysis: Annualized trailing three-year performance of most-often hired managers *less* S&P 500 performance for that same three-year period.

that gained the most large accounts were those that outperformed the market by an average of more than eight percentage points per year. (If the market was up 10%, these firms were up more than 18%.)

However, this study also revealed that performance faltered for the top-performing managers during the following three-year period. On balance, they *underperformed* the market averages by almost two percentage points per year.

The period of the study included both rising and declining markets. Some years, inflation rose dramatically. In other years, inflation declined. We experienced an oil crisis and, later, an oversupply. During all of these different economic environments, two observations stand out:

- Fund sponsors clearly choose managers who have top recent performance.
- Managers who have achieved top recent performance are unable to sustain that performance advantage. They gravitate back toward trend-line performance that is similar to most other managers over the long term.

The Fiduciaries' Paradox

Stratford Advisory Group, Inc. refers to this phenomenon as the "Fiduciaries' Paradox." Fund sponsors expend effort to "beat the market" because the reward or payoff is so great. They think the way to accomplish this is to select a past winner. Yet, the clear evidence is that 75% (or more) of fund sponsors fail to achieve their objective. But they still try, in spite of clear evidence of overwhelming failure.

Fund sponsors "buy" investment managers based on a promise of performance—and "sell" managers based on reality. This is the continued triumph of hope over reality.

From our vantage point, trying to beat the market is not the underlying problem. We firmly believe that fund sponsors *can* beat the market. It is the process embraced by fund sponsors that is the crux of their difficulties. And this process is rooted in antiquated belief systems.

Who's at Fault?

As fund sponsors continue to seek out better investment-managers, many have questioned the factors underlying their apparent failure.

- From the fund-sponsor perspective, this failure is due to the investment managers themselves. They believe the managers sold them a "bill of goods"—that the managers misrepresented their inherent abilities.
- The investment managers' point of view is that they are not given enough time to prove their capabilities. They believe their clients should stay with them over a complete market cycle. However, in the competitive field of investment management, fund sponsors continually feel an obligation to seek out improved investment returns. When an investment manager underperforms for several years—even if the period has been less than a complete market cycle—the fund sponsor will likely replace the manager.

What is really going on? More important, can a fund sponsor do anything to improve long-term investment returns?

What we believe is occurring is a fundamental misunderstanding of two critical elements:

- Why investment managers outperform or underperform

- How fund sponsors should go about selecting investment managers

The Fund-Sponsor Perspective

From the fund-sponsor viewpoint, managers that perform well are "smart." Managers that perform poorly are "stupid." In fact, our research—consistent with the analyses of many academicians and practitioners—reveals that neither designation is truly accurate.

A fund sponsor seeks top-performing managers. It wants a firm that excels in the "four Ps": philosophy, process, pedigree, and performance.

- Philosophy—The firm must have an investment philosophy that makes sense to its clients or prospective clients.
- Process—The firm must have a definable and understandable process for selecting securities. It must communicate this clearly to its clients.
- Pedigree—The principals of the firm must have excellent credentials. Fund sponsors seek portfolio managers who have attended the most prestigious universities and trained at well-known investment-management organizations.
- Performance—Fund sponsors may look at many factors in assessing which investment managers meet the appropriate criteria. Yet, no single factor counts as much as performance. *During the past quarter of a century, as observers of fund sponsors selecting some investment managers and rejecting others, we have concluded that past performance counts for as much as three-quarters of the manager-selection decision.*

The Performance Obsession

Why do fund sponsors fixate on past performance? The reason is quite simple. Philosophy, process, and pedigree are subjective. Performance is quantitative. You can "hang your hat" on the numbers. (What fiduciary would be criticized for hiring a top-performing manager?) Numbers tell the truth (so they believe). The truth is that the selected manager has outperformed. He or she must be very "smart."

Performance measurement universes were first compiled about 30 years ago. This gave fund sponsors the tools to compare their manager(s) to other firms in a seemingly unbiased manner. A natural extension was for fund sponsors to learn who were the top managers and to seek them out.

The paradigm is that fiduciaries search for managers who rank within the top quartile (top 25%) of all other managers within that asset class. In effect, fund sponsors attribute "capability" to portfolio managers based on achieved past performance.

- Those with recent top-quartile performance are judged "smart" and worthy of being hired.
- Those unfortunate enough to fall into the bottom quartile are deemed "stupid" (i.e., ineffectual) and become candidates for replacement.

Fund sponsors reward a manager's "smartness" (top performance) with new accounts or the flow of additional assets to an existing account. Fund sponsors penalize "stupidity" (poor performance) by reducing assets or by outright dismissal. This appears to be a very rational, almost Darwinian system. It rewards success and penalizes failure. The "strong" survive.

However, the reasons a manager may appear "smart" or "stupid" often have very little to do with capabilities. Other forces are at work beneath the surface, either enhancing or detracting from the manager's capabilities.

The Investment Managers' Perspective

Managers claim that it is their unique stock-picking ability that results in their ability to outperform other managers. They have obviously done a great job in convincing fund sponsors of this because fund sponsors are constantly seeking out great "stock pickers."

How do investment managers go about picking stocks? They use computers to access huge databases of corporate financial history.

FIGURE 19-1.　Managers' Stock-Selection Process

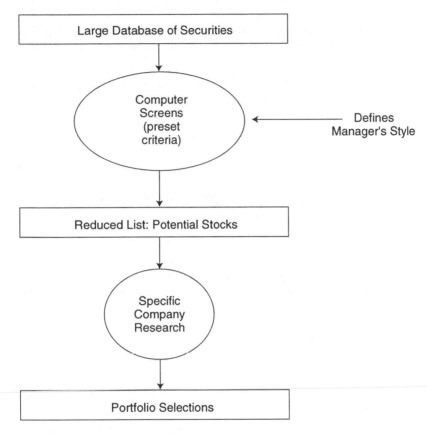

© 1989, Stratford Advisory Group, Inc.

As portrayed in Figure 19-1, criteria are selected to screen thousands of securities. The objective is to create a "focus list" of 100 to 200 securities that meet their specifications.

From the managers' viewpoint, it is their ability to conduct subjective research into those few hundred companies that creates a performance advantage. This analysis includes in-depth research by analytical staff as well as visits to company management, suppliers, vendors, and competitors.

If we step back and examine the criteria that managers use for screening, we discover that large numbers of firms use virtually identical parameters. The attributes of the companies that fall into these "focus lists" are reasonably similar.

In actuality, it is the *criteria* the manager establishes at the initial stages of the screening process that are largely responsible for the resultant performance—not the individual stocks selected. Often these screening processes find not just mispriced securities, but mispriced industries or sectors. Change the screening criteria and you change the performance—and, the performance *pattern*—of that manager over a market cycle. Managers with virtually identical screening criteria have very similar performance patterns over time—even if they own different stocks.

Belief Systems and the Self-Fulfilling Prophecy

In investment management, there are many unseen factors beneath the surface that managers won't often admit and of which many fund sponsors are unaware. But, these factors have a robust impact on managers' results—and on fund sponsors' decisions regarding the perceived adequacy of the results.

This dilemma is what Nobel laureate Douglass North (professor of economics at Washington University in St. Louis), refers to as "belief systems." Applying North's work to investment management, the authorities in power—in this case, large pension funds that have the most dollars to allocate to managers—determine what they believe is important and act upon it. They create a self-fulfilling prophecy.

In examining history, we look back in humor at some of the belief systems considered universal. It was not uncommon during Columbus' time to believe that the earth was flat. During Galileo's life, the consensus was that the sun revolved around the earth. Today, we consider these beliefs to be utterly ridiculous. Yet, at the time, these beliefs were universally embraced.

In our own lifetimes, we have seen the repudiation of certain belief systems. Think back only a generation ago when authority figures taught us that eating red meat and cheese was "good for you." Now we discover that this diet produces excessive weight gain, clogged arteries, and is a prime cause of strokes and heart attacks.

George Soros, managing general partner of the $6 billion Quantum Fund, addressed this concept of self-fulfilling prophecy. In a highly conceptual book on his investment perspective,[2] Soros referred to the dominant mental model operating within the investment community as "reflexivity." Reflexivity is an analysis system that assumes reality affects perceptions. Perceptions, in turn, may alter reality.

Let's use as an example the exchange rate between the Japanese yen and the U.S. dollar. If enough market players believe that the dollar will rebound, they buy dollars and short yen. When others see the dollar rising, they jump "on board." This reinforces the original investors' perceptions. Stratford believes markets move rapidly for short periods of time because of this closed-loop process.

In the investment realm, there is widespread acceptance—a belief system in North's parlance—that a manager's stock-picking capability is the differentiating factor between achieving superior returns and average returns (or inferior returns). There are more than 20,000 investment-management firms registered with the Securities and Exchange Commission. These managers each make many sales calls. They attempt to differentiate their capabilities from their competitors by promoting the belief system that stock-picking ability is the key variable.

The underlying truth is that it is a firm's investment philosophy and process—not stock-picking capability—that determine its performance pattern. Nevertheless, as long as investment managers continue to promote this stock-picking belief system, fund sponsors will continue to make poor manager-selection decisions. In spite of overwhelming new evidence, the stock-picking myth is alive and well.

Let's explore an example. One of the most renowned investment managers during the past 25 years is Peter Lynch. Lynch was the portfolio manager of the Fidelity Magellan Fund during the 1970s and 1980s. In his books, articles, and public appearances, Lynch claims that his superior stock-picking was the reason for his investment success.

Stratford agrees that Lynch was very successful. Yet, extensive statistical analysis by Nobel laureate Professor William F. Sharpe (Stanford University)[3] reveals that more than 95% of Lynch's performance superiority is attributable to correct investment style-allocation—not

---

[2] Soros, George. *The Alchemy of Finance* (New York: John Wiley & Sons, Inc., 1987).

[3] Sharpe, William F. "Asset Allocation: Management Style and Performance Measurement." *The Journal of Portfolio Management*, Winter 1992, p. 7.

superior stock-picking. (Figure 19-2 graphically depicts the results of this analysis.)

Lynch's brilliance occurred through shifting the allocation of his fund's many holdings to investment styles with superior future potential. (How *could* stock picking have been that important when the Magellan Fund held more than 1,000 stocks?)

The good news is that those investors who understand the myth of the stock-picking belief system can exploit their advantage. These investors can choose managers on a totally different belief system to enhance long-term returns. This myth-shattering belief system is the concept of "regression to the mean."

Regression to the Mean

After years of extensive analysis, Stratford believes that the most powerful force in the investment management field is "regression to the mean." What this means is that there is a strong tendency of stocks, economic sectors, and investment managers (who invest in these stocks and economic sectors) to go through cycles where they outperform and then underperform. Managers outperform for a while (in sports parlance, a "streak"). Afterwards, they find them-

FIGURE 19-2. Sharpe Case Study: Fidelity Magellan Fund*

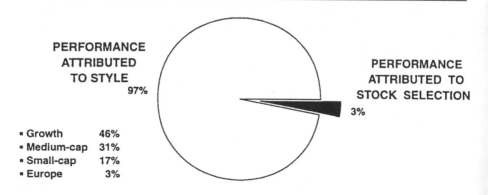

PERFORMANCE
ATTRIBUTED
TO STYLE
97%

- Growth   46%
- Medium-cap   31%
- Small-cap   17%
- Europe   3%

PERFORMANCE
ATTRIBUTED TO
STOCK SELECTION
3%

* William F. Sharpe, "Asset Allocation: Management Style and Performance Measurement." *Journal of Portfolio Management*, Winter 1992.

selves in a period where they underperform (a "slump"). Over a long period of time, the performance of different managers converges to a definable trend line.

Stratford and others are discovering that fund sponsors can exploit these periods of outperformance and underperformance to enhance long-term returns. The characteristics of these trends are summarized below:

- Cycles are of long duration. Periods of manager outperformance and underperformance each last for several years. Complete cycles may take 10 to 15 years.
- Cycles are of significant amplitude. Periods of manager outperformance and underperformance differ substantially from the overall-market trend line. Over long-term periods, the stock market has averaged a total return of 10% per year.[4] Wilshire Associates'[5] research indicates that investment style-trend differences may be as much as 10 percentage points or more per year. The style "in favor" might return 15% on average per year for several years. The "out-of-favor" style might return just 5% per year during that same period. If one can "tilt" successfully toward the style in favor, the compounding effect of this performance differential is enormous.
- Manager returns cluster within a "style peer-group." As previously mentioned, the performance of managers employing certain similar stock-screening criteria cluster. *Over a several-year period, managers within a defined style-grouping have a very similar performance pattern.*

It is this last point, the clustering of managers' returns, that opened up an entirely new area of inquiry—the analysis of investment styles. Before Sharpe published his myth-shattering research during the winter of 1992, Stratford and a few other organizations discovered that different managers constructing portfolios with totally different stocks had very similar performance patterns. Both anecdotal evidence and in-depth research contributed to this discovery.

What is the fundamental implication if the stock holdings of a

[4] Ibbotson Associates, Chicago, Illinois.

[5] Wilshire Associates, Santa Monica, California.

number of managers are different but the performance patterns of the managers are nearly identical? The logical deduction is that the managers' investment-selection *process* is clearly more important than the specific *stocks selected.*

To analyze this premise, Stratford's first step was to group managers according to their similar stock-selection criteria. We referred to these groups as "style peer-groups." The next step was to assess the degree to which the performance patterns of the managers within those peer-groups coincided. We discovered that the overlap among managers *within* a style peer-group was significant. And, we discovered that the performance patterns among different style peer-groups was significantly different.

This is intuitive. And, it is borne out as we analyze the performance patterns and stock holdings of large groups of managers.

Capturing Opportunities through Style Tilting

Stratford Advisory Group, Inc. began to examine these style peer-groups of managers more closely. We attempted to draw hypotheses as to why this phenomenon occurred. The result was an enhanced understanding of what factors contribute to investment performance. We discovered how we could exploit these trends to enhance our clients' performance. Over several years

- An outperforming manager is likely to regress to the mean (begin to underperform)
- An underperforming manager will also likely regress to the mean (begin to outperform)

This is the essence of Stratford's approach to "style tilting." Stratford attempts to capture opportunities through the recognition that both style outperformance and underperformance will eventually balance out through the passage of time. If one can identify the style cycle "in favor" and the factors that determine style-trend dominance, one can select a manager representing the in-favor style to capture enhanced returns.

In order to profitably exploit manager tendencies toward "streaks" and "slumps," certain conditions must be satisfied:

- The style cycle must be long enough—five to 10 years. If the cycle were just a year or two, it would be too short to efficiently capture valuation discrepancies. Market timing would be too crucial. (Evidence abounds that no one can time the market successfully.)
- The magnitude of the performance differential of one style of managers vis-à-vis a second style must be sufficiently large to compensate for inevitable errors due to inexact timing. If the performance differential is significant, it will compensate for brokerage-commission costs incurred to sell one manager's portfolio—or a style index fund—and buy another.

Stratford's research provides reasons for optimism that style trends can be exploited successfully. We studied both style index data[6] as well as data collected through our own internal research efforts. Complete style-cycles appear to occur over periods as long as 10 to 15 years. Cumulative performance differentials between contrasting styles have been as much as 50% to 100%. Our research indicates the average manager in an in-favor style may outperform the average out-of-favor manager by about eight percentage points *per year for several years.* This large performance-differential is a powerful inducement to embrace style tilting.

Potential Impact of Style Tilting on Performance Rankings

What is the potential impact of style tilting on relative performance rankings for a fund? Competition in the investment management field is intense. Portfolio managers work long hours to try to beat their competitors. By examining performance databases, we discovered that over the long term—seven to 10 years—the difference between a median (or 50th percentile) manager and a top quartile (or 25th percentile manager) is about one percentage point per year in added performance.

[6] Wilshire Associates, Santa Monica, California; Frank Russell Company, Tacoma, Washington.

If style trends are responsible for an eight-percentage-point-per-year performance increment—and we believe this is a low estimate—then capturing only one-eighth of this style impact (1/8 of 8.0% equals 1.0%) through style tilting could thrust an average- or median-performing fund into the top quartile. This is a significant potential payoff! Taking this one step farther, if one could capture one-quarter of this style impact, the positive performance-increment would be 2.0%—placing otherwise average performance into the top 10% of comparable funds.

There is more good news for those interested in exploring the impact of investment styles. Not only is the potential performance-impact large; the duration of style cycles is sufficiently long. This permits an astute institutional fund sponsor the opportunity to capture excess returns. Exact timing of a style-trend "bottom" or "top" is unnecessary to capitalize on style differences. One can invest a year early or a year late from the market bottom and sell a year early or late from the market top. The length and amplitude of the style cycle allow investors to exploit a significant proportion of the performance advantage.

Stratford's approach avoids market timing. When guiding clients' assets, we know we will often not catch the exact market bottom or top. So, we gradually buy in to an investment style when we believe it is in a zone of extreme undervaluation. And, we gradually sell out of an extremely overvalued investment style. The entry and exit processes extend from one to two years.

Defining Investment Styles

As recently as five years ago, style definition and understanding were rare. Today, many financial journals frequently refer to style trends. Investors can access sophisticated quantitative tools to help define manager style. In addition, Stratford and others have defined style benchmarks.

As noted earlier, some firms—ours included—have created groupings of investment managers that use a similar investment approach ("style peer-groups").

- One group of investment managers searches for companies with "value" characteristics—low P/E multiples, low price/book characteristics, and high relative dividends. These managers try to buy stocks at a large dis-

FIGURE 19-3.   Clustering of Selection Criteria

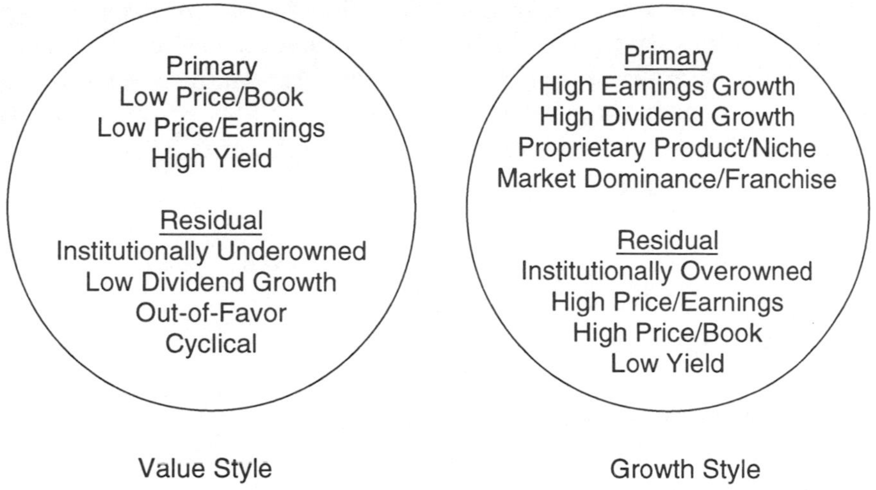

Primary
Low Price/Book
Low Price/Earnings
High Yield

Residual
Institutionally Underowned
Low Dividend Growth
Out-of-Favor
Cyclical

Primary
High Earnings Growth
High Dividend Growth
Proprietary Product/Niche
Market Dominance/Franchise

Residual
Institutionally Overowned
High Price/Earnings
High Price/Book
Low Yield

Value Style   Growth Style

© 1989, Stratford Advisory Group, Inc.

count from consensus estimates of fair value. We refer to this group as "Value-style" managers.

Some managers in this group focus on larger companies. Others seek out similar characteristics among medium- or smaller-sized companies. So, we further subdivide this style into large-, mid-, and small-capitalization approaches.[7]

- In contrast, a second group of managers looks for companies with "growth" characteristics. Growth companies tend to exhibit higher-than-average return on equity, earnings momentum, and long-term product or service growth prospects. The companies dominate their particular market niches or industry segments, leading to pricing flexibility. We refer to this group as "Growth-style" managers. (These Value- and Growth-style characteristics are shown in Figure 19-3.)

As with Value-style managers, we further subdivide Growth-style managers into large-, mid-, and small-capitalization groups.

---

[7] These designations are the service-marked property of American National Bank, Chicago.

Some managers resist style categorization. They comment that it represents an oversimplification of their investment philosophy and process. Managers fear that these "classifiers" miss important distinguishing factors that characterize the uniqueness of their firm compared with its competitors. However, extensive analysis reveals that most investment-management firms are very style-specific. Ironically, those managers that most resist style classification use "style" as an excuse for underperformance.

Categorizing Investment Managers into Style Groups

There are several methods of categorizing an investment manager's style. The first method is interrogative. It involves asking the investment manager to define its style. Some managers are forthright. At other firms, marketing professionals may claim the firm uses the style that is "hot" that year—sort of the "flavor of the year." Consequently, this rather naive interrogative method is not always reliable.

A second analytical method is more qualitative. It requires delving into the philosophy and process that the manager uses to construct portfolios. By asking questions—in-depth questions best asked by a trained investment professional with superior interviewing skills—the key investment-criteria become apparent, thereby identifying the manager's style. An evaluation of portfolio characteristics and sector weightings often helps to confirm the qualitative assessment. This method is superior to the first interrogative approach. It has a much higher probability of success.

The third method is quantitative in nature. It involves performing a statistical regression analysis of the manager's past investment performance compared to the investment performance records of many groups of other managers organized into style peer-groups. The manager's specific style emerges when its performance pattern correlates strongly with a predefined peer-group of managers. The underlying rationale is simple. If a manager exhibits a performance pattern similar to a certain style peer-group—that is, its performance clusters with that style peer-group—then its style is likely similar to that of managers within that peer-group.

In order to make this quantitative method work, a statistically-valid style peer-group is necessary. This requires tracking the monthly performance of each manager and each style grouping. It is a costly, time-consuming effort for most fund sponsors because it requires tracking close to 1,000 managers' results. One might ask, why go to this trouble? Why not use style indices as a proxy for style peer-groups?

Why Style Peer-Groups Are More Useful than Style Indices

Stratford believes that style peer-groups provide more meaningful indications of a manager's capabilities than style indices for several reasons:

- Style indices are "capitalization-weighted" while managers' portfolios tend to be more "equal-weighted." This difference can result in distortions when comparing a manager's returns to a specific style-index.
- Some style indices are too restrictive. They filter out many stocks, leaving indices more concentrated in certain economic sectors than most managers would permit. Other style indices are so broad as to be "contaminated" by stocks that are not purely of that style.
- No single style-index is "right" for comparison with all managers of that style, particularly over short periods.
- Managers cannot buy or sell stocks at a moment's notice. They have to plan their entry and exit strategy to minimize market impact. Market impact and other transactions costs detract from performance. As all managers have these "real-world" problems, comparing one manager to other managers may be a more relevant comparison than to a style index.

We believe that the best reference point for a given manager's performance is its competitors with a similar investment approach. Would anyone with knowledge of opera compare the talents of a tenor with a bass or a soprano? Why, then, should a large-cap growth manager be compared with a large-cap value manager? Or a small-cap growth manager? (A comprehensive "apples-to-apples" comparison helps distinguish the "apples" from the "oranges"!)

Maintaining Style Consistency

Fund sponsors often ask us why investment managers don't change their styles when they go through a period of underperformance. For both business and philosophical reasons, managers are unlikely to changes their styles..

The first reason is business related. When an institutional investor hires a specific manager, it is "buying" a specific investment philosophy and approach. That manager would jeopardize its relationship with its client if it violated its stated philosophy and approach by embracing a different investment style. Some institutional investors would fire a firm that changed its approach—even before waiting to determine if the manager's performance would excel. This is a strong business reason for managers to adhere to their specific investment approaches.

Managers also maintain a consistent style because they believe it represents the best way to "beat the market." Just as individuals do not find it easy to accept the precepts and practices of other religions, managers stay true to their investment styles.

Evaluating Underperformers through In-Depth Surveillance

We believe the best method to evaluate underperformance is through a detailed surveillance of that manager. Following an in-depth visit with the firm, one might conclude the organization is intact and its key professionals remain vitally involved in the organization; its investment philosophy and process seem to be unchanged.

Perhaps, then, the underlying reason for underperformance is style related. The manager's style may be "out of favor." One clue that the underperformance is style related would be to examine the performance results of different investment-management firms emphasizing a similar investment style—the style peer-group. If those managers are also performing poorly, this is a strong indication that the underperformance is style related.

If, indeed, the major reason for underperformance is style based, then perhaps the fund sponsor should *not* fire its manager. In fact, at some point in the cycle, it may make sense to award that manager *additional* assets!

Style Trends During the Past Decade

Let's take a look at investment style-trends in more depth to understand the magnitude of investment style-performance differences. We will also see more clearly how these cycles could have caused fund sponsors to make disappointing manager-selection decisions.

Figure 19-4 graphs average annual equity-manager returns for the five-year period ended in December 1988. The left side of the

FIGURE 19-4. Equity Universe Comparisons
Five years ended December 1988

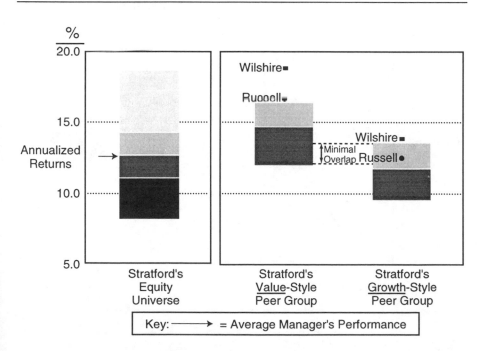

graph shows all equity-manager returns, irrespective of investment style. Obviously, there is a wide variation between the best-performing manager (about 17% on average per year), the median manager (about 13% per year), and the worst manager (about 8% per year).

On the right side of Figure 19-4 are the Value- and Growth-style peer-groups. (Note that we show only the middle quartiles for the style peer-groups to avoid outlying managers that may be inappropriately classified or a blend of styles.)

Value-style managers clearly outperformed Growth-style managers during this five-year period. The top-performing Growth managers performed about the same as the worst-performing Value managers. Obviously, it was more important to be in the right investment-style than to be with the right manager within a style.

In contrast, if it was the end of 1988 or early 1989 and you were looking for a new manager, which style do you think you might have

FIGURE 19-5.   Equity Universe Comparisons
Three years ended December 1991

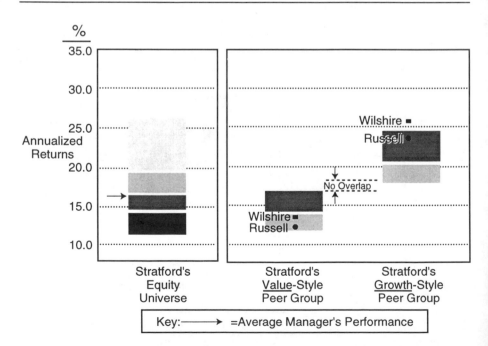

picked? Most fund sponsors looked for a top-performing manager and selected a Value manager. Figure 19-5 illustrates what happened in the following time period.

If you guessed that the Value managers began to underperform, you were right. For the three-year period ending 1991, the growth style outperformed. There are many reasons for this. However, remember that the Growth style tends to outperform when the economic cycle is maturing. It continues to outperform as we move into and during a recession. Investors are more willing to pay higher prices for earnings growth when earnings become scarce. The United States entered a recession in late 1989 or early 1990. Economists say the recession ended in 1991. The Growth style did very well during that time.

Value managers—the top-performing managers in late 1988 and early 1989—were very disappointing during the recession. Money chasing yesterday's top performers only served to push their stocks to overvaluation. This accentuates style-trend cycles and distorts valuations. While economic fundamentals are critical to a style's performance patterns, it is the popularity—and resulting asset flows—that drive a style to overvaluation and its style-cycle peak (Figure 19-6).

FIGURE 19-6. Cycles Are Valuation Based

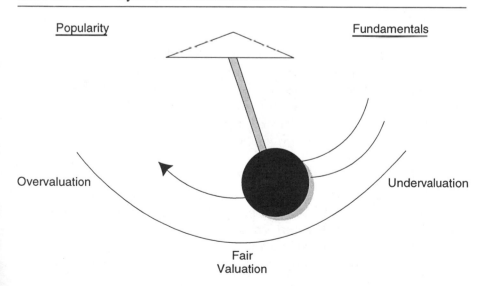

© 1989, Stratford Advisory Group, Inc.

Consequences of Chasing Past Performance

What are the consequences of the fund sponsor selecting managers the traditional way—by chasing past performance? As we have seen, the traditional method is to select investment managers who have had the best most recent performance. Fund sponsors expect top-performing managers to continue to excel. However, the consequence is that one is emphasizing overvalued, overpopular styles. In essence, one is buying into an investment approach that has been on a streak and is more likely to suffer a slump.

When one consistently invests with the latest top-performing managers, he or she significantly increases the chance of disappointment as that manager—and that manager's style—shifts out of favor. This traditional approach leads to periodic manager-turnover and high associated costs. These costs include hiring a consultant to conduct additional manager searches, brokerage commissions incurred in selling stocks of the manager being fired, commissions on buying stocks for the new manager's portfolio, and bank trustee's transaction fees.

A More Rewarding Approach to Manager Selection

There is another approach to manager selection that may be counterintuitive but works. The foundation of this approach is the recognition of style cycles and "clustering" of performance among managers within a similar style.

The objective of the more rewarding approach to manager selection is first to identify which styles are "in phase" and likely to remain so for several years. The second step is to select competent managers within those styles and allocate assets to them. While these managers may have recently underperformed relative to all other managers, they may indeed be top performers *within* their style peer-groups. The expectation is that the slumping style and the slumping managers will regress to the mean and will emerge as the new "hot" investment style.

As noted earlier, there are substantial performance gaps between styles in favor and styles out of favor. A fund sponsor need only capture 10% to 20% of this performance differential to elevate a fund's performance ranking from average into the top quartile. This, we believe, is a more rewarding method to select investment managers and allocate fund assets.

Managing Equity Style Exposure: A Plan Sponsor's Experience

Robert A. Birch, Assistant Director of Finance
Central Pension Fund, International Union of
Operating Engineers and Participating Employers

Over the years, the Central Pension Fund of the International Union of Operating Engineers and Participating Employers (CPF) has witnessed firsthand a peculiar relationship. As we have endeavored to retain some of the industry's most successful active equity-advisors, our execution of the investment-management agreement has proven with inexplicable consistency to be a leading indicator of prolonged poor performance for these advisors. Often the ink on the agreement is barely dry before the favorable long-term performance record starts to erode. CPF, like so many institutional investors, has experienced the frustration with active managers' attempts to add value relative to a market index.

It is against this backdrop of relatively disappointing results with active equity-management that CPF embarked upon an effort to establish an equity program which provides a high likelihood of achieving broad equity-market-like returns, while preserving opportunities to add incremental value in a very structured way. In doing so, we acknowledged that, while we can't reliably control return, we can certainly improve our capacity to control risk. The staff of CPF was intrigued with the early work related to style characterization and management. Over the past two and a half years, CPF has implemented and refined an equity style characterization and bias-offset program with the objectives of better explaining active manager performance and offsetting unintended equity style exposures.

Structuring an Equity Program

In determining the appropriate equity allocation for CPF, our market expectations are predominately influenced by the historic risk premiums and volatility experienced in the broad equity-market and the correlation with other asset classes. The objective, therefore, of the Fund's equity program is to earn the rate of return of the broad U.S. equity-market as defined by the Wilshire 5000 without incurring uncompensated risk. The management approaches utilized by the Central Pension Fund in pursuing this objective include:

- Passive management, which delivers the return and risk characteristics of a broadly diversified market index by holding all of the securities in that index in their appropriate market weight.
- Traditional active management, which attempts to consistently add value through market research, security selection, and portfolio construction with the objective of outperforming the market as a whole.
- Enhanced indexing, which seeks to add incremental value over a stated market index while exhibiting essentially the same risk characteristics.

Since CPF's equity investment objectives are tied so closely to the pursuit of market-like returns, a compelling case can be made to index a considerable portion of the equity assets to the Wilshire 5000. In fact, that is precisely what has been done for a number of years. Figure 20-1 illustrates the structure of CPF's equity program. Approximately 70% of the CPF's equity assets are indexed. This provides CPF with a low cost and predictable means of achieving market-like returns without incurring particular style-biases relative to the market. It is with the remaining 30% of equity assets, which are actively managed to varying degrees, that significant opportunities exist to improve our management of risk.

Observations about Active Equity Management

The process of selecting active equity-managers in the past focused on identifying superior talent without particular regard to style

FIGURE 20-1. Equity Allocation

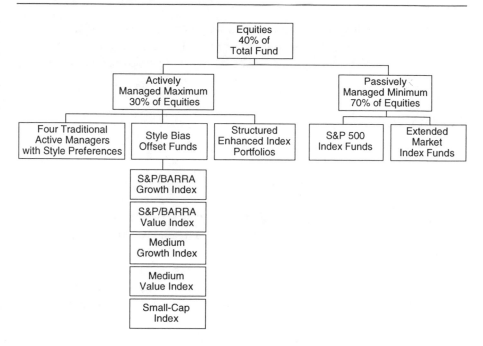

emphasis. In fact, we were largely dependent upon qualitative judgments in determining manager style, including the acceptance of managers' self-ascribed styles. The difficulty was not necessarily finding a manager or two capable of turning in strong performance, but in assembling a team of active equity-managers which in the aggregate could outperform the market through multiple cycles. In fact, a significant portion of the poor performance experienced by CPF with active equity-managers was attributable not to stock selection, but to style emphasis, for which no reliable and cost-effective process existed to facilitate style exposure management.

CPF's experience with traditional active equity-managers has led to a number of general observations:

- Active managers tend to embrace certain style preferences which potentially expose CPF's equity program to unintended style biases.
- The single largest determinant of active-management performance is not specific security selection, but style

emphasis, typically explaining in excess of 90% of manager performance.
- Individual investment styles perform differently during
  various stages of a market cycle. No single style or mix
  of styles can definitively be said to be optimal over all
  periods.

Determining an Appropriate
Style-Management Approach

It became apparent that evaluating and managing style-emphasis is
essential in order to successfully meet the objectives of CPF's
domestic-equity program. Deciding upon the proper approach to use
in determining manager style was not particularly difficult. The alternatives included relying on managers' self-characterized style, using
one of the many multifactor models to painstakingly examine the
industry and sector exposure of portfolios, or to employ a returns-
based approach of attributing performance to effective style-
exposures. The objective in selecting a style-management approach
was to maximize explanatory power without requiring an entourage
of mathematicians and statisticians to interpret the results.

The first approach, relying on managers' own assessments of
their style, was quickly dismissed as managers tend to characterize
their style as one of a number of styles as opposed to some mix of
styles. While the use of a multifactor model to evaluate the fundamental characteristics of individual portfolio holdings was appealing,
it was recognized that the collection of portfolio holdings for multiple
periods was enormously time consuming, costly and complex. It was
determined that a returns-based approach offered both conceptual
elegance and signifiacnt explanatory power at a reasonable commitment of resources. A frequent criticism of returns-based style-analysis
systems is that they may imply that a manager is holding securities of
certain styles which the manager in fact has never held. However, our
objective in assessing style-emphasis is not to identify specific security exposure but effective style-exposure, which returns-based systems do extraordinarily well. The returns-based style-analysis
approach offers a powerful yet pragmatic solution.

Once the general approach to identifying style exposure was
determined, a two-fold process of controlling risk through the use of

style analysis was adopted. First, the effective style-mix of each active equity-manager was determined with the objective of creating a benchmark which represent the manager's style. The second aspect of the process involves identifying the style biases brought to the total equity program by the active managers in aggregate. If these biases can be reliably identified and quantified, they can be offset through the allocation of assets to passively managed style funds without interrupting the portfolios managed by active managers.

Selecting a Style-Characterization Framework

Perhaps the most challenging aspect of implementing a style evaluation and management program is the determination of an appropriate style-characterization framework. With a plethora of style indices to choose from, selecting the appropriate indices can be a daunting job in itself. The selection process began with the premise that the most important dimensions of a style framework are size (market capitalization) and relative valuation. The process continued by identifying style indices which met the following criteria:

- Passively replicable
- Collectively exhaustive (all securities in universe should be represented)
- Mutually exclusive (no overlap of securities among indices)
- Commercially available to accommodate investment
- Sufficiently liquid to facilitate frequent rebalancing transactions
- Low cost (minimal management-costs and accommodative of crossing opportunities)

The style indices ultimately selected by CPF to define the domestic-equity universe are compiled and maintained by S&P/ BARRA. With relatively minor conversion procedures, these indices are commercially available for investment. Table 20-1 provides a snapshot of the composition of these indices as of December 31, 1993.

Figure 20-2 illustrates the framework within which these style indices are viewed. Effective manager-styles are characterized as some mix of these investment styles plus cash. In fact, to the extent

Chapter 20

TABLE 20-1. Style Index Characteristics

	S&P/ BARRA Value Index	S&P/ BARRA Growth Index	Medium Value Index	Medium Growth Index	Small-Cap Index
Number of issues	310	190	702	679	4,085
Percent of U.S. equity market	34.62%	34.59%	11.03%	11.91%	5.28%
Median capitalization (mil)	$3,044	$4,442	$464	$491	$40
Volatility	13.72%	15.33%	15.75%	17.73%	18.18%
Yield	3.27%	2.15%	1.96%	0.78%	0.83%
Price/book	1.89	4.37	1.44	4.22	1.96

Source: WFNIA.

that a manager selects from among the high-beta stocks in his or her respective style universe, cash is permitted to be leveraged to capture this volatility. The coordinates marked by the five boxes define the edges of the characterization framework.

Creating Custom Style-Benchmarks

In determining each manager's effective style mix, performance is attributed to two sources: (1) the mix of those investment styles which best characterizes the manager's historic returns, and (2) specific security selection. From this process, a customized style benchmark is developed which incorporates the manager's effective style mix as well as a premium for the residual variance not explained by the style mix. Again, the objective is to be compensated not only for style exposure but for the relative riskiness of the stocks selected within those styles. To date, the custom benchmarks have, in each case, done a better job in explaining past performance than the market alone. Particular attention is given to each manager's style evolution or drift over time. The evidence suggests that most managers operate within a relatively tight style domain. CPF's managers have yet to experience significant style drift, either in terms of size or relative value.

In the end, the style-benchmark construction process produces a benchmark which better explains manager performance than the

FIGURE 20-2.   Style-Analysis Framework
Manager style, September 1994

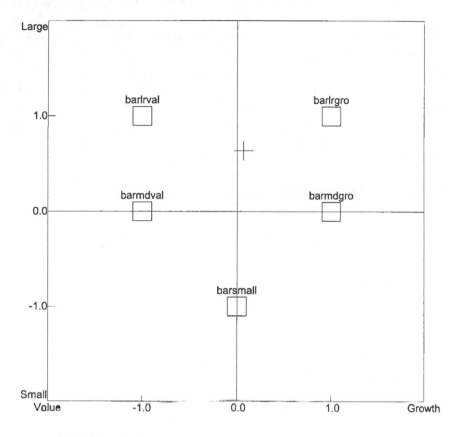

+ Wilshire 5000 Value-Weighted Total Perf Index
□ Style Map

Style Advisor: Central Pension Fund

market index or peer-group comparisons, and provides an assessment of the manager's ability to add value within his or her respective style. The benchmark is clearly defined, passively replicable and reflective of the universe of stocks from which the manager selects. To ensure this latter point, each style benchmark is thoroughly reviewed with the managers prior to introduction. This benchmark then forms the basis of performance evaluation moving forward.

Assessing Overall Style-Biases

As suspected, the use of active equity-managers has brought certain, quantifiable style biases to the total equity program. For example, as illustrated in Figure 20-3, the aggregate active equity-component of the portfolio had meaningful deficiencies in large-growth and medium-growth stocks while exhibiting a significant bias toward small stocks relative to the market. Interestingly, none of the managers were previously thought of as predominately small-cap managers. However, two managers generally regarded as large-cap value managers in fact possessed notable commitments to small-cap issues.

Offsetting Unintended Style Biases

The extent to which these biases can be offset is a function of the dollars available to commit to the style indices. With a sufficient pool of assets available for this purpose, the style biases could be perfectly offset. In the absence of sufficient assets to perfectly offset the biases,

FIGURE 20-3.   Effective Style Mix of Total Active Managers

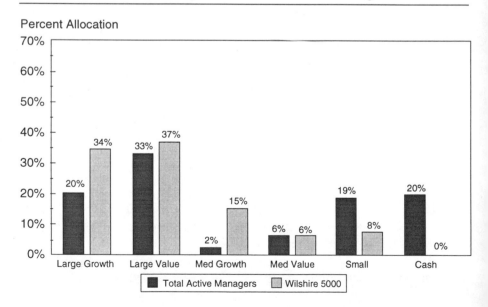

an allocation can be derived which minimizes residual variance relative to the market index subject to this constraint.

If the style biases relative to the market index are large, as was the case with CPF, a perfect offset may require more assets than the total managed by active managers. Figure 20-4 illustrates the allocation among the style bias offset funds which minimizes tracking error to the Wilshire 5000 given the money available to deploy in this process.

While the commitment of funds to the style-bias offset program did not eliminate style biases within the active equity program, it did significantly reduce those biases. As expected, the optimal solution calls for increasing exposure to larger stocks in general and growth-oriented stocks in particular. A substantial portion of the bias offset funds are allocated to the medium-growth component.

Figure 20-5 depicts the combined effective style-mix of the active equity-managers and the allocation to the style bias offset-funds. Again, although the biases in the total equity program are not entirely eliminated, the effective style exposures are much more similar to those of the market than was the case prior to actively managing style exposure.

FIGURE 20-4.   Optimal Allocation of Style-Bias Offset Funds

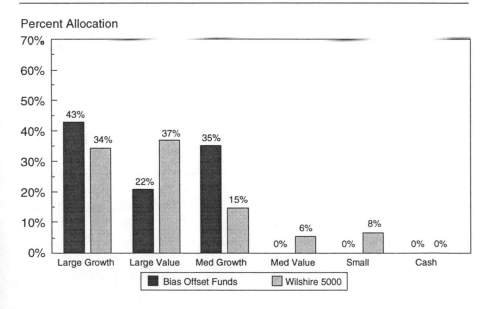

FIGURE 20-5.   Effective Style-Mix of Total Equity Program after Allocating Bias-Offset Funds

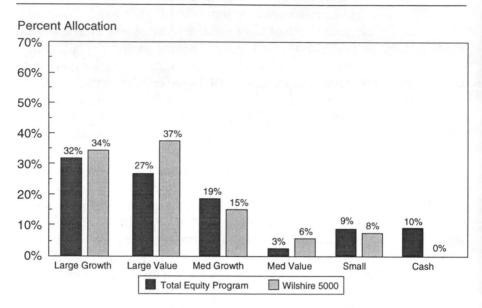

Percent Allocation

Figure 20-6 provides a map of the evolution of CPF's equity program as active manager-style exposures are identified and compensated for. By investing available assets in the appropriate mix of bias-offset funds (shown in Figure 20-6 as the Custom Core Portfolio), the total equity program (shown as 50% in Custom Core) moves closer to the Wilshire 5000 index in terms of effective style-exposures.

Evaluation of Results

The process of constructing customized style benchmark for active equity-managers and aggressively managing total equity program style-exposure has enabled CPF to better control risk within its equity portfolio. It has provided a more appropriate delineation of responsibilities between the plan sponsor and the investment manager. The plan sponsor assumes responsibility for the style biases brought to the equity program by the active equity-managers selected, while the managers assume responsibility for maintaining consistency in

FIGURE 20-6.   Evolution of Effective Style Mix
Manager style, September 1994

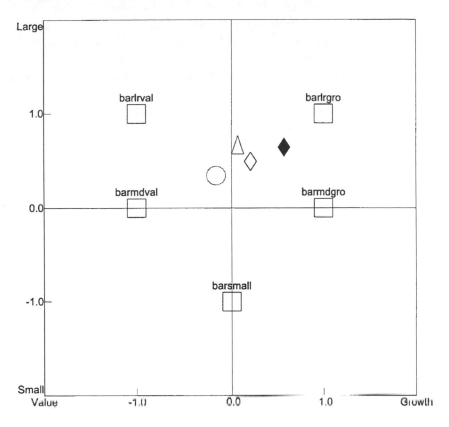

△ Wilshire 5000 Value-Weighted Total Perf Index
○ Total Active Managers
◇   50% in Custom Core
◆ Custom Core Portfolio (50%)
□ Style Map

Style Advisor: Central Pension Fund

employing their strategies and selecting stocks within their styles
which provide added value.

   In the performance-evaluation process, active managers are no
longer penalized for emphasizing an investment style which happens
to be out of favor for a period of time. Similarly, strong performance
attributable to security selection is distinguished from favorable per-

formance attributable solely to style emphasis, thus enhancing the sponsor's confidence in evaluating the skillfulness of the manager.

The approach effectively provides for the identification of custom style-benchmarks that better explain performance than the market index alone. Equally important, the style biases of the total domestic-equity program relative to the equity benchmark are minimized *without interrupting the active managers.* In essence, to the extent managers who outperform their respective styles are retained, CPF is left with superior stock-selection within assorted styles with no biases relative to the market in any style.

Controlling Misfit through the Use of Dynamic Completeness Funds

Jeffery V. Bailey, Principal
Richards & Tierney, Inc.

David E. Tierney, Ph.D., Principal
Richards & Tierney, Inc.

This chapter discusses misfit—the situation that arises when a plan sponsor combines multiple managers within an asset category whose investment styles in aggregate are inconsistent with the plan sponsor's choice of an investment target for that asset category. Our objectives in writing this paper are several-fold:

- To introduce basic investment management concepts relating to misfit
- To offer potential solutions to the misfit problem
- To describe how a dynamic completeness fund (DCF) is constructed and the relationships that should exist between various parties involved in its management
- To provide a case study that illustrates the potential benefits of controlling misfit to discuss various DCF implementation issues

This chapter is intended to be a practical complement to the theoretical misfit control discussion presented in Tierney and Winston [1990]. Much of the chapter's content is based on material presented by David Tierney and Jeffery Bailey at the Franklin Portfolio Associates' client conference in June 1994.

Part I: The Problem

Multiple-manager investment programs have become fixtures at virtually all large pension funds in the last 20 years. For a variety of reasons, plan sponsors have concluded that their investment objectives are best realized by assigning their investments within specific asset categories to more than one manager. The plan sponsors typically reserve the decision concerning allocation of funds among the asset categories to themselves, with the managers limited to investing in their designated asset categories.

The merits of this multiple-manager approach have received surprisingly little discussion.[1] Unquestionably though, it has produced several unintended consequences. Our focus will be on one particularly important outcome: the risk introduced when the investment "styles" of a plan sponsor's multiple managers are inconsistent with the plan sponsor's investment objectives for a particular asset category. We contend that this risk considerably reduces the effectiveness of many plan sponsors' investment programs. Our discussion begins with a definition of the problem. We then consider potential solutions to the problem. Finally, we conclude with a case study examining how one plan sponsor implemented a particularly effective risk-management technique.

The Asset Category Target

When establishing an investment policy, plan sponsors invariably separate the universe of investable securities into broad asset-categories. Standard examples include domestic and foreign equities, real estate, venture capital, and so on. Further, within a specific asset category, plan sponsors have some concept, either explicitly or implicitly, of the scope of their potential investments. In most cases, that scope is formalized by the selection of an *asset category target* (ACAT).

The ACAT represents the set of feasible investment opportunities that the plan sponsor believes best achieves the purposes for which the asset category is included in the plan's investment policy. We can think of an ACAT as the *single* portfolio in which the plan would be invested were it required to have all of its assets in that asset category *passively managed*.

Plan sponsors typically choose broad-market indices as their ACATs. For example, the S&P 500, the Russell 3000, or the Wilshire

---

[1] See Sharpe [1981] for a discussion of the rationale for possible reasons underlying the use of multiple managers. Jeffrey [1991] discusses some of the implementation problems of multiple-manager investment programs.

5000 are the preferred domestic equity ACATs. We note that these popular choices are based more on conventional wisdom rather than any thoughtful reflections on the part of plan sponsors. That is, market indices do not incorporate any restrictions on a plan sponsor's investments (for example, corporate pension-plan prohibitions against owning company stock). In addition, they often exclude certain types of securities in which a plan sponsor's managers regularly invest and include other securities in which the managers rarely, if ever, invest.[2] Moreover, there are reasons to suspect that alternative well-diversified portfolios offer superior long-term risk-reward characteristics relative to the standard market-indices.[3]

An appropriate ACAT should satisfy three conditions:

1. It should be consistent with the plan sponsor's tolerance for risk. If the ACAT is too defensively or aggressively positioned relative to the plan sponsor's willingness to bear risk, then eventually the plan sponsor will be dissatisfied with either the returns on its investments in the asset category, the volatility of those returns, or both.
2. It should be preferred to all other alternative targets. The *expected* long-run risk-adjusted returns from the ACAT must be superior to any investable passively-managed alternatives. If not, then the plan sponsor has settled for an acknowledged inferior focal point for its investments in the asset category.
3. It should provide an investable alternative. The plan sponsor must be able to own a passive portfolio that adequately tracks the ACAT's performance.

An ACAT serves both prospective and retrospective functions in a plan sponsor's investment policy. In its retrospective role, the ACAT is as an evaluation tool. It is the benchmark against which to assess the performance of the plan's *aggregate* investments in the asset class. The plan sponsor should only deviate from a passive investment in

---

[2] On occasion, examples of the former include large American Depository Receipts (ADRs). On occasion, examples of the latter include various small-cap, illiquid issues.

[3] For example, see BARRA [1989], Grinold [1992], Haugen and Baker [1991], and Winston [1993].

the ACAT if it believes that alternative investment strategies offer positive incremental returns relative to the risk incurred in pursuing those strategies. In hindsight then, the plan sponsor's investments in the asset category are successful only if they at least match the ACAT's returns (after all fees and expenses).

In its prospective role, the ACAT is a planning tool. It possesses a risk profile that the investment styles, or benchmarks (more on these shortly), of the plan sponsor's multiple managers should maintain, *in aggregate.* Recall that the ACAT reflects the plan sponsor's preferred risk posture, exclusive of active management. Therefore, whether one views risk in a CAPM, APT, or some other framework, unless the managers' benchmarks in aggregate are similar in risk to the ACAT, then a fundamental inconsistency exists.

Investment Style

Investment style is a commonly used, albeit nebulous term. Many practitioners define investment style qualitatively. In this context, investment style refers to distinguishing and continually-applied aspects of a manager's investment process. Such terms as *top-down, bottom-up, quant, growth, value,* and *sector rotator* are often used.

Although these qualitative terms are useful in many situations, for purposes of analyzing the effects of combining managers' investment styles, we prefer a more rigorous and quantitative definition. In particular, we define a manager's investment style as a set of prominent investment-characteristics that the manager's portfolios persistently exhibit. By "prominent investment-characteristics" we mean measurable financial attributes of the portfolio that are significantly correlated with its returns.[4] For example, equity managers may be categorized in terms of their portfolios' average market-capitalizations, dividend yields, or earnings-growth prospects. Fixed-income managers may be categorized by their portfolios' durations or quality ratings.

We and many other practitioners believe that most managers pursue distinct investment-styles that set their portfolios apart from one another and from the broad-market indices. Figure 21-1 gives an

---

[4] For example, Fama and French [1992] found significant relationships between a firm's size and a firm's price/book ratio and the return on the firm's stock. Chen, Roll, and Ross [1986] specify several Arbitrage Pricing Theory factors that they believe systematically affect common-stock returns.

FIGURE 21-1.   Style Distribution of Managers' Portfolios

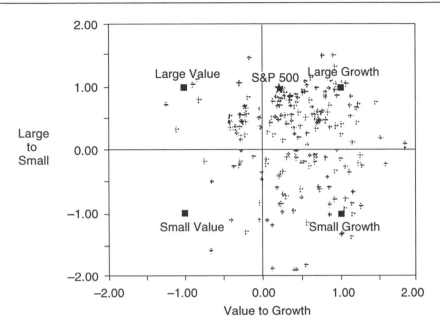

indication of these tendencies. As of December 31, 1993, the portfolios of over 200 domestic equity managers are plotted relative to four "generic" style portfolios: large-capitalization growth and value, and small-capitalization growth and value. In this "style" space, distance equates to forecast correlation of returns.[5] Thus the closer two portfolios are, the more their returns are likely to move in concert. Clearly, most managers do not hold portfolios similar to the S&P 500, which is also plotted on the graph as a reference point. (Interestingly, there appear to be many more growth managers, particularly large-cap growth managers, than there are value managers. We leave that observation for investment anthropologists to consider.)

Do these differences in investment style really matter in terms of investment performance? Figures 21-2 and 21-3 answer the question

---

[5] Tierney and Winston [1991] describe the intuition and mathematics underlying this two-dimensional "style" space.

FIGURE 21-2. Rolling Three-Year Annualized Returns Relative to the S&P 500 (Value/Growth)

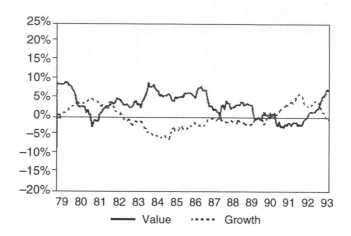

with a resounding "Yes." Those figures illustrate the performance of four domestic-equity generic-style portfolios (defined in this situation as value, growth, small, and large) relative to the S&P 500 over three-year rolling windows. The long trends in relative performance are fascinating to observe. More important, the differences in returns among the styles are dramatic; in many 36-month periods, the gap between the highest-performing style and the lowest exceeds 10 percentage points *per year*.[6] In the short term, no domestic equity manager could ever hope to overcome these style effects with his or her active-management skills. Furthermore, if a plan sponsor inadvertently concentrates its allocations with managers employing a similar investment style, then the aggregate manager-returns are likely to differ considerably from those of the ACAT.

How can we effectively convey a manager's investment style? One approach is to assign the manager to one of a group of predetermined style categories. (We refer to such benchmarks as *assignment-based benchmarks*.) For example, in terms of Figure 21-1, we could place domestic equity managers with the generic styles to which their

---

[6] For annual periods, differences in the returns on the generic style portfolios of over 30% have been observed.

FIGURE 21-3.   Rolling Three-Year Annualized Returns Relative to the S&P 500 (Large-Cap/Small-Cap)

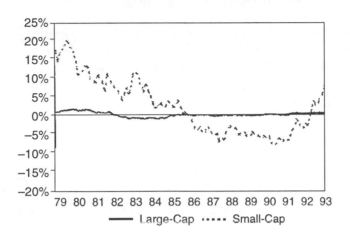

portfolios tend to be aligned. This is the essence of the qualitative approach to defining investment styles. It has the advantage of simplicity and ease of implementation, and for those reasons, it has been highly popular among performance-evaluation consultants. However, as is frequently pointed out by the managers, this approach rigidly "pigeonholes" a manager, ignoring the unique elements of the manager's investment style.

Manager Benchmarks

We believe that a more desirable approach to specifying managers' investment styles is to design *custom asset list* benchmark portfolios (hereafter simply called "benchmarks") to reflect those styles. More specifically, we define a benchmark as a passive, investable representation of the manager's prominent investment-characteristics. Fundamentally, it represents the manager's area of expertise—the group of securities, appropriately weighted, from which the manager typically selects his or her portfolio. In a broader sense, a benchmark reflects all investors with similar business interests, knowledge bases, risk tolerances, and operating constraints. Thus a properly constructed benchmark is actually the ideal "manager universe."

What defines an acceptable benchmark? No simple answer exists. Nevertheless, we contend that a valid benchmark should possess several basic attributes. It should be

- *Unambiguous*. The names and weights of securities comprising the benchmark are clearly delineated.
- *Investable*. The option is available to forego active management and simply hold the benchmark.
- *Measurable*. The benchmark's return can be readily calculated on a reasonably frequent basis.
- *Appropriate*. The benchmark is consistent with the manager's investment style.
- *Reflective of current investment opinions*. The manager has current investment knowledge (be it positive, negative, or neutral) regarding the securities that constitute the benchmark.
- *Specified in advance*. The benchmark is constructed prior to the start of an evaluation period.

Just as an ACAT reflects the plan sponsor's desired risk posture in a particular asset category, a benchmark represents the manager's desired risk posture prior to the implementation of active-investment strategies.[7] A well-designed benchmark serves many functions. Most important, for purposes of our discussion, combining the benchmarks of a plan sponsor's managers within an asset category conveys valuable information to plan sponsor decision-makers concerning the *aggregate* investment style of the plan's managers.

Investment Skill

Investment skill is the ability to outperform an appropriate benchmark consistently over time. We call a manager's excess returns relative to his or her benchmark the *value of active management* (VAM).[8] No manager is omniscient and therefore managers' VAMs will be positive in

---

[7] For a discussion of basic custom-benchmark issues, see Bailey, Richards, and Tierney [1988] and Divecha and Grinold [1989].

[8] A manager's value of active management (VAM) is also referred to as the manager's alpha or risk-adjusted return. See for example, Sharpe, Alexander, and Bailey [1994], p. 928.

some periods and negative in other periods. Relative to their less talented brethren, however, skillful managers on average will produce relatively large positive VAM compared to the variability of their active-management results. The ratio of VAM to the variability of VAM (on either an *ex post* or *ex ante* basis) is referred to as the information ratio.[9] That is:

$$IR = VAM/\sigma_{VAM}$$

Even skillful managers have a surprisingly high probability of underperforming their benchmarks over what most plan sponsors consider to be reasonable evaluation intervals. For example, a manager with an information ratio of 0.4 (= 2% VAM/5%σ_{VAM}) has a one in four chance of underperforming his or her benchmark over any three-year period.

It is important to distinguish between the returns derived from investment *style* and the returns derived from investment *skill*. The situation is analogous to the difference between one-time and sustainable corporate earnings. Investment style is not proprietary. By definition, it can be replicated by a benchmark portfolio that is based on publicly available information concerning the manager's investment process known in advance of an evaluation period. Therefore, just as extraordinary sources of corporate earnings should not be expected to repeat regularly, a particular investment style should not be expected to outperform the ACAT persistently on a risk-adjusted basis. Investment skill, on the other hand, represents the unique and proprietary aspects of a manager's investment process. Just as sustainable corporate earnings can be counted on to recur predictably, investment skill should be expected to produce positive results in both good times and bad for the manager's investment style.[10]

Realistically, superior domestic equity managers can be expected to outperform their benchmarks, after all fees and expenses, by at most 100 to 200 basis points per year. As we have seen, however, differences between various domestic-equity generic-style returns can exceed 3,000 basis points per year. Consequently, investment style

---

[9] The information ratio is discussed at length in Grinold [1989] and Sharpe [1994].

[10] In mathematical terms, the manager's VAM process is *orthogonal* to the manager's investment style.

tends to obscure the abilities of even the most skillful managers, making the task of identifying superior managers problematic for plan sponsors.

Some Simple Portfolio-Management Algebra

At this point, we can begin to apply the concepts that we have discussed in a simple mathematical framework. Start with the identity of an investment manager's portfolio:[11]

$$P = P \tag{1}$$

Now, consider an appropriately selected benchmark B. Adding and subtracting B from the right side of Equation (1) gives:

$$P = B + (P - B) \tag{2}$$

If we define the manager's active investment-judgments A as being the difference between the manager's portfolio P and the benchmark B, so that $A = (P - B)$, then Equation (2) becomes:

$$P = B + A \tag{3}$$

Equation (3) states that the manager's portfolio can be partitioned into two elements: the manager's benchmark (or investment style) and the manager's active-management decisions (or investment skill).

If we now introduce an asset category target T and appropriately add and subtract it from the right side of Equation (3), then we have:

$$P = T + (B - T) + A \tag{4}$$

The manager's portfolio can be viewed as being composed of a systematic element T, an element $(B - T)$ that represents how the manager's style differs from the ACAT, and the active-management element A. All managers operating within the ACAT are exposed to the systematic source of returns, as reflected in T. However, managers'

---

[11] Equation (1) and the various equations that follow can be thought of as referring to returns or security holdings, as the context of the discussion dictates.

unique investment-styles, as represented by their benchmarks, determine their biases relative to the ACAT. (We will refer to these style biases as *misfits* and shortly discuss the concept in detail.) Finally, the plan sponsor pays the manager to take active bets that both parties anticipate will add value to the benchmark's results, as reflected in A.

Benchmark Misfit

Benchmark misfit, or simply *misfit*, is the difference between a manager's benchmark and the ACAT. If the benchmark and ACAT are properly specified as unambiguous, investable portfolios, then we can calculate misfit on a security-by-security basis, thereby creating a misfit portfolio. This misfit portfolio will contain both long and short positions. Consider the simple example shown in Table 21-1. The table shows the holdings (stated as percentages) of the benchmark, the ACAT, and the misfit portfolio. Security 1 is held in the benchmark at a 21% position, while it constitutes only 13% of the ACAT. As a result, the misfit portfolio contains a positive 8% position in Security 1; the manager's investment style emphasizes Security 1 relative to the plan sponsor's ACAT.

The weights of the securities in either the benchmark or the ACAT, of course, must sum to 100%. On the other hand, the weights of the misfit portfolio's securities must sum to 0% as the long positions exactly offset the short positions (thus the misfit portfolio is a

TABLE 21-1. Example of a Misfit Portfolio

Security	Benchmark Holdings	Asset Category Target Holdings	Misfit Portfolio Holdings
1	21.0%	13.0%	+8.0
2	0.0	9.0	−9.0
3	24.0	15.0	+9.0
4	30.0	6.0	+24.0
5	0.0	5.0	−5.0
6	0.0	16.0	−16.0
7	0.0	8.0	−8.0
8	8.0	11.0	−3.0
9	0.0	10.0	−10.0
10	17.0	7.0	+10.0
Total	100.0%	100.0%	0.0%

hedge portfolio). If the manager's benchmark overweights a particular security relative to the ACAT, then the benchmark must necessarily underweight one or more other securities.

Figure 21-4 illustrates the misfit concept. Manager A's benchmark is placed in "style" space relative to a particular plan sponsor's ACAT. Because the two portfolios lie apart from one another, they can be expected to produce different investment results in any given measurement period.

We can calculate the misfit portfolio's return, which we call *misfit return*. In any given period, misfit return for an individual manager, or a group of managers, is likely to be some nonzero value. In fact, that misfit return in many cases will exceed the VAM produced by the manager or the group of managers. Nevertheless, a plan sponsor should not expect that the manager's benchmark (or aggregate benchmark of the managers) will outperform the ACAT or vice versa. Indeed, if such an expectation existed, then the plan sponsor has misspecified the ACAT. Therefore we operate under the assumption that the expected misfit return is zero.

FIGURE 21-4.   Misfit Concept

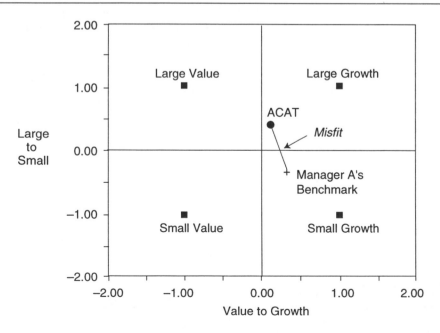

In contrast, the variability of misfit return is always positive. We refer to this variability as *misfit risk*. It too can be measured for an individual manager or a group of managers. Further, it can be contrasted with *active-management risk,* or the variability of VAM. For the typical plan sponsor, the misfit risk of the managers in aggregate is often greater than their aggregate active management risk.

Capital-market theory teaches that unproductive risk should be avoided. A plan sponsor hires active managers with the expectation that the VAM that they produce will more than compensate for the active-management risk they generate. As a plan sponsor has no expectation of gain by incurring misfit risk, then misfit return volatility can only serve to reduce the plan sponsor's utility. We conclude that the thoughtful plan sponsor should adopt investment policies that minimize the magnitude of the misfit present in the plan's investment program, up to the point where the costs of those minimization efforts equal the benefits.

The Magnitude of Misfit Risk

How large is the misfit risk experienced by plan sponsors? That is a difficult question to answer empirically. Measuring misfit risk involves, among other things, establishing valid benchmarks for each of the plan sponsor's managers within the asset category under consideration, assigning policy allocations to each of the managers, and selecting an appropriate ACAT. Only a few plan sponsors to date have implemented the disciplined and sophisticated investment policies necessary to facilitate such a detailed analysis. Further, those plan sponsors who have in place the required investment policies have generally concentrated their efforts in the domestic-equity asset category. Nevertheless, to provide a sense of the magnitude of the misfit problem, it is instructive to examine the domestic-equity misfit exposures of several large plan-sponsors.

We collected data on the active-management components of five plan-sponsors' domestic equity programs. At year-end 1993, their investments in U.S. common stocks totaled almost $11 billion. Using a multifactor risk-model, we computed the forecast misfit-risk, active-management risk, and total volatility of those domestic equity programs. Whereas active-management risk is intended, and misfit risk is not, plan sponsors should seek to maintain high levels of the former relative to the latter. However, the results of our analysis, shown in

TABLE 21-2.   A Comparison of Active Management and Misfit Risk

Plan Sponsor	Active Management Risk	Misfit Risk	Misfit Risk As a Percent of Total Volatility	Ratio of Active Management Risk to Misfit Risk
Fund #1	1.115%	1.277%	56.75%	0.873
Fund #2	2.618	1.434	23.08	1.826
Fund #3	2.724	3.901	67.21	0.698
Fund #4	1.620	2.213	65.11	0.732
Fund #5	1.954	2.635	64.53	0.741

Table 21-2, do not support that contention. (All risk figures are reported as annualized standard deviations.)

Contrary to expectations, the misfit risk incurred by four of the five plan-sponsors was greater than their active-management risk. In fact, the average ratio of active-management risk to misfit risk was only 0.974 (excluding Fund #2, the average was even lower at 0.761). Consequently, the majority of the forecast return volatility of the active-management components of these domestic-equity programs can be traced to their misfit risks, as opposed to the active-management risks assumed by their managers.

As a rule of thumb, we prefer to see domestic-equity misfit risk be under 1%, while active-management risk should exceed misfit risk by a factor of at least 2. Without such risk exposures, the biggest decision affecting the performance of a plan sponsor's active-management program becomes the structuring of the managers' investment styles rather than the investment decisions of the managers. The benefits of any successful active management are likely to be lost in the noise of misfit.

Part II: Potential Solutions

Having presented the basic concepts underlying the misfit problem, we now want to turn our attention to potential solutions. To highlight the critical issues involved, we will examine a hypothetical plan-sponsor with a simple multiple-manager investment structure.

Consider a plan sponsor who has retained three domestic-equity managers and assigned specific allocations of the total investment

FIGURE 21-5.   A Simple Multiple-Manager Alignment

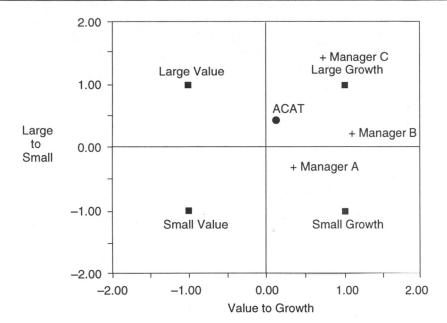

program to each of them. All of the managers have developed benchmarks that accurately reflect their investment styles. The positions of those benchmarks in "style" space are illustrated in Figure 21-5.

Each of the managers' benchmarks differs materially from the ACAT in terms of risk characteristics, as indicated by their different locations on the graph. As a result, each of the managers exhibits a misfit relative to the ACAT. How should the plan sponsor treat this problem?

Solution #1: Ignore the Problem

Certainly, the simplest approach to dealing with the misfit problem is to ignore it. In this case the plan sponsor, perhaps explicitly or through omission, assigns each manager the ACAT as his or her benchmark. With a stroke of the pen, misfit is eliminated. Viewed in the context of our discussion, this approach may seem hopelessly naive. However, consider how many plan sponsors insist on using the S&P 500 or the EAFE index as the universal benchmarks for every one of their domestic- and foreign-equity managers, respectively.

In various aspects of life, ignorance may truly be bliss. In the world of investments, however, this is rarely the case. Ignoring misfit does not make it go away. Unexpectedly large and negative misfit returns will still appear on occasion to bedevil the plan sponsor's investment program. While such negative misfit returns may be offset by positive misfit returns over the long-term, Figures 21-2 and 21-3 indicate that the "long term" may be very long indeed. The drawn-out bear market for small-cap growth stocks that many plan sponsors suffered through in the mid and late 1980s amply demonstrates the folly of ignoring misfit risk.

Solution #2: Transport Alpha for Individual Managers

The growth of over-the-counter swap markets to exchange portfolio returns has been one of the most fascinating developments of the early 1990s. The return on virtually any identifiable portfolio can now be swapped for the return on another portfolio. One possible solution to the misfit problem therefore is to exchange the return on each manager's benchmark for the return on the ACAT.

Consider Equation (4) again:

$$P = T + (B - T) + A \tag{4}$$

For each manager, the plan sponsor prefers that:

$$P = T + A \tag{5}$$

That is, the plan sponsor desires that each manager's return simply be that of the ACAT plus the manager's VAM. Confounding the achievement of this objective is that most managers exhibit misfit relative to the ACAT ($B - T \neq 0$). However, suppose that the plan sponsor could add T and subtract B from the right side of the Equation (4). The plan sponsor could do this by swapping the manager's benchmark return for the return on the ACAT. That is:

$$\begin{aligned} P &= T + (B - T) + A + T - B \\ &= T + A \end{aligned} \tag{6}$$

The result is that the manager delivers the ACAT's return plus his or her VAM as Equation (6) reduces to Equation (5).

Conceptually, a series of such swaps for each manager resolves the misfit problem. However, in practice this is likely to be a very high-cost solution. Market-makers, of course, charge a fee to carry out swaps. The more exotic the swap the greater the fee as the market-maker's hedging risk increases. The cost of implementing swaps for managers with benchmarks very dissimilar to the ACAT is likely to be prohibitively expensive.

Just as important, the cost of this solution is exacerbated by treating each manager as an individual misfit problem. That is, when considered in aggregate, the misfits of the managers may tend to offset one another as diversification of managers' investment styles mitigates the misfit problem. For example, in Figure 21-5 the small-cap bias of Manager A relative to the ACAT is offset by the large-cap bias of Manager C. Swapping Manager A's and Manager C's benchmark returns for the return of the ACAT is largely unnecessary along the small-large dimension. The message is: *Investment style and investment skill should be evaluated from an aggregate portfolio perspective.*

With that thought in mind, consider the individual managers' benchmarks and the aggregate of their benchmarks in Figure 21-6.

FIGURE 21-6. The Aggregate of the Managers' Benchmarks

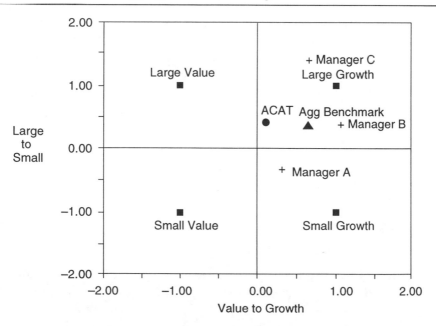

The aggregate benchmark is the weighted combination of the individual managers' benchmarks, with the weights being the plan sponsor's policy allocations to the three managers. In this example, the aggregate benchmark has less misfit than any of the three managers' benchmarks, although it retains a growth bias relative to the ACAT due to the growth biases of all three managers.

Approaching the issue more generally, Equation (4) can be extended to cover the multiple-manager situation. Consider an aggregate-weighted (denoted by the subscript ∗) portfolio composed of m managers' portfolios, where the weights (w_i's) are the managers' assigned policy allocations in a plan sponsor's investment program. That is:

$$P_1 = T + (B_1 - T) + A_1 \qquad w_1$$

$$P_2 = T + (B_2 - T) + A_2 \qquad w_2$$

$$P_3 = T + (B_3 - T) + A_3 \qquad w_3$$

$$\vdots \qquad\qquad\qquad\qquad \vdots$$

$$\underline{P_m = T + (B_m - T) + A_m \qquad w_m}$$

$$P_* = T + (B_* - T) + A_* \qquad 100\% \qquad\qquad\qquad (7)$$

In the same way that each manager's portfolio can be segmented into systematic, misfit, and active-management components, so too can the aggregate of the managers' portfolios. The plan sponsor prefers that the performance of the managers in aggregate reflect only the performance of the ACAT and the managers' aggregate investment skills. That is:

$$P_* = T + A_*$$

The plan sponsor's problem is that, in aggregate, the managers exhibit misfit relative to the ACAT. That is, $B_* - T \neq 0$.

Solution #3: Transport Alpha for the Aggregate Portfolio

The third solution to the misfit problem follows directly from Equation (7) and the second solution: swap the aggregate benchmark's return for the ACAT's return. This solution avoids the redundant expenses of the second solution, while eliminating misfit, before transaction costs.

Unfortunately, while this is a less expensive alternative, there exists no natural other side to the transaction. No other investors stand ready to accept the aggregate benchmark's return in exchange for providing the ACAT's return. As a result, a plan sponsor would have to turn to a brokerage firm to implement the swap—undoubtedly an expensive proposition (we have heard anecdotal estimates of 2% to 3% per year), with the cost depending on the nature and magnitude of the misfit. Further, the plan sponsor would have to be acutely aware of counterparty risk, as it would be entrusting a prominent portion of its investment returns to a private organization.

Solution #4: Reallocate Funds among Existing Managers

If the current allocations to the managers produce an aggregate benchmark with misfit relative to the ACAT, then perhaps some other set of allocations may relieve the problem. Such a solution would be desirable for several reasons. First, it is simple and easy to explain to the plan's trustees, who may only vaguely grasp the nature of the misfit problem. In fact, as it does not involve hiring or firing managers, a plan-sponsor staff might be able to undertake such a reallocation without engaging in a major policy-review with the plan's trustees.

We believe that a reallocation of funds among the existing managers can be a useful first step, as it directly focuses attention on the nature of the misfit problem. Unfortunately, in most cases a reallocation is unlikely to significantly reduce misfit, particularly without requiring unacceptably extreme allocations to certain managers. This situation is illustrated in Figure 21-7.

Analyzing portfolios in "style" space has the convenient feature that they combine linearly, in the same way that security betas combine. Thus a 50/50 combination of benchmark portfolios A and B in Figure 21-7 would lie halfway along a straight line connecting the two benchmarks. This makes it a simple process to examine the set of reallocation alternatives open to a plan sponsor.

In our example, the plan sponsor can produce an aggregate benchmark with style exposures lying anywhere in the triangle

FIGURE 21-7.   Reallocating among Managers

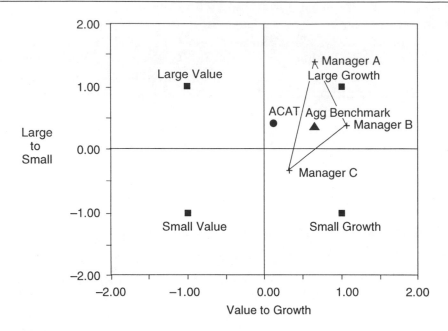

formed at the corners by the three managers' benchmarks.[12] Note that in this example, there is *no* combination of the managers that will cause the aggregate benchmark to lie on top of (that is, have the same style-exposures as) the ACAT. For plan sponsors that have managers with style biases all in a particular direction (as the managers of this hypothetical plan-sponsor all have a growth bias) it is not possible through reallocation among the managers to eliminate misfit entirely.

In some situations, a plan sponsor may be able to eliminate misfit through reallocation among existing managers, but only at the cost of giving uncomfortably large allocations to one or more managers and significantly reducing allocations to other managers. That is, a particular manager's investment style may effectively complement the investment styles of the other managers. (For example, a large-cap value manager may offset the styles of several small-cap growth man-

---

[12] This analysis assumes that the policy allocations to the managers are limited to non-negative values. Allowing for negative allocations (that is, "shorting" a manager or managers) would theoretically permit a plan sponsor to reach any desired point on the quadrant graph.

agers.) However, to achieve the desired style combination may take so large an allocation to the one manager that the plan sponsor becomes concerned that a mistake on the part of that manager might unacceptably diminish the total portfolio's performance. In other words, manager reallocation to control misfit may compromise the goal of maintaining adequate diversification of judgment.

The other serious problem with the reallocation solution is that misfit control becomes the dominant factor in manager-allocation decisions, instead of basing those allocations on expectations concerning managers' value-added capabilities. Consequently, the managers with the largest allocations may be relatively low expected value-added managers. A plan sponsor may find the resulting diminution of total portfolio-expected VAM to be too high a cost to pay to eliminate misfit.

Solution #5: Hire an Additional Active Manager

If allocations to the existing managers cannot be altered to produce a desirable level of misfit, perhaps an additional active manager can be hired to offset the current style-biases. Such an alternative would be attractive because it provides not only considerably more flexibility to control misfit, but, if properly implemented, it has the potential to virtually eliminate misfit. Further, like the reallocation solution, this alternative is simple to explain to trustees, who need only approve the addition of one more "horse" to the multiple-manager stable.

Figure 21-8 illustrates how the additional-manager solution would work. Manager D has the value exposure that the plan sponsor's other managers lack. Creating a box connecting all four managers indicates that there is a feasible allocation to the managers that will produce an aggregate benchmark with the desired characteristics.

Despite its appealing simplicity, the additional manager approach has several serious drawbacks. First, the allocation to the additional manager may have to be quite large to offset the misfit created by the other managers, thereby allowing the manager to have too much influence on the total investment-program's performance. In our example, roughly 60% of the total portfolio would have to be allocated to Manager D to offset the growth biases of the other three managers. This lack of diversification of judgment could be controlled by hiring even more managers, but this would add significantly to the costs of misfit control in terms of time expended in manager searches and management fees paid.

FIGURE 21-8.   Hiring an Additional Manager

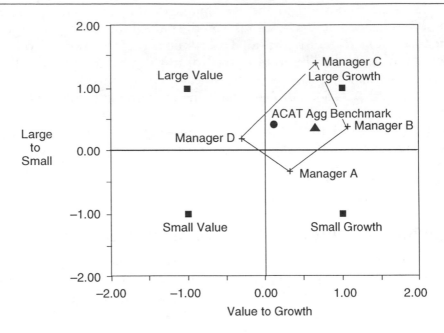

Second, it may be difficult to find a skillful active manager who coincidentally helps the plan sponsor control misfit. That a manager would provide the right style-exposures to offset the misfit created by a plan sponsor's other managers would seem fortuitous indeed. However, to expect that the manager also would be a value-added contributor to the total investment-program seems much less likely. As a result, the plan sponsor may be forced to hire a manager who provides little or nothing in terms of active-management skills to achieve acceptable misfit reduction. The misfit horse has been put before the VAM cart!

Third, and perhaps most important, the misfit problem is dynamic, potentially changing from period to period. What happens if the plan sponsor chooses to alter the manager alignment, perhaps firing an existing manager and replacing that manager with another, or simply deciding to allocate more funds to one existing manager and allocate less to another? The manager hired to control misfit may no longer solve the puzzle as the aggregate manager-benchmark will have changed along with the manager-alignment change. Should the misfit-control manager now be fired and another hired? Although possible, such a process would seem to be irresponsibly expensive both in terms of transaction costs and time spent in manager searches.

Solution #6: Use an Index Fund

By definition, if a plan sponsor retained no active managers and instead placed all of its assets in a passive portfolio designed to track the ACAT, then the investment program would have no misfit. Extending this logic, we might conclude that investing a portion of heretofore actively managed assets in an index fund is a viable misfit-control option.

Although such an approach will certainly reduce misfit, it does so inefficiently and at a high price. That is, viewed in "style" space, the index fund lies on top of the ACAT. Consequently, it cannot be as effective at offsetting misfit as the additional manager solution (or other solutions, as we will see shortly). If a boat is listing to one side, then shifting weight to the center of the boat will relieve some of the tilt, but not as efficiently as shifting weight to the other side of the boat. Further, as an index fund has zero (actually, slightly negative) expected VAM, taking assets from the active managers and placing them in an index fund will reduce the investment program's total expected VAM.

If the plan sponsor previously has not employed passive management, then it makes little sense to now sacrifice positive expected VAM to control misfit through the use of an index fund. Other solutions will do a better job at a lower expected VAM cost. If the plan sponsor already has an index fund in place, then the plan can actually increase its expected VAM and (or) reduce its misfit by replacing the index fund with a customized misfit-control portfolio. Those types of solutions are discussed below.[13]

Solution #7: Combine Style Portfolios

As institutional investors have come to understand the impact of managers' investment styles on performance, a number of organizations

---

[13] The inefficiency of using an index fund to control misfit is discussed in Tierney and Winston [1990].

have created generic style-portfolios similar to those used in the style graphs shown in this paper. In several instances, enterprising managers have created passively managed portfolios designed to track the performance of these generic investment style-portfolios. A plan sponsor can now mix and match investment style-portfolios to create a wide range of style combinations at relatively low management-fees. As a result, one possible means to control misfit is to create a combination of style portfolios that specifically offsets any misfit present in the investment program.

Figure 21-9 shows how style portfolios might be applied to the misfit problem. Given the aggregate benchmark of the plan sponsor's three managers, a combination of the four style-portfolios is produced such that the joint allocations to the three managers and the style combination creates investment-style exposures precisely equal to those of the ACAT.

The style combination solution has several important advantages over the previously discussed alternatives. It focuses solely on the misfit problem. The plan sponsor is free to concentrate on hiring the most proficient active managers, knowing that the style-combination port-

FIGURE 21-9.   Combining Style Portfolios

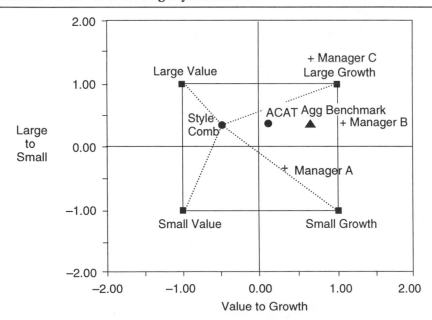

folio will be able to correct for any subsequent misfit. Further, this solution provides a customized approach to controlling misfit that can be adjusted to accommodate changing circumstances.

The style-combination solution does have several disadvantages, however. The required style combination may lie "outside of the box." That is, no positive-weight combination of the style portfolios may off-set the misfit of the plan sponsor's managers. If so, then short selling one or more of the style portfolios may be necessary. Given the rela-tively concentrated positions held by these portfolios, shorting the component securities in large volume may prove difficult.

Further, the style-combination solution is a complex approach that is not easily explained to trustees. They must understand that a portion of the total portfolio's assets are being devoted to misfit risk-control, with no expectation of value-added. Moreover, the style-combination portfolio is likely to produce returns quite different than those of the active managers. These differences may cause consider-able discomfort among the trustees during periods when the style-combination portfolio underperforms the active managers' managed and benchmark portfolios.[14]

A more subtle, but nevertheless important, disadvantage of the style-combination solution is that it can generate considerable indus-try and stock-specific risk relative to the ACAT. That is, the style port-folios tend to have very specific concentrations in various types of stocks. For example, the small-cap value portfolio tends to be heavily concentrated in banks and utilities. Consequently, although the com-bination of style portfolios may display acceptable common risk char-acteristics, the underlying industry and stock-specific misfit risk may still be present and compromise the performance of the misfit-control portfolio.

Solution #8: Create a Dynamic Completeness Fund

At this point let us return to Equation (7), where the aggregate portfo-lio of a plan sponsor's managers was segmented in the following manner:

$$P_* = T + (B_* - T) + A_* \tag{7}$$

---

[14] This discomfort is due to a natural myopia on the part of the trustees. They tend to look at the misfit-control portfolio in isolation, instead of recognizing it as a hedge that is only a part of the plan's total investment-program.

Now define a pure hedge-portfolio (that is, no net dollar investment) that has the following attributes:

$$H = T - B_*$$

If we were to combine this hedge portfolio with the plan sponsor's aggregate portfolio, the result would be:

$$P_* = T + (B_* - T) + A_*$$

$$\underline{+\ H =\qquad (T - B_*) + 0}$$

$$P_* + H = T + 0 +\qquad A_*$$

That is, misfit has been eliminated and the joint portfolio becomes the ACAT plus the managers' value-added, which is the plan sponsor's desired solution as specified in Equation (5). We call this hedge portfolio H a *dynamic completeness fund* (DCF). Figure 21-10 illustrates the application of a DCF.

FIGURE 21-10.   DCF Solution

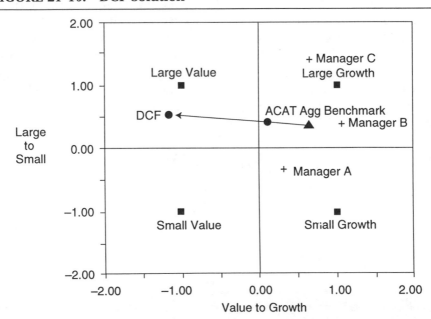

In many ways, the DCF solution is similar to the combined-style portfolio approach. In both cases, a customized portfolio is created that is directed solely toward misfit control. Like the combined-style portfolio, the DCF can accommodate changes in the plan sponsor's manager alignment. However, the DCF has a significant advantage over the combined-style portfolio in that by definition it has no industry or stock-specific risk relative to the ACAT. That is, the DCF is constructed to precisely offset the stock-by-stock over- or underexposures of the aggregate benchmark relative to the ACAT.[15]

Referring back to Table 21-1, if the benchmark were the aggregate benchmark of the plan sponsor's active managers and Security 1 had a weighting of 21% in the benchmark and 13% in the ACAT, then the DCF would have a holding of –8% in that security.

Because it addresses the misfit problem on an individual-security basis, the DCF approach is the most effective method to eliminate misfit. Further, as it is a pure hedge-portfolio, it requires no cash outlay on the part of the plan sponsor. Thus all of the plan sponsor's assets can be directed to the most productive active managers, thereby allowing the plan sponsor to maximize the investment program's information ratio.

The DCF solution does have its drawbacks. As a hedge portfolio, the DCF carries sizable short positions in securities that are overweighted in the aggregate manager-benchmark relative to the ACAT. In practice, implementing these short sales may prove difficult. (An alternative to this hedge portfolio DCF is discussed in the next section.) Further, like the style-combination approach, the DCF solution suffers from a greater level of complexity than the less sophisticated approaches. Moreover, the DCF portfolio, like the style-combination portfolio, may produce returns quite different than any generated by the plan's other managers, thereby causing discomfort among the plan's trustees.

Many plan sponsor decision-makers confuse the DCF misfit-control methodology with attempting to offset the active-management decisions of the managers. They become concerned that the DCF will lead to an "expensive index-fund." Nothing could be further from the truth. The DCF is designed strictly to eliminate the unintended style

---

[15] The DCF is a true nonparametric solution to the misfit problem. No risk model is required to construct the DCF.

biases of the plan sponsors' active managers, as embodied in the aggregate of their benchmarks.[16]

Thus the DCF operates at the benchmark level, not at the active-portfolio level. Therefore the composition of the DCF has no effect on performance of the active managers. In fact, use of the DCF permits the plan sponsor decision-makers to be more aggressive, if they so choose, in selecting the most skillful active managers, without regard to their respective investment-styles. The DCF compensates for any unwanted style biases created in the selection of active managers.[17]

Part III: Building a DCF

Implementing any of the misfit-control options described in Part II of this chapter requires that the plan sponsor follow certain basic procedures consistent with establishing a formal investment-policy, such as selecting an ACAT and assigning allocations to individual managers.[18] Further, due to its intricate design, the DCF approach necessitates several additional steps. The DCF construction-process is outlined and described below.

The DCF Benchmark Construction-Process

1. Establish the asset category target (ACAT).
2. Develop valid benchmarks for all the plan's managers.
3. Assign policy allocations to the managers.
4. Construct the aggregate managers' benchmark.
5. Create a long-short DCF.
6. Produce a positive-weight DCF.
7. Set the policy allocation to the positive-weight DCF.
8. Rebalance the DCF periodically or when required by a manager-alignment change.

[16] The orthogonality property of the relationship between the managers' active management processes and their benchmarks, mentioned in footnote 10, ensures that the DCF will not counteract the managers' active-investment judgments.

[17] The theory of dynamic completeness funds is presented in Tierney and Winston [1990].

[18] The components of a plan sponsor's investment policy are discussed in Ambachtsheer [1986] and Ellis [1985].

Step 1: Establish the ACAT

As described in Part I of this chapter, the ACAT represents the focal point of the plan sponsor's investment program within the particular asset category. Consequently, the plan sponsor should not treat the choice of an ACAT as a perfunctory decision. Instead, the plan sponsor's decision-makers should carefully consider their beliefs regarding the opportunities and risks offered by the capital markets and the financial circumstances of the plan. The ACAT should represent the one portfolio that the plan sponsor would be willing to own passively if that were to be the plan's only investment in the asset category.

Further, the plan sponsor should consider the investability of alternative ACATs. While the issue is beyond the scope of this chapter, many broad-market ACATs are constructed in ways that make it difficult for a passive-investment manager to closely track the ACAT's results.

Step 2: Develop Valid Manager Benchmarks

Similarly, the plan sponsor decision-makers should pay close attention to the selection of benchmarks for each of the managers retained to invest assets for the plan. Inappropriate benchmarks will misrepresent the investment style-exposures of the plan's managers. Thus, to the extent that managers' benchmarks are significantly misspecified, misfit-control efforts will be misguided. As in most areas of investment management, the GIGO (garbage in, garbage out) paradigm prevails.

We have long advocated that managers be responsible for creating and distributing their own benchmarks to interested parties. Managers are in the best position to understand and represent the persistent elements of their investment processes that appropriately belong in their benchmarks. Plan sponsors should play a due-diligence role, requiring the managers to verify that their benchmarks meet certain minimum-quality criteria.[19]

Step 3: Assign Manager Policy-Allocations

The plan sponsor must determine the appropriate allocation of assets to the various managers. Many plan sponsors refuse to take formal

---

[19] Criteria used in the evaluation of benchmark quality are described in Bailey [1992].

responsibility for this decision, preferring to let the seemingly random course of events set the allocations to managers. Of course, _no decision is still a decision._ The managers will end up with some allocations. It makes eminently more sense for those allocations to be based on explicit expectations regarding the managers' value-added capabilities, their active-management risk, their investment styles, and the correlations of their investment styles and active-management skills among one another. The scope of this chapter does not permit a discussion of the _manager structuring_ process. Nevertheless, it should be an integral part of a plan sponsor's investment program.

Step 4: Construct the Aggregate Benchmark

As discussed previously, the aggregate benchmark is the weighted combination of the managers' benchmarks, with the weights being the policy allocations assigned by the plan sponsor. Thus the aggregate benchmark is an asset-list portfolio created by multiplying each security in each manager's benchmark by the manager's policy allocation and summing all stocks in all of the managers' benchmarks.

Step 5: Create the Long-Short DCF

As noted earlier, the DCF is created by a straightforward comparison of the aggregate benchmark with the ACAT. Securities that are overweighted in the aggregate benchmark relative to the ACAT are held in the DCF in negative (short) positions. Conversely, securities that are underweighted in the aggregate benchmark relative to the ACAT are held in the DCF in positive (long) positions. The holdings of the DCF are of the same absolute value, but opposite sign, as the holdings of the misfit portfolio (an example of which is contained in Table 21-1). We refer to this form of the DCF as a long-short DCF. It has a zero investment-weight (and thus is a pure hedge-portfolio) because the long positions are exactly offset by the short positions.

Step 6: Produce the Positive-Weight DCF

If plan sponsors were free to sell short securities with no administrative problems and no significant additional expenses, then the long-short DCF would be the most effective solution to the misfit problem. Although the market mechanisms for creating low-cost long-short portfolios are advancing, most plan sponsors are understandably reluctant to commit sizable assets to such portfolios, particularly if those portfolios involve short positions in small, illiquid names. For that reason, it is usually impractical for a plan sponsor to invest in a long-short DCF. Instead, a *positive-weight* DCF is designed to track the performance of the long-short DCF.

A positive-weight DCF, as the name implies, is composed of only long positions in securities. Through optimization techniques (or, less effectively, stratified sampling techniques) a portfolio is created that mimics the performance of the long-short DCF within a prescribed tracking tolerance. Although the positive-weight DCF cannot eliminate all misfit as can the long-short DCF, if well-constructed, it will perform better than any other alternative misfit-control approach (as we will demonstrate shortly). Further, the optimization techniques used to construct the positive-weight DCF can address the problems of transactions costs inherent in carrying out misfit control.

Step 7: Assign the DCF's Policy Allocation

The plan sponsor must also determine a desired allocation to the positive-weight DCF. Here the plan sponsor faces an important tradeoff. The larger the allocation to the DCF, the more effective will be the misfit-control effort. On the other hand, as the DCF has a zero VAM, any funds allocated to it will reduce the expected VAM for the total investment-program. The ultimate choice of a DCF allocation will depend on the unique circumstances of the plan sponsor. The decision regarding the DCF's allocation ideally should be made simultaneously with the decision to allocate funds to the active managers. In general, our experience has been that a 20% to 30% positive-weight DCF allocation is desirable for an investment program with aggressive, skillful active managers.[20]

---

[20] The allocation assigned to the positive-weight DCF will affect both its composition *and* the composition of the long-short DCF. This can be seen by noting:

$$w_{DCF} \times DCF_{L/S} = T - (1 - w_{DCF}) \times B.$$

That is, when the plan sponsor sets the allocation to the positive-weight DCF (w_{DCF}), the same allocation also applies to the long-short DCF. As w_{DCF} changes, so will the right side of the equation, which defines the misfit. Therefore, changing the allocation to the DCF will affect the weights of individual securities in the misfit portfolio and the resulting DCF portfolio, both long-short and positive-weight.

Step 8: Rebalance the DCF

Finally, the DCF should be updated periodically or in the event of a shift in the manager alignment. In the normal course of business, market movements and changes in security characteristics will cause changes in the position of the aggregate benchmark relative to the ACAT. Quarterly or semiannual rebalancings can effectively deal with these changes. Occasionally, a plan sponsor will hire additional managers, terminate existing managers, reallocate funds among existing managers, or perform some combination of all three. Usually, such changes typically will materially affect the composition of the aggregate benchmark and hence require an immediate and coordinated change in the composition of the DCF.

Part IV: DCF Roles and Relationships

Management of a DCF is essentially a three-party relationship. The parties involved are the plan sponsor, the DCF builder, and the DCF manager. Due to various specialized skills, usually three separate organizations play these three roles.

The Role of the Plan Sponsor

The plan sponsor is the owner of funds and thus has final authority in any DCF-related decision-making. Nevertheless, the plan sponsor is most effective when focusing on the following tasks:

- Define the ACAT.
- Establish policy allocations.
  —Active managers
  —DCF manager
- Evaluate manager performance (both active and DCF) and the DCF builder's effectiveness.

The Role of the DCF Builder

The DCF builder acts as a consultant to the plan sponsor in both the design of the DCF and potentially the structuring of managers within the total portfolio. As a result, the DCF builder has the following tasks:

- Recommend an efficient structuring of manager policy-allocations.
  —Active managers
  —DCF manager
- Build and rebalance the long-short DCF.
- Build, rebalance, and deliver the positive-weight DCF to the DCF manager.
- Monitor and evaluate DCF performance outcomes relative to expectations.

Note that the benchmark for the DCF builder is the long-short DCF. That is, the DCF builder is charged with creating a positive-weight portfolio that reduces misfit to levels agreed upon in advance with the plan sponsor. The effectiveness of that process can be measured by comparing the performance of the positive-weight DCF with that of the long-short DCF. On the other hand, the DCF builder creates the benchmark for the DCF manager. That is, the DCF manager will be evaluated on his or her performance relative to the positive-weight DCF. In both cases, the relevant benchmarks are unambiguous standards against which to evaluate the performance of the total misfit risk-control program and its constituent elements.

The Role of the DCF Manager

The DCF manager is responsible for creating and maintaining a portfolio of securities that adequately tracks the performance of the positive-weight DCF. As a result, the DCF manager has the following tasks:

- Receive and process the positive-weight DCF benchmark.
- Manage the tradeoff between trading costs and tracking error.
- Match or exceed the performance of the DCF benchmark within prespecified tracking-error tolerances.

The DCF manager is on the front lines of the misfit-control effort. Thus the manager must face the reality that trading securities involves costs. At periodic rebalancings, the manager must design a portfolio construction-strategy that holds trades to a minimum, while simultaneously maintaining adequate ability to track the positive-weight DCF. To effectively accomplish this task, the DCF manager must have access to a large securities-database and to sophisticated optimization technology that permits a comparison of the relative benefits and costs of buying and selling securities from the DCF portfolio.

The DCF manager may take a passive approach to investing the DCF portfolio, in which case the portfolio will be designed to match the performance of the positive-weight DCF benchmark, less trading-costs and management fees. Alternatively, the DCF manager could take an active approach, in which case the portfolio will be expected to exceed the performance of the positive-weight DCF benchmark after all fees and expenses. Typically, this active management is carried out under very strict risk-control policies designed to prevent unacceptable volatility relative to the benchmark. (The term *semipassive management* is often applied to this approach.)

Part V: A Case Study

The concepts of investment styles and misfit control have been discussed for well over 15 years. Nevertheless, it has only been in the last few years that a number of plan sponsors have taken the misfit problem to heart and attempted to systematically resolve it. The longest-running DCF was implemented in 1988 by Owens-Illinois (OI). From the perspective of understanding how effective the DCF solution can be, it is instructive to examine the results of the OI misfit-control efforts.

The Pre-DCF Situation

Prior to mid-year 1988, OI had applied a domestic-equity manager structure that was typical by the standards of other large institutional investors. OI had hired nine active equity managers to manage its $1.1 billion of domestic equity assets. Figure 21-11 illustrates the situation in terms of the styles of the individual managers' benchmarks and the aggregate manager-benchmark.

The misfit present in the OI domestic equity program is evident. That misfit had an effect on the program's results, both in terms of actual returns and in terms of the additional risk added to the program. Those effects are summarized in Table 21-3.

FIGURE 21-11. **Pre-DCF Manager Situation**

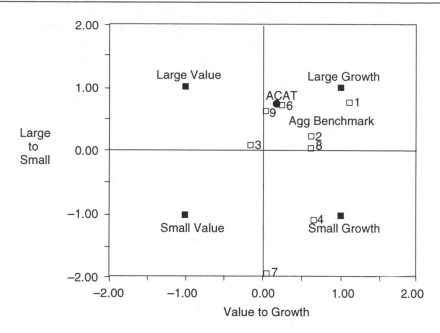

TABLE 21-3. **Performance Attribution**
Five years ending June 30, 1988

	Incremental Value	Cumulative Value	ROR	
Beginning market value	$876,124,690.45			
Net contributions	−310,010,187.83	$566,114,502.62	0.00%	
Risk-free asset	338,063,645.54	904,178,148.16	7.90	
Domestic equity target	248,296,060.76	1,152,474,208.92	13.50	⎫ −1.69% Misfit
Manager benchmarks	−57,384,223.45	1,095,089,985.47	11.81	⎬
Managers' value-added	33,051,269.55	1,128,141,255.02	12.80	⎭ +0.99% VAM
Allocation tactics	−9,709,004.22	1,118,432,250.80	12.53	
Ending market value	$1,118,432,250.80			

The analysis in Table 21-3 breaks down the OI domestic equity fund's change in total assets over the time period June 30, 1983 through June 30, 1988. Over these five years, the fund grew from $876 million to $1.118 billion. Net contributions over this period were a negative $310 million, as shown in the second column. If the original funds, less these net withdrawals, had gone uninvested, the fund would have been worth only $556 million at the end of the period, as shown in column 3.

The OI fund's decision-makers had a number of investment options. They could have placed all of the fund's assets in a risk-free asset—namely, 90-day Treasury bills—and maintained the purchasing power of the fund's assets. Taking into account the timing of cash flows, investing the fund's original $876 million and the associated contributions and withdrawals at the prevailing 90-day Treasury bill rates (which averaged 7.90% over the period) would have resulted in an incremental $338 million to the fund, or a total accumulated value of $904 million.

If the OI fund's decision-makers had chosen to invest in the fund's domestic equity ACAT, then an average 13.50% return would have been earned over the five-year period. This would have resulted in a $248 million incremental increase in value over the risk-free strategy, or a total accumulated value of $1.152 billion.

Instead of this "pure index-fund" strategy, the OI fund's decision-makers chose to hire a number of active managers. One means to quantify the historical impact of the fund's misfit is to calculate what the fund would have earned if all of its assets (accounting for contributions and withdrawals) had been passively invested each month in the managers' benchmarks at the policy allocations then in effect. Table 21-3 shows that the fund's domestic equity program would have produced a total accumulated value of $1.095 billion, *$57 million* less than the pure index-fund strategy. In rate-of-return terms, the fund's return would have been 11.81% versus the ACAT's return of 13.50% over the period. Thus the fund's domestic equity misfit-return was *–1.69%* per annum over the five years.

If, instead of passively investing in each of the managers' benchmarks, the OI fund's decision-makers had invested in each of the managers' actual portfolios at the managers' assigned policy allocations, then the fund would have earned *$33 million* more than it would have by investing in the managers' benchmarks, for a total accumulated value of $1.128 billion. In other words, the managers outperformed their benchmarks by (had a positive VAM of) *0.99%* per annum over the five years.

Finally, the OI fund's decision-makers never funded the managers precisely at their assigned policy allocations. Over the five years, this cost the fund $10 million, or 0.17%, from what it would have earned had the policy allocations been followed exactly. This last step brings us to the OI fund's ending domestic equity market-value of $1.118 billion.

From this type of analysis, it is apparent that the OI domestic-equity managers were actually performing well, yet the investment program as a whole was falling short of its target. Misfit was the culprit, as summarized in Figure 21-12.

The DCF Results

In June 1988, OI instituted the first dynamic completeness fund (DCF). The DCF was designed to reduce misfit risk to acceptable levels, with the expectation that the fund's investment managers would continue to demonstrate positive VAM relative to the ACAT. The intended result was to be that the total domestic-equity program, including the DCF, would outperform the ACAT. Figure 21-13 por-

FIGURE 21-12.   Pre-DCF Misfit and VAM Returns

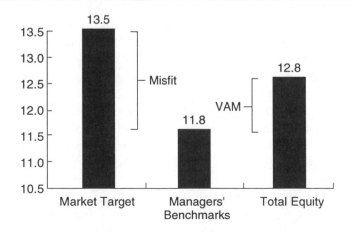

FIGURE 21-13. Post-DCF Manager Structure

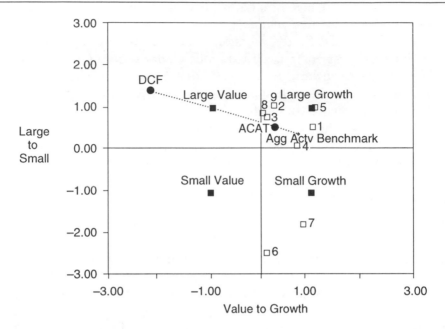

trays the OI domestic-equity manager structure as of December 31, 1993.

As shown in Figure 21-13, the DCF offset the small-cap growth bias of the OI active equity-managers. From the quadrant graph, the large-cap value orientation of the DCF is evident. Interestingly, referring back to Figure 21-1, we can see that no active manager in the sample offers the extreme style-bias necessary to complement the style bias of the active managers. Only a custom designed portfolio could have provided the misfit offset.

How did the DCF perform? In the same format as Table 21-3, Table 21-4 provides an attribution analysis of the OI domestic equity program's performance, from June 30, 1988 through December 31, 1993 (5.5 years), when the DCF was in place. The results are striking. The active managers continued to perform well relative to their benchmarks, with an aggregate positive VAM of 1.15% per annum, quite similar in magnitude to the active-management returns pro-

TABLE 21–4.   Performance Attribution
Five years ending December 31, 1993

	Incremental Value	Cumulative Value	ROR	
Beginning market value	$1,118,432,250.80			
Net contributions	–1,038,287,509.00	$80,144,741.80	0.00%	
Risk-free asset	382,066,406.51	462,211,148.31	6.01	
Domestic equity target	399,048,476.00	861,259,624.31	13.10	} +0.44% Misfit
Manager benchmarks	25,070,701.58	886,330,325.89	13.54	
Managers' value-added	72,910,734.43	959,241,060.32	14.69	} +1.15% VAM
Allocation tactics	–12,948,724.47	946,292,335.85	14.44	
Ending market value	$946,292,335.85			

duced in the earlier five-year period. (The dollar impact of this supe-rior performance was $72 million, net of all fees and expenses.) The managers' aggregate benchmark, on the other hand, now including the effects of the DCF, actually outperformed the ACAT. Although this outperformance was unintended, the more important result was that the level of misfit was significantly reduced, so that it was much smaller in absolute value than the VAM contributed by the active managers.

Figures 21-14 through 21-16 provide more detail on the DCF's performance. Figure 21-15 shows the 12-month rolling performance of the aggregate active-manager benchmark, the positive-weight DCF benchmark, and the combination of the two benchmarks. Several aspects of the figure are of interest. First, deflated by the ACAT's per-formance, the DCF benchmark is very negatively correlated with the aggregate active-manager benchmark. Over the 5.5-year period, the correlation coefficient for the two-return series was –0.897. Second, the combination of the two benchmarks provides a much smoother set of returns (has less misfit risk) than either of the benchmarks indi-vidually. Finally, the combined return series is much closer to the hor-izontal axis, which represents the return on the ACAT, indicating that

FIGURE 21-14.   Dynamic Misfit-Management
July 1988 through December 1993

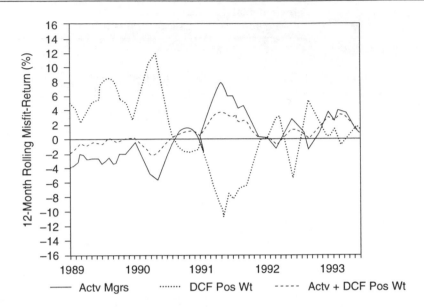

FIGURE 21-15.   Misfit Risk-Control

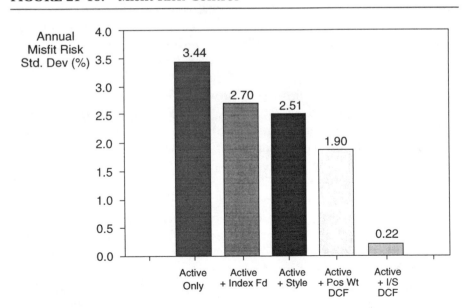

FIGURE 21-16.   Pre-DCF versus Post DCF Equity Performance

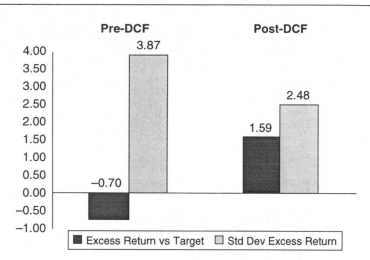

the combined return series in any given 12-month period is closer to the ACAT (has less misfit-return) than either of the benchmarks individually. The message is therefore that the DCF acts to significantly control misfit-return and reduce misfit-risk.

Figure 21-15 amplifies this message, presenting the misfit risk produced by several misfit-control options. For example, the misfit risk of the aggregate active-manager benchmark alone is 3.44% per year. An index fund in conjunction with the aggregate active-manager benchmark reduces misfit risk to 2.70% per year, while the combined style portfolios and the aggregate active-manager benchmark reduces misfit risk even further to 2.51% annually. The best solution is the long-short DCF, which together with the aggregate active-manager benchmark virtually eliminates misfit. The positive-weight DCF cannot do as well, but nevertheless brings misfit risk down to 1.90% over the 5.5-year period of analysis, a 55% reduction from the misfit present in the active managers' aggregate benchmark.[21]

Figure 21-16 presents the bottom line as far as the plan sponsor is concerned. With the DCF in place, for 5.5 years the OI domestic-

---

[21] Owens-Illinois allocated roughly 15–20% of its domestic-equity assets to the DCF over the 5.5-year period, less than what we believe is appropriate for most plan sponsors.

equity program experienced higher returns and less variability relative to the ACAT than it did in the five-year period prior to the inception of the DCF. Specifically, before the DCF implementation, the domestic equity program produced a –0.70% annual return relative to the ACAT, while the variability of that excess return was 3.87% per year. With the use of the DCF, the domestic equity program's excess return relative to the ACAT was +1.59% annually, with a 2.48% standard deviation. The post-DCF period clearly dominates the pre-DCF period.

Part VI: Implementation Issues

Misfit poses a problem for plan sponsors who desire an investment program in which the skills of their managers are allowed to flow unimpeded to the bottom line. Among the many options available, a dynamic completeness fund provides the most effective means for controlling misfit.

Plan sponsor decision-makers implementing a DCF must face several implementation issues. First, they must recognize that managing a DCF portfolio is neither simple nor costless. In particular, implementation difficulties arise because the DCF benchmark is not capitalization-weighted and because its composition is dynamic over time. As a result, passive managers may not be well suited to DCF management. Active managers with tightly disciplined risk-control procedures, on the other hand, may actually be more effective DCF managers. Further, their active management skills may permit them to defray some of the costs of managing a DCF (which are greater than the costs of managing a standard index fund).

Whether a passive or active DCF manager is hired, a plan sponsor should insist that the manager have access to a large internal securities-database. Further, the DCF manager should utilize a multifactor risk-model and state-of-the-art optimization techniques to minimize tracking-error relative to the DCF benchmark. The manager's construction process should take into account the tradeoff between the forecast tracking error of a particular DCF portfolio and the costs of trading into that portfolio. Essentially, as the DCF benchmark changes over time due to either manager realignment changes or simply market movements, the DCF manager should be capable of evaluating the marginal costs and benefits of adding and subtracting individual securities from the DCF portfolio. In addition, the DCF manager should have access to low-cost trading facilities, including internal and external crossing-systems. Finally, the DCF manager should be in the business of regularly accepting custom-portfolio assignments.

Although the primary purpose of a DCF is to efficiently control misfit, a DCF can also offer several secondary benefits to a plan sponsor.

A DCF can accommodate "tactical" ACATs established by the plan sponsor. That is, the plan sponsor may consciously desire that the investment program tilt temporarily away from the long-term ACAT due to a strong belief about the near-term attractiveness of a particular investment style. To effectively implement that strategy, the plan sponsor will want to avoid any misfit between the existing active managers' benchmarks and the tactical ACAT. In such a situation, the DCF can play the role of a "swing" manager, with its benchmark adjusted to offset any new misfit created by the selection of a tactical ACAT.

A DCF also permits a plan sponsor to pay less attention to the misfit effects of changes in the active-manager alignment. Investment skill is a scarce resource. It is difficult enough for plan sponsor decision-makers to identify what they believe are effective active managers, let alone worry about controlling misfit as well. With a DCF in place, a plan sponsor can make manager hiring decisions based solely on the managers' perceived investment skills.

The use of a DCF also enhances the discipline involved in establishing and maintaining a formal investment-policy. The DCF requires that explicit statements be made regarding the investment program's ACAT, the managers' benchmarks, and the managers' allocations. Plan sponsor decision-makers are often reluctant to make these choices and periodically revisit them. The DCF permits no such reticence.

Finally, the DCF can be applied in innovative ways to enhance the active-management decisions of a plan sponsor's managers. For example, the plan sponsor might create an "augmented" DCF designed to magnify the active bets of the managers, while still maintaining control of the investment program's misfit. The plan sponsor could follow a simple rule of never shorting the DCF stocks in which the managers hold positive active positions relative to their benchmarks. Similarly, the plan sponsor would never go long the DCF stocks in which the managers hold negative active positions. The result is that the DCF would effectively "double up" on the managers' active decisions.

References

Ambachtsheer, Keith P. *Pension Funds and the Bottom Line: Managing the Corporate Pension Fund as a Financial Business* (Dow Jones-Irwin, Homewood, IL, 1986).

Bailey, Jeffery V., Thomas M. Richards, and David E. Tierney. "Benchmark Portfolios and the Manager/Plan Sponsor Relationship." *Journal of Corporate Finance,* Winter 1988, pp. 25–32.

Bailey, Jeffery V. "Evaluating Benchmark Quality." *Financial Analysts Journal,* May/June 1992, pp. 33–39.

BARRA. "Comparison of the Capitalization- and Equal-Weighted S&P 500." *BARRA U.S. Newsletter,* February 1989, pp. 9–12.

Chen, Nai-fu, Richard Roll, and Stephen A. Ross. "Economic Forces and the Stock Market." *Journal of Business,* July 1986, pp. 383–403.

Divecha, Arjun, and Richard C. Grinold. "Normal Portfolios: Issues for Sponsors, Managers, and Consultants." *Financial Analysts Journal,* March–April 1989, pp. 7–13.

Ellis, Charles D. *Investment Policy* (Dow Jones-Irwin, Homewood, IL, 1985).

Fama, Eugene F., and Kenneth R. French. "The Cross-Section of Expected Stock Returns." *Journal of Finance,* June 1992, pp. 427–465.

Grinold, Richard C. "The Fundamental Law of Active Management." *Journal of Portfolio Management,* Spring 1989, pp. 30–37.

———. "Are Benchmark Portfolios Efficient?" *Journal of Portfolio Management,* Fall 1992, pp. 34–40.

Haugen, Robert A., and Nardin L. Baker. "The Efficient Market Inefficiency of Capitalization-Weighted Stock Portfolios." *Journal of Portfolio Management,* Spring 1991, pp. 35–40.

Jeffrey, Robert H. "Do Clients Need So Many Portfolio Managers?" *Journal of Portfolio Management,* Fall 1991, pp. 13–19.

Sharpe, William F. "Decentralized Investment Management." *Journal of Finance,* May 1981, pp. 217–235.

———. "The Sharpe Ratio." Stanford University, January 1994.

Sharpe, William F., Gordon J. Alexander, and Jeffery V. Bailey. *Investments* (Prentice Hall, Englewood Cliffs, NJ), 1995.

Tierney, David E., and Kenneth J. Winston. "Enhancing Total Fund Efficiency with Dynamic Completeness Funds." *Financial Analysts Journal,* July/August 1990, pp. 49–54.

————. "Using Generic Benchmarks to Present Manager Styles." *Journal of Portfolio Management,* Summer 1991, pp. 33–36.

Winston, Kenneth J. "The Efficient Index' and Predictions of Portfolio Variance." *Journal of Portfolio Management,* Spring 1993, pp. 27–34.

CHAPTER 22

Driving Factors Behind Style-Based Investing

Kenneth L. Fisher, President and Chief Executive Officer
Fisher Investments, Inc.

Joseph L. Toms, Senior Vice President and Director of Research
Fisher Investments, Inc.

W. Kevin Blount, Research Analyst
Fisher Investments, Inc.

"We're lagging the index, but the index doesn't reflect our style." You hear it all the time. Most indices have biases which exclude or minimize unique market segments and render them less than fully useful for measuring changes in the stock market. How can you measure and adjust for this? Do certain families of stocks have unique characteristics which create underperformance or overperformance? How can you break the market into reproducible sets which allow you to anticipate the future correlation of those sets in a semipredictable fashion? We believe semipredictable relationships exist which allow style-based market analysis to be used as the basis for timely shifts in subasset allocations that outperform the overall domestic stockmarket while maintaining a fully invested exposure to the market. All of this falls under the heading of style-based investing.

Eugene Fama and Kenneth French conducted research into stock market returns and demonstrated that the two most important determinants of a stock's performance are market capitalization and valuation.[1] They concluded that the market's return over the past 20 years can be explained by these two variables.

---

[1] See "The Cross-Section of Expected Stock Returns" by Eugene F. Fama and Kenneth R. French, Graduate School of Business, University of Chicago.

But this raises the question of how to best measure the market. Historically, investors have used the Dow Jones Industrials or the S&P 500. In the past decade, many began using indices such as the NASDAQ Composite or the Russell 2000. These indices, and the others available, have fundamental weaknesses. Primarily, these indices are market cap-weighted (or, in the case of the Dow, price-weighted), making their representation of the market suspect.

Any cap-weighted index gets its impact from the largest stocks in the index, thereby underrepresenting the majority of the stocks due to their smaller size. For example, the 10 largest stocks in the S&P 500 (less than half of one percent of all the companies in the index) represent 17.8% of the market value of the index, and consequently contribute almost one-fifth of the index return. Clearly, the performance of the smaller stocks is obscured by a few huge companies. An example is seen in the first quarter of 1992, when the S&P 500 index was down 2.5% but the equal-weighted return of all the stocks in the index was a positive 3%. Clearly the vast majority of the stocks' performance was not reflected in the index's return.

A second characteristic in market cap-weighted indices is that, over time, they become biased by the "hot" companies or industries. Since market cap is determined by the stock price and the number of shares outstanding, as a stock's value increases, so does its market cap and its subsequent weighting in the index. If, for example, technology stocks are "in," as they appreciate their market caps rise accordingly, until the industry represents a disproportionate amount of the index. Simultaneously, depressed industries, due to low or decreasing prices, have smaller weights and are underrepresented. One must look beyond traditional indices to accurately isolate equity style returns.

Six-Style Analysis

Rather than using one of the standard indices, we avoid their inherent weaknesses by using what we term *six-style analysis*. This allows us to eliminate the problems described above while dividing the market by valuation and capitalization into investment styles based on the Fama/French determinant variables.

We see the market as being composed of six distinct styles. First, via *Standard & Poor's Compustat Database*, we identify the 2,500 largest market-cap U.S. stocks.[2] The aggregate value of this group is over 97% of the total value of the stock market and is the only truly liquid part in an institutional sense. The rest of the market consists of thousands of publicly traded companies whose total value is less than the market cap of the two largest stocks! Many term this segment of the market "microcap."

We take the 2,500 largest stocks and separate them on the basis of cap size—the 250 largest-cap stocks (the traditional big-cap stock universe), the next 750 stocks (the mid-cap universe, stocks 251–1,000), and the bottom 1,500 (the small-cap universe, stocks 1,001–2,500). The next step is to divide each group into equal halves based on a four-factor valuation methodology using price/book (P/B), price/earnings (P/E), price/sales ratio (PSR), and dividend yield. The result is six distinct equity styles in the U.S. market: 125 big-cap value stocks, 125 big-cap growth stocks, 375 mid-cap growth stocks, 375 mid-cap value stocks, 750 small-cap growth stocks, and 750 small-cap value stocks. All returns and valuations are calculated on an equal-weighted basis. The median market-capitalization and median P/B, P/E, PSR, and dividend yield for each style are shown in Table 22-1.

[2] Primary source for all research data and graphs is *Standard & Poor's Compustat Database*, unless otherwise indicated. All total-return data were calculated on an equal-weighted basis.

TABLE 22-1.   Median Market-Capitalization and Valuation of the Six Equity Styles

	Number of Stocks	Capitalization	P/E	P/B	PSR	Dividend Yield
$81.3 billion						
Big-cap value	125	6.48 bil	11.43	1.61	0.94	3.48
Big-cap growth	125	7.80 bil	19.31	3.80	1.66	1.89
$3.8 billion						
Mid-cap value	375	1.34 bil	12.08	1.52	0.83	2.93
Mid-cap growth	375	1.24 bil	21.62	3.41	1.85	0.10
$0.7 billion						
Small-cap value	750	0.27 bil	11.75	1.43	0.70	2.02
Small-cap growth	750	0.29 bil	21.23	2.97	2.06	0.00
$0.1 billion						

Source: Standard & Poor's Compustat Services, Inc.

As you see, the characteristics of each style are quite different. Each is distinct from the others in median market-capitalization, valuation, and the type of firms that make up the style. The industry weights in each style may also vary significantly. For example, the number of biotechnology stocks will be vastly larger in small-cap growth and mid-cap growth than in big-cap value because of the nature of their business and the valuations the market gives them. Once this is understood, it is apparent that many managers who invest in specific industry sectors are making de facto style choices as well.

The beauty of the separation of the market into six styles is that it not only "purifies" each specific style, allowing you to isolate performance, but also allows you to equal weight each stock to see how each area is truly performing. It avoids the inherent problem of market-cap weighting, where a few big stocks may totally mask the performance of the majority of the stocks.

Next is the issue of small versus mid versus big. It is generally accepted that big-cap stocks and small-cap stocks perform in alternating multiyear cycles. Figure 22-1 gives a visual perspective. It takes the performance of the smallest 50% of the New York Stock Exchange (NYSE) and subtracts from it the performance of the big-cap S&P 500. The resulting number represents the "spread" between small-cap and big-cap stocks. When the spread is positive, small-cap is outperforming; when it's negative, big-cap is outperforming. This is measured over three-year periods to minimize single-year aberrations.

By graphing the performance spread between small-cap stocks and big-cap stocks over three-year rolling periods, a clear cyclical picture emerges. There have been four distinct periods of small-cap outperformance and four periods of big-cap outperformance. One timeframe, the 1950s, was mixed. Mid-cap will also show a cyclical pattern in a similar comparison. Our research has shown mid-cap's returns typically split the gap between small-cap and big-cap returns. It follows that the size of the overperformance and underperformance, the peaks and valleys on the graph, will be less extreme in the mid-cap cycle.

Market Share

Another way to differentiate between the styles is to determine the "market share" each has today and what it has had in the past. What

FIGURE 22-1. Small-Cap versus Big-Cap: Three-Year Relative Performance Spread
Three-year rolling periods

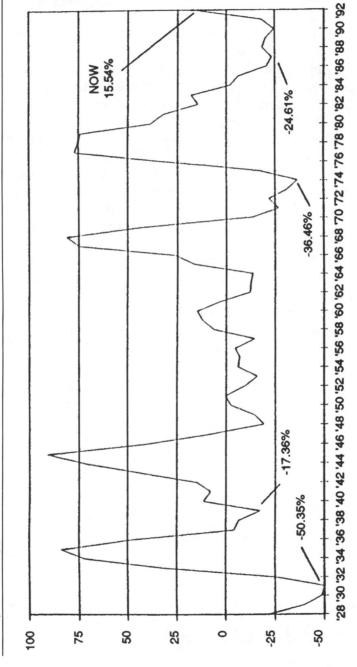

Source: Fisher Investments, Inc. Based on Ibbotson Associates data.

we mean by market share is the percent of the aggregate value of the total stock-market represented by each style. Using the six-style approach, this becomes a very easy task by just summing the market values of the stocks in an individual style, or any combination of styles, and comparing it to the whole. Consider the case of small-cap as an example. We take the combined value of small-cap growth and small-cap value and compare it to the total value of all six styles. This lets us examine small-cap's market share over time, as shown in Figure 22-2.

Note that when small-cap has done well, it has started with a low historical market-share relative to the market (the 2,500 stocks). In 1974, the greatest opportunity to own small-cap stocks since the end of the Great Depression, small-cap's market share was only 14%. By the time small-cap peaked in 1983, it had grown to 22% of the total market. At the end of the 1989–1990 small-cap bear market, it reached a 15-year low of 15%, not seen since 1976. Not surprisingly, small-cap has been the dominant performer since October, 1990.

Low market-share for a style relative to its historic market-share is one indication of low popularity, a limited down-side risk, and substantial upside opportunity. When a style has a high market-share relative to history, its value has been bid up and the majority of the stocks are typically fully valued or overvalued.

FIGURE 22-2. Small-Cap's Capitalization as a Percent of the Market's

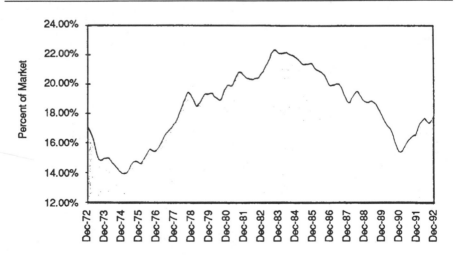

Source: Standard & Poor's Compustat Services, Inc.

Just as big-cap and small-cap stocks perform in alternating cycles, many pension plans have long known that an alternating cycle exists between value and growth stocks in big-cap. This is why so many plans have both big-cap growth and big-cap value managers. You can see these cycles by taking the low 30% of P/E big-cap stocks and subtracting the high 30% of P/E big-cap stocks to again derive a spread. And again we use three-year rolling periods to smooth performance. When the spread is declining and becomes negative, growth stocks lead. When it's rising and positive, value stocks dominate. Figure 22-3 shows distinct periods of value and growth dominance. As you see, big-cap value stocks dominated from late 1974 to 1978. Then big-cap growth took over, leading value from 1979 to 1980. Value again led from 1981 to 1986, after which growth dominated, from 1987 to 1991.

Furthermore, what surprises many investors is that the same cyclicality between value and growth holds true for small-cap and mid-cap stocks. The same analysis applied to the 1,500 stocks from the two small-cap styles produces the graph shown in Figure 22-4.

In the same time-periods, value dominates from 1974 to 1978, growth from 1979 to 1980, value from 1981 to 1986, and growth again from 1987 to 1991. If you overlay the two, you get the graph shown in Figure 22-5.

What this shows is that the magnitude of the swings between value and growth is larger in small-cap than in big-cap, a misunderstood and greatly underappreciated point. Mid-cap is nearly always in the range between, more volatile than big-cap, but not as extreme as small-cap.

Another way to put this into perspective is to examine value's historical market share. In this case, we aggregate the market value of big-cap value, mid-cap value, and small-cap value and compare the aggregate to the market as a whole. The result is the graph in Figure 22-6.

Figure 22-6 shows that value's market share has fluctuated from a low of 37% in 1975 to a high of 53% in 1984. There have been two main value-cycles, 1975–1979 and 1981–1984. Both of these value cycles started when value's market share was below 41%. In December of 1991, value's market share was 38%, the second lowest in the last 20 years, actually lower than the 1981 dip. In 1992, value did better than growth, suggesting a reversal in trend. Owning value when

FIGURE 22-3. Big-Cap Value versus Growth: Three-Year Value Return Minus Growth Return

Three-year rolling periods

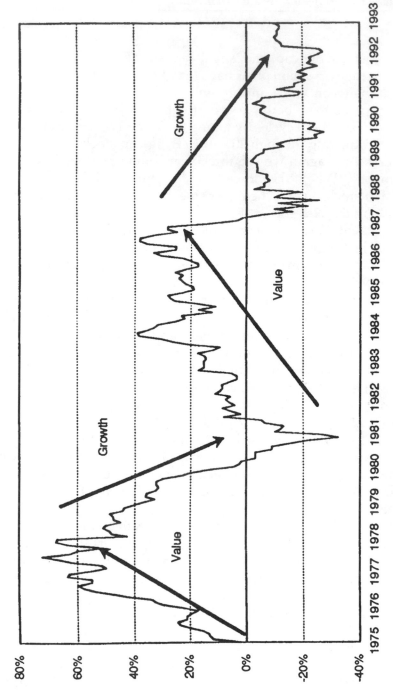

Source: Standard & Poor's Compustat Services, Inc.

FIGURE 22-4. Small-Cap Value versus Growth: Three-Year Value Return Minus Growth Return

Three-year rolling periods

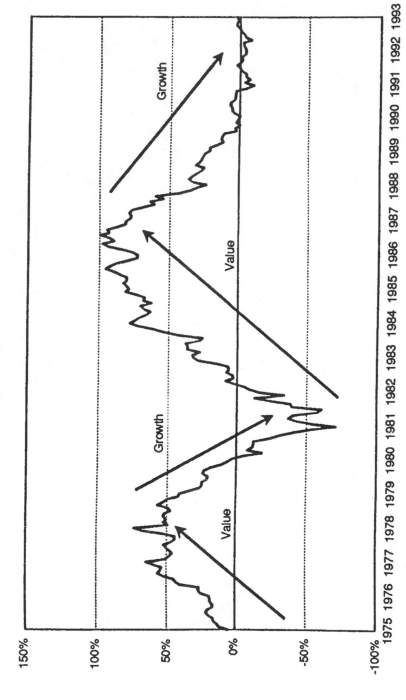

Source: Standard & Poor's Compustat Services, Inc.

FIGURE 22-5. Value/Growth Cycles for Big-Cap and Small-Cap Stocks
Three-year rolling periods

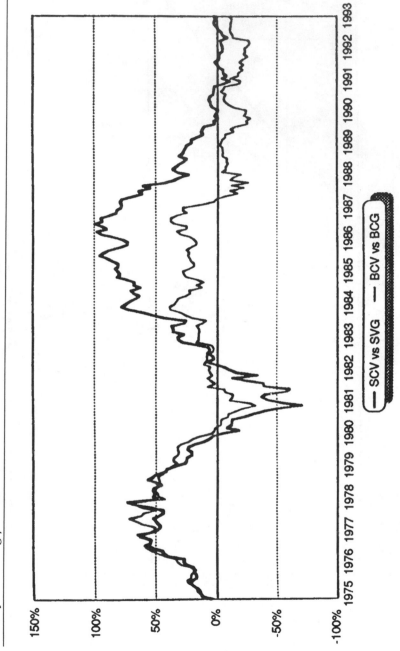

Source: Standard & Poor's Compustat Services, Inc.

FIGURE 22-6. **Value's Capitalization As a Percent of the Market's**

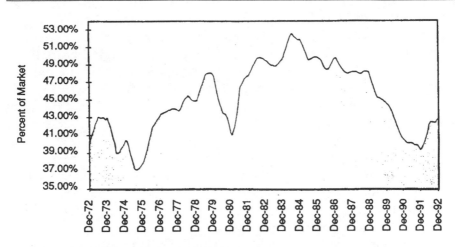

Source: Standard & Poor's Compustat Services, Inc.

its market share has fallen below 41% has resulted in these returns relative to growth:

	May 1975–July 1979	*Dec. 1980–Nov. 1984*
Value	+26.5%	+19.6%
Growth	+20.3%	+1.9%

As the numbers show, when value's market share fell under 41%, the result has been an average gain over growth of 12% in the value cycle that followed. Not surprisingly, the same basic pattern applies when moving to the small-cap value style and mid-cap value style.

Before we examine performance, it is necessary to see that when any one style dominates in terms of returns, the opposite style performs worst. This should logically follow. If big-cap growth is the "hot" style, then the opposite style—small-cap value—should be the worst. Big is the opposite of small, and growth is the opposite of value. The elements that make big-cap growth attractive will be lacking in small-cap value, which will perform poorly as a result. The same holds true for big-cap value versus small-cap growth, so in terms of styles, diagonal styles will be the best and worst performers.

A look back to the early 1980s shows how the opposite style impact works. From January 1981 through January 1984, small-cap value was dominant. Styles rotate—much like a clock. If you imagine a clock with only one hand, you would see it sweep in this time frame from 6:00 (January 1981) to 9:00 (January 1984), through the small-cap value style and into the mid-cap value style. Figure 22-7 is a graphic representation with the specific returns for each style.

The number-one style was small-cap value with a total return of 120.93%. The worst performer was big-cap growth with a return of 12.89%.

Using the same analogy, as the clock's hand sweeps through the mid-cap value and big-cap value styles from 9:00 (February 1984) to 12:00 (January 1989), it is not surprising to find that the best performance came from the big-cap value style (see Figure 22-8). The worst? Of course, small-cap growth.

The next stage of the cycle logically follows. From February 1989 to October 1990, the big-cap growth style leads with the small-cap value style having the lowest return (see Figure 22-9).

FIGURE 22-7. Top 2,500 Market Cap Stocks' Performance
January 1981 through January 1984

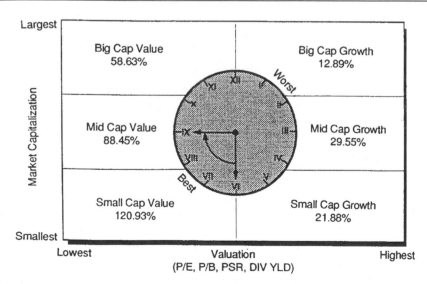

Data provided by Standard & Poor's Compustat Services, Inc.

FIGURE 22-8.   Top 2,500 Market Cap Stocks' Performance
February 1984 through January 1989

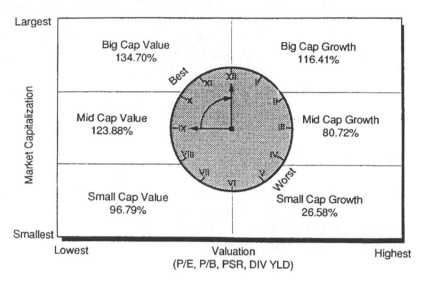

Data provided by Standard & Poor's Compustat Services, Inc.

FIGURE 22-9.   Top 2,500 Market Cap Stocks' Performance
February 1989 through October 1990

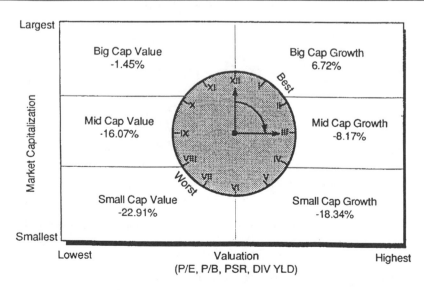

Data provided by Standard & Poor's Compustat Services, Inc.

The clock continues. From 3:00 (November 1990) to 6:00 (December 1991), the clock sweeps through the small-cap growth style (see Figure 22-10). The best performer was small-cap growth. The worst, of course, was big-cap value.

But what happened in 1992? For the first time since 1981, small-cap value did best (see Figure 22-11). The worst style was big-cap growth. Note that the style returns depicted here exclude those of the financial sector—an industry whose 1992 return was such an aberration that it tends to distort longer-term reality.

Interest Rates

What provides the impetus for cycles to change? More specifically, what causes value cycles to start? We believe the answer relates heavily to interest rates and the yield-curve spread between short and long rates. First let's consider interest rates.

FIGURE 22-10.   Top 2,500 Market Cap Stocks' Performance
November 1990 through December 1991

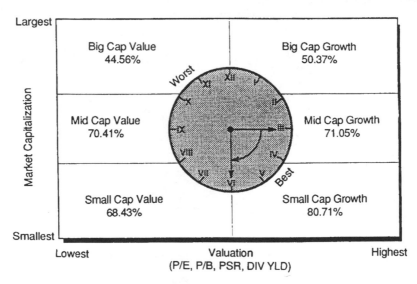

Data provided by Standard & Poor's Compustat Services, Inc.

FIGURE 22-11. Top 2,500 Market Cap Stocks' Performance
January 1992 through December 1994

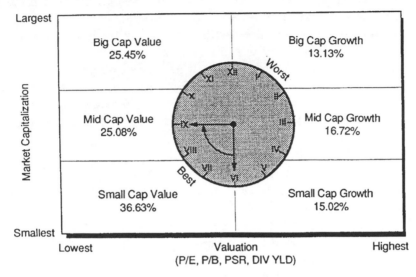

Data provided by Standard & Poor's Compustat Services, Inc.

Whenever interest rates drop significantly, if you wait a couple of years, a value cycle results. Whenever they rise significantly, with a time lag, the result is a growth cycle. This is exactly the opposite of what most market students expect tied to the dividend discount model, which is a nice theory, but empirically wrong, and in fact, backwards. Longer-term cyclical interest-rate fluctuations seem to tie in directly with whether value or growth will be the dominant style.

Why do falling interest rates benefit value stocks? For many investors this seems counterintuitive. Many argue, particularly those weaned on the dividend-discount model, that when rates fall, growth stocks will do better than value stocks. Were all else equal that would be true. But the real world is not *ceteris paribus*. The data prove otherwise. It's true that about 50% of the time, growth stocks perform better initially (over the first year or so) as investors scurry to own "quality" in a time of typical economic concern. But this impact is temporary, and by the end of the three-year cycle, value clearly wins. The reason is quite simple. It relates to the overall level of debt (both short- and long-term) that value companies carry relative to growth companies.

This extra leverage and debt-financing sensitivity is a result of the fact that it makes more sense for growth companies to raise capital by offering equity than by issuing debt. The tradeoff is quite simple. If a growth company is selling at 30-times earnings, that translates into an earnings yield of 1/30 or 3.3%. Selling stock at this level is, in essence, borrowing money at a 3.3% interest rate, as compared to current long-term rates of over 8%, saving the company over 4.7%. This tradeoff doesn't work as well for value companies, which sell at much lower valuations and thus have higher earnings yields—a company with a P/E of 10, for instance, would have a 10% earnings yield, making an 8% rate on debt very attractive. The result is that value companies tend to look to debt for additional capital while growth companies look to equity.

The impact of this difference in leverage is that when rates rise, with a time lag to work through maturity schedules, the interest costs of value companies rise faster than growth companies, negatively affecting earnings of value companies relative to growth companies. With suppressed earnings, value stocks perform more poorly than their growth counterparts. The opposite effect occurs after rates fall. Value stocks' earnings improve—because of reduced interest costs— on an absolute level and also relative to growth stocks. For instance, in the small-cap value style, assuming no dramatic economic changes over the course of the next 12 months, the potential improvement in earnings is a whopping 17% as a result of the drop in rates in 1991 and 1992. With *any* economic recovery (slow or strong), the relative potential earnings increases on the value side become dramatic.

So it's not surprising to find that when you take Treasury rates and overlay growth and value cycles, they tend to follow reasonably closely the longer-term direction of interest rates. Often there is a lag as it takes time for the interest-rate change to translate into investor expectations. But as this happens, and with interest rates as the catalyst, the cycle changes.

The Yield-Curve Spread

As important an indicator to the value and growth cycles as the interest rate, and directly related to it, is the difference in the three-month

T-bill rate and the 30-year Treasury bond rate—the *yield curve spread.* The difference between these rates has an important impact on availability of credit, cost of debt, and the earnings potential of different stocks and investment styles.

A shrinking yield-curve spread forces bankers to make credit more available to lesser creditworthy customers. Imagine it's 1990 and you're a banker. The government (through the Federal Reserve) allows you access to low-interest money. As you borrow you ask: "To whom do I most want to lend?" The answer is simple—to the U.S. government by buying its Treasury bonds. You know the U.S. government is the best credit-risk available. With 1990's sad economy, you are uneasy making loans to riskier customers, despite the potential for higher profit. If you lose money on a loan, you get fired. With long rates high, the solution is easy—avoid all risk while making tremendous money by playing the spread between the short and long rates by buying Treasuries. As long-term rates started to drop faster than short-term rates in 1993, bank operating-margins started dropping too. What to do to keep your earnings up? Wait for the spread to widen again? It may not, and even if it did, it would take a long time.

Instead, you start looking for safe customers—big, stable ones with good reputations. Not as safe as Uncle Sam, but safe. These firms will pay higher interest rates than the government. This begins the process of pushing "money out the door" and is your only real chance to keep growing your bank's earnings. Initially, you look toward the best and most creditworthy corporate customers you can find. But as the yield curve flattens, your desire to maintain earnings will ultimately send you throughout the rest of corporate America.

To illustrate how bankers actually use this logic, look at the level of free reserves in the banking system as depicted in Figure 22-12.

Note several points. Consider 1990–1992. Bank reserves skyrocketed, and it was also the period of widening yield-curve spreads. Bank earnings and stock prices soared. The economy bounced its way to minimal growth, but banking-system liquidity improved steadily.

By 1994, reserve levels were still very high—yet the yield-curve spread diminished. It's like a dam holding a body of water, a dam that is showing signs of cracks. Eventually, the dam crumbles and water rushes out. This is the case with the credit available in the United States. As it becomes more available, it provides opportunities for firms to take on projects they were previously unable to finance. This creates economic growth.

FIGURE 22-12.   The Stock Market and Free Reserves

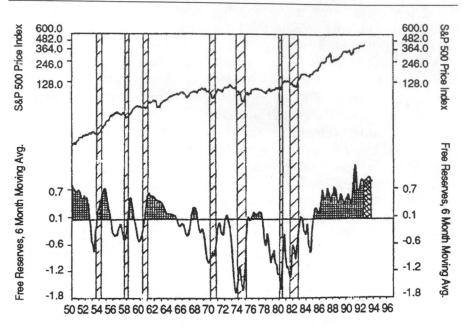

Source: Garzarelli Capital, Inc., 1993.

If short-term rates rise, but long-term rates don't, the yield-curve spread shrinks further, forcing the dam to crumble even more, and that's bullish for the economy and the market—even with rising rates. The implication of rising rates is an economy needing more cash—and, looking at the free reserves, the cash is available. In this situation, don't fret about rising short-term rates—they are bullish, foretelling continued economic growth. Bull markets of sizable duration (like the 1950s, 1962–1968, 1982–1989) saw plentiful free reserves most of the time, and rising interest-rates more often than not.

Understanding the effect of the yield-curve spread on corporate debt, interest costs, and earnings allows us to make predictions on the effect of the yield-curve spread on the performance of the stock market. When the spread narrows it makes capital more available as the banking system looks for more customers. Capital is deployed, the economy grows, earnings increase, and the stock market rises.

Figure 22-13 looks at the yield-curve spread since 1955. The top half of the graph shows the price performance of the S&P 500; the bottom half shows the spread between the three-month T-bills and the 30-year Treasury bond. When the number is negative, it means the 30-year bond is higher by the corresponding numerical value found at either side of the chart. When it's positive, it means the yield curve is inverted—short rates are higher than long rates.

Note that from 1955 to 1957, the spread diminishes and stocks rise. From 1958 to 1960 the spread diminishes and stocks rise. From 1961 to 1966 the spread diminishes and is briefly interrupted in 1966-1967 before inverting in 1969. Stocks rise following the same basic pattern. Again the spread diminishes from 1971 to 1973 before inverting, and stocks rise. The same is true for 1975–1980 and 1982–1989, and the result is the same: rising stock prices.

Also note at times of inverted yield curves or when the spread is widening, stocks do poorly. This is true for 1957–1958, 1960–1962, 1969–1970, 1973–1975, and 1980–1982. While the timing of each isn't perfect, they correlate well.

FIGURE 22-13.   The Stock Market and Yield Curve Spread
Three-month T-bill versus Treasury bond rate

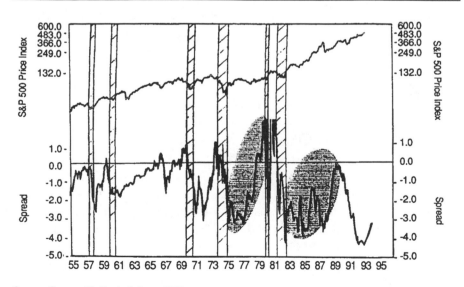

Source: Garzarelli Capital, Inc., 1993.

Just as the yield-curve spread affects the market as a whole, its effect on the value and growth cycles of the market can be shown even more dramatically.

The key for a value/growth cycle is a narrowing or widening of the yield curve. When the spread widens or inverts, banks stop lending, whereas when it is flattening, they lend aggressively. Since value firms are much more debt-dependent, when credit is tight they become defensive and do poorly; when credit is more easily available, they do well. Figure 22-14 shows the history of yield-curve spreads back to 1953.

The vertical axis represents the yield spread. When it is high, long-term interest rates are higher than short-term rates by the corresponding number. As the line falls to the graph's bottom, it indicates a flattening spread. When the line is below zero, it is an inverted yield curve (like 1979–1981). In 1994, the spread was historically high, at about 350 basis points, but it has been falling since 1992. Figure 22-15 is the history of the value/growth cycle since 1953. Here we take the performance of each group and use three-year rolling averages. We then subtract value's return from growth's and plot the spread.

When the line rises above zero, value is outperforming growth. When it falls below zero, growth is outperforming value. Three obvious growth spikes exist in 1973, 1979–1981, and 1990–1991. Overlaying the two graphs gives the result shown in Figure 22-16.

Confusing? Yes and no. Until 1971, no relationship appears. From 1972, they track well. Breaking the study into these two periods and running correlation coefficients, you get the two graphs shown in Figures 22-17 and 22-18.

Surprise! A negative correlation from 1953 to 1971. A good correlation of 0.60 for 1972 to 1993. The 0.6 number is statistically meaningful since it occurs with two phenomena not normally thought of by market participants as related.

The obvious question: Why has the correlation become meaningful since 1971 when it wasn't before? Answer: The United States abandoned the gold standard in late 1971. This step began when currencies decoupled from a gold base. Monetary policy had been tied to gold. Without the gold standard, yield-curve changes could be felt immediately by the banking system—resulting in a quickly responding financial system where credit flows were more easily controlled. In this environment, yield-curve spreads have a heavy influence on

FIGURE 22-14. Yield Curve Spread: Long Bond Minus Three-Month T-Bill
1953 to 1993

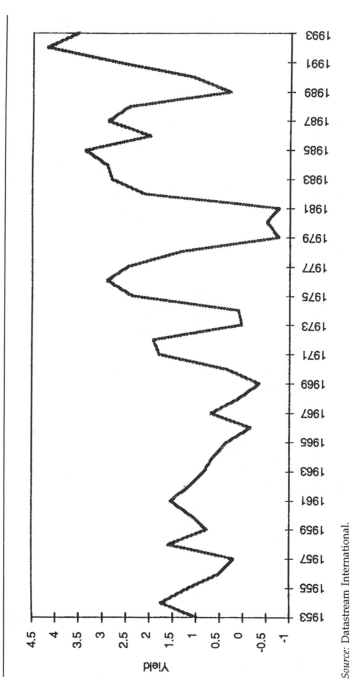

Source: Datastream International.

FIGURE 22-15.   Value versus Growth: Three-Year Rolling Spread
1953 to 1993

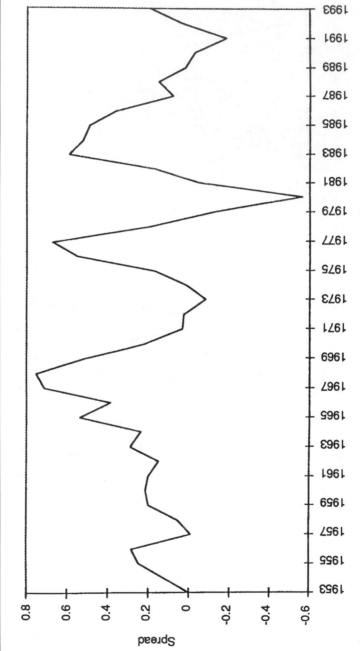

Source: Standard & Poor's Compustat

FIGURE 22-16. Yield Curve Spread versus Value-Growth Cycle
1953 to 1993

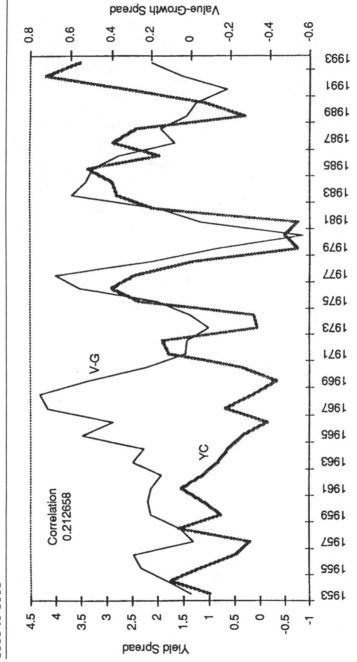

Source: Datastream International; Standard & Poor's Compustat Services, Inc.

FIGURE 22-17. Yield Curve Spread versus Value-Growth Cycle
1953 to 1971

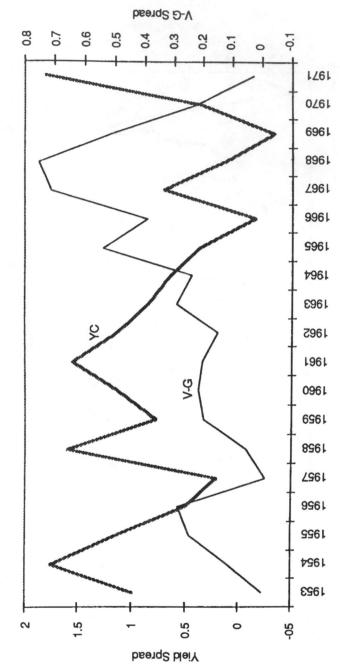

Source: Datastream International; Standard & Poor's Compustat Services, Inc.

FIGURE 22-18. Yield Curve Spread versus Value-Growth Cycle
1972 to 1993

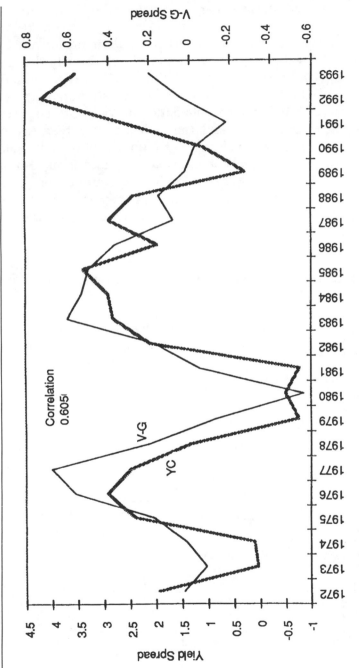

Source: Datastream International; Standard & Poor's Compustat Services, Inc.

the value/growth cycle as banks respond immediately to any yield-curve shifts.

We've argued that expansions create demand for money which in turn flattens the yield curve. Figure 22-19, by Charles Clough at Merrill Lynch, shows this basic relationship. He uses unfilled nondefense capital-goods orders to measure future strength in the economy. Its predictive ability in terms of a flattening yield curve is excellent.

While interest rates and the yield-curve spread are excellent indicators of changing cycles, they are not the only ones. Many other drivers exist, both macroeconomic and microeconomic, fundamental and technical. For example, the foreign exposure of the style plays a role. Big-cap stocks derive over 40% of their revenue from foreign markets. In a global environment where the U.S. economy is trailing

FIGURE 22-19.   Yield Curve and Nondefense Capital Goods Orders

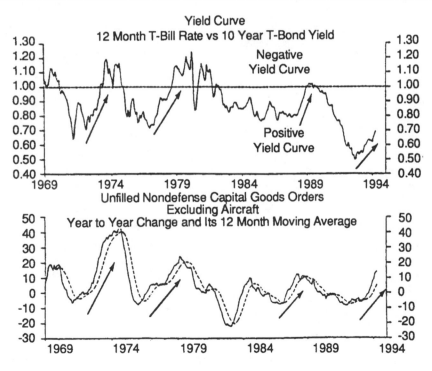

Source: Merrill Lynch Investment Strategy, July 6, 1994. Reprinted by permission of Merrill Lynch, Pierce, Fenner & Smith Incorporated. Copyright 1994.

its foreign partners, big-cap stocks have a distinct advantage over mid-cap and small-cap stocks because of this foreign income. In periods when the percentage change in U.S. gross-domestic product lags our economic rivals, the big-cap style, all else being equal, will outperform the small-cap and mid-cap styles. The opposite will apply during the eras when the U.S. economy is expanding at a faster rate than those of our trading partners. Nonetheless, interest rates and the yield-curve spread are excellent primary indicators of style swings.

Conclusion

Six-style analysis is a simple and effective way of isolating the distinct equity styles within the stock market. It clearly illustrates the variations in style valuations and characteristics, as well as the cyclical nature of the styles' performance. To truly replicate the U.S. market requires exposure to all six styles, while performance superior to the market is possible with accurate selection of the styles in which to invest and those to avoid. Rotating a portfolio among the different styles, or adjusting the weights of the styles, can yield significant performance gains over the broad market. Unlike tactical asset-allocation and other market-timing methodologies, a style-rotation or style-tilt portfolio is always fully invested in equities and can maintain exposure to the entire market. In this case, just as a manager might make a bet on utility or telecommunications stocks, the style-tilt portfolio will make a bet by putting an emphasis on, say, big-cap growth or mid-cap value. The analysis of market share, interest rates, and yield-curve spreads are some of the ways to help determine the equity allocations among the six styles.

Index

A

Allocation, equity style, 297–331, 399–420
Asset allocation, relation to, 7–8

B

Babson, David and Thomas, 67–69
BARRA Global Equity Risk Model (GEM), 85–95
Benchmarks
custom style, 426–427
growth, 149–151
large-cap growth, 149
large-cap value, 151–152
mid-cap growth, 150
mid-cap value, 152–153
small-cap growth, 150–151
small-cap value, 153
value, 151–153
Bernstein, Peter, 67–68
BIA (Boston International Advisors) Indices
aggressive-value indices, 134–135

country weights, 125–131
methodology, 118–120
performance, 120–125
performance attribution by sector, 132–134
rebalancing interval, transaction costs, and performance, 135–138
Biases
assessing overall, 428
offsetting unintended, 428–430
Bonds, synthetic convertible
motivation for creating, 386–388
uses, 388–393

C

Capaul, Carlo, 96–97, 138
Country selection style, 333–352

D

DCF, *see* Dynamic completeness funds

Dynamic completeness funds
  benchmark construction
    process, 460–464
  benefits of, 446–460
  case study involving, 466–474
  dynamic completeness fund
    roles and relationships,
    464–466
  implementation issues,
    474–475
  role of, 433–446

E

Expense control, 15

F

Fama, Eugene F., 4, 262–263,
    479
French, Kenneth R., 4, 262–263,
    479
Financial Times Actuaries
    World Index (FT Index),
    85–95

G–H

GEM, *see* BARRA Global Equity
    Risk Model
Global Equity Risk Model, *see*
    BARRA Global Equity Risk
    Model
Growth and value
  Capaul, Rowley, and Sharp,
    96–97, 138
  constructing indices, 72–75 ,
    118–120
  economic considerations,
    78–80

French and Fama, 139–140
  history, 67–68
  international, *see*
    International investing
  Lakonishok, Schleifer, and
    Vishny, 138–140
  performance of small-cap
    stocks, 219–229
  predicting index
    performance, 75–78
  Salomon Brothers forecasting
    model, 80–82
  Shefrin and Statman, 139
  small-cap value, 235–247

I–K

Implementation issues, 9–13
Indices
  aggressive-value indices,
    134–135
  BIA (Boston International
    Advisors) Indices,
    118–138
  definitions of, 145–146
  descriptions of, 146–148
  evolution of equity index-
    ation in the United States,
    251–257
  Financial Times Actuaries
    World Index (FT Index),
    85–95
  predicting index
    performance, 75–78
  S&P/BARRA, 72–75
  S&P MidCap 400, 192–199,
    204–212, 213
International investing
  BIA (Boston International
    Advisors) Indices, 118–138

Capaul, Rowley, and Sharpe
study, 96–97
correlation of returns across
countries, 95–96
relative strength, 107–109
return seasonality, 105–107
small cap stock results,
98–104
value/growth results, 88–95

L

Large-cap
large-cap growth
benchmarks, 149
large-cap value benchmarks,
151–152
mutual fund returns, 28,
30–43
Salomon large cap growth
index, 73–75
value investing compared
with small-cap, 243–246

M–O

Malkiel, Burton G., 3
Market timing, 8–9
Mid-cap investing
adding value to, 212–214
as a specialized sector,
181–190
as an alternative to small
stocks, 200–203
definition of, 182–183,
196–198
mid-cap growth benchmarks,
150
mid-cap index effect,
203–205

mid-cap value benchmarks,
152–153
return factors, 214–216
role of futures, 194–195
S&P MidCap 400 Index,
192–199, 204–212, 213
Misfit
building a dynamic
completeness fund,
460–464
case study, 466–474
dynamic completeness fund
roles and relationships,
464–466
implementation issues,
474–475
origins of the problem,
433–446
potential solutions, 446–460

P–Q

Portfolio construction,
13–14
Portfolio characteristic
approach to style
determination, 20
Price, T. Rowe Jr., 67
Requirements for management
process, 15

R

Return-based analysis,
21–29
analysis inputs, 22–27
cyclicality, 267–275
seasonality, 265–267
validity of results, 27–29
Rowley, Ian , 96–97, 138

S

S&P/BARRA index, 72–75
S&P MidCap 400 index,
192–199, 204–212, 213
Salomon Brothers forecasting
model, 80–82
Sharpe, William F., 3–5 , 96–97,
138, 261–262
Small-cap
international investing in,
98–107
mutual fund returns, 28,
30–43
performance cycles, 217–233
small-cap growth
benchmarks, 150–151
small-cap value benchmarks,
153
value in, 235–241, 243–248
Small stock effect, 201–202
Static tilt, 6–7
Stock selection across styles,
289–296
Style benchmarks, *see*
Benchmarks
Style determination techniques
manager tilts, 37
portfolio characteristic
approach, 20
return-based analysis, 21–29
style shifts, 37–38
validity of results, 27–34

Style identification
fundamental characteristic
approach, 51–53
of managers, 414–415
qualitative assessment
approach, 51
statistical time-series
approach, 53–54
Style management, active,
357–366
Style maps, 54–66
Style neutral, 5–6
Style prediction, 275–287

T–U

Tactical versus dynamic
allocation, 16
Tilting, 6–7, 34–37, 336–343,
410–412
Timing, equity style, 297–331,
343–352
Timing models, 305–330
Total allocation, styles and
38–43
Trends, style, 367–384,
417–420

V–Z

Value versus growth, *see*
Growth and value